*Writing Well*

## BOOKS BY DONALD HALL

### Books of Poetry

*Exiles and Marriages*, 1955
*The Dark Houses*, 1958
*A Roof of Tiger Lilies*, 1964
*The Alligator Bride: Poems New and Selected*, 1969
*The Yellow Room: Love Poems*, 1971
*The Town of Hill*, 1975
*Kicking the Leaves*, 1978
*The Happy Man*, 1986

### Books of Prose

*String Too Short to Be Saved*, 1961
*Henry Moore*, 1966
*Writing Well*, 1973, 1976, 1979, 1982, 1985, 1988
*Playing Around* (with G. McCauley et al., 1974
*Dock Ellis in the Country of Baseball*, 1976
*Goatfoot Milktongue Twinbird*, 1978
*Remembering Poets*, 1978
*Ox-Cart Man*, 1979
*To Keep Moving*, 1981
*The Weather for Poetry*, 1982
*Fathers Playing Catch with Sons*, 1985
*The Ideal Bakery*, 1987
*Seasons at Eagle Pond*, 1987

### Edited Works

*New Poets of England and America* (with R. Pack and L. Simpson), 1957
*The Poetry Sampler*, 1961
*New Poets of England and America* (Second Selection) (with R. Pack), 1962
*Contemporary American Poets*, 1962; Second Edition, 1971
*A Concise Encyclopedia of English and American Poetry and Poets* (with Stephen Spender), 1963
*Poetry in English*, 1963; Second Edition (with Warren Taylor), 1970
*The Faber Book of Modern Verse* (New Edition with Supplement), 1965
*The Modern Stylists*, 1968
*A Choice of Whitman's Verse*, 1968
*Man and Boy*, 1968
*American Poetry*, 1970
*A Writer's Reader* (with D. L. Emblen), 1976, 1979, 1982, 1985, 1988
*Oxford Book of American Literary Anecdotes*, 1981
*To Read Literature*, 1981, 1983, 1986
*Claims for Poetry*, 1982
*The Oxford Book of Children's Verse in America*, 1985
*To Read Fiction*, 1987

# Writing Well
## Sixth Edition

## Donald Hall

**SCOTT, FORESMAN/LITTLE, BROWN COLLEGE DIVISION**
**SCOTT, FORESMAN AND COMPANY**
Glenview, Illinois     Boston     London

*To Gerard McCauley*

Library of Congress Cataloging-in-Publication Data

Hall, Donald, 1928–
  Writing well.

  Includes index.
  1. English language—Rhetoric.  I. Title.
PE1408.H312    1988      808'.042      87-23396
ISBN 0-673-39723-8

Cover art: "New York Dawn," 1977 by Elizabeth Murray. Courtesy, Saatchi Collection, London.

1 2 3 4 5 6 7 8 9 10—MPC—93 92 91 90 89 88 87

Printed in the United States of America

## ACKNOWLEDGMENTS

*James David Barber.* Quotation on page 296 from *The Presidential Character* by James Barber. Copyright © 1972 by James David Barber. Published by Prentice-Hall, Inc., Englewood Cliffs, N.J. Reprinted by permission.

*Wendell Berry.* Quotations on pages 236–237 reprinted by permission of Sierra Club Books from *The Unsettling of America* by Wendell Berry, copyright © 1977 by Wendell Berry.

*The Boston Globe.* "Women's Work is Never Done" on pages 304–305 from the op-ed page of *The Boston Globe,* April 19, 1984. Reprinted courtesy of The Boston Globe.

*Marvin Cohen.* Quotations on pages 263–264 from *Baseball the Beautiful* by Marvin Cohen. Copyright © 1974 by Marvin Cohen. Reprinted by permission.

*John Collier.* Quotation on page 262 from *Indians of the Americas* by John Collier. Copyright 1947, © 1965 by John Collier. Reprinted by arrangement with The New American Library, New York.

*Joan Didion.* Quotation on page 70 excerpted from "On Going Home." Reprinted from *Slouching Towards Bethlehem* by permission of Farrar, Straus and Giroux, Inc., and William Morris Agency, Inc., on behalf of the author. Copyright © 1967, 1968 by Joan Didion.

(*Acknowledgments continue on page 485*)

# *Preface to the Sixth Edition*

*The Premise*

When I make a new edition of *Writing Well*, I need continually to consult and reaffirm the premise from which I started. It remains my intention that *Writing Well* not only recommend good prose but exemplify it.

Some composition texts describe correct prose in language stiff, drab, passive, shallow, boring, and trite. But we learn by observing actions not by memorizing advice. "Do as I say, not as I do," fails in child-raising as it does in composition teaching. A textbook that praises "effective communication" resembles a father who screams at his son: "DON'T RAISE YOUR VOICE!"

In *Writing Well*, I mean to teach correctness and originality at the same time. It is nasty to teach the correctness of cliché; it is pointless to teach expression without the correctness that allows readers to understand what is being expressed. Good writing makes passages from one human being to another. To carve a passage we require both correctness and originality.

A naive view proposes that invention precludes revision, or that revision negates invention. Experience shows that we need both, and both continually. As I put it elsewhere: "Writing is acquiring material (the floating memory, the rapid daily writing) and it is also ordering and cutting that material. The writer must be a paradoxical combination of opposites, the big spender and the miser." In the process of writing, these two qualities sometimes come in sequence: invention followed by revision. More often, in the reality of composition, the writer goes back and forth between revision and creation so rapidly that it is hard to tell the one from the other.

We combine these opposites in order to open passages to the reader—and audience is at the heart of everything. Teaching a vigorous and combative class of composition, we meet this defense of the cliché: "But it's *exactly* what I mean!" The answer to this defense brings audience in. If the purpose of writing is to make passages to other people, the narcissistic defense—". . .what *I* mean . . ."—is irrelevant. As with bad mechanics, bad style obscures. The trouble with trite expressions, passives, dead metaphors, vague intensives, jargon, and modish words is that these stylistic mistakes block the passage from person to person.

### Writing to Write

It is commonplace to notice that when we enter college, these days, we lack experience in writing. We don't write thank you notes to our grandparents; we use the telephone instead. Someone fluent in speech may remain stiff and inhibited in writing, for reasons that are virtually physiological. We are not illiterate but lacking practice we lack fluency. The neural path from mind to mouth is open and clear from constant use; the path from mind to the small muscles of the fingers is dusty, cobwebbed, narrow, and unused.

Continual application of pen to paper is the first necessity in a composition course. The student who makes one theme a week is practicing writing for only a few hours, and the muscles do not develop. Writing resembles athletic skill; it comes more naturally to some people than to others, but it always and only improves with practice.

### Metaphysics of Organization

*Writing Well* begins with a chapter that introduces its values and methods, using for example mostly essays of personal reminiscence. The new second chapter speaks of reading, and reader response, sketching the relationship between language and audience. The third chapter presents ideas of process, the practicalities of essay writing, and tells the life story of one composition.

In its crucial center, *Writing Well* goes from small to large—from words to sentences to paragraphs. Most readers find "Words" the best part of *Writing Well*. Some teachers follow a different order, going to patterns of rhetoric before they enter the world of the verb and the modifier; teachers must consult their own passions. However, my small-to-large ordering exists for reasons, and I would like to argue the point.

The baby in the crib makes noises that are pleasing to him, autistic utterance without discernible message. Then he begins to associate sounds with responses: "mm" brings milk; another sound gets his diapers changed. Later, the articulation of words becomes the magic of naming, and the magic mind of the child thinks metaphorically because that is the way it knows of thinking. The child sees the leg of the table as a leg like his own or his father's. The table might run away if it wanted to; it stands still, as if under a spell.

Mother Goose and fairy stories perpetuate magic and transformation, sometimes by sheer incantation, as in the great poem:

Ba, ba, black sheep,
Have you any wool?
yes, sir, yes, sir,
Three bags full,
One for the master,
One for the dame,
And one for the little boy
That lives down the lane.

Here to autistic pleasures of the mouth we add pleasures of dance and rhythm. The muscles of the leg begin to move, whether we notice it or not.

And sometimes, as the level of discourse moves *toward* that of the grownup, we have sequences or stories, but stories in which the nightmare and the seer's dream find embodiment in a beauty or a beast, or a boy who plants a seed and confronts a giant. Words have extended into narration without losing their transformative power.

We are educated to take part in civilization and education puts down the magic world, as people rising in social class are ashamed of clothes or accents that give away their origins. And so instead of incorporating the old uses of language—which have inherent power and intuition—into our new use of language for reason, for conscious control of environment, for order, and for shape, we bypass the primitive modes of thinking entirely. This bypass creates a profound problem in our use of language; that is, in our feeling and in our thinking. It has created the mess we have made of technology and civilization.

No sane man thinks he will accomplish anything by doing away with lightbulbs and appendectomies. The man who substitutes an oil lamp for a lightbulb merely replaces a newer invention with an older one. We do not need to junk civilization to recover a part of the powerful intuition we lost when we disavowed our primitive past. We can go beyond; we can include both; the wisest men have been doing it for years. Creativity requires returning—in part—to the magic of the crib.

I once met a woman who had taught grade school for many years and was concerned, like Wordsworth, with the diminishing imagination of the growing child. She told me—more or less; I must paraphrase—that if you asked a nine-year-old to do a report on Magellan, he might begin, "Magellan got eaten by cannibals!" If you asked the same child, at eleven, for a report on Magellan, the child knew better; the report would begin, "Magellan was born in 1480 in Portugal."

Conventional order has won out over the order of intensity. After chronology come the forms of logic and argument, all creations of the cerebral cortex, strongly suppressing messages from the world of nursery rhyme and fairy story. "That was when I was a kid."

In telling a story, whether true or false, the order of chronology is often the most appropriate order; in persuasion, logic is a component of argument. But no reasonable idea of order satisfies or expresses the whole complex of human thought and feeling. It expresses a portion of human potential, and it would be ridiculous to ignore it. But it is equally and tragically ridiculous to ignore the order of color and intensity: "Magellan was eaten by cannibals!"

As a painter at the turn of the century, when he finished art school, had to set out by forgetting what he had learned, so I think most of us need to build our prose again from the start. Ultimately, shapeliness—the general order within a piece of writing, or the focus I talk about in the first chapter—is part of the style we must reach for, but this order says only: Exclude everything that is not really to the point! Know thyself, and know thy point. The ultimate shapeliness, of the finished essay or the finished Chinese pot, depends on the ingredients we bring to the shaping. In writing the first ingredient is always the word.

To attempt in a composition textbook to reconstruct growing-up-with-language is doubtless overambitious. We cannot undo and redo, in four hundred pages, twenty years of experience. But perhaps we may set an example for *rethinking* writing: otherwise, we merely give rules and suggestions, Hall's Helpful Hints; otherwise, we avoid the fundamental issues of writing well. No one can emphasize too much that good writing depends on abilities, thoughts, and feelings which are the difficult but available sources of psychic and social health.

Donald Hall

# Author's Note

The people from whom I derived my ideas of style are the writers whose work I have loved. I quote many of them here, so that they may speak in their own voices, and need not depend upon the articulation of an admirer. I do not quote them all. I owe my sense of style, as well as some ideas of it, especially to the modern writers I read and imitated when I was young: Ernest Hemingway, Ezra Pound, Marianne Moore, George Orwell, Gertrude Stein, James Joyce.

In earlier editions of *Writing Well*, I benefited from the help of many people, and mention their help in my notes. Because their assistance persists in this sixth edition, I want at least to list their names again. At Little, Brown, I was greatly aided by Margaret Zusky, Rab Bertelsen, Jan B. Welch, Dale Anderson, Elizabeth Philipps, Donna McCormick, and David W. Lynch. I used editorial help by Lawrence Russ and Rosemary Yaco in earlier editions. Some of the teachers whose suggestions informed earlier editions were Donald Butler, Terrence Collins, Steven V. Daniels, H. Ramsey Fowler, Neita Gleiker, Frederick Goff, Richard Larson, Thomas Lux, Russell J. Meyer, Marcia Stubbs, M. Elisabeth Susman, Barbara Wicks, and Peter T. Zoller. For their help on the fifth edition, I especially want to thank Sally Crisp, Mark Halperin, Carole Hayes, Celest Martin, Alan McKenzie, and

Barry Weller. In the fourth, fifth, and sixth editions, the editorial assistance of Linda Howe has been extraordinary. I learned much from the students to whom I taught Freshman English at Colby-Sawyer College in New London, New Hampshire. I have special reasons for thanking Sandy Bielunis, David Martinez, and Joyce Robinson. Traveling around the country, I have profited from many conversations with teachers of Freshman English, and with directors of writing programs. I think particularly of visits to Ball State University, to Oakland University in Michigan, to the University of Wisconsin at Stevens Point, to the University of Vermont, to Syracuse University, to Orange Coast College, to Macon Junior College, to the University of Pittsburgh at Bradford, to C. W. Post University, to the University of Wisconsin at Eau Claire, to Jamestown Community College, to Behrend College, to Mercer College, to the University of Utah, to Lynchburg College, and to the Modern Media Institute. I cannot list the names of everyone with whom I have conversed—and from whom I have taken instruction—but here are a few: Thomas Carnicelli, Peter De Blois, William Hiss, Frederick Bromberger, Joann Mercer, Diana Anderson, Charles Berger, Muriel Allingham-Dale, Doug Carlson, Lynn Matson, Lawrence Mobley, Margaret Woodworth, Richard Lindner, John Coates, Joseph Trimmer, Susan Bartels, Mary Jane Dickerson, Sally Ronsheim; and Sandra Donaldson and Celia B. Diamond who spoke by letter. With the sixth edition I appreciate the help of Lisa Ede of Oregon State University and David Skwire of Cuyahoga County Community College.

I am also grateful for the many suggestions from Thomas Adler, Linda Albright, Robert Aldridge, Nell Altizer, Nancy G. Anderson, Maureen Andrews, David Baker, Barry Bakorsky, Anna M. Barnes, Richard Bausch, J. Charles Berger, William W. Betts, Jr., Dorothee Bowie, Margaret Brady, May Brown, Carl Brucker, Ingrid Brunner, Nancy Bunge, Edward Byrne, Harriet Carr, Fern Chertkow, T. L. Clark, Jerry Coffey, Steve Connolly, Mary Copeland, Edward Corbett, Gary Culbert, Paul Dameen, David Dawson, Miriam Dow, Helen Dunn, Oliver Durand, Anne Elam, Mary J. Elkins, Thomas Elliott, Richard Fine, Gala Fitzgerald, William T. French, Michele Giannusa, Peggy Gledhill, Robert M. Gorrell, Barbara Griffin, Richard Grounds, Mark Halperin, Norman Hane, Joan C. Haug, David R. Hauser, Joyce Hicks, Kathryn Holmes, D. Howard, M. Huyser, Walter Isle, Thomas Johnson, Paul Kameem, Sighle Kennedy, Sharon King, Opal A. Lanett, Jim Ledford, Karen B. LeFerre, Merrill Lewis, Sherry McGuire, Alan T. McKenzie, Peter W. Mackinlay, Lynne McMahon, Ann Maioroff,

Andrew Makarushtra, Silvine Marbury, Doreen Maronde, Timothy Materer, Celest A. Martin, Michael Martin, Paul F. Michelson, Sr., Jean Michaupt, Patricia Moody, Jim Moore, C. R. Moyer, Fred Muramunco, Helen Naugle, Kenneth Newman, Richard O'Keefe Steve O'Neill, Janice Philbin, Adele Pittendrigh, George Pittman, Martha Rainbolt, Kate Reavley, Kenneth Requa, Elizabeth G. Richards, Chris Rideout, Florence Roberts, Judy Rogers, Monroe Roth, Sherod Santos, Charlotte W. Sargeant, Ted Schaefer, Michael Sexon, Susan Simpson, Harriet Susskind Spiegle, Sandra Stancey, Diane Stege, J. Stege, Pamela Stith, Margaret A. Strom, Sharon Stuut, Kathleen Sullivan, J. C. Taylor, Charles L. Tilgham, George J. Thompson, Darlene Unrue, Linda Venis, Lucien A. Waddell, Ricki Wadsworth, Nancy Walker, Martha S. Waller, James Watt, Richard Widmayer, Diane Williams, Louis Williams, Thomas Wilson, and George Wymer.

Students who mailed in completed questionnaires helped me revise this text for future students. From the second edition on, I was helped by Clayton Hudnall of the University of Hartford. For the sixth edition, he has also provided the Instructor's Manual and prepared the Indexes, for which I am grateful.

In all editions, I am greatly indebted to Richard Beal, of Boston University, who has supplied strengths in the areas of my own weakness, who has been tireless and good-natured and relentless and kind. In all editions, I am most grateful to my former editors Charles Christensen, and Carolyn Potts, to my present editor, Joe Opiela, and their assistants Virginia Pye, Adrienne Weiss, Amy Johnson and Nan Upin. Mike Moran of the University of Rhode Island helped me out and from the same institution Robert Schwegler contributed mightily to the changes I have made in this new edition; I am especially grateful to him.

# Contents

## 1

**INTRODUCTION: WRITING, AND WRITING WELL  1**

# 2

# 3

# 4

# 5

# 6

## PARAGRAPHS 219

# 7

## FORMS FOR THE ESSAY: RHETORICAL PATTERNS IN EXPOSITION 265

# 8

# 1

## Introduction: Writing, and Writing Well

**WRITING TO MAKE CONTACT**

Students write essays and answer questions on tests, scientists write reports on their work, teachers write evaluations of their students, people make lists to remember what they must do, some of us keep diaries to remember what we have done, executives address reports to their fellows, salespeople write messages from the field to the office, and we write notes and letters to keep in touch with relatives and friends. There are practical reasons for writing. The reasons for writing *well* are practical also.

But not at first. First comes the spoken message: *I want milk*. As our brains develop, our messages become more complicated. We give emphasis to outloud messages by gestures and facial expressions. Learning to write well is harder than learning to talk, but it can bring pleasures deeper than the satisfaction of immediate needs. It can bring us the pleasures of discovery and of contact; writing well, we must think clearly; writing well, we must understand both feelings and ideas; writing well, we reach across the space of our difference and touch other human beings.

A good writer uses words to *discover*, for we use words to think with. We do not first have a thought and then find words to express that thought; we think in the act of finding words—accepting some and rejecting others. Our thought is incomplete until we find a language and a shape by which we can transmit our thought to other people. An essay reflects the shape of our thought; its sentences develop thought and carry it across to others. We write well when our prose gives pleasure while it carries knowledge. That pleasure-carrying knowledge comes from understanding, which includes self-understanding, and creates understanding in the minds of others.

Here is a passage from a student essay about registering for freshman courses:

> Hey, I got a hard time all over the gym, a totally unbelievable experience, and a bad way to begin anything as important like college.

This writer has problems in mechanics, in levels of diction, and in generality of language. A message comes through, but inferior writing garbles the faint sound of complaint. The words may express something for the writer, and maybe it was a relief to utter them, as it is a relief to cry out when we feel pain. But the words do not reach out to make contact with readers. Later in the term, the student rewrote the passage.

> There were long lines at every table, during registration at the gym. It took me one hour to find out that a class was closed and I could not take it. Some teachers didn't know the rules for their own departments. After half a day of feeling frustrated, I went back home and told my mother I wasn't sure about going to college after all.

This version gains clarity through detail, through improved mechanics, and especially through the writer's developed sense that he writes for someone who reads him. He does not merely cry out; he gives examples and pictures by which his reader can locate the source of the complaint. Any reader will respond to stories of institutional incompetence. A short version could have read:

> Registration took a long time and I felt frustrated.

This version is brief and correct, better than the first version, but not good enough. Because it only *tells* us a feeling but does not *show* us anything, it will not create the feeling in the reader. It is not constructed by the writer with the reader's response in mind. Details *shown*, like illustrations, carry feeling from writer to reader; the mere names of feelings, *told* in summary, carry no feelings at all. The short version tells its message abstractly, making a message purified of character and feeling, like a slice of bread purified of nutrition and taste.

When we write, we make a contract: *my words are addressed to the outside world; I construct sentences in order to reach someone else.* Too often we write as if we ourselves were our only reader. If we leave out punctuation or use a cliché, then, it does not matter—*we* know what *we* mean. But neither the first version with its errors and its vagueness nor the third version with its meagerness tells enough to someone besides the writer. The middle version quoted, on the contrary, is sociable: it enters the world of other people, and by using detail and conventional mechanics, it speaks to an audience.

Writing well means making contact with an audience. Every piece of advice in this book—about argumentation and about commas, about paragraph structure and about spelling, about avoiding clichés and about inventing transitions—helps the writer make contact with the reader.

## THE IDEA OF AN AUDIENCE

Writing well is a social act.

The better our language, the more we may connect with other people whether by speech or by writing. Although we may communicate *something* with a grunt, although we may give tone and feeling by gesture or facial expression, on the page we have words alone, and we require every resource of good writing to cross the space between people, to make contact. Writing well, as well as *Writing Well*, exists for a social purpose.

In writing and revising, writers face a thousand choices that they resolve by *the idea of an audience.* It helps to pinpoint an audience in the mind, as we write, the way a lecturer may pick out one face to address, as if everything were intended for the one face only. Sitting at a desk alone, with no listening face to remind us, we need imagination to sustain the idea of an audience. In other contexts we constantly imagine audiences: walking alone, or driving, most of us daydream encounters and conversations; we invent speech and counter-speech; we imagine contact and communication. For that matter, watch anyone talk on the telephone: even though we talk with someone a thousand miles away; even though we *know* that we use ear-contact (words in their many meanings; also emphasis by pitch, volume, and rhythm) with no eye-contact at all; yet everyone in the world, talking on the telephone, bodies forth an eye-audience in imagination. Everyone gestures, smiles, frowns, raises eyebrows, and makes faces. We do these things not because we forget that our friend cannot see us but because we communicate more thoroughly when we imagine complete contact. *The idea of an audience generates contact.*

When we write words on a page we cannot raise and lower the volume of our speech, or make faces, but by keeping the idea of an audience steadily in the forefront of our minds, we use the gestural resources of language to make contact with another person across the space of our difference.

## HONEST AND DISHONEST EXPRESSION

An idea of an audience implies that we have something to say to someone else—and that it is something worth saying. Alas, much human language seems to serve the purpose not of making contact, or revealing, but of concealing or of providing the appearance of communication instead of the real thing. Much language serves dishonest purposes; and much of this dishonesty is unintended. The phrase *honest expression* implies an opposite, dishonest expression, which no one admits to but which we sometimes see clearly in others. We are all aware of honest and dishonest expression. We have grown up on the false laughter of television, the fake enthusiasm of advertising, the commercial jollity and condolences of greeting cards, and the lying assertions of politicians. If some falsity has not entered our prose, we are made of aluminum.

We can be false in a thousand ways. We do it with handshakes and we do it with grunts. We do it by saying outright lies and we do it by keeping silent. But in these examples we understand our own falsity. When we fool *ourselves* we are in more trouble. We fool ourselves with words that can mean almost anything. How much have we said when we call someone *liberal?* We fool ourselves when we avoid blame by leaving *I* out of the sentence, as when we knock over a lamp and claim, "The lamp was knocked over" or "The lamp fell," as if it acted by itself. We also fool ourselves by using clichés, trite expressions that have become meaningless substitutes for feeling and thought:

| | |
|---|---|
| impressionable age | bottom line |
| startling conclusion | name of the game |
| a vital part of our future | get a point across |
| made it what it is today | a changing society |

Clichés are little cinder blocks of crushed and reprocessed experience. When we use them in writing, we violate our agreement to construct sentences in order to reach someone else. We appear to make contact, but the appearance is not a reality. Clichés are familiar and comfortable; they *seem* to mean something, but when I reach the *startling conclusion* that the *bottom line* is the *name of the game* in a *changing society*, I say nothing to anyone. Clichés prevent true contact by making false contact in its place.

Every profession—medicine, law, theater, business—has its own clichés. We call the clichés that belong to a profession its *jargon*. One set of clichés appears especially at graduations, from primary school through graduate school:

> The future belongs to you.
> The challenge of new . . .
> In today's world . . .
> Responsibility, good citizenship, service to the community . . .

The university, in fact, is a great source of jargon. Here are two paragraphs from a letter addressed by a newly elected college president to his faculty.

> Dear Members of the State College Community:
>     I am deeply honored and challenged by the opportunity to join State College as its seventh president. The hospitality and spontaneous warmth of everyone we have met has made both Barbara and me feel very welcome. We look forward to making State our home as quickly as we can arrange an orderly transition from our current responsibilities.
>     State College is rich in tradition: it is an institution with a past, and, more importantly, it is a College with a future. Building on its heritage, and maximizing its resources, State College can continue to achieve distinction by providing educational opportunities for young men and women.

This is the language we expect from officials—from politicians and bureaucrats, from the presidents of colleges and the presidents of corporations. It says nothing, and it says it with maximum pomposity. It took this man years to learn the trick of empty jargon, the style of interlocking cliché. Every phrase is trite, and the phrases are stuck together with mortar like *is* and *and* and *with*. The edifice is reprocessed garbage.

deeply honored
challenged by the opportunity
spontaneous warmth
making . . . our home
orderly transition
current responsibilities
rich in tradition
Building on its heritage
maximizing its resources
achieve distinction
providing educational opportunities

One should mention as well the trite and meaningless contrast between the past, as in *heritage*—a word as hokey as *home*—and *a college with a future.* The contrast says nothing. Unless the collegiate doors are closing tomorrow, of course it has *a future.* The word *future*—like *heritage* and *home*—carries vaguely positive connotations. A candidate for president of the United States used as a slogan *The future lies before us,* trying to associate himself with this positive connotation; no one found the slogan offensive, but he lost.

In the college president's letter, the smoothness of the masonry is exceptional, but the passage is almost without content. If I call the paragraphs insincere, it is because they express only conventional notions, not anybody's own ideas or feelings. Of course the author did not *intend* insincerity, nor did he feel that he was lying.

We must look closely at the notion of sincerity; otherwise, we use it to justify its opposite. The worst liars sincerely say, to themselves and to the world, that they are the most honest. Yet sincerity can be a valuable idea if we think clearly about it, and sincerity has everything to do with the reasons for writing well. Peter Elbow says:

> I warn against defining sincerity, as telling true things about oneself. It is more accurate to define it functionally as the sound of a writer's voice or self on paper—a general sound of authenticity in words. The point is that self-revelation . . . is an easy route in our culture and therefore can be used as an evasion: it can be functionally insincere even if substantially true and intimate. To be precise, *sincerity is the absence of "noise" or static—the ability or courage not to hide the real message.*

The static is the distance between what the words say and what we sense lies behind them. The person with a pose of sincerity fixes us with his eyes, saying, "I am going to be wholly honest with you. I am a bastard. I cheat on my girlfriend and I steal my roommate's tooth-paste." The real message has designs on us: "Love me, I'm so *honest.*"

The distance between the meaning (the apparently stated) and the expression (the really implied) ruins the statement and prevents real communication between people. Triteness and insincerity prevent true contact by substituting false contact. In the college president's letter, the meaning has something to do with expressing pleasure in a new task; the expression is an exhibition of academic smoothness; it is a little dance performed by a well-trained educationist seal. It says, "Look at me. Admit me to your ranks. I am one of you."

We cannot accept sincerity as a standard if we are going to take the writer's word for it. We can take it seriously if we listen to his *words* for it. Sincerity is *functional* (Elbow's word) if we believe it, if we hear the voice of a real person speaking forth in the prose—whether of speech or of the written word. We must speak in a voice that sounds natural, to reach the ears of other people. But finding this natural voice is not easy; the natural voice is usually not the spontaneous voice, for when we write without examining our words we often speak words that are trite and ordinary or even institutional. Writing well requires self-criticism, hard thinking, and analysis. It is worth it. Socrates made the commitment: the life that is unexamined is not worth living.

## PLAGIARISM

We have been talking about the kind of dishonesty in writing that anyone can slide into without meaning to. This falsity resembles the social lie, or exaggeration, when we act enthusiastic in order to seem agreeable. Although this falsity is forgivable, surely we do best as moral beings, as citizens, as bosses, or as employees when we learn to say what we mean. But there is also the deliberate dishonesty of plagia-rism, which we should speak of early in our approach to writing: steal-ing someone else's good writing is not an acceptable form of writing well.

Plagiarism is stealing the words or ideas of others and presenting them as our own. It is like cheating on tests; it is trying to steal a better grade. Obviously plagiarism is self-defeating because we cannot learn if we use somebody else's accomplishments as a substitute for our own endeavors.

It is also wrong.

Now I call it deliberate dishonesty and it is usually just that: the plagiarist props open a book beside the typewriter and copies word for word. However, some people come to college unsure of what plagiarism is, or from schools where plagiarism has become a way of life, or with an unconscious habit of mimicry or copying. It is important for everyone in a composition class to know what plagiarism is. It is good to discuss it in class, and then it is up to everyone to avoid it.

When we consult any printed source, on any subject we write about, we should take a note of that source (book, encyclopedia, magazine, newspaper, radio program, television show) and list this source when we hand in our paper. (See the pages on documentation late in this book, 338–344.) If we quote from a source, we should use quotation marks *and* identify the source. But also, *if we use an idea from a source, even though we put it in our own words, we must always give the source of the idea.* If we take these precautions, no one can ever accuse us of plagiarism.

Some people need to be especially careful not because they are criminal sorts but because they have good if unconscious memories and tend to mimic or repeat whatever they hear or read. Some of us, hearing a joke from friend A, find ourselves repeating it almost word for word when we tell it to friend B. Others who repeat a story will make it over into their own words. There is nothing better or worse about these different personalities; but the apt repeater or mimic is the one who must *be on guard, always, against unconscious plagiarism.* If this person writes a theme about cigarette smoking in public places, he or she might repeat ideas and even phrases from a newspaper editorial, read a week earlier, without being aware of it. But once this is said, ignorance is no excuse. We must be on guard; we must make the unconscious conscious. It is up to each writer, whatever the personality.

NEVER REPEAT ANYBODY ELSE'S IDEAS OR WORDS WITHOUT ACKNOWLEDGMENT.


## EXAMINING THE WORDS

Writing well can be a starting point for all thinking. Self-examination finds what we have inside us that is our own. Understanding the self allows us to move outside the self, to read, to analyze, to define, and thus to make contact outside the self, with others. Self-examination, which sounds convoluted and maybe egotistical, can provide the basis for moving outside the self; looking inward is the basis for looking outward; writing is a social act that begins in privacy.

Of course we are stuffed with clichés—we have been exposed to them all our lives—but clichés are not "our own." We have swallowed everything that has ever happened to us: we dropped the bottle to the floor at the age of eight weeks and cried for the lack of it; the telephone did not ring last week, and we cried for the lack of it; the toy shines under the tree, the toy rusts behind the garage; the smell of bacon, the smell of roses, the smell of kittens that have been careless; the flowers and the beer cans emerging from the snow. Everything that ever happened to us remains on file in our heads. As a professor at MIT put it: the human brain is a big computer made of meat.

If the brain is a computer, we are all engaged in learning how to operate it. For the college president quoted above, the task of writing was simple: he was programmed to write that kind of prose; he pushed the right keys and his brain computer turned out preassembled units of academic jargon. Usually the commencement speaker or the student writing home for money presses other keys for printouts of ready-made pseudothoughts and pseudofeelings. But let us suppose that we are interested in something genuine, the voice without static, the utterance in which expression and meaning are the same. We must learn new ways to use the accumulation of words, sense impressions, and ideas that we keep in the floppy disks of the brain. Our words must not make rows of identical houses like the subdivision prose of cliché. "New" is fresh, genuine, ourselves, our own experience. Making it new, we make contact with the reader.

Freshness is not, however, the inevitable result of spontaneity. Writing freely, without pausing for correction, is a good way to practice writing, to learn to flow, and to uncover material you didn't know was in you. It can be important to develop a sense of freedom in writing. But then there is the second half of genuine expression, the half that applies the mapmaker's self-examination to the new country of self-exploration. Examination and analysis, leading to revision, allow the writer to communicate with other human beings. Revising the map, we think of the reader; we revise to make contact with the reader. The idea of an audience must govern us. Writing well is a social act.

## REVISING THE MAP

Almost all writers, almost all the time, need to revise. We need to revise because spontaneity is never adequate. Writing that is merely emotional release for the writer becomes emotional chaos for the reader. Even when we write as quickly as our hand can move, we slide into emotional falsity, into cliché or other static that prevents contact. We make leaps by private association that leave our prose unclear to others. We often omit steps in thinking or use a step that we later recognize as bad logic. Sometimes we overexplain the obvious. Or we include irrelevant detail. First drafts remain first drafts. They are the material that we must shape, a marble block that the critical brain chisels into form. We must shape this material in order to pass it from mind to mind; we shape our material into a form that allows other people to receive it. This shaping often requires us, in revising, to reorganize whole paragraphs, both the order of sentences and the sentences themselves. We must drop sentences and clauses that do not belong; we must expand or supply others necessary to a paragraph's development. Often we must revise the order of paragraphs; often we must write new paragraphs to provide coherent and orderly progress.

Good writing is an intricate interweaving of inspiration and discipline. A student may need one strand more than the other. Most of us continually need to remember both sides of writing: *we must invent, and we must revise.* In these double acts, invention and revision, we are inventing and revising not just our prose style but our knowledge of ourselves and of the people around us. When Confucius recommended, "Make it new," he told us to live what Socrates called "the examined life." It was a moral position. By our language, we shall know ourselves—not once and for all, by a breakthrough, but continually, all our lives. By our language we connect with other human beings; as we read them (or read their tones and facial expressions) we understand and make contact in reciprocal social exchange—or we don't. The necessity to write well arises from the need to understand and to discriminate, to be genuine and to avoid what is not genuine, in ourselves and in others. Human connection by way of language is not the most important thing: it is the only thing.

## THEMES AND REVISIONS

On the first day of class, the assignment was to write for twenty minutes on the topic "How I Came to College." Here is an impromptu theme by Jim Beck.

> Education is of paramount importance to today's youth. No one can underestimate the importance of higher education. It makes us well-rounded individuals and we must realize that all work and no

play is not the way to go about it, but studies is the most important part, without a doubt. Therefore I decided when I was young that I would go to college and applied myself to studies in high school so that I would be admitted. I was admitted last winter and my family was very happy as was I. Coming here has been a disappointment so far because people are not very friendly to freshmen and everyone has their own clique and the whole place is too big. But I expect that it will get better soon and I will achieve my goal of a higher education and being a well-rounded person.

Repetition at the end of the impromptu gives it some unity. When Jim says that "people are not very friendly to freshmen," the reader glimpses a real Jim Beck. But through most of the paragraph, the writer is not being himself. You can tell that he is not being himself because he is sounding like so many other people. Doubtless he thinks that he writes for a teacher who wants to hear this sort of language. Therefore in a sense Jim works from an idea of audience. The trouble is, it's a bad idea of audience and, really, he makes contact with no audience at all. Jim is assembling an impromptu from the cliché collection in the why-I-want-to-go-to-college box. When he says *paramount importance*, does he really know what *paramount* means? Does he mean that *today's youth* is genuinely different from yesterday's or tomorrow's? And how far into history does *today* extend? What does *well-rounded* mean? Why say *individual* instead of *person* or *people*? *Importance* is vague, and saying it twice makes it vaguer. In the sentence of complaint, where the reader briefly senses an actual writer, Jim would have done better to *show* his loneliness in an anecdote, instead of just *telling* us about it. Showing makes contact; telling avoids it.

Later in the term, when he had a free theme, Jim wrote an essay which was not so much a revision of his impromptu as a new start and which *really* told how he came to college.

*The Race to College*
Jim Beck

It's horrible now, and I don't know if it will get any better. The only people who pay attention to me are the people who are trying to beat me out for the track team. My roommate is stoned all day and gets A's on his papers anyway. I hate him because he hates me because I'm a jock. My classes are boring lectures and the sections are taught by graduate students who pick on the students because the professors pick on them.

But I remember wanting to come here so bad! Nobody from Hammerton named Beck had ever been to college. Everybody knew the Becks were stupid. This went for my father, who never got through high school, and for my grandfather, who died before I was born, and who was the town drunk. It went for my two older brothers who went bad, as they say in Hammerton. Steve got a dishonorable discharge from the Marines and he works on a farm outside town and gets drunk on Fridays and Saturdays. Curt stole a car and did time at Jackson and nobody has heard from him since. My sister had a three-month baby and the town liked to talk about that.

I was different. Everybody told me I was. My mother told me I wasn't a Beck. My father told me I was going to bring back the family's good name. (I never knew it had one.) In grammar school the teachers all told me how much better I was than my brothers. By the time I was in sixth grade my father and the school Principal were talking about the University.

My father isn't really dumb. Sometimes people look dumb because it's expected of them. He's worked at the same grocery for twenty years, I guess. Now that I made it to the University, he wants to be called Manager, because he's the only man there besides Mr. Roberts who owns it. (The rest of the help are—is?—kids who bag and an old lady cashier.) When I went back for a weekend everybody treated me as if I won the Olympics.

I said the Principal and my father were talking about my going to the University. All through junior high I said I didn't want to go. I was scared. No Beck could do that. Bad things kept happening to my family. My father had an accident and totaled the car and lost his license and for a year we didn't have a car at all. He had to walk home two miles every night pushing a basket of groceries. When I said I would quit school and get a job, everybody jumped on me.

It wasn't that I was an A student. It was just that I tried hard at everything I did. I got B's mostly. Now with B's, the counselors kept telling me, I could be admitted to the University, but I wouldn't get a scholarship. I needed mostly A's for that, and then when I got to the University I would lose the scholarship if I couldn't keep the grades up. Then my brother Steve, who was a pretty good athlete once, suggested athletics.

I was too skinny for football, too short for basketball, I could barely swim and my school didn't have a swimming team anyway. There is one sport you can practice with no money and no equipment. I started to run when I was in my last year of junior high. It felt good right away. I ran to and from school. I went over to the high school and did laps. The high school coach noticed me and asked me to go out the next year. Running long distances hurts a lot. Sometimes you get a stitch in your left side and suddenly it shifts to your right side. I didn't exactly mind the pain. I studied it. I studied it in order to go to the University, the way I studied every-thing else.

In my Senior year I was all-state and held two high-school rec-ords (600 and half-mile) and I had an athletic scholarship to the University. Now I am here, the first Beck to make it. I don't know why I'm here or why I ran so hard or where I go from here. Now that I am here, the race to get here seems pointless. Nothing in my classes interests me. I study, just as I did before, in order to pass the course or even get a good grade. I run to win, but what am I running for? I will never be a great runner. Sometimes when I cannot sleep I imagine packing my bags and going back to Hammerton. But I can't do that. They would say, "He's a Beck, all right."

Jim's essay has several important features of good writing: it has unity, which means the focus, the point, the coming together of many details; and it has the voice of a real person speaking out of experience with a minimum of tired phrases, of borrowed clothing. It has disci-pline, and it has feeling. Although Jim is discouraged and feels aimless and melancholy, his mind has made an enormous stride toward know-ing and being able to present itself. He revised, using his own experi-ence in his own language. *And* he was disciplined; he used tighter sentence structure, and he found a narrative structure that contained and shaped his thought. Therefore he made contact with his readers; and he made contact at least partly because he believed in his readers. He developed an idea of an audience chiefly from work in class, where students responded as readers to one another's essays. For Jim the shape of his thought came from an analogy—the struggle to attend college compared to a footrace—and this analogy helped him to think, to embody the shape of his thought, and to reach his fellow-student readers.

This revision was the product of much hard work, of which only a portion went to the actual revision. Jim's daily writing—with which he struggled at first and which he later enjoyed—was a source of improve-ment. He began to find his own, unpompous voice. He also revised other essays after reading his teacher's comments and after discussing these comments in conferences. Jim Beck also talked with his English teacher during office hours and thought about his writing and his ideas while he ran cross-country in the autumn of his freshman year.

## EXAMPLES FROM PRINT

Jim Beck's original essay was impromptu, and the revision printed here came two months later. People who spend their whole lives writing often take longer still and struggle with the same enemies, disunity and evasion. Habitual writers differ from beginners in many ways. For one thing, they know that they are likely to fail at first. Some writers know that they may be weak in details; to succeed they must struggle to generate more of them. Others know that they often generate too many details and lose clarity of organization; to succeed they must pare words and organize. Whatever their problems, professionals learn to be patient. They expect writing to be hard work. They struggle with the same materials as beginners do and strive for a voice that makes contact with others.

People who write well begin by reading well. Reading good prose with close attention, we can acquire the manners that make the good writing we admire. It is like learning a foreign language by living with a family that speaks it, by shopping in it, and by listening to television shows with dialogue in it. Of course there is reading and reading. (See the next chapter.) By way of introduction, take this passage from a book by the anthropologist Margaret Mead. She starts by making a contrast.

> For many people moving is one kind of thing and travel is something very different. Travel means going away from home and staying away from home; it is an antidote to the humdrum activities of everyday life, a prelude to a holiday one is entitled to enjoy after months of dullness. Moving means breaking up a home, sadly or joyfully breaking with the past; a happy venture or a hardship, something to be endured with good or ill grace.
>
> For me, moving and staying at home, traveling and arriving, are all of a piece. The world is full of homes in which I have lived for a day, a month, a year, or much longer. How much I care about a home is not measured by the length of time I have lived there. One night in a room with a leaping fire may mean more to me than many months in a room without a fireplace, a room in which my life has been paced less excitingly.
>
> Margaret Mead, *Blackberry Winter*

If we learn to read Margaret Mead, maybe we can learn to write as well as she does. In the first sentence she contrasts two words as they function "For many people." Then she spends one long sentence on each of the two words that she has contrasted. She defines travel as a positive thing, then as the opposite (*antidote*) of a word (*humdrum*), and finally combines negative and positive definitions by calling travel the journey to a *holiday* from *dullness.* This sentence makes a definition by repetition. When Mead defines *moving,* she uses a similar doubleness.

All along, we have been held in suspense by the phrase "For many people" that began the passage. If we hear that a definition is true "For many people," we are surely going to hear a contrasting definition for other people. Mead's second paragraph begins with a contrasting "For me" that provides the transition, or stepping-stone, from one paragraph to the other. We learn that the words that contrast for many people do not contrast for Mead. But, conscious that she writes for an audience, wishing to make contact with that audience, Mead is not content simply to *tell* us that contradictions disappear for her; she *shows* us by repeating earlier expressions jumbled together—"moving and staying at home, traveling and arriving"—and then by detail and example from her life—"homes in which I have lived for a day."

Or take another paragraph, from fiction this time. One of the models of prose style in American literature is Ernest Hemingway, who worked carefully on rhythm and sound. When he began writing as a young man, he studied style and practiced and revised, to learn the way to his own voice. A short story called "In Another Country," about some wounded soldiers in a hospital in Italy during World War I, opens with this paragraph:

> In the fall the war was always there, but we did not go to it any more. It was cold in the fall in Milan and the dark came very early. Then the electric lights came on, and it was pleasant along the streets looking in the windows. There was much game hanging outside the shops, and the snow powdered on the fur of the foxes and the wind blew their tails. The deer hung stiff and heavy and empty, and small birds blew in the wind and the wind turned their feathers. It was a cold fall and the wind came down from the mountains.

Such a simple style! And if we try to imitate it, we are likely to lace one shoe to the other. Reading it, we may notice that the grammar is simple, yet the length of sentence and clause—the units of rhythm— varies continually. The vocabulary is simple—*the fall, cold,* and *wind* repeated, *wind* four times in the last five lines—yet expressive. The effect of the whole is hypnotic or dreamy; the war is around us, but *we* are not in it. Then the paragraph ends with the corpses of animals, described in loving detail. Look at the word *pleasant;* normally, we might find this word too general and want to ask *how,* exactly, did you feel? But here, in the emotions of the paragraph, the vagueness is an accurate understatement; it embodies the emotional restraint in this removal from war, the tentative acceptance that *we* are alive, unlike the animals outside the shops and the unmentioned combatants among whom *we* used to count ourselves.

### DISORGANIZED WRITING, POMPOUS WRITING

For a perverse sort of fun, let us rewrite the Hemingway passage in a couple of bad versions. Let me call this exercise *downwriting,* turning something good into something bad. This practice can be instructive as we learn how to write. Mostly, we will try to improve bad writing; but sometimes we will imagine how we might have flubbed the opportunity for good writing that someone else took advantage of.

First, a parody (an imitation of a style, for the sake of mockery: a kind of downwriting) of the disorganized writing that most of us start with:

> September through December, in the fall, at any rate, the war still went on, but we ourselves weren't doing the fighting by this time. It got chilly then in the Italian city of Milan. It started to get dark earlier in the day. When it got dark they turned on the lights. It was nice to look in the windows of stores. There were a lot of dead wild animals outside of the stores. When it snowed it snowed on the animals' fur too. There was a lot of wind and it blew the animals' fur and it even blew the little ones around. It was really cold because the wind was coming down from the mountains, which were cold.

Actually, this parody is better than the prose most of us write at first, because the writer observes real things. Most bad writing omits anything that might be interesting and expressive. The whole paragraph might be reduced to

> It was fall in Milan, Italy, one year during World War I. It got colder and the days got shorter.

But the short version omits all feeling. In the real paragraph, details of image and action carry the scene to the reader. You cannot reduce *War and Peace* to a telegram.

Or we could try it in Pompous Institutional Moderne.

During the autumn, the hostilities continued to ensue, but we personally no longer engaged in them. The daily temperature declined in Milan as the autumn continued, and the hours of daylight gradually contracted. When darkness ensued, lights were illuminated. It was altogether agreeable to promenade and investigate the contents of shop windows. There was considerable unrationed meat available at this particular time, by reason of the prevalence of slaughtered wild animals. Precipitation in the form of snow, as the months progressed, accumulated on the fur of these slaughtered beasts, and the cold breeze that accompanied the snow caused the tails of the animals to wave. Venison was at the present time available, as was small fowl. The extreme cold of this autumn is attributable to the fact that the prevailing winds came from the direction of the mountains which, because of their elevation and the snow which had already accumulated thereon, were lower in terms of temperature than the temperature which normally prevailed in the city.

This last writer, if he or she existed, might be elected chairperson of the Senior Class Gift Committee but would never by such language make contact with another human being. We learn to write well, if we learn, for good reason. If we write with the chaos of the first parody or with the pomposity of the second, we are in trouble in our heads and our hearts, not just in our writing. If we learn to write well, we will sharpen our wits on the one hand and point our imagination on the other—both together, or neither at all.

## LEARNING TO WRITE WELL

How then do we learn to write well? This whole book tries to answer the question. Here at the beginning let us mention three things, at least. First, we can read well, which helps slowly but keeps on helping; we can think about what we read, in a way that helps our writing. After we have read a page or two, we can pause to consider *how* the author has shown us what we have taken, *how* the writer has assembled details, organized them, and led us from one thing to another. If we talk in class about essays we have read, either student work or professional models, we can compare our successes and failures of reading; by improving the way we read, we will improve our writing. See the next chapter for more about reading.

Second, we can study writing and think about it and discuss it with others; mostly, we will discuss it in class with a teacher and with other students. Among our friends we may discover one or two willing and able to act as audience for our drafts and revisions. We discover not only by analyzing the finished products of the writing process but by studying the process of writing itself, our own and other people's. (See Chapter 3 for some models of process.)

Third, and most important, we can write and rewrite and rewrite. Because rewriting our own work is most useful, we must have writing to rewrite. We can keep a notebook. Keep a journal. Keep our old themes. We can keep copies of papers or exams we write for other courses. In this collection of our own prose, we will find ideas for expanding and rewriting. We may notice, the tenth time we read something, that we have written to hide something from ourselves instead of to discover. After thinking about clichés or paragraph organization or passive verbs, we will find examples in our own prose, and we will see how to revise them.

## DAILY WRITING

While we are learning to write, it is essential to write every day. Constantly applying pen to paper will ease the work of writing and will give us a collection of words in which to look for ideas to develop and for sentences to revise. Writing is a skill, like an athletic skill, which comes more naturally to some people than to others but which improves with practice for everyone. Practice is a necessity. Maybe the best method is to write daily dated entries in a notebook. This notebook sounds like a journal, but for most people a journal is like a diary and records merely the day's events:

> Had pancakes for breakfast. 9 o'clock boring . . .

Little entries that set out our daily schedule do not help us. Better are memories, whole anecdotes, ideas, and queries. Or it may help to concentrate on the world outside the self.

Doing daily writing means writing a page or two a day, every day, seven days a week, working rapidly and without trying to impose a direction on it, without conscious control or focus. Nor should a daily entry be continuous, necessarily. Some days one has apparently unrelated flashes of thought or memory. Some days one seems to have no ideas at all. On such a day, you may let your hand flow over the page with disconnected words and phrases.

Daily writing helps fluency, ease and supply, but it gives us no practice in making shapes directed toward a reader: our work toward an audience, and our work on organization, will derive from social occasions like classes and conferences and from imagining social encounters. But in the meantime, daily writing will improve the fluency that we will later use for contact with others.

Many lifelong writers keep notebooks. The American poet Theodore Roethke left two hundred and seventy-seven notebooks behind when he died. Some entries were lines and images for poems; some were used, some were not. Others were prose notes to himself about writing poetry and might have been seeds for unwritten essays. At other times, he made a conventional journal entry.

> Today, or tonight, I realized finally at the age of 40, for the first time, that it is really possible for me to think, and even get pleasure from the process. Not that my efforts—or effects—are spectacular. Perhaps four consecutive related thoughts at present is the absolute top of my form—and that only just before falling asleep, or just after eating a fine breakfast, when I'm too lazy to write anything down. But still, even this is a beginning. And such excitement!

The novelist F. Scott Fitzgerald kept a notebook in which he recorded situations, observations, jokes, and anything else.

> Family quarrels are bitter things. They don't go according to any rules. They're not like aches or wounds, they're more like splits in the skin that won't heal because there's not enough material.

> Jules had dark circles under his eyes. Yesterday he had closed out the greatest problem of his life by settling with his ex-wife for two hundred thousand dollars. He had married too young, and the former slavey from the Quebec slums had taken to drugs upon her failure to rise with him. Yesterday, in the presence of lawyers, her final gesture had been to smash his finger with the base of a telephone.

> Run like an old athlete.

Daily writing can loosen minds. Our minds are muscle-bound, not by intellect, but by formulas of thought, by clichés both of phrase and of organization. Our minds do not need to remain restricted. An economics student wrote this entry one day:

> Blue clouds in Arizona. I was hitchhiking last August, at the edge of the desert waiting for a ride that would take me across state. A little tree, a little shade. Sun so hot it melted turtles. Blue clouds of Arizona. Because there were no clouds at all, just blue glaring

and turning white toward the sun. Like an egg only a lot brighter and hotter. Got a ride with a truck driver. "Never went to college myself. The war came along and then I had kids, you know. My daughter's at State." Jiggle. Oil. Hot. We had cheeseburgers in an airconditioned diner and I never felt so good in my whole life as when that ice-air hit me. Then the heat outside. Walking into the oven. (cliché.)

There is no point to his story, or maybe no story. No one said he had to make a point. All he had to do was write a page. He was practicing.

Practice was the first thing for him, sheer practice in putting pen to paper, letting the words follow each other across the page; if the habit of writing remains alien to us, we will never learn to write with any naturalness. Second, he was learning to loosen up. No one was going to correct his spelling, or argue with his logic, or tell him that his clauses were not parallel; he felt free to let the images follow each other loosely by association. Until the last phrase, his loosened mind provided fresh images. But if he had written a string of clichés, nobody was going to bother him about it. Earlier in his notebook, before he trusted himself to loosen up, his prose had been rigid and trite.

Beginning a notebook of daily writing, almost everyone is shy and stiff, as if this private writing were a public performance. One student began her notebook:

> I am not "an emotionalist," if such a word exists. I feel as if I'm taking a step forward in saying that I tend not to be sincere in my writing. From this point forward I shall try to do so. I feel that I'm honest with myself, but when I know that others will read my work I unconsciously become dishonest as I write.
>
> If I were to write a short essay on any topic and hand it to a person to read, I wouldn't stay in the same room while the person read my work. Whether this is because of shyness or embarrassment, or both, I don't know.

Two months later, her prose was less self-conscious and more relaxed, and she seemed to enjoy herself more.

> They try to give something special every week. When I read eggrolls listed on the menu, I thought, great, my favorite thing in the world. But to my dismay, I was shocked at what the Stockwell Cafeteria had done. How could they destroy *my* eggrolls? I bit into one of them and I noticed *black,* inside my eggroll. Shortly later, I

discover that *raisons* had been planted in the eggrolls! Raisons! How could they! It seemed that they just sat around saying, "What can we put in the eggrolls to make them terrible? We can't lose our image!" Of all the stupid things. That's enough to start a new war with China!

Nobody leaned over her shoulder, drew a red circle around "raisons," and wrote "raisins" in the margin. Over the term her writing improved, perhaps because she wrote ninety-two pages of daily writing; her spelling stayed about the same.

Everybody who starts daily writing at first fears running out of material. Really, we have enough memory packed away, by age eighteen, to keep us writing until we are seventy. We gradually discover tricks that keep the pages coming. We should stop writing while we still have something to say; it is even wise to make an arbitrary rule: stop at the bottom of a full page, even in the middle of a sentence, and write nothing more until the next day. The next day, you will not have to sit and wait for the words to start.

Many students find that they work best with large categories of reminiscence, writing many pages—weeks of daily writing—on one general subject: my six best friends and their families; fishing trips with my mother; Christmas vacation; jobs I have had; my teachers in grammar school; pets; relatives; the Little League; 4-H clubs; fights with my brother; learning how to repair my ten-speed bike; my favorite meals; and my favorite jokes (one student remembered forty pages of jokes!). Some students interested in science and technology try to write about science in a language that nonscientists can understand—a difficult and useful kind of writing.

> I talked with another freshman yesterday who made the same old mistake. Arguing about science and history, and what you could know for sure, he told me that some physicist had discovered that even in science you don't know anything for certain. And I tried to tell him about Heisenberg's uncertainty principle, but it's hard to explain it when people don't know some mathematics. Heisenberg showed that it's impossible to measure, accurately and at the same time, both the momentum and the location of a subatomic particle. This indeterminacy is totally insignificant with big things like baseballs and spaceships, but with an electron or a neutron, for instance, Heisenberg proved that knowledge of simultaneous momentum and position is impossible.

Daily writing is a means and not an end, however. Daily writing without an audience must prepare us to write for an audience. Our fluency is the tool by which we embody the shape of our thought, to reach out and connect with the reader. Unity, clarity, and the discipline of the sentence and paragraph—all are necessary to move the message from the writer to the reader. Once we have found an idea or an image or a secret lode of language, then we must learn to shape and control in order to communicate.

We need to learn all about language—choosing words, inventing metaphors, phrases, clauses, and sentences, and constructing paragraphs—before we can establish control over our writing. Of course we must try to make whole shapes, like the revision by Jim Beck, from the very beginning, even before we have learned the names of what we do. It makes sense to look at what happens when we write an essay, and in Chapter 3 we will investigate the process of writing and look into suggestions for stimulating that process. But first, we must take a look at the more general problems of language and communication. We know that reading and writing are twins. If we investigate what happens when we read, it will help us to understand what should happen when we write.

------ **EXERCISES** _____

1. Write a page in a notebook, every day, for the rest of the term. Bring your notebook to conferences for your instructor to inspect, but not to correct. Bring it to class, if your instructor asks you to, with a page or a paragraph marked to read aloud. Discuss in class the problems and rewards of daily writing, giving each other suggestions for subjects.

2. Write a brief impromptu essay on the events of your first few days in college. You might write about motives and ideas like Jim Beck, or write a narrative like Marian Hart (see Exercise 12). Work to find unity and focus that will hold your essay together. Use specific details, examples, and anecdotes. Consider other students as your audience.

3. Write a brief essay about writing or reading. Pick one thing you have learned, about either writing or reading, which allowed you to improve your practice. Tell what it is, give at least one example, and describe how you learned it.

4. Who was the best teacher who taught you in high school? (Do not choose merely the most agreeable but the one from whom you learned most.) How did the teacher do it? What did you learn? Be specific and show what you learned.

5. Pick one sentence from the two paragraphs by Margaret Mead on p. 14. *Downwrite* it (see pp. 16–17) to achieve one of these failures: disorganization, emptiness, or pomposity.

6. We discover ourselves by the language we use. Write a dialogue, or a conversation, in which two people reveal their characters by their language.

7. Analyze the language of this essay. Try revising the first paragraph.

*My Big Moment*

In my humble opinion, after all is said and done, opportunities for people to show what they are made of are conspicuous by their absence at this university. Because of this sad truth, the day I gave my report stuck out like a sore thumb. It was a red letter day. I had spent the entire year at college burning the midnight oil and leading a precarious existence earning my tuition working for a professor who was a veritable mine of information. I was very much interested in the finer things of life. My hope to do things that would make me stand out from the crowd were usually doomed to disappointment. As I wended my way from class to class each day, and then to the job where I put my nose to the grindstone, I often thought that the events in my life at which I could point with pride were few and far between. But today would be different.

Today I, a rank outsider, would be the center of attention. People would realize that I was smart as a whip. They would listen with bated breath. At ten o'clock I stood as scared as a rabbit before the class. Although I was hungry as a bear because I had not eaten breakfast, I was calm and collected. I stood before them and I told the unvarnished truth about Man's mistreatment of Mother Nature. I explained that the powers that be must sit up and take notice of the fast and furious pace of pollution, and that there was a crying need for immediate action. I viewed with alarm the future of society when the purity of the very air we breathe hangs in the balance. When I concluded my few remarks, there was thunderous applause. I could tell I had hit the nail on the head. I was tired but happy. I had hit one out of the ball park.

8. Earlier you were asked to *downwrite* a passage. *Upwrite* these sentences. Use your imagination if you need to supply details.

a. The nature of marketing practices in the dry cleaning field at the present time is not to be believed.

b. We visited the Radio Shack. It was fun. The man talked a lot. He told us all sorts of things.

c. Swimming lots of lengths in a pool is good for toning muscles but you get tired of the chlorine and I don't like the fact that they are always out of towels at the Y.

9. In *The Atlantic*, a writer discussed some schools he disapproved of. In one paragraph, he wrote:

> In such places students are taught clichés. In one college a test consisted of stories with blank spaces to be filled with adjectives, the "correct" answers arcane or phony words used by *Time* magazine during the era of Henry Luce (but no longer used even by *Time*). In another college the blanks to be filled were the most hackneyed phrases, so that fires were always "raging," heavy rains always "torrential downpours," and recriminations always "bitter."
>
> Ben H. Bagdikian,
> "Woodstein U.: Notes on the Mass Production
> and Questionable Education of Journalists"

Make a short paragraph in which you leave blanks for parts of clichés—usually an adjective or an adverb. Read it aloud in class to see if other students can fill in the "correct" clichés.

10. Here is another "How I Came to College" impromptu. (a) Criticize it for language and for structure. (b) Edit it. Rearrange and rewrite. Avoid clichés. Aim for a consistent idea of audience.

> I looked for work waitressing or anything last summer. Not finding anything school seemed like the best thing. Besides my family wants me to go. Learn a trade or skill I guess. So thats how come I am sitting here writing this!
>
> My girlfriend had already gotten in here and so she told me how to do it. I sign up and they tell me what I had to do. Just before I started classes I got the job I was looking for! But my father says you go to school. That's life.
>
> I can't tell yet how I like it or not. But I had a hard time getting here every morning because I don't have a car and, my mother doesn't drive and my father needs it except on Thursdays. My girlfriend has a car, she drives me here MWF. Tuesday I take buses for one hour or so.

11. Here is a better example. (a) What makes it better? (b) In what ways could this student learn to improve her writing? Pay attention to mechanics, to focus, and to word choice. Pay attention to the author's idea of audience and think how it might be improved.

> All my life I have known that I would, some day, go off to school. By the end of my senior year in High School I knew where and when I'd be leaving and spent the summer getting used to the idea. But getting

used to the idea was all I did—I did not begin to think or worry about what college was really going to be like. I did not spend hours contemplating the importance of "going off into the big wide world." I did not even speculate what things would be like, what if I hated my roommate, what if the work was too hard, what if I'm unhappy. I did not think about specifics, I had told myself that I would have time to get psyched the week before I left.

But a week before the day I had planned to leave, before I had prepared myself I got a phone call from my father. He had to give a lecture at a convention on the west coast in five days. For him to make it we had to leave that day and he would drop me off in Michigan on his way to California. I had one hour to pack. One hour to collect all my belongings and somehow fit them into a car that looked like it could not hold half the things I wanted to take. It happened so fast I did not have time to think, I did not even have time to say goodby to my mother who was out shopping. We left in a hurry leaving behind many things I had forgotten to pack and a small note to my mother that simply said good-by.

If I had more time I'm sure my goodbye to my mother and friends would have been a long, emotional scene. Driving through my town I had no time to look at my Elementary School, my High School, the house of my best friend and get sentimental. It was pouring and concentrating on the driving was all I could do.

The eleven hour drive also left no time for thought. I drove most of the way so that my father could prepare his speech. Every so often he would read parts to me to try them out. Our talk consisted of whether injection-lasers was a hyphenated word or not. (I still don't know.)

Then I was here, in the dorm, with my roommate, in my classes. It seemed as if I had been here all my life and the trauma of leaving home was over. I did not even have time to think about it until later and then I could not even remember how it felt to leave home.

12. Here is an impromptu followed by a revision made late in the term. Compare the two essays. Correct the first version. What has the student learned? What is good about the revision? Can the improvements be explained by the writer's attention to an idea of audience? Find places in the revision where the writer could make further improvements. Rewrite two sentences in the revision to make them better.

I always wanted to go to the University because my Dad went here.

I remember how it got started. I had a job as a car-hop in a drive in, an A & W in Flint where I make my home. Business was slack because it was about 3:30 Saturday afternoon so I was talking away with Barb and Karen who were working there too and I knew them from school of course. We had to wear these very tight stretch pants because Boss said it was good for business. A car came in and because it was my turn I picked up a pad and started out for it, then I saw it was my Dad. He jumped out of the car and hugged me. I knew what it was and so did Barb because we were all waiting to hear about admissions. I told him he could open it and he did and that's why he drove out, to tell me. Barb had to wait until she got off, the Boss wouldn't let her go and there was nobody at home to call up.

So! We got here three days ago, in the same car, only loaded to the roof with my stuff. I was petrified with fear. My Dad kept telling me what to do, and then he kept saying he knew it had changed a lot in 25 years. I wished he'd be quiet. My Mom cried. We couldn't find the dorm. Everybody we asked didn't know either. The boys all had pink hair and Nikes and looked exactly the way I expected them too. My Dad hated it. Then when we found my dorm and we found my room my Dad was all out of breath, and mad, and he just pushed the door open with his shoulder and busted in. There was a naked girl standing there, with no clothes on, my roommate (whose very nice, named Terri, but I didn't know that yet) and he made a funny noise and dropped the suitcase and ran back out into the hall.

*My Father's Place*
Marian Hart

It is about an hour and a quarter from my house in Flint to the dormitory in Ann Arbor. All the way, as we drove here last August to move in, my Dad was talking about the class of 1959. I tried to listen. I had heard him talk about the University since I was a little girl, and since I was a little girl I had wanted to come here to college. But in the car I was shy and frightened. I was going to meet a roommate named Terri who was from Detroit. She would be sophisticated and have long hair. All the boys would be crazy about her. I would be the invisible frump from Flint.

I tried to think about the happy things. I tried to think about how happy I was, as I sat there feeling stupid and ugly. I remembered how happy I was to be accepted. It was a Saturday last Spring when I was working at the A & W, being a car hop in the stretch pants that the boss made us wear "because it's good for business."

It was a slack time of day, and suddenly a car rolled up, parking across two parking places, and rocking with the brakes put on too fast. I picked up an order pad and headed out, and then I saw that it was our car and that my Dad was jumping out at me waving an envelope and grinning. He didn't have to say anything. We hugged and he called me his sweetheart. The three of us went out to dinner that night and celebrated.

Now my mother was sobbing and my teeth were chattering and my father was talking about hula hoops! I groaned a little, and he said—for the twelfth time—that of course he knew that everything was different now, with student rights and politics and ecology and (he gagged a little) co-ed dormitories. But . . . and he was off again. He was as nervous as I was.

When we drove into town my Dad's composure fell apart completely. He didn't know where he was. We asked directions but everyone else was as lost as we were. The whole place had changed, he said; none of the old landmarks were there. And he obviously hated the new landmarks. Girls with pink hair and bare feet were throwing frisbees with boys with blue jeans and earrings and pink hair. My father's jaw went tight, and from the back seat I could see the tenseness of his neck that happened when he was worried or angry.

We found the dorm. My father carried the four suitcases. I carried a portable stereo and a box of indispensable records. My mother had three garment bags full of clothes which I knew I would never wear. Of course my room was on the third floor. Every time we passed a boy in the hallway my father's neck, which was red with carrying four suitcases, got tenser.

When we got to the door of my room, he didn't set down the suitcases to knock. Puffing and snorting, he pushed open the door with his shoulder and strode in, me and my mother close behind. Then he dropped all four suitcases, crash, and made a weird little noise. I thought: My God, he's having a heart attack. Then I looked past him and saw a girl standing facing him with her mouth flopped open in surprise—Terri, I thought, even then, and she's *not* too beautiful—and stark naked.

---

# 2

## _Reading, and Reading Well_

There is no writing well without reading well.

One writer puts it with a pun, which I set into lines as if stitched on a sampler:

> No skillful composition is possible
> without that prior act of decomposition
> practiced through reading models
> of composition by others.

Reading, writing, and thinking are not separate activities; talking is nothing but writing out loud—with gesture and expression as aids to emphasis, like SMALL CAPS or _italics_. Reading, thinking, and writing-talking are a single thing: we use them in combination or we do not use them at all.

### READING, WRITING, AND THINKING

We may learn a sport part by part, backhand now and serve later; or we may learn a musical instrument by fingering a melody before we learn to make chords. But we play the game or the song only when we put things together. Because we have learned to consider reading, thinking, and writing as separate, we need to unlearn this lesson in order to proceed—and in order to sing the song or win the game.

When we write we read—that's easy to see—but when we read we write, which takes more seeing. My first draft of this chapter began like this:

> The act of reading resembles the act of writing, as the way out resembles the way in. Both are social acts, attempted connections between persons, and resemble the two sides of a conversation.

As I read it now, I understand what I intended to say, but only because I wrote it. To improve my chapter, in my attempt to reach you, I tried to become the reader of my own writing. I tried to question my writing as if someone else had written it. Why should I say *the act of* twice? It sounds pedantic or pompous. Why not say "Reading resembles writing"? I answered myself: for one thing, because I don't mean *writing* as in "Southern writing today," where it means *literature*. Also the phrase omits talking and thinking. I tried rewriting it:

> Reading resembles writing. When we read we do something that resembles what we do when we write. It also resembles what we do when we talk and when we think.

When I read this attempt a day after writing it, it seemed even less clear than it was before. "What we do when" is words of one syllable but the syntax is hard to follow; also it begs the question of what, in fact, we are doing. While I was puzzling over how to begin, I ran across a sentence by J. Hillis Miller (the sentence set out in lines above) that seemed useful to me.

At some point I noticed that I could use my new chapter title to suggest the identity of reading and writing; I could use the same words as the first chapter's title, except to substitute *Reading* for *Writing*. After five drafts I showed my chapter to a friend. He liked the sentence quoted from J. Hillis Miller but found it hard to follow; it was he who suggested setting it out as I have done. Thus my friend's reading helped my writing. But it was my own reading of my own writing that came first, as it always does.

Nothing resembles a bump so much as a hollow; the act of reading traces the same map-journey as the act of writing. Reading and writing are social acts that we often accomplish in solitude. Although each is solitary, each resembles *both* sides of a conversation. While we write we read what we have written as if we heard another speak; while we read we interpret words by our own experience, which means that we contribute to the writing in the act of reading, or more properly the *acts* of reading.

Our third term is thinking, not a separate item. We need to understand: we do not *think*, as we commonly use the word, except by means of language. It is possible to speak or write without thought, but it is nearly impossible to think without words. Maybe an architect thinks in spatial relations; but the word *thinking* as we use it, ninety-nine times out of a hundred, requires words. Thinking is a function of language.

## THE DIFFERENT ACTS OF READING

When we read, our eyes habitually translate letters into words, then words by the linkages of syntax into sentences that carry meanings. But this sentence—the one I just committed—leaps from objective to subjective without attending to the leap. Look at the first three words, "When we read. . . . " Perhaps we all read the same *When*; perhaps we all read the same *we*; I am sure that we do not all read the same *read*.

Experiences differ and make for different responses in different readers. If reading has been a pleasure for X since X was little, the word *read* will carry easy and pleasurable associations for X. For Y, on the other hand, *read* may be associated with crabby teachers, with hard and unrewarding labor, with school failure, with the blame or scorn of siblings and parents—a small intense universe of pain. In a class of twenty students there may be twenty different responses to the word *read*.

Last year in a classroom in Greeley, Colorado, I read a paragraph aloud to a group of students. I asked the students to listen carefully as I read and to write down their uncensored responses to the words they heard—so that we might take a look at how we are reading. The paragraph included this sentence:

> When the full moon rises in late winter, shining over rags of snow,
> it wakes bears in the hemlock woods who stagger sleepily to ex-
> plore our compost.

Then we listened to each other's responses. For one boy the word *moon* triggered *astronaut* and then *Challenger*—it was the anniversary of the disaster—and said that he never really heard the rest. Hearing something read aloud differs from silent reading because you cannot stop and go back when you know you've missed something.

A young woman liked the images in the sentence except that *rags* did not make sense to her. Two other people raised their hands consulting their own notes, because they responded to *rags*. One said that *rags* was like the filthy cloths you wiped an oilstick on; March snow rotted; covered with dust, March snow looked filthy and raggedy; therefore, he said, *rags* was a good image. The second student laughed: "No, no," she said—she understood that she contradicted a response and not a meaning—"*rags* means torn-up sheets and pillowcases, white from bleach, waiting piled in a laundry basket to use for dusting." Therefore, she said, *rags* was a good image.

As visiting teacher I used these responses for happy examples. Neither was right or wrong, or, rather, both were right, because both students read actively into the text, letting a word blossom and grow in the soil of their own experience, responding to the text by reading with their imaginations. The sentence itself could accept either rags-white or rags-dirty. Other students in the class, upon questioning, mostly felt that they hadn't paid much attention to rags—and we discussed whether their inattention implied superficial reading, on the one hand, or less experience of the word *rags*. One said, "Hell, no. That's my dog's name! And it *is* a dog's name!"

One boy brought class discussion to an end, finally, by telling us—embarrassed but amused—that when he heard "bears" he misheard it "bares" and lost himself in speculations about frozen nudity.

When the boy said that *rags* meant *dogs*, mocking his own dogmatism, someone in the class addressed him as "Mr. Grumbacher," because of a story I had earlier told. It is a story from my schooltime that I have told many times when I have tried to show that different responses can be valid. Our eighth-grade teacher was sick; then the substitute got sick: I don't think that Mr. Grumbacher had taught for a long time, and I don't think he wanted to teach; he did it as a favor. In a sense, he did me a favor, for he taught us for a whole week and I will never forget him; he was the most dogmatic teacher I ever knew. The subject was a poem by Robert Frost, "Stopping by Woods on a Snowy Evening," which our old teacher had assigned us. Mr. Grumbacher was not reluctant to teach the poem, for he knew what every syllable in the poem meant; he must have been inside Robert Frost's head when Frost wrote it. If you don't remember the poem, here it is:

*Stopping by Woods on a Snowy Evening*

Whose woods these are I think I know.
His house is in the village though;
He will not see me stopping here
To watch his woods fill up with snow.

My little horse must think it queer
To stop without a farmhouse near
Between the woods and frozen lake
The darkest evening of the year.

He gives his harness bells a shake
To ask if there is some mistake.
The only other sound's the sweep
Of easy wind and downy flake.

The woods are lovely, dark and deep,
But I have promises to keep,
And miles to go before I sleep,
And miles to go before I sleep.

When Mr. Grumbacher read it aloud to us, he said, "Tell me what that poem's about." Nobody spoke for a while; then somebody said that it was about a person who couldn't afford to waste any time because he had so much to do; somebody else said it was about a man with a horse and a cart, maybe delivering milk. (This happened so long ago so that milkmen still used horses and wagons.) Mr. Grumbacher looked impatient. I said that the poem was about how pretty the woods were with snow falling in the dark night. Then Mr. Grumbacher told us: Robert Frost was a farmer so that's what the man was and he was fed up with snow and cold so he wanted to go to Florida. We didn't argue, he sounded so convinced.

Now when I read this poem, if I remember Mr. Grumbacher, I respond not to the poem but to my own private memories. Of course there is nothing in the poem about going to Florida; nor do we need to think that Robert Frost speaks it or that he is a farmer. The children who thought of milkmen and mailmen were reading well—and Mr. Grumbacher wasn't. He must have wanted to go to Florida himself. Of course I think of him when I see the poem, but I would have to be crazy to tell you that my experience *is* part of the poem; *for me* it is part of the poem. Everyone reads a different poem and there are different valid poems. All readings are subjective. Let us enjoy our differences—but let us also work on our ability to understand what we do, to discriminate private from public. We read well when we imagine particulars that fit—milkman, mailman—and we read badly when we imagine nothing or when we imagine something that isn't there, like a desire for a trip to Florida in Robert Frost's poem.

Associations that arise from personal history make for different responses, and maybe these individual biographical differences account for the greatest disparities. But also, different associations can derive from philosophical or political differences. Apparently *Democracy* differs for readers in Communist and capitalist nations. Two of us in conversation may agree that we are each *conservative*, but on further discussion we may find that one of us wishes to conserve liberty by locking the other in jail.

We differ as readers not only by the associations or definitions of individual words but in how we receive or respond to tone and irony, which is usually a matter of whole phrases or of sentences. When one person uses a cliché ironically, thinking that it's funny to say, "It's not the heat, it's the humidity," another will take the assertion literally and ponder the relative importance of temperature and dampness. For one reader, long sentences with dependent clauses help bring across an author's sense and expression. For another reader, such complexity seems not a tool for expression but an assertion of superiority. Reading, we may find that a colon or semicolon provides us with information about the relationship between parts of sentences; or we may find a colon as obscure as a Chinese character.

All readers have problems: some will miss small clues like punctuation but be good receptors of larger clues to structure—beginnings and turning points and conclusions. Others may pick up little clues but show something like color-blindness for transitions. Certainly all of us read with limitations or biases that derive from experience, age, race, religion, culture, and region: we can become alert against our own limitations only when we recognize them.

Lest we end in discouragement, remember the two *rags*. Our differences are real and let us enjoy them. If we read well, with imagination, we will make our own differing texts out of our own creativity.

## FROM SUBJECTIVE TO OBJECTIVE

If we worry about our differences, we should appeal to common sense: language *exists* because we need to consult each other, originally to hunt the elephant together, to protect ourselves from the tiger, and to negotiate claims over territory. If there were as many *tigers* as there were Fred Flintstones, still a tiger's eyeteeth remained objective: we needed to invent language or die.

And we still do. We must use language for reading, thinking, talking, and writing—or we cannot be human, or civilized, or lovers or citizens or makers of a living. We must acknowledge our separateness but then we must work to overcome our separateness as well as we can. There is another ground besides passivity on the one hand and denial (sometimes miscalled heroism) on the other. When we think— and read and speak and write—in order to touch each other *despite* our real separateness, we use language for its social connection, to string wires of communication from each to each.

## PRIVATE AND PUBLIC: THE PARADOX

We acknowledge that by necessity we are separate and that each reader's response differs from every other reader's. Second, we assert that language exists for social purposes, that we think by language and connect by it. We connect—therefore—by the same device that separates us.

When we study ways to connect, classroom work is probably more useful than homework. We can learn about our own responses by listening to the responses of others—and by hearing the responses of others to our own. If we cannot eliminate private response, we can learn to discriminate the private from the public. Working together, disagreeing, we can work toward a community of ideas; we can negotiate a consensus. First each of us separately responds to what we read; then as a community we scrutinize our responses, looking to tell the more subjective from the more objective, realizing that our responses will occupy a continuum from the extremely private to the extremely public, and finding what we can agree about in common.

We will always ask the question How much of my reading is me and how much is the author? When twenty different *me*'s expose their responses in a classroom, many responses will occur only once, and we will understand them, not necessarily as wrong, but as individual or even eccentric: we must always remember that the singular, unusual response—when it is exposed to others—may by its insight reveal something that the others originally missed in their reading; one of us can sometimes add to the responses of others. Other responses will occur to a handful of students; still others will occur to all or almost all. By and large, the curve of frequency describes the range from individual to general, from subjective to objective.

These responses remain subject to the negotiated consensus of a community.

## VALUES OF CONSCIOUSNESS

It is a preconception of this book—it must be a preconception of this course, of the teaching of English, of the university itself, of the teacher's life devoted to the classroom, of the students' undertaking when he or she comes to the university—that knowing is better than not knowing. Thinking is preferable to not-thinking, and for thinking we need words and we need agreement or consensus about the meanings of words.

There are forces in any society that assert the values of unconsciousness—the less people understand, the easier people are to handle—but education promotes consciousness. Study of composition is basic because words are fundamental to thinking or consciousness. When we read and speak we are unconscious grammarians, using our previous experience of grammatical structures from speech and from reading as a way to understand the grammatical structures made by writers: but if we consciously learn the names and behavior of grammar in English, we will learn syntax more securely and with greater usefulness. If we understand alternatives in constructing paragraphs, or the differences in tone between passive and active moods in verbs, we will read paragraphs and sentences with more sensitivity. Therefore our awareness of other people will increase.

The more we read, the more imaginatively and actively we read; the more we reflect on our responses, the more experience we will gather for further reading.

## WORDS ARE SOCIAL

Language exemplifies our separateness but it exists to alleviate that separateness. If we need the condiment yards away down the table, we may retain our separateness by standing up and walking down the table to get it; or we can use language for communication and ask our neighbor, "Please pass the salt."

Here is a homely example of the utility of language. But what about the other extreme, for instance the poem that uses language to embody something ineffable, like Andrew Marvell's "a green thought in a green shade," that makes an object out of language that most readers or hearers will find obscure? Or what about the philosopher's distinction between *being* and *existence,* or Einstein's thinking about space, time, and energy?

These uses of language differ from "Please pass the salt," and they make three sorts of hard reading. But should we say that poet, philosopher, and physicist use language *not* for communication with other people? Maybe the poet uses language partly to make an aesthetic shape with it, as if it were stone and he a sculptor; we must admit that the shapeliness itself does not exist *for* communication; but if the poem communicates something to some readers and hearers, and if it communicates something otherwise unsayable, then even at this extreme we use language for communication. If philosopher and physicist use language to reach someone else, this social use does not imply that their language can reach everyone in society.

## READING AS RE-READING

Whenever this book speaks of writing it speaks of revision, and not only when it concentrates on process; writing *is* revision. When we become conscious of the act of written revision, we may learn to hear ourselves revise even as we *speak,* even in casual conversation: almost everyone speaking crosses out one word and substitutes another, saying, "Those banners were really red, I mean *crimson.* . . . " Sometimes we may say the same sentence over again, repeating it almost exactly but making little changes in word-choice, in grammar, or in emphasis by pitch and volume—trying for more exact shades of meaning as we reach out to the listener.

It is less obvious but equally true that reading requires revision.

As writing is revising reading is re-reading. Even the most experienced of readers will misread on occasion. If we read actively, demanding coherence from the page before us, we will from time to time realize that we have lost this coherence—and we will need to return to the text, to go back and start again. We lose track because our minds wander when we are tired, because a car backfires or a clock strikes, because a roommate makes a telephone call. We lose track because of imprecise knowledge of a word, because we miss the force of a grammatical turn or the sense of a transition, or because we do not share an association with the author.

We misread because we do not share experience with the author. If an Argentinian uses the word *July* with the implication of a frigid climate white with snow, we from the northern hemisphere may miss something at first reading. Also we misread because of bias or because we do not want to hear something the author wants to tell us. For all these reasons and a thousand more, we always need to revise as we read; we must return to the text and question it; we must try to pick up again where we left off.

Students get the notion that texts are too difficult for them because they see their teachers reading with apparent ease, gliding over the text as if skating on an icy pond. But the teacher reads something that the teacher already knows, something read before perhaps many times.

For this reason, many teachers will sight-read an essay for the first time in front of their students. They will show themselves encountering new sentences, responding, thinking, misreading, and revising their reading. If then teachers make mistakes, as they must, they provide a model for correcting mistakes—for revising reading.

## PUT THE BLAME ON BLAME

People often lose sight of the issues—readings and misreadings—by assigning fault. When we have trouble reading, we often think *either* "This is a stupid/obscure/lousy writer" *or* "I am stupid/This is not the kind of thing I can read/I don't connect to this kind of writing." Casting blame lets us off the hook of the text. Casting blame is a kind of laziness, because it suggests that we surrender.

We should ignore whose fault it is, writer or reader; we should go back and revise our reading, instead of assigning blame.

But when we turn into writers, it can be useful to remember how readers tend to blame writers.

## ACTIVE AND PASSIVE READERS

We must be active not passive readers. Much in our culture encourages passivity. When we grew up watching cartoons on weekend mornings, we bathed in the glow of animations created to entertain us in order to sell us something. If we felt bored we would switch channels: therefore no one allowed us to feel bored. If we read the way we watch television, we never get past Archie Comics.

Maybe I should call not merely for active reading but for aggressive reading. We should look the text in the eye; if it will not look back at us we should take it by the scruff of the neck and shake it. Or we should sit it on a chair with a thousand-watt bulb glaring in its eyes and repeat our questions: "Where were you on the night of May 23? Admit it!" But we must not merely question a suspect text; if we grill our reading like a detective, we must also be sure to investigate the investigator.

Here my analogy breaks down. The active or aggressive reader is a series of detectives, one of them interrogating the text and the rest interrogating the interrogator. Suspect, detective, judge, and jury are all the same—which makes for difficult justice. If we ask the text to confess how it gets from A to B, or why it lacks detail in support of Z, we must also ask if the question itself is appropriate, or if the interrogator is not making the mistake (omitting to notice a connective; missing the support offered) that it accuses the text of making.

Be the actor singular or plural—better an inward plural—the point is to be active not passive, to be aggressive not merely to accept. When we read that E. M. Forster gives two cheers for Democracy, we must not simply record the number as datum; after we register the number we must inquire *why?* Why does Forster use the figure *two* instead of *three* or *one* or *twenty-seven?* Out of our experience we should recollect that the traditional number of cheers is triple, three cheers for the old school, and understand that Forster's approval of Democracy implies limitation. Then we can inquire about the writer's reasons for limitation, but if we merely registered *two cheers* without actively inquiring about the phrase, without questioning the number of the number—if we had been passive to it, or if we had switched channels— we would have no limitation to look for. We would be passive readers or not readers at all.

The more active or imaginative we are in our reading, the more we tend to make our own essay as we respond to the writer's. This invention is not only inevitable with active readers, it is even a good thing—always with the proviso that we recognize what we are doing. Avoid the Grumbacher Effect! Reading E. M. Forster on "two cheers," I always wonder what happened to the third cheer. I think, "Maybe the third cheer is for the English class system!" This is *my* conscious notion, not E. M. Forster's.

## READING FOR WRITING

When we have responded and discriminated, as well as we can, subjective from objective, we can then analyze the text, reading aggressively—and reading analytically to see how the writer has caused our responses.

So reading leads back to writing. Reading and writing are a continual conversation, a transaction sometimes immediate and always potential. Reading old writing is conversation with the dead, almost miraculous; maybe all communication is a miracle, certainly when we feel that the author has reached out and touched us. By analysis we decide how well the author has performed. We are the audience. Has the writer reached us? Was the writer aware of us? By making this judgment about the transaction between the writer and ourselves we develop an idea of audience that ought to help us in our own writing.

*Reading and Writing are Social Activities.* When we talk about audience, about reader response, about the objective and subjective, we talk about the *social* use of language, which includes business letters and résumés as much as poems or histories of the world in twenty volumes.

When we interview someone for a club or a job, we form opinions of the person based on appearance, gestures, and accent, as well as on the words he or she uses. Although these judgments may be poor or superficial, we make them. When we write without the aid of gesture or voice, the words (sentence, paragraph structure, transitions) are all-important. Anyone reading listens to the tone of the transaction. Therefore, when we study our own reading we study what happens when others read us.

Reading is composing. Reading we make a whole. If we cannot make a whole our reading fails or the writing does. When our reading fails to make a whole, it is the same failure as when our writing fails.

## PRACTICE IN RESPONSE

A class at a university in Rhode Island practiced and compared its own responses by reading Edward Hoagland's editorial "Walking the Dog" reprinted from the *New York Times.* Beginning the exercise, the teacher identified the essay as an editorial. After all, any reader encountering it under normal circumstances would come to it with such information. She also reminded her class that editorials speak like Kings and Queens, using *we* where the writer normally would say *I*. Otherwise, she said to her class, you're on your own.

She asked the class to write a page or so of notes as they read it. She asked them not to read through the whole editorial before beginning their notes, but to write as they went along, pausing after every paragraph to write about what they had just read—and to predict what would come next if they had any notion. She told her students: Don't spend more than ten minutes on this; you don't have to be correct; but be prepared to read it aloud and to each other. She reminded them that in such an exercise there are no right answers, though it is always possible to misread. No one would be graded on correctness of response; the point of the exercise was to explore *differences* of response. This exploration, she said, should help us not only as readers in trying to understand our response and discriminate between the more subjective and the more objective, but it should help us as writers who try to predict the responses of our readers. Here's the editorial she used:

### Walking the Dog

We are in favor of cleaning up after them, but we are also in favor of dogs. Manhattan was once the home of whistling swans and seals and moutain lions, and, walking the dog, we remember this in our bones. Walking a dog, we feel occasionally that we are with a living ancestor, as children seem to do also. Children are born with a liking for dogs; and when we are out with the family dog, we seem to remember aptitudes of nose and leg that we no longer have.

For the dog, one purpose of our walks is checking out the gutter—the chicken knuckles and Reuben sandwiches there. As a student of fermentation (wine and cheese buffs have nothing on him), he is immensely cheerful as we go around the block. Also, he marks his territory. You might say it's like the trappings of wolf territoriality without the territory, just as for us it is a walk in the woods without the woods. He looks particularly for irregularities to mark: a shovelful of dirt next to a Con Ed excavation, a clump of grass, houseplants or Christmas trees that have been thrown out but still smell of earth. Males found females by the process, but the other social function—when dogs were wolves—was to reinforce the order of rank and rule within the pack, increasing the pack's efficiency on a hunt.

We are animals too. We confront a cold wind with our backs, and turn grumpy if somebody unexpectedly grabs hold of us while we are bent over a steak. But the spirit of both man and dog is sociable, and most people will never be too old to get a kick out of whistling to a dog and seeing him wag his tail. The point of having a descendant of the Lost Wolf for company is not to crush his spirit but rather to direct it so that he can live in, even delight in, the city. The eagles and wild swans are gone, and we have an idea that dogs and the saving irregularities they look for add life to New York City.

At the next meeting of the class the instructor asked two students to read their responses aloud. Bill Julio read:

This "we" business sounds affected even if it's an editorial. Dogs mean a policedog when I read the word, one called Bessie with a lame rear leg that never lived in Manhattan in her whole life. Why do swans whistle? Do they whistle at other swans?

This slows me up, about moutain lions in Manhattan. Are we talking about zoos? Stupid to say the children are all like dogs.

He is going to say that we shouldn't keep dogs in the city.

Litter. Don't litter. This writer is showing off about "students of fermentation," fancy talk. And I'm confused about who is who. And who is Con Ed, Constance Edward, for that matter? Edward Hoagland. Is this science or is this crap?

If we are animals how come we write editorials. This argument for keeping dogs in the city is stupid if that's what it's all about. Do swans migrate in the winter?

Hands went up; people started talking. Someone said: "It's not talking about zoos; it's about prehistoric times when animals really did live in Manhattan, or where Manhattan is now." Bill Julio answered that now he knew that, but he was writing down what he thought at the moment he was reading. His instructor said that he did what he was supposed to do. The student who had corrected Bill said that she didn't get it at first either. After some further comparison of notes, the instructor asked Rachel Goldberg to read what she had written:

Cleaning up after being sick? Shedding hair? What does cleaning up have to do with seals? Is a living ancestor like a grandfather or like a caveman? I cannot believe that this is an editorial because it doesn't. . . . Is it our own "aptitude" that this is about? Dogs in Manhattan—pooper scoopers!

I bet this comes from when they passed the law about dog doodoo on the sidewalks.

In the suburbs it's telephone poles and fire hydrants not sandwiches.

He marks off territory. This is by lifting his leg, right? Why can't he say so? The New York Times can't use bad language like piss. I don't see why he talks about the pack.

Grabs steak. Like a kid protecting a popsicle. Like being in McDonald's and protecting your French fries. Natural I suppose. Why is it animal? Is this an argument for keeping dogs in NYC? For the sake of people. What about the dog's sake?

When Rachel's notes were finished everybody wanted to talk at once. "Not all dogs are policedogs and lots of city dogs are tiny dogs." "When a dog wags its tail it means it's happy, so whistling at a dog is not just for the human being's sake." "This piece is about cities and civilization." "He is saying really how we are all savages." "He says how civilized we are but we have some old savage inside us whether we are people or dogs." "He says how cities and civilizations are no good because all the wild things are gone."

The instructor let the discussion flow and then brought her class to quietness again. She asked everyone, around the room, to compose one phrase of no more than five or six words to describe a response to *dogs*, when each student read it first in the editorial. After two minutes, going around the classroom, there were these responses:

Mutts, mongrels / Brown dog in a fenced yard. / A Great Dane. / Lots of little dogs, brown and white. / Something like a collie, maybe a sheepdog. / A dog show. / Lassie on television. / Cute white dog on a leash. / Grandmother's old brown mutt, sleeping all day. / Two China dogs on a mantlepiece. / *101 Dalmatians.* / Three old dogs one after the other. / A derogatory expression for human beings. / A dog on a postcard with its head cocked wearing a pink ribbon. / James Herriot. / Policedog named Bert that nipped a mailman. / Postcard of a spotted hound on a firetruck. / Maizie with puppies. / Hot dogs. / Scottie next door. / Wirehaired fox terrier named Phoebe. / A part golden named Gussie on a purple leash.

So—said the instructor after a sigh—when you look *dog* up in the dictionary, does what you find have anything to do with what the word *dogs* meant when we read it on the page?

Nobody answered the question because they knew it was not a question. Several sighs rose in the classroom.

## NEGOTIATING MEANING

To continue the work and to look for consensus, after something like discouragement, the instructor divided her class into five small groups dispersed around the room. They passed their notes to each other; they compared; they argued a little but mostly they managed to see how each read differently. From time to time there was laughter.

## SIGHT-READING

For the next class meeting, three days later after a weekend, the instructor asked for volunteers to bring in another editorial, so that the instructor herself could read something aloud to the class—trying to speak out her responses as she read it for the first time. They would continue their investigation of reader response with the teacher as Exhibit Number Two. Three students agreed to bring something in.

On Monday she picked one of the three, noted that she had read this editorial on the weekend, and said so. Glancing at the second one, she realized from the typeface that she had not read this newspaper. It was a small-town paper that a student had read on a weekend home. She would leave the room for a moment, she explained, while the student who brought it in read it aloud twice. When her students became familiar with it, she would return and encounter it for the first time.

When her students let her back in, she performed the following text. Here the newspaper editorial is in italic, and the instructor's improvised outloud associations follow each sentence, in parentheses and quotation marks:

First she read the title:

*Downtown Merchants Association?*

("The question mark seems old fashioned to me. 'Downtown' makes me think of growing up outside Cedar Rapids in the country. 'Downtown' for me meant one street especially with a big old department store and places that sold sporting goods and shoes and clothes. 'Downtown' means hot chocolate with my mother after shopping before taking the bus home.")

*Talk has once again begun to surface about forming a Downtown Merchant's Association.*

(I'm always glad to see an apostrophe in the right place!")

*Seems we had one a few years back but it died due to bickering and lack of cooperation between merchants at the east end of Central and those at the west end.*

("When they start without a subject—maybe they don't like *we* the way Bill doesn't—it sounds folksy to me. I mean it sounds sort of *affected.* I cannot see the word *bickering* without thinking about a radio program when I was a kid, 'The Bickersons.' When I read a sentence that goes on too long I want to cut it down. I'm just reading like an English teacher—but I can't help that, can I?")

*Funny but I always thought the intent of an association was to bring people, even competitors, together to promote a common cause or to overcome common problems.*

("I . . . I'm resisting making jokes about this but that's what I feel like doing because that's a terrible sentence. I don't mean it's incorrect, it's just loose. Also I think of associations just as places where people make speeches.")

*After all, before you can even attempt to "make the horse drink" you've got to first "lead it to the water."*

("What's wrong here? Oh. You've got to lead a horse to water before you can make him drink. They switched *the horse* and the *it* around. OK. But what does it mean? I don't understand about horses and water and the Downtown Merchant's Association! Wait a minute. . . . Oh . . . . I guess that if they talk together, associating without bickering, it would be like taking a horse to the water— and then getting results from the talking together would be like the horse drinking. That's right. That's it. I think it's a good analogy. I don't know why I was so slow to get it.")

*So this time around what would make a downtown association different?*

("Again I cannot help being an English teacher but the cliché of *this time around* bothers me. Isn't this whole editorial trying to sound like *folks,* like something that the editorial writer thinks he isn't? It sounds condescending.")

*Not anything I've uncovered so far.*

("So all of a sudden it is *I.* Isn't that weird all of a sudden? He has been avoiding it so carefully—why do I think it is a he? I think it's a man writing.")

*Comments like "those guys don't care about this city," "I'd never join in with those snobs," "don't have the time" and "we don't want them involved, they're owned by outside interests" were recently expressed to me.*

("This is another horrible sentence but it is understandable. It's horrible because it's passive—isn't the man trying *not* to say who spoke?—and because it's much too long and he quotes too many people.")

*Don't know about you, but I get the feeling another downtown association would serve about as much purpose as taking a long walk off a short pier.*

("I'm hating this guy—and if it's a woman you can laugh at me all you want! Here's this phony friendly 'Don't know about you' stuff, followed by the oldest joke in the universe.")

She continued. (See Exercise 3 for the whole editorial.) Afterwards, and in conference, many students referred to this class hour; several said that they understood the instructor's notions of cliché for the first time when they heard her respond to the editorial. Several seemed amused to discover that the instructor's reading resembled their own. When students brought new themes into conferences, or more often revisions of old themes, the instructor tried sight-reading while her students watched and listened: this had the effect of making her marginal comments more meaningful, because students watched her arriving at them.

A week later, mostly studying other matters, they reviewed the subject of reader response by working together, instructor and students, on another editorial brought to class by one student but unread by anybody else. For the rest of the term, when the class talked about student essays or essays read in a reader, they analyzed their own responses as readers. Writing they tried to remember the potential responses of others—and to respond to their own writing, and they re-read and revised their own work.

Writing they tried to remember that language is a social act.

## CONSENSUS ON EDWARD HOAGLAND

The class wrote papers, read essays, did impromptus, and re-viewed grammar—in the classic manner of English Comp, doing every-thing at once or trying to. Part of doing everything is repetition. Several weeks after the class exercise on "Walking the Dog," the instructor asked her students to read it again at home, to work on watching their own response—and to bring to class a brief written summary of their reading. We will see, she said, how close we have come to each other in reading this piece of prose—how close and how far apart. Then we will see how close we *can* come.

As it happened, the first summary read aloud was a response out of step with the rest of the class. Ed Folaro took from the editorial the notion that the author disliked dogs:

> At first I thought he liked dogs because he said "we are in favor of dogs." Gradually I got to see that he didn't like them, not really, although I don't think he was very clear about it. Dogs not only make messes, you can't keep them out of stuff at least in the city. He would rather have wild animals around but he knows that's out of the question.

Students disagreed with Ed's reading but remained polite about it, per-haps because their instructor made a habit of finding merit in diverse responses. One girl said that Ed heard Hoagland's tone as ironical but she couldn't hear it that way. Another said that when she felt squeam-ish, reading about the Reuben in the gutter, she was mad at people who littered, not at the dogs who sniffed it. Then Jennifer Gutwillig read her summary:

> Edward Hoagland says a lot in a few words. He *sounds* sort of humor-ous but there are deep thoughts here too. When he says "We are animals too" is when I realize that he is writing philosophy and not just about walking dogs. But when I go back to read it again, I can see that this sort of thinking goes right through the whole thing. At the start he says that mountain lions used to live in Manhattan. Really, that's the same thing—the old and new together—that he does with the animal-person later. The Manhattan jungle is like the animal inside us. About the fifth reading I saw the connection between the whistling swan at the beginning and the whistling for a dog at the end.

"What connection?" said her instructor, adding that she had never no-ticed the repeated word. Jennifer having noticed a connection found that she could not explain it. Roger Rappert said: "It's the same thing she said. In the old times swans whistled, now we whistle. It is being animals and being humans at the same time. Comparison and contrast!"

The instructor called for another response, something different. No one put up a hand. Finally, timidly, Tom Dragon read his summary:

> Newspaper editorials are about the day's news and so this must have been a time when a city—New York City—decided to enforce the law about curbing dogs. Most newspaper editorials are serious or pompous. They tell how to negotiate with the Chinese or something. But every now and then you get one—usually the bottom one in a whole column of edits—that's silly or funny. I worked for a paper last summer and I think I might try to go into it. This is a good example of the light editorial. It is relaxing, it is light and good-natured, it is not going to offend anybody.

Their instructor pointed out that Jennifer and Tom read the same editorial; neither of them misread anything; but Tom read it as a professional job of work, expert at being lighthearted, while Jennifer read it as profound philosophical speculation.

Now, said the instructor, we will separate into five small groups, pass written comments back and forth, and each group work for consensus. After fifteen minutes, each choose a chairman, and we will see how we do as a class, negotiating a consensus together—as if we were the diplomats of five different countries, getting together to negotiate a treaty.

"Remember," she said, "you are not trying to be *right* but to find honest agreement. A treaty isn't the truth; it's what people can agree on."

_____ **EXERCISES** _____

Here are two more editorials by Edward Hoagland:

*There Go the Clowns*

The word "clown" probably derives from *klunni*, which meant "loutish" in Old Norse. There have been three kinds of clowns. The whitefaces had sunny, quick, boyish souls. The pink-and-red-and-white "august" clowns were foolish guys, bumpkins, scapegoats, and stuffed shirts. The character clowns, playing cops, farmers, ethnics, and so on, depended upon costuming and frequently wore darker makeup to add complexity to their temperament.

In America the best character clowns were two hoboes invented during the Depression by Emmett Kelly and his good friend Otto Griebling. Kelly, who died in Florida last Wednesday, wore blackish, reddish, grayish makeup on his cheeks and chin, white and black on his mouth, and a polka-dot derby. He was broke and sad and seedy—in short, a tramp. Griebling projected an angrier, "crazier" idea of humanity and of those times, but both were men for the 1930s, not for our more prosperous, fast-paced decade. Slow in all his movements, Emmett Kelly would fall in love with ladies in the crowd, turn out his ragged pockets, weep unashamedly at supposed slights—none of which we like to see ourselves as doing, lately. He would hit a peanut with a sledgehammer, or juggle while balancing a feather on the tip of his nose.

There is a dearth of clowns today. Ringling Bros. and Barnum & Bailey has had to establish a Clown College to fill its need for replacements, and almost all the young talent is either white-faced or "august." They wear painted overalls or neon suits. Though nothing is wrong with that, we miss the tramps. And we will particularly miss "Weary Willie"—Emmett Kelly's creation—for his leisurely sweetness and his vulnerability.

### Banking for Winter

Applemen prune their trees "so that a crow can fly between any two branches," as the adage goes. And now is the time when they want some apples of the winter varieties, "keepers" for the storage bin. Brussels sprouts, beets, and carrots can still be got from the garden and stored down in the cellar too.

But before there were beets and apples there were beavers—and trappers before farmers. A good trapper hardly needed a rifle to feed himself. His wolf traps would as conveniently catch a deer; his bear traps were just right for moose or buffalo. Mainly, he lived on beavers, and mostly on the tails of the beavers, which were a frontier luxury on a par with buffalo tongues and moose noses.

Beavers rudder or scull themselves, as they swim, with their foot-long, tongue-shaped, broad, scaly tails. They also use the tail to brace themselves as they stand up to gnaw a tree, and as an extra leg for balancing as they clasp mud in their arms and walk upright when dam-building. Warning each other of danger, they whack their tails on the water. The tail provides a means of regulating body temperature in the summer and a place to store fat for the winter.

It was this combination of fat and muscle that made for delicious eating. And now is the time when beavers are stacking poplar branches underwater for winter feeding—ramming them into the mud or piling stones on them to keep them from floating up and freezing in the ice that forms.

For the trapper, all this busy preparation before the ponds closed over added to his own larder as well. The more poplar and birch he saw them haul into the water for winter meals of bark, the fatter he knew their tails were going to grow, to sizzle in his campfire, and the more money John Jacob Astor would pay him for his catch of furs, when he came out of the woods next April.

1. For homework, read "There Go the Clowns" and write notes while you read it, following the instructions given on page 41. Come to class with your notes, prepared for classwide discussion or for work in small groups.

2. In class divide into groups of three to five. Read "Banking for Winter" together, a paragraph at a time—underlining words and making small marginal notes. After you read each paragraph, and before you continue, spend a few minutes talking about what you have read and speculating on what will follow. When you have finished the editorial, see if your group can reach a consensus about meaning. Elect a chairman to present your group's consensus to the whole class.

3. Here is the whole newspaper editorial, part of which was printed with the instructor's responses on pages 44–46.

*Downtown Merchants Association?*

Talk has once again begun to surface about forming a Downtown Merchant's Association.

Seems we had one a few years back but it died due to bickering and lack of cooperation between merchants at the east end of Central and those at the west end. Funny but I always thought the intent of an association was to bring people, even competitors, together to promote a common cause or to overcome common problems. After all, before you can even attempt to "make the horse drink" you've got to first "lead it to the water."

So this time around what would make a downtown association different? Not anything I've uncovered so far. Comments like "those guys don't care about this city," "I'd never join in with those snobs," "don't have the time" and "we don't want them involved, they're owned by outside interests" were recently expressed to me. Don't know about you, but I get the feeling another downtown association would serve about as much purpose as taking a long walk off a short pier.

Obviously there are some Franklin merchants that would welcome an association, not just downtown, but Town Line Plaza, Franklin Shopping Center and West Franklin as well. There are also civic leaders, attorneys, doctors, media people, politicians and even just plain residents that would like to see an association of some sort. You guessed it! A good old down to earth, American as apple pie, Chamber of Commerce to serve and promote the entire community, not just one self-serving group.

How about it? It's high time *we all* get together and promote the common interest of Franklin as a place to live, work, play and shop.

Imagine the instructor's responses to the last two paragraphs.

4. Further exercises may come from your reader, if your class uses one, or from the text of *Writing Well.* For instance, study your responses to paragraphs from "The Insides of Words," pages 91–107, or "Verbs," pages 110–117.

Throughout this book exercises print whole paragraphs for analysis, especially in the chapter about the paragraph, where examples are collected for study of structure. These paragraphs will do as well for investigation of reading habits and as subjects for collaborative learning.

Take any of the paragraphs on pages 260–261. Let the class divide into groups of three to five students and work on negotiating a consensus or a community of meanings, one paragraph at a time. Let each group collaboratively write a one-sentence summary of its consensus on a paragraph. Let each group find two examples of subjective responses that needed correction in the pursuit of objectivity and consensus. If there are significant differences among the consensuses arrived at by different groups, let the whole class try to negotiate a super-consensus.

5. Let students work together to bring to class a brief essay (perhaps an editorial) for the instructor to encounter for the first time in front of the class. See the classwork described on pages 44–46.

6. Here is a letter printed a week later in the small-town paper that published "Downtown Merchants Association?"

Dear Editor:
Whoever wrote your Downtown editorial doesn't know much about our town or at least our downtown. A Chamber of Commerce got tried out thirty years ago but nobody paid any attention to it and it up and died. What we need is more gumption and less kooky ideas from strangers. A Downtown Merchant's Association will do what it can to put the townline folks out of business and that's the trouble with a Chamber of Commerce. People who care about this town care about downtown and those plazas are made by flatlanders for flatlanders.
Concerned Citizen

Collectively read. Collectively revise. Criticize language and logic.

# 3

## _Writing An Essay_

"Students write essays and answer questions on tests. . . ." So I began this book, naming an immediate and practical necessity for the student writer. Then I talked about the idea of an audience and other matters essential to good writing and matters that good writing leads to. In the second chapter I talked about how we read and about interconnections among reading, thinking, and writing—even their identity. Now we must move to a matter of the moment. In most composition courses the student is asked to write a complete paper at the very beginning and to write additional complete papers every week or two throughout the term. It is time for some practical advice on writing an essay.

In the first chapter we named some qualities, like focus and unity, that we look for in a paper. Now we must investigate the _process_ of writing a paper, how a writer achieves focus and unity, and makes contact with a reader. For many students, daily writing will increase their fluency, and fluency will help them revise their papers. But daily writing—spontaneous, undirected, and uncorrected—is a means to an end, not an end in itself. The end is good writing, and the occasion for good writing in a composition class is the essay. The essay is _controlled, disciplined,_ and _directed_ by the student writer.

_A paper has a purpose_—to give information, to define or to contrast, perhaps to persuade. A paper _shows_ its purpose, both in its shape and in its statement, or the paper fails. In beginning a paper, we *find* that purpose, often in the act of writing; revising and finishing the paper, we make that purpose *clear* to the outside world.

*In a paper we must support our purpose by detail;* we must provide sufficient detail, and we must arrange the details into an order that expresses purpose. If we are writing five hundred words, we must find a purpose limited enough to be supported adequately in two pages of typing. If we try brief surveys of grand topics—"Nuclear War," "The Problem of Welfare"—our five hundred words will remain thin and superficial, abstract and general, lacking detail. If we choose a more limited topic—"Recruiting High School Seniors for the Army," "Applying for Food Stamps"—we can organize adequate detail into a shape that reaches an audience. We must limit not only topic but purpose.

<u>Writing an essay we need to use both the critical and the creative sides of our brains.</u> To accumulate detail, we can use the spontaneity we cultivate in daily writing. But to cut and to shape, to narrow and to focus, we need to cultivate other qualities of mind. We must develop a sense for order and shape, a sense by which we understand the whole paper as several units organized to become one larger unit controlled by one purpose. Finally the shape of an essay is the shape of our purposeful thought.

We must also understand that <u>our whole paper</u>—from our choice of words for the opening paragraph to our choice of detail for the concluding paragraph—<u>directs itself to the eyes and ears of other people.</u> We do not write for ourselves only. We need to persuade, to inform, to please, to convince, to charm, to arouse, to make an impression on *other people.* Writing intended for the writer alone is by definition of the writer's business. By definition a composition class presumes—as much as a newspaper presumes by publishing—that its writing directs itself from inside out, from writer to reader, from individual to world. Acts of language are social acts; it takes two to talk.

Once we understand that writing is directed elsewhere—and not inward, where we can be sure that a generous interpretation will accept our intentions—then we can understand the function of good style and even of mere correctness. <u>Good style smooths the passage from reader to writer; good style is a convincing clarity.</u> Mechanical correctness removes impediments to understanding; even a mistaken *it's* for *its* can throw a momentary monkey wrench into the machine of comprehension. We must write well in order to make contact with our readers. We avoid clichés, or extraneous information, or misleading abstractions, or dangling modifiers, or incomplete arguments, *for one reason:* all these flaws, errors, imperfections block the passage between the writer and the reader.

In later chapters, we will look into the choice of words, the making of sentences, the construction of paragraphs, and at the different types of writing a student may undertake. First we must investigate how the whole essay is made. We must look into the process that will be the student's classroom task throughout the term: writing papers single in purpose, whole and adequate in shape, and clear to others.

## GETTING IDEAS FOR PAPERS

Writing begins with invention. Many writers find that getting started is the hardest part and feel discouraged about learning to invent. Beginning writers commonly suspect that organization and clarity are qualities that can be learned by study but that originality depends on luck or genius—the inventor's spark of inspiration. Fortunately, however, this common idea is untrue; anyone can learn procedures that generate ideas. We need not be Thomas Alva Edison to invent a good paper, but even for a literary genius, inspiration is 99 percent perspiration.

When an instructor assigns a free paper, both topic and organization are up to the writer. When an instructor assigns a general topic like "public transportation," we need to invent and organize ideas on the topic. When an instructor assigns a form of organization—comparison and contrast, for instance—we need to generate a topic appropriate to the form and an idea by which to organize the topic. Then we must discover and organize the best details. Whatever the assignment, we need to discover details and set them in order.

Maybe the mind feels blank, at first, with an open assignment. Total freedom suggests no starting place. If we do daily writing we can read over the pages to find a suitable subject to rewrite into a shape that will embody a purpose to the reader. Otherwise, it is a good idea to consult our recent interests, or subjects of discussion or argument in other classrooms, at breakfast with family, or with other students. It is also true that we should simply keep our eyes open: essay topics float around us like motes in the air.

When the instructor assigns a topic or a pattern, the direction simplifies the process of invention. We generate ideas on a topic by narrowing it; reducing "Student Politics" to "Running for Senate Vice-

President" begins the choice of detail. When form is assigned, we must filter possible topics through this special entry-gate: although we could contrast a small college with a large university, do we know enough about life in a large university (or a small college) to provide fair comparison? If we do not, we cannot write a decent comparison and contrast paper on this topic, which therefore fails to pass through the gate. If we are to analyze a process and think of writing a recipe for spaghetti sauce, can we really generate enough detail for a paper? Hot pepper and chopped carrots are not enough.

The true beginning of the essay waits for desk and paper, concentration on the task. Writers find many ways to begin, and in a moment we will look at several of them. First, we must emphasize how *not* to begin: *do not sit down with a few notes and a vague notion of topic and form to write the paper.* Many papers fail because beginners try to improvise the final paper at first sitting, attempting to find ideas at the same time as they organize and shape them. Too often, vaguely aware of shortcomings but despairing of large changes, the writer merely copies this rough draft—improving only mechanical matters like spelling and capitalization—and hands in a messy, disorganized, incoherent paper.

Time spent in preparation is time well spent. It is wise to figure how much time we have and allot half to preparation and half to execution. When we begin by writing a whole draft, we start without a full complement of detail; thinking of detail later, most of us either omit it (leaving the writing thin and general) or misplace it (leaving the writing chaotic and unclear). Of course if we have the time and energy, we can look at a premature first draft as raw material, take it apart, rewrite and reorganize it thoroughly. But it takes less time and effort if we prepare patiently and thoroughly before attempting a draft. A delayed draft is more likely to generate the material for a complete and coherent final revision.

Any advice on writing a paper, however, must carry the acknowledgment that different writers follow different processes. The same writer, at different times, may find different procedures useful. Some writers, or maybe all writers on some occasions, will find it best to begin by writing several pages before the plan of the paper becomes clear, in order to generate material. Some people think best in the act of writing. Later, they must return to what they have written in haste, to mine this material for the real essay. Attitude is important. If we do not wait, think, and plan before attempting the paper, we must write with the knowledge that we are generating <u>raw material</u>. We must not write expecting merely to polish this material into a final draft. Revision more radical than polishing will be necessary.

Whatever procedure we follow, two things are worth knowing. First, it helps to know that we can go about writing a paper many ways, to be aware of the many options. Second, we must acknowledge that however we go about writing a paper, it will always take *work*—we will not get it right, or close to right, the first time we try.

Here are some ways to prepare for writing an essay, ways to get ideas, develop them, examine them, analyze them, and expand them. Later we will mention ways to select and organize these ideas.

### Brainstorming

To brainstorm is to list rapidly ideas and details without self-criticism, without attending to formalities or parallelisms or mechanical considerations—and without worrying about being silly: no one else need see the product. Brainstorming fills a blank sheet of paper with fragmentary notes that we hope may lead to ideas on a topic. When brainstorming, we write rapidly and uncritically, receiving the brain's topical snow flurries without trying to make sense or to give shape. The uncritical mind generates good ideas and bad ones together with a broad generosity.

Suppose the topic is comparing and contrasting bicycles and cars at a residential campus. Sitting down with a blank sheet, a student might list:

> bikes quicker no parking trouble
> but bike theft—chains and combinations
> healthy, keep in shape
> but carrying groceries?
> more car accidents; more serious?
> bikes ecology, energy saving
> winter ugh salt jeans
> bike cheap car expensive
> insurance gas parking fines
> car status symbol
> kind of car?
> old car repairs
> vans, hearses, old buses

When the mind compares and contrasts, it brainstorms ideas by flipping back and forth like a Ping-Pong ball—bikes are healthier, *but* you don't carry a lot of groceries on bikes; bikes save energy, *but* riding them in winter can be unpleasant. These alternatives are good for invention, but if we wrote an essay that swung from side to side so rapidly, the to-and-fro would only confuse the reader. After we list alternatives, we can organize coherently, often putting like with like—the advantages of cars in one paragraph perhaps and the advantages of bicycles in another.

It is useful after brainstorming to look back at the list and circle ideas that need thinking out. The creator lists; the critic reads the list and responds to it. We may put question marks by some notes to acknowledge that we are only guessing; are we really more likely to have an accident driving a car than riding a bicycle? To make such an assertion, we would need the authority that comes from research. Sometimes we find an item, like "car status symbol," which can head a list for further brainstorming:

> car status symbol
> rich students—rich-seeming?
> money and parents
> but—doing errands for others
> weekends? not on campus—
> sports cars, antiques

When we brainstorm, we list a few words, sensing that if we needed to, we could expand any item. Each phrase stands for something possible to develop. We are generating material for later expansion, generating the seeds from which we will cultivate our gardens. Often we begin with a general area for investigation, and as we investigate we generate possible ideas and purposes. When we glimpse a purpose for a paper—perhaps to demonstrate the superior utility of the bicycle—purpose will allow us further brainstorming. After we have accumulated much material, we could try organizing our notes and writing a draft—but chances are we will do better if we continue to delay the first draft, preparing further.

### Sprinting

Sprinting is another technique for loosening the mind into discovery or invention; we can use it instead of brainstorming or in addition to it. Sprinting, we write a quick paragraph on our topic, writing as fast as we can for five minutes or so, beginning with the first thought that occurs to us and hurtling forward by association of ideas without pausing for logic or correctness. Before beginning an essay, we may try sprinting on our essay topic for our daily writing.

Sprinting resembles the method Peter Elbow calls "looping," writing a series of ten-minute passages, each loop circling out of the passage before it. This technique is especially appropriate for endeavors longer than a weekly paper. We may follow Elbow and loop a second sprint onto our first one. Pausing to look back at our spontaneous prose, we should extract the essence of what we have written. Do these sentences lead toward something in particular? Is there a leading idea? Trying to answer such questions, we should write one more sentence that captures the best or most interesting idea of our paragraph. And next, using this sentence as our beginning, we should sprint again. Often a brainstorming list provides an initial range of topics, and a sprint or two will generate detail within the narrowing topic.

### Cross-examining

There are questions we need to ask ourselves when we gather materials for writing. If we cross-examine our notes and ideas before we begin a draft, we will save ourselves revising time. Not all questions will apply to all topics. But usually an array of questions directed at the topic undertaken will generate new ideas, details, and directions.

*The Journalist's Six.* Anyone who writes for a newspaper or takes a journalism course learns to answer six questions at the beginning of a news story: Who? What? When? Where? Why? How? Here is how a news story in a Detroit daily begins: "A Grosse Pointe systems analyst missed out on a $1,000 first prize at a Pontiac radio station yesterday because he could not remember the lyrics of 'America the Beautiful.' " *Who?* "A Grosse Pointe systems analyst"; *What?* "Missed out on a $1,000 first prize"; *Where?* "At a Pontiac radio station"; *When?* "Yesterday"; *How?* "Because he could not remember the lyrics of 'America the Beautiful' "; *Why?* "Because he has a rotten memory." The journalistic formula anticipates the questions any reader might ask; newspapers fail quickly without an audience.

Although essays for freshman English are seldom news stories, if we ask the six questions before we begin to write, they will help us make contact with our audience. If we write about the antique televi-sion series *Hogan's Heroes,* we may find ourselves easily telling what it was, why it was the way it was, how it formulated itself—but we may forget to tell when it was on the air, which will leave a question hanging for our readers. If we remember to answer the six questions, we will satisfy our audience's curiosity.

*Questions of Form.* In planning any paper, we should scrutinize our topic by making questions out of rhetorical forms (discussed more fully in Chapter 7), and shake ideas out of our brain like apples out of a tree. We can phrase *comparison and contrast* by asking: What is it like or unlike? *Definition* asks: What *is* it? *Division:* What is it composed of? What are its parts? *Classification:* What kind of thing is it? *Process:* How does it work? *Cause and effect:* What causes it? What effect does it have? The same questions can help us to develop paragraphs when we revise (see Chapter 6).

Thus, if we were preparing to write about leaves changing color in autumn, consideration of rhetorical forms might lead us to write about the chemical *process* by which chlorophyll drains from the maple tree, or about the temperature-related *cause* of the change, or about the *classification* of different maples, or about the *comparison and con-trast* between two parts of the country or two kinds of maple tree. Considering these forms, not unlike the journalist's six questions, al-lows us to consider alternatives for the structure of our paper. We may choose a rhetorical form for our whole paper—*comparing and contrast-ing Hogan's Heroes* and *M\*A\*S\*H* or *defining* the national debt—or we may simply use *analysis* or *classification* in a paper; calling something a "situation comedy," we classify a form of popular entertainment.

## More Hints for Inventors

Always begin thinking about a paper early, because much of our best invention happens after we have chosen a topic but when we are not consciously thinking of it: sometimes in dreaming sleep, more often in daydreams while we are lightly occupied driving a car or walk-ing from parking lot to class, or—let us admit it—while we are attend-ing a lecture in another course.

Internal dialogue can become an exercise of mind and imagina-tion, for we can talk things over, not just with a friend or a roommate, but with an ideal friend or roommate that we keep inside ourselves.

This invisible voice can embody a teacher, a whole stable of teachers, a priest, an aunt, or friends back home or at other colleges. It is our brain's attempt to find in itself An Other. The Critic Inside may raise useful objections: *That's a dumb way to say it!* Or it may make polite suggestions: *But what about the problem downtown merchants have with suburban shopping malls?* Everyone can find such a voice. Much of our idle thinking or daydreaming occurs in dialogue. For the sake of our brains, it is wise to cultivate a sometimes crabby voice. Let it argue its heart out as we listen to it carefully. It is the closest we can come to taking an audience inside, an internal critic whose opinions help us to see what we have not said or what we have said badly.

Even at an early stage, the idea of an audience may generate further ideas. If we have not thought of whom we address, that thought may bring to mind special responses that we may expect from our audience, and therefore generate material shaped to meet these responses.

### Selecting Detail

Invention generates detail; next we must select and organize what we have generated. To write a good paper, we have to organize details in the best order, and we must leave out any details, however attractive, which do not contribute to the whole. The whole essay embodies our purpose in writing it. The essay's shape is the shape of our thought, and focus or concentration is the architecture of purpose. The idea of focus, in Chapter 1, is perhaps the most important *structural* idea in making a paper, unless it is the related idea of a thesis. With many essays it is possible to boil our purpose down to a single sentence that states a thesis: a summary or kernel of purpose, that our detail and argument support. A single governing thesis allows us unity and focus.

Sometimes—before we write or during revision—we find ourselves oppressed with too much detail. Writing is acquiring material (the floating on memory, the rapid daily writing), and it is ordering and cutting that material. The writer must be a paradoxical combination of opposites: the big spender and the miser, the nymphomaniac and the virgin. Cutting can take place when we organize our notes before writing, or it can come later. When we start to write, it is often hard to know which details are going to prove relevant. Many writers consciously write too much in their first drafts, knowing that they do not yet know what will be useful and knowing that they will later cut for focus and form, often with the help of a discovered thesis directed to a specific audience.

Suppose you describe a particular day. At the end of a vacation, you had a perfect (or perfectly horrible) day. On that Thursday, when you woke up, it was 8:35. You ate scrambled eggs with catsup. These details could be relevant, or they could be mere padding. Cut what does not contribute to the whole. But first, you must have a whole. The point of your paper could be a triviality of your day: a dog barked, the mail was junk, nobody was home when you telephoned your friends. The point is to have a point. Find one—or even make one up. The truth we want is truth-to-feeling; we are not under oath in a court. If we are remembering a sequence of events—A, B, C, and D—we can rearrange the sequence to make a piece of writing true to the feeling we want the whole to give. If event B happened second, but we see in retrospect that it was the emotional climax, we can *lie* a little in order to tell the emotional truth. We can use C, A, and D in that order and save B for last. We are still writing out of our own life. We are telling the truth in a serious sense. Within the limits set by credibility, we can even combine different events into one, or different people into the same character. Suppose in a family anecdote two uncles move in and out of a story, doing approximately the same things. In telling the anecdote, it might be more shapely and pointed—and just as true—to turn them into one person. This advice does not apply, or course, when the writer's relationship to audience—a report to a committee investigating a problem, a journalist's account of an event—implies a contract to tell the literal truth.

To make a point, and to give our writing a shape, we must limit our material. Here we are back to unity. If we try to write about a whole summer, we are most likely to write disjointed paragraphs and be boring and superficial. We should find one event, or one unifying device (a place, a person, an automobile, a time of day, a kind of food), to tie together different details. Contrast can make a glue as adhesive as similarity. We must find the detail and form that combined will embody the summer's spirit.

When Jim Beck decided to make a theme out of his drive to attend college, he knew that he had accumulated detail in his daily writing. In fact, he had too much detail. At first, when he looked over thirty-six pages of undisciplined writing, he felt elated because he had so much to write about; then he felt depressed because he had too much to write about. Should he tell about his father's parents? The story of their troubles was background to his father's diffidence. Should he tell about his brother Steve's dishonorable discharge? In two pages of daily writing, he had told only half the story, but he suspected that Steve's life story contributed to local opinion of the Becks. In a way, it belonged.

Of course *everything* belongs. Everything that ever happened to us contributes to how we are, how we act, and how we feel at this moment. But because Jim had to condense his idea into three pages, he had to narrow his topic. He had to focus on his purpose, to seek out the proper order for his thoughts. The idea of focus helped him begin to narrow. In this paper, the topic was his personal feelings; he realized that he must concentrate on himself and keep his family at the side, mentioning his parents and his brothers only so far as details about them promoted his purpose. The essay's shape was the shape of his thought, and his thesis used an analogy to express the difficult ambition of his race for college; his disillusion as he begins college only emphasizes his struggle to get there.

Reading over his daily writing, he listed the topics covered, as if he were outlining a chapter in his reading. When he crossed out the topics he did not require, he found focus. Right away, he could cut thirty-six pages down to eight or ten. The rest of the cutting came when he chose details that would be most felt by a reader. He decided that accounts of races by which he won his athletic scholarship would mean little to a reader. He decided with regret to omit an anecdote about a vice-principal.

## WRITING THE DRAFT

To write the draft, we first try setting our notes in order, notes derived from brainstorming, sprinting, or cross-examining. Orderly notes resemble an informal outline, reminders of what we need to say in the best order of saying. Writing a first draft, we waste time worrying about finding the perfect beginning. If we do not immediately know how to begin our paper, we should plunge ahead anyway and worry about the introduction later.

What matters is the paper's shape-of-thought: *the shape we give the paper*, like the motion in the paragraph, *is the structure formed by our thought.* Our matter and our purpose determine our manner—or they ought to. An anecdote or a historical summary or an exposition of a process must use chronological order. In an argument that advances a thesis, the paper's order embodies persuasion—accumulating detail, proceeding by logic, and using various forms of persuasion or argument.

Our writing's purpose reflects itself in our paper's order of development. A different order of ideas can make a different statement, even when the ideas or details remain the same. In a reminiscence, if we begin with pleasant associations and move to horrid ones, we leave the reader with a negative impression; if we move from horrid to pleasant, we leave the reader feeling positive. We could accumulate identical details for each paper but make a different impression by our organization. There are insides to the order we give details, as there are to words and syntax. In a history paper, one student wrote:

> The rainfall in the Southern provinces is approximately two inches a year. On the average. What this means is that most years the country people starve in a drought; one year in five, they drown in a flood. However, the combination of a surviving Indian ritual, and a local brand of Roman Catholicism, keeps the people remarkably cheerful and content.

For the same assignment, writing from the same source, another wrote:

> Indian rituals which still survive, combined with a peculiar indigenous Catholicism, keep the natives of the South apparently contented. However, the climatic conditions are deplorable. The rainfall averages two inches a year. This means that the peasants parch for several years in drought, and are drowned in floods the next one.

Both students' original notes for this passage were, approximately,

> Catholicism and Indian stuff
> happy
> rainfall
> floods
> starvation, drought

The two students were heading in different directions—the first toward an expository essay on daily life in the tribe, the second toward an argument for public works such as irrigation and flood control—but they started from the same information, which they organized or pointed in different ways. Their paragraphs embody the different shapes of different thinking.

We need to make an order that is lucid and expressive. Too often, essays lack lucidity because they lack orderly development, one sentence leading into another and leading the reader to follow the track of thought. Lucidity and expression carry our thought, writer to reader; we are not expressive if our message is garbled by repetition, by lack of transition, or by afterthought. We need orderly progress in all our writing in order to engage the reader. We must always address a reader incapable of knowing our intentions; a lucid structure makes intentions clear.

The development in Jim Beck's paper is deceptively simple. He started with a paragraph telling us how much he hated college, with details to make sure the reader understood the feeling.

> It's horrible now, and I don't know if it will get any better. The only people who pay attention to me are the people who are trying to beat me out for the track team. My roommate is stoned all day and gets A's on his papers anyway. I hate him because he hates me because I'm a jock. My classes are boring lectures and the sections are taught by graduate students who pick on the students because the professors pick on them.

But this would not be news. Lots of people are unhappy in college. He then constructed his second paragraph to make a contrast to the first. He not only told us how much he wanted to come to college, but gave us reasons.

> But I remember wanting to come here so bad! Nobody from Hammerton named Beck had ever been to college. Everybody knew the Becks were stupid. This went for my father, who never got through high school, and for my grandfather, who died before I was born, and who was the town drunk. It went for my two older brothers who went bad, as they say in Hammerton. Steve got a dishonorable discharge from the Marines and he works on a farm outside town and gets drunk on Fridays and Saturdays. Curt stole a car and did time at Jackson and nobody has heard from him since. My sister had a three-month baby and the town liked to talk about that.

In the third, fourth, and fifth paragraphs, his writing made us understand his separateness from the rest of his family and from his home town, and then the easy and appropriate order of chronology began to organize the paper. Jim began a paragraph speaking of athletics in general and moved on to his own ambitions as a runner; he carried us with him, right up to the paper's conclusion, with ease and clarity.

> I was different. Everybody told me I was. My mother told me I wasn't a Beck. My father told me I was going to bring back the family's good name. (I never knew it had one.) In grammar school

the teachers all told me how much better I was than my brothers. By the time I was in sixth grade my father and the school Principal were talking about the University.

My father isn't really dumb. Sometimes people look dumb because it's expected of them. He's worked at the same grocery for twenty years, I guess. Now that I made it to the University, he wants to be called Manager, because he's the only man there besides Mr. Roberts who owns it. (The rest of the help are—is?—kids who bag and an old lady cashier.) When I went back for a weekend everybody treated me as if I won the Olympics.

I said the Principal and my father were talking about my going to the University. All through junior high I said I didn't want to go. I was scared. No Beck could do that. Bad things kept happening to my family. My father had an accident and totaled the car and lost his license and for a year we didn't have a car at all. He had to walk home two miles every night pushing a basket of groceries. When I said I would quit school and get a job, everybody jumped on me.

It wasn't that I was an A student. It was just that I tried hard at everything I did. I got B's mostly. Now with B's, the counselors kept telling me, I could be admitted to the University, but I wouldn't get a scholarship. I needed mostly A's for that, and then when I got to the University I would lose the scholarship if I couldn't keep the grades up. Then my brother Steve, who was a pretty good athlete once, suggested athletics.

I was too skinny for football, too short for basketball, I could barely swim and my school didn't have a swimming team anyway. There is one sport you can practice with no money and no equipment. I started to run when I was in my last year of junior high. It felt good right away. I ran to and from school. I went over to the high school and did laps. The high school coach noticed me and asked me to go out the next year. Running long distances hurts a lot. Sometimes you get a stitch in your left side and suddenly it shifts to your right side. I didn't exactly mind the pain. I studied it. I studied it in order to go to the University, the way I studied everything else.

## Beginnings

It remains in considering structure to think about beginnings and endings for papers. Sometimes we overexplain at the beginning of a paper and begin too far back. Trying to talk about something that we did last weekend, we realize that it resembled something we did last summer; then we realize that last summer's feelings were like the feelings we had at age five when we started kindergarten or at age three when we moved to a new town. All these details may be valid, but to include them all would destroy the paper's shape. The bridge into the country of last weekend would be longer than the country itself. With enough self-questioning, we could begin every autobiographical paper with "I was born," or "My grandparents emigrated from Lithuania in 1905," or "Life for my peasant ancestors in medieval Turkey must have been difficult." Too much detail prevents the reader from perceiving the shape of thought. This malady or origins and causes might be called the house-that-Jack-built syndrome.

Long bridges curse not only autobiography; the same malady can afflict all writing. In discussing how World War II began, we can begin with the fall of the Roman Empire. In assembling a research paper, we can go backward in time or laterally in comparisons. Wanting to write about ecology, we may pick the disappearing whale as our topic; we can begin the paper with the general topic of man's destroying his environment, narrow it to his destroying species, narrow it to his destroying whales, and then narrow it to the decline in population of one type of whale. The last category is the paper's focus; if we are not careful, we can spend three-quarters of our paper walking the bridge to our topic.

The good, sharp beginning narrows the topic. When we understand our writing's purpose, we can begin with reference to that purpose, or with a thesis we propose to explain. We can begin with something that arrests the reader and points to the main topic.

> Humpbacks are mammals, as all whales are; they breathe into huge lungs, bear live young, which they nurse for the better part of a year, and have vestiges of hair. . . .

In this research paper, the author catches our attention immediately with facts that will interest almost anyone, probably because they interested her and she shows it: *huge lungs, for the better part of a year.*

Editors of magazines sometimes refer to *zingers,* beginnings (or *leads*) to articles constructed to grab the reader by the hair. *Time* is good at zingers. Here are two opening sentences from one issue.

The United States was founded on a complaint.

When the young Chinese woman heard a mysterious voice asking, "What's under your pillow?" she felt sure that the answer was a "biological radio apparatus" put there by a special agent who suspected her of crimes against the state.

In the *Saturday Review*, Gordon Lish began an article:

Like every interesting American, I live in New York City—

All immediately involve our interest, and none has a preamble. Two begin with a startling short sentence. At other times a definition of the subject may be essential before we can begin.

In its widest possible extension the title of this book—*Adventures of Ideas*—might be taken as a synonym for The History of the Human Race. . . .

A. N. Whitehead, *Adventures of Ideas*

Whitehead builds a swift bridge into his topic.

Purpose and context determine the kind of beginning. But in any piece of writing, the beginning focuses our writing; it requires special attention, and it requires brevity and incisiveness. Some information we need quickly; information which may be pertinent but not wholly necessary should be suppressed; information which is both pertinent and necessary but which might make a tedious beginning can often be put off until later in the essay, when its relevance becomes obvious and it ceases to seem tedious.

One kind of opener, the overt announcement of what is to be done, is often boring: "I am going to show that the government of the United States is split into three branches, the executive, the legislative, and the judicial." Papers may be constructed analytically by delineating parts, but they should show and not tell. The paper that begins with the sentence above will probably take a paragraph each for the three branches and end, as boringly as it began, "I have shown that the government of the United States is comprised of the executive, the legislative, and the judicial branches." It is structure for people who have difficulty following the story line of a Disney movie.

Once he had discarded the thought of beginning with his grandparents, Jim Beck tried several opening sentences.

When I was daydreaming about college it scared me, but I didn't have any idea how I would hate it. I thought that it might be too hard but I never suspected that it would be horrible. It's horrible now, and I don't know if it will get better. . . .

> Since I first came to the university, I haven't slept more than four hours in a row. . . .

Giving up on getting the beginning right in his first draft, he went on to the rest of his paper. When he looked at his draft the next day, he decided to start with the third sentence of his first attempt:

> It's horrible now, and I don't know if it will get any better.

principally because he thought it would arouse curiosity; it was a bit of a zinger.

## Endings

Endings are nearly as important as beginnings, and the same cautions apply. We often make them too long, summarize facts that are already obvious, reargue a point already established, say abstractly what we have shown concretely—and by all these methods dilute the intensity our conclusion should have. Our endings often drag and decline into blank space, dwindling instead of concluding. This diminishment is bad organization. Usually the dwindling can be cut, just as most bridges at the beginning can be removed. If the dwindling qualifies the conclusion, the qualification can come before the conclusion.

There are exceptions. In a long complicated argument, we may be pleased to find at the end a succinct summary of the author's argument. It is like seeing an aerial photograph of country we have just walked through. But the short paper—the kind in which we are most interested in this book—rarely profits from summary and often withers by it. We should point the whole essay toward the last sentence, and when we have written it, stop writing. Often we conclude an essay and then continue writing. The essay writer must develop the confidence to let facts and arguments stand by themselves without epilogue. People who moralize at the end of a story or summarize at the end of an argument are the same people who kill jokes by explaining them. In a report about Tracy Kidder's *The Soul of a New Machine*, which recounts the invention of a computer called "Eagle," a student concluded:

> Kidder makes an adventure story out of unlikely materials, the marriage of business and technology, the interrelationships of a corporation and its research engineers. Both in the book and in the marketplace, the Eagle flies.

Unfortunately, this student felt the need to continue after her conclusion:

> *The Soul of a New Machine,* by Tracy Kidder, is a book that tells a story both unusual and exciting.

Her paper improved when, at her instructor's suggestion, she revised by crossing out her final paragraph.

Usually we should conclude a topic without seeming to draw attention to the conclusion. Part of a paper's unity is the resolution it comes to, all details organized toward an end, a coda felt by the reader. Paradoxically, this resolution can be violated by obviousness. Anything that feels tacked on destroys a sense of unity.

Joan Didion, in an essay called "On Going Home," writes about the fragmentation of American family life. Visiting her parents in the house where she grew up, she encounters familiar details of her old life. She feels that she was "born into the last generation to carry the burden of 'home' " and clearly finds a value in the burden. Her feelings are complex, and she ends her essay not by summarizing her feelings or reducing them to abstraction, but by turning to her own child and enacting her ambivalence.

> It is time for the baby's birthday party: a white cake, strawberry-marshmallow ice cream, a bottle of champagne saved from another party. In the evening, after she has gone to sleep, I kneel beside the crib and touch her face, where it is pressed against the slats, with mine. She is an open and trusting child, unprepared for and unaccustomed to the ambushes of family life, and perhaps it is just as well that I can offer her little of that life. I would like to give her more. I would like to promise her that she will grow up with a sense of her cousins and of rivers and of her great-grandmother's teacups, would like to pledge her a picnic on a river with fried chicken and her hair uncombed, would like to give her *home* for her birthday, but we live differently now and I can promise her nothing like that. I give her a xylophone and a sundress from Madeira, and promise to tell her a funny story.
>
> Joan Didion, in *Slouching Towards Bethlehem*

When Jim Beck first drafted his essay, he had no title and no ending. His last paragraph trailed off.

> Sometimes when I cannot sleep I think about going back to Hammerton but I can't do that. Sometimes I think about getting a gold medal in the Olympics. Both of them are happy dreams except that I *know* I'm not Olympic class and if I went home it would be a

disgrace to everybody. So all I am doing is sticking it out and hating
every minute of it and hoping that things will get better sometime.

When he reconsidered his essay in terms of focus and thesis, he discovered his title by turning his actual running into a metaphor for his drive
to get to college. Then he saw that by cutting and shaping his original
last paragraph, he could make the paper's ending strike the reader and
refer to the beginning without being obvious about it .

> In my Senior year I was all-state and held two high-school rec-
> ords (600 and half-mile) and I had an athletic scholarship to the
> University. Now I am here, the first Beck to make it. I don't know
> why I'm here or why I ran so hard or where I go from here. Now
> that I am here, the race to get here seems pointless. Nothing in my
> classes interests me. I study, just as I did before, in order to pass the
> course or even get a good grade. I run to win, but what am I running
> for? I will never be a great runner. Sometimes when I cannot sleep I
> imagine packing my bags and going back to Hammerton. But I can't
> do that. They would say, "He's a Beck, all right."

## Revising and Invention

Usually it takes several drafts to arrive at an essay that is worth
finishing. Later in this chapter we will follow a student through typical
changes. We have already looked at Jim Beck proceeding from an impromptu to a finished essay. Usually we will need to revise our first
draft in major ways, for focus and clarity, removing some paragraphs
and adding others, altering the order of details or paragraphs, developing and expanding. Finally, if we are persistent, we will accomplish a
draft which is almost there—a roughly finished object which we may
now polish and perfect.

In the next chapter we will concentrate on words, sentences, and
paragraphs, providing tools for final revisions. But in this chapter on
Writing an Essay, we must anticipate some advice. To revise, as to
compose, we must invent. But in order to revise we must find fault
with what we have written, and it is difficult to find faults that we have
just committed. If we have started writing our paper early enough, we
can put time between the latest draft and the final revision; nothing is
so helpful as a night's sleep.

First, we should check the drafted paper against the teacher's
assignment; it is easy to forget a directive and fall into silly errors.

Second, it helps if we make a checklist of our own typical errors—we can collect them from our teachers' corrections on old papers—so that we can be on guard against them. Spelling? Look up every word that seems doubtful. Incomplete sentences? Comma splices or run-on sentences? Parts of sentences not going together? Check the review chapter (pages 377–421). Examine the length of your paragraphs. Have you denied your reader the pause of paragraph breaks? Or have you made your paragraphs too short, only three or four lines long? Look at your paper for its sentence structure. Many beginners make their papers boring by using too many simple or compound sentences; their prose sounds childish. Vary your sentence structure by using long sentences as well as short ones, complicated ones—with clauses beginning *when, although, because*—as well as simple and straightforward ones.

At the suggestion of your instructor, it may be useful at this time to get together with one or two other members of the class, to read each other's drafts and criticize each other. You can provide examples of audience for each other—models, anticipations.

Finally, look closely at your prose for clichés and empty expressions. Summon the Critic Inside for internal dialogue. A cliché discovered is an opportunity for new invention. If you have written that something is the *basic foundation* of something else, and you detect the cliché *basic foundation,* consider what kind of building-base you are talking about. Is the *basic foundation* made of granite? Concrete block? Cinder block? Frozen baloney? Empty expressions give us the same opportunity. If you have written that a teacher was *awfully nice,* as critic you should cross it out; then as inventor you should fill the empty space. You should invent, out of memory, a detail or a story or a fresh expression or some quoted speech that *shows* the quality which *awfully nice* tried to *tell.*

### A Note on Impromptus

This survey of essay writing emphasizes preparation over several days and advises sleeping on ideas, brainstorming, sprinting, cross-examining, daydreaming, drafting, and revising. It is good to have the time to follow these steps. Sometimes in the real world we are required to write thirty-minute essays on final exams or to put a letter in the mail by five o'clock—or to write an impromptu paper in an English class with only forty minutes for invention, drafting, self-criticism, and revision. We are unlikely to be able to sleep on an impromptu, much as we might like to. Nor are we able to spend much time brainstorming, sprinting, or consulting the Critic Inside. But this chapter's advice is not useless, even when time is short.

The components of invention, organization, drafting, and revision remain the same whether we have a week or a quarter hour. If our time is brief, all components are reduced in length, and we must remember to follow our habitual methods *in proportion.* If we have learned to spend half of our time in preparation and half in execution, we should keep the same proportion when we find ourselves with forty minutes instead of four days. Many beginners make the mistake of changing their methods entirely, feeling so cramped for time that they try to write a final draft right away. The result is messy.

If we have forty minutes, we should spend twenty minutes thinking and organizing and twenty minutes writing and correcting. Try brainstorming a list; try sprinting one small paragraph; circle the most inventive idea, make another list, and organize it into an informal outline. Try daydreaming the Critic Inside for a minute or two. Try remembering the responses of other students to your earlier writing; if there were ways you missed your audience earlier, these are ways to watch out for. We should do everything we would do at our desks over an optimal period—only squeeze the time.

Writing an impromptu in the time remaining, we should write slowly and deliberately, crossing out and correcting—but be legible. If we write on alternate lines of lined paper, when we spend the last minutes revising we can add missing phrases or sentences in the blank lines.

## Biography of a Theme

Frank Rodriguez took composition in the second term of his freshman year in 1987, doing daily writing, exercises in and out of class, and an essay a week. His first grades frustrated him: a C minus, a D, and a C minus minus. When he was assigned a fourth paper, he decided to get an early start and try the suggestions for getting ideas and for inventive revising that his teacher had made and that he found in his textbook.

Frank's instructor assigned the paper on a Monday, due one week later. This time, the instructor said, his students should write about something besides their own experiences. They had been writing personal narratives, trying to make their own actions and feelings clear to an audience. For this paper they should attempt more objectivity; in pursuit of that objectivity, their instructor asked them to write a five-hundred-word essay making use of comparison and contrast.

The class asked questions. The instructor referred his students to a definition of comparison and contrast (pages 278–283). He reminded them that an essay must be governed by its purpose and that therefore they must find a comparison which could legitimately make a point, fulfill a purpose. Frank raised his hand; if they were not to write out of personal experience, he asked, how were they supposed to know what they were talking about? His instructor replied that the assignment did not prohibit writing about something they had experienced; the injunction was to be objective about it, to avoid subjectivity or autobiographical narrative. Don't tell us your feelings about the election of 1986 or what you did on election day; tell us what happened in the election of 1986.

Frank walked from class to dormitory to kill an hour before lunch. He started jotting ideas for paper topics on the inside cover of his daily writing notebook:

> Hot Dogs Boiled and Grilled
> McDonald's versus the Hamburger

He must have been hungry. In the dormitory lounge, someone was playing solitaire. Frank's list continued:

> To Cheat or Not to Cheat at Solitaire

He opened his daily writing and glanced over the twenty-four filled-up pages about hitchhiking to Arizona, about playing defensive tackle in high school, about an old girlfriend, about a poly sci class, about rock-climbing, about loyalty, friendship, and two old friends. All of it was autobiographical. Maybe he could write objectively about rock-climbing. . . . But comparison and contrast? He tried rapidly brainstorming a list:

> washouts
> vegetation: don't grab!
> Arizona vs. Massachusetts
> equipment: shoes
> seasons
>   fall
>   summer
>   spring
>   winter tough

> park rangers
> bear tracks
> other animals

Lunch was approaching fast; he closed his notebook, aware that most of this list led to personal anecdotes out of his own experience. . . . Possibly *"Arizona vs. Massachusetts"* could lead to an objective comparison and contrast of terrain, difficulty, and equipment needed. He circled *"Arizona vs. Massachusetts."*

After lunch he did a two-hour chemistry lab, and while he performed mechanical tasks, his mind returned to rock-climbing and flitted over several other topics as well, like the *objective* boredom of Chemistry 101. When the lab was over, he stopped in the lounge again before going up to his room. The television set was on, one student watching late afternoon reruns on a UHF channel. He was surprised to see the old situation comedy *Hogan's Heroes* still on the air. Frank saw Colonel Klink humiliate Sergeant Schultz and found himself thinking how different *Hogan's Heroes* was from *M\*A\*S\*H*—and pulled out his chemistry notebook to take notes for five hundred words on comparison and contrast on two television comedies with a background of war.

> *Hogan* childish
> unrealistic
> watching after school with Kenny
> *M\*A\*S\*H* real war, blood, death
> *Hogan*—no dead?
> *M\*A\*S\*H* real
> *Hogan*—beautiful women spies
> Germans WWII / Koreans
> Germans always stupid, play tricks on
> in *Hogan* everybody same
> *M\*A\*S\*H* characters change
> Audience *Hogan* kids? *M\*A\*S\*H* grown-ups?
> Hogan impossible

When he ran out of thoughts, it was almost time for supper, and then Frank studied for a history quiz and played Ping-Pong for an hour. Just before going to bed, he looked at his notes again. He felt uncertain that he could compare the shows at all—they were so different. Did he have anything to say? Was there any purpose to comparing them? He did not know. How could he find a thesis or focus when he chose to compare marshmallows with circuses? He did not know. He went to bed telling himself that he would look at his notes in the morning.

In the morning before breakfast, he opened his daily writing note-book and wrote for five minutes without pausing to think:

> *Hogan's Heroes* was a rerun when I first heard of it—1973? I was five—when I came in from playing after school it was on at four-thirty or so and I watched it every afternoon with Kenny who was about three and a half or four and we both laughed at it until we were sick, Shulze (?) especially who Hogan always convinced of anything he wanted to, and Klink was just as stupid as Schultz—like recess!! G.I. Joe doll on TV ads. It's lousy when you think about it that kids got an idea of war from *Hogan's Heroes . . .*

After breakfast and poly sci, in the library before chemistry lecture, he read over his rapid paragraph and circled "like recess" and the word "war." Then he wrote one final sentence: "Instead of the reality of war, *Hogan's Heroes* was just like babies." Then he tried sprinting on *M\*A\*S\*H*.

> I never saw the movie *M\*A\*S\*H*—it's the TV show I'm comparing *Hogan* to. No comparison? *M\*A\*S\*H* is funny, not mostly about the war but you never completely forget that the war is there all the time, with all the blood in the operating room. The people are real. Realistic. They don't just say funny things all the time. People die on it, in the hospital and off-camera in accidents or the war. Its still going so I can watch it this week, maybe reruns too. They all want to get home—guy who wears women's clothes? Klinker?—Always two plots going at once.

That night he set aside an hour to work on his paper. In his second paragraph, he circled "Always two plots" and "People die" and wrote this sentence: "Using two plots at once helps *M\*A\*S\*H* be real, with real ups and downs, death and comedy." Then he wrote another five-minute sprint:

> *M\*A\*S\*H* is more serious than most sitcoms I guess. There are always (?) two stories flipping back and forth in every episode, maybe one of them more serious and the other one just funny. They always have the other plot to fall back on when things get too serious or sad. But it *is* funny. I remember watching it every afternoon for two weeks on vacation and laughing myself silly. I think the *words* are funny in *M\*A\*S\*H*, I mean not just what you see but the way they say things. How to compare the two things? *Hogan* is all one way, all jokes like the Three Stooges—The only thing not jokey is the danger—will they get away with it again?—and even

when you're a baby you know that they will. In *M\*A\*S\*H* you don't know because sometimes somebody dies—a patient or once the old Colonel in a plane crash . . .

He circled "*Hogan* is all one way" and "two stories flipping back and forth." He hoped he might be coming to a focus for his paper. Trying to make the point in one sentence, he wrote:

> *Hogan's Heroes* is childish and simpleminded in its humor but *M\*A\*S\*H* tries to bring in more of life in all it's complexity.

He tried again.

> In *Hogan's Heroes*, a whole show serves one purpose which is comedy appealing on a low level but *M\*A\*S\*H* is adult and tries to show the dark side of life as well as . . .

He tried again.

> *M\*A\*S\*H* is comedy for adults, because although it is funny it tries to show the complexity of war and human feelings. *Hogan's Heroes* is simply comedy, with no attempt to be realistic about war or . . .

He stopped because he realized he was about to begin a draft of his paper, and he did not feel ready to begin. For one thing, although the contrast was clear and becoming clearer, he was not sure that he had found a purpose for making the contrast. How could he find a thesis to support or a single focus to develop? He could contrast apples and oranges—clearly enough—but what good would that do? Yet he had the notion that if he continued to think he would discover a purpose.

He tried the journalist's six questions: Who? What? When? Where? Why? How? *Who* should include the names of characters. *What* was the body of his paper, to define the programs by comparison and contrast; should he say what a situation comedy is? *When* was the dates of programming, which he must somehow discover; or it was the settings of World War II and the Korean War. *Where* seemed irrelevant, except as Germany and Korea, which was also *When*. *Why* was difficult; how could he decide the motives of television networks? Maybe *Why?* would be a clue to his purpose. *How* was like *What*—how the plotting and structure of each series contrasted.

He decided to try to organize his ideas by listing topics he might cover, in some sort of order—an informal outline. Then he realized that he lacked information he needed—especially dates—and decided that he should gather everything together before trying to organize. Consulting a television schedule he discovered reruns of *M\*A\*S\*H* on the same channel showing *Hogan's Heroes;* he could do his research in the dormitory lounge any afternoon. Watching reruns he could record the correct spellings of characters' names, and could use plots or lines of dialogue as details for his paper. But how could he discover the dates when the comedies started to broadcast, or when *Hogan's Heroes* stopped? He knew *approximately* when. If *Hogan's Heroes* was already a rerun by 1973, it must have started earlier, maybe in the sixties. Because he was occasionally allowed to stay up for the regular show, he remembered that it was still being broadcast new when he was in second grade; and he remembered staying up to watch *M\*A\*S\*H*—he was almost positive—when he broke his arm in the sixth grade, in 1980. But being "almost positive" was not going to satisfy his English teacher; the word *vague* would fill the margin of his paper with red ink. He wondered if some encyclopedia could tell him what he needed to know.

For a moment it seemed that he might have to abandon a good comparison and contrast just because he lacked a couple of dates. Then he had a bright idea. The UHF channel broadcasting these reruns was only a few miles away. Frank looked up the call letters in the paper, found the channel listed in the telephone book under its call letters, and telephoned it. An obliging woman in public relations left the phone for a moment and returned to tell him that *Hogan's Heroes* had run from 1965 to 1971, and *M\*A\*S\*H* had started broadcasting in 1972. Frank had seen its last program in February 1983. The woman at the TV station also answered his surprise by telling him that *Hogan's Heroes* still appeared regularly as of 1987 in every major American market on UHF; so did shows that started and ended on regular network television even earlier, like *I Love Lucy* and *The Honeymooners*.

Now he was ready. Using the lists and paragraphs he had generated, Frank sketched a preliminary organization for his paper.

1. Sitcoms, war comedies, network
2. Watching *Hogan*, watching *M\*A\*S\*H*
3. Definition of *Hogan*
4. Definition of *M\*A\*S\*H*
5. Similarities
6. Obvious differences
7. Wars
8. Attitudes to war

9. Kinds of humor
10. Characters
11. Plot
12. Examples
13. Conclusion—childhood and maturity?

He put numbers in the margins of his notes that corresponded with the numbers on his informal outline. He set his notes on his desk in a semicircle around a fresh pad of paper and began writing a first draft.

> The situation comedy television show gets its humor from a continuing set of characters in the same place with a plot which begins and ends in each episode.
>
> When I was about seven I watched a situation comedy called *Hogan's Heroes* every day when I came home from school. For a long time I thought it was the funniest thing I had ever seen, it was slapstick like a cartoon more than it was like a movie, with Germans being fooled all the time by Americans in a prison camp. My brother who was only three and a half laughed as much as I did, which shows the level it was on.
>
> I don't remember when I saw *M\*A\*S\*H* first. I think it was partly over my head when I first saw it, because it was about things that are over your head when you are ten years old. But as I got older—and it was on reruns in the afternoon—I got to love it and really appreciate it. . .

Frank stopped writing. He realized he was describing himself, not *Hogan's Heroes* or *M\*A\*S\*H*, and this paper was supposed to be objective. It was a false start. Even the first paragraph, which was at least objective, was a waste of time; to compare two television shows, he did not really need to define *situation comedy* any more than he needed to define *television*. He decided to start again on a fresh page.

### *Two War Shows*

> Two television situation comedies have war in the background. *Hogan's Heroes* was on from 1965 to 1971. *M\*A\*S\*H* was in 1972 and still does new episodes. Each of them is funny although there backgrounds are killing. The two programs sound just alike but they are totally different in every way.
>
> All you have to do is watch *Hogan's Heroes* once or twice and we can tell what will happen next. An American in a prison camp makes a fool out of the Germans. They believe everything he says. He gets away with it every time and he never gets caught.

*M\*A\*S\*H* is different. It is in the Korean War. Its stars are doctors and nurses. Its got two plots usually in each episode. Something like life and death contrasted with something silly. *M\*A\*S\*H* is called a comedy but it has everything in it, all kinds of feelings.

*Hogan's* characters are always the same and the German officers are always stupid. *M\*A\*S\*H's* humor is not childish but wisecracks.

In *Hogan's Heroes* war is an easy game which the good guys always win. In *M\*A\*S\*H,* war is hell and the show's stars hate it.

Frank stopped without an ending. At least he had started.

He picked up his draft a day and a half after putting it down.

It was terrible. It was too short. It was thin. It said nothing. His paper had no hint of a purpose. As his teacher had written about his earlier papers, it was vague and general, without detail or development. It had no shape of thought, he decided, because it had no thought. As for audience, he had not even thought about it. Discouraged, he was tempted for a moment to give up, just to copy it out and hand it in—and then summoned his resolve again and started to read it over slowly. This time as he read, he pretended to be his own teacher, the Critic Inside, and wrote in the margin his own nasty comments to himself. *What movie?* he wrote beside the first paragraph. Next to "they are totally different in every way," he wrote, *Says nothing.* When he found himself saying both "you" and "we" in the second paragraph, he wrote, *Make up your mind. Thin,* he wrote halfway down the page. When he read the third paragraph, we wrote, *What's* M\*A\*S\*H *mean? What's it* about?

Beside every paragraph he questioned himself on detail. *Who? Like what?* He changed punctuation here, altered a word there—but concentrated mostly on structure and detail. When he came to the end, he wrote a new paragraph that just entered his head:

The differences between the shows must be because of one thing in particular. *Hogan's Heroes* started before most Americans even knew about the Vietnam War. By the time *M\*A\*S\*H* started in 1972, after the protest movement in the United States, Americans were ready for a television show that was against war.

He sat back: he did not yet have a paper, but he had thought of an answer to the journalist's Why? He had found a purpose for his comparison and contrast, and as soon as he recognized it, he realized that it had been there all the time, waiting for him to see it. He always knew that his high school course Social Issues in Contemporary History would come in handy.

Now Frank began his most difficult draft. He had assembled and roughed out his material; he had a comparison and contrast which led to a conclusion, which served a purpose. Now, with the help of his critical notions about his first draft, he would write a version that would do what he wanted it to do. He would concentrate on detail, on organization, and on making better sentences.

This time he wrote in less of a hurry, because he was more confident of where he was going. This time when he found a sentence going wrong, he crossed it out and tried again before he went further. When he needed to move from one subject to another, he experimented with transitions. Slowly, with much rewriting, searching for detail and color, trying to move gracefully between his two subjects, Frank drafted his theme. He did not rewrite his first draft so much as write the theme over again from start to finish, with the Critic Inside's marginal questions as reminders. When he had finished this draft, he set it aside again; then on Saturday he revised yet again. Again the Critic Inside made marginal comments: *trans., fragment, Germans 3 times, more detail, parallel.* He repaired to satisfy the Critic Inside. Then he checked over the margins of his three earlier essays to list errors he was likely to make: comma splices, apostrophe with *it's,* repeated simple sentence structure, transitions, lack of detail, lack of color imagery. He made the list and returned to his essay—correcting, replacing, changing compound sentences into complex ones, adding an adjective, making a noun or a verb more particular. He had used *fool* twice as a verb for what Hogan did to his captors. He looked up *fool* in his *Roget's Thesaurus* and found "deceive, beguile, trick, hoax, dupe, gammon, gull, pigeon . . . "—and in a series of words and phrases near the end of the entry discovered for his purposes either *outwit* or *outsmart.*

On Sunday he went over his manuscript one more time, checking for mechanical errors and for spelling. Then he typed a clean copy, checked over his typing, and on Monday handed in his paper.

On these two pages are Frank Rodriquez's next-to-final draft, with the Critic Inside's marginal comments, and, on pages 83–85, his finished essay, on which he received his first A in freshman English.

*Two War Comedies*                    *boring title*

*unclear*          Two television situation comedies, which are still seeable on afternoon reruns, have war as a background. *Hogan's Heroes* ori-

*short sentences*

*trans.*

*you/we*

*German 3 times*

*longer sentences*

*trans. It?*

*not stars*

*how?*

*detail parallel?*

*repeats*

*revise parallels*

*rewrite*

ginally showed in seasons from 1965 to 1971.[footnote] *M*A*S*H* premiered in 1972 and continues to film new episodes. Each makes jokes out of war. The two programs sound similar. But they are as different as kindergarten and college.

All you have to do is watch a few episodes of *Hogan's Heroes* and we can predict a plot. An American colonel named Bob Hogan is in a German prison camp during World War II. He makes a scheme against the Germans. With other American prisoners, he fools the Germans. He flatters them and they believe him. Then something is going to spoil his plan—he wants to blow up a bridge for example—but he manages to get past the trouble and win. Every time.

But *M*A*S*H* is unpredictable. It stands for Mobile Army Surgical Hospital and it takes place during the Korean War. Its stars are doctors and nurses. When a doctor works over a wounded soldier, he may not live. *M*A*S*H* has two plots usually in each episode. Something like life and death contrasted with something like bathwater. *M*A*S*H* is called comedy but it mixes comedy and sadness, horror and laughs. In this mixture *M*A*S*H* shows its grown up.

Hogan's characters are always the same stereotypes. Hogan's flattery fools the German officers who are always stupid. We laugh as they trip and fall, or as Klink hits his head. We laugh at people as predictable as cartoons. In *M*A*S*H* on the other hand, there is a nurse we don't like because she is all for No. 1. But then we see she is human after all. *M*A*S*H*'s humor is not childish but wisecracks. Somebody tells a soldier who is toying with his dinner, "Don't pick at your food. It will never heal."

Perhaps the greatest contrast lies in realism. *Hogan's Heroes* uses war as a play-

*awk.*

*more particulars*

*fragment*

*make one sentence*

*clarity ambiguous*

*it's!*
*word?*

*so what?*
*other word?*

*details*

*more detail*

*names?*

*what kind?*
*war*

*trans.?*

*repeats—*
*"Changing*
*channels–"*

*logic?*

ground, with no sense of the horror of World War II—genocide and saturation bombing. On the other hand, *M\*A\*S\*H*'s operating tables are covered with blood. In *Hogan's Heroes* war is an easy game which the good guys always win. In *M\*A\*S\*H*, war is hell and the show's stars hate it.

*heroes?*

The dates of the two series show why they are different. In the seven years between *Hogan's Heroes* of 1965 and *M\*A\*S\*H* of 1972, America made its major commitment of troops to Vietnam. Tens of thousands of our soldiers died in the jungles. As a result, this country was torn apart by protests—many of them led by college students who grew up on *Hogan's Heroes.*

*one sentence?*

*do you know?*

## Two Comedies, Two Wars, Two Worlds

You can watch reruns of both in the same afternoon, in many cities—two situation comedies with a background of war. <u>Hogan's Heroes</u> was produced from 1965 to 1971; <u>M\*A\*S\*H</u> premiered in 1972\* and continues to film new episodes. Each recounts humorous plots, in dialogue interrupted by "canned" laughter, although the reality behind each is tragic. Thus described, the two programs sound similar; but they are as different as kindergarten and college.

After we have seen a few episodes of <u>Hogan's Heroes</u>, we can predict each plot. An American colonel named Bob Hogan, incarcerated in a German prison camp during World War II, conceives an intrigue against his captors. With the aid of other allied and American prisoners, he outwits a stupid sergeant and a vain colonel, often by flattering them. Some accident seems to thwart his intention

\*Dates supplied by public relations at Channel WYBS.

(for stealing plans, for blowing up a bridge)
but he overcomes adversity and succeeds—in every episode.

The plots of M*A*S*H on the other hand
are unpredictable. The show's initials stand
for Mobile Army Surgical Hospital, it takes
place during the Korean War, and its heroes
are doctors and nurses. When a surgeon struggles to save a wounded soldier, we are not
certain that the soldier will live. Usually,
M*A*S*H works two plots against each other in
each episode, something as serious as a soldier's life contrasted with something as
frivolous as the availability of bathwater.
Although M*A*S*H is called a comedy, it mixes
laughter and tears, horror and happiness; in
this mixture M*A*S*H shows its maturity and
realism.

Hogan's characters never change, and its
humor comes from exploiting stereotypes. Hogan's flattery manipulates the vain Colonel
Klink and the gullible Sergeant Schultz to
act against their own interests. We laugh as
an officer of the Gestapo bumps his head; we
laugh at characters as simple as cats and
mice in Saturday cartoons. In M*A*S*H, on the
other hand, we feel compassion for an apparently overambitious nurse ("Hotlips") when
she reveals her vulnerability. Humor in
M*A*S*H is not childish slapstick but verbal
wit; a surgeon ("Hawkeye") speaks to a soldier ("Radar") who is depressed and toying
with his dinner: "Don't pick at your food. It
will never heal."*

Perhaps the greatest contrast lies in
the realism of the war used as backdrop. In
Hogan's Heroes, World War II is a playground;
there is no genocide, no saturation bombing.

*Heard on rerun, February 3.

Switching channels, M*A*S*H's operating tables are red with American and Korean blood.
In <u>Hogan's Heroes</u> the good guys always win—
and no one dies. In M*A*S*H, war is hell and
the show's protagonists hate it.

Perhaps the dates of the two series reveal the reason for the difference. In the
seven years between the start of <u>Hogan's He-</u>
<u>roes</u> in 1965 and M*A*S*H in 1972, America com-
mitted a huge army to Vietnam, tens of thousands of our soldiers died in the jungles,
and this country was torn apart by antiwar
protests—many of them led by college students
who must have watched <u>Hogan's Heroes</u> as children.

---
### EXERCISES
---

1. In class, imitate collectively how we choose a subject and narrow a topic. Narrow these general subjects into topics.

| | |
|---|---|
| the arms race | funding social security |
| the plight of the aged | alternate energy sources |
| the Saturday-night special | women's athletic programs |
| coming to college | legalizing marijuana |

Some subjects are broader than others, but all can be narrowed further.

2. In class, brainstorm details for a paper on a recent local controversy (housing rules? parking regulations? faculty unionizing? recruiting athletes?). Then try to organize the details, using the blackboard. Or take the details home and elaborate and organize them for the next class.

3. Write a paragraph rapidly (sprint) in class, taking as a starting point the list brainstormed in question 2. Read the paragraph aloud for class discussion. Which sentence or phrase would profit from expansion and development?

4. (a) On your own, work up an idea that might be developed into a theme. (b) Accumulate details, brainstorming or sprinting if you wish. (c) Organize details, eliminating those which seem irrele-

vant, tailoring your material to your purpose. (d) Bring all material to class. Students can read their material one at a time for general discussion. Or the instructor may want to collect the material and machine copy some of it to use in the next class meeting.

5. Here is a student essay. (a) Does this essay answer the journalist's six questions? (b) How well does this student accomplish comparison and contrast? Might questions of form have helped this student revise? Does the theme show a purpose? Is it addressed to an audience? (c) Pretending that you are a teacher, correct this paper in the margins. Give it a grade. (d) Revise and improve one of the paragraphs of this essay.

*Night and Day*

There is a small ski area about five miles away from my home town of Easthampton, Massachusetts, called the Mt. Tom Ski Area. Besides its excellent slopes and trails, Mt. Tom is the only ski resort in my neighborhood that offers both night and day skiing. Although night skiing is convenient and fun, there are many advantages to skiing during the day.

One annoying problem that can be avoided by skiing during the day is the large crowds. In the daytime, most people are in school or working and therefore, aren't able to go skiing. That means the parking facilities are less crowded and the lift lines are shorter, giving you more time on the ski slopes. Usually the conditions of the mountain are best during the daytime. The surface powder is still deep and fluffy. At night, the slopes often become icy because the deep powder has been worn away.

Also, feeling the sun's warmth as you glide down the slopes makes daytime skiing quite enjoyable. When the sun is warm, you can shed some of those layers of clothing. Who knows, maybe you'll even get a suntan!

With all that daytime skiing has to offer, there are still some disadvantages. For example, because your friends are either in school or working, you have to ski alone. Skiing just isn't as much fun unless you have a friend to fall down and look like a fool with! The view when riding the chairlift is much more glamorous at night than in the day. The bluegreen and white lights you see from above look like the flashing eyes of some Hollywood monster!

However, I still haven't mentioned safety, the most important advantage to skiing during the day. In the daytime, the trails are much more visible. At night, they are dimly lit and can be dangerous if you're not careful. In case of injury, it is much easier to locate an emergency telephone than it is at night. For these reasons alone, I feel that daytime skiing is best.

6.  Revise this beginning:

Every Easter we drove to my great Aunt's house in Troy to eat a ham for Easter dinner. Even when my father was a little boy, they had gone to Troy for Easter. Sometimes it would snow and we would be late. Once we blew a tire about half way, and the spare was soft, and we took at least an hour and a half to get it fixed.

Last year was my Senior year in high school, and my great aunt thought graduating from high school was a big deal, so I knew I would get a lot of attention when I got there. We have to pack because we actually stay over Friday and Saturday nights. Fortunately, for some reason, I packed my tennis shoes and my jeans. If I hadn't, I wouldn't have been able to play touch football decently, I wouldn't have wound up in the emergency ward, and I wouldn't have met Linda.

7.  Which of these beginnings are interesting and which seem potentially boring? Why? How might different purposes be served by different beginnings?

a. When the United Nations met in September, its members were already agitated, anxious, and almost apoplectic.

b. The origins of the missile crisis are already well known to the informed reading public.

c. Bang!

d. When I was born I lived in Cleveland. Then my family moved to Akron when I was two years old. After that we moved to Muncie, Indiana.

e. The goat had three eyes.

8.  Consulting the margins of essays your teacher has returned with corrections, make a checklist of repeated errors. Bring it to class or conference to see if your instructor agrees with your self-assessment. Use your revised list when you write your next paper.

9.  Correct Frank Rodriquez's draft on pages 79–80.

10.  Look over "Two War Comedies," Frank's next-to-last draft on pages 81–83. Make further comments in the margins. Do you see improvements in the final draft that are not accounted for by Frank's self-criticisms?

11.  Here is another essay in two drafts. The next-to-last draft is followed by the last draft. Notice differences between the two versions. Is the last draft better? Why? Find faults in the earlier draft that are repaired in the final. Is the final perfect, or can you find ways to improve it? Consider the two versions, thinking of purpose and audience.

### Two Wheels Are Better Than Four
Sharon Rustig

Bikes are better than cars, at least on this campus. Although cars protect you against bad weather, and take you on long trips, they cannot compare with bikes for practical daily use. You can pedal from dorm to class, lock up outside the door, and backpack your books upstairs—ten minutes from bed to classroom! If you have an hour's break between classes, you can go back to your room instead of wasting your time hanging around the hallways. Or you can zip downtown and do an errand and zip back to your next class.

But with a car, you would get to class half an hour late, because you couldn't find a place to park. If you park legally, you feed a meter. If you park illegally, you feed more than that. If your car is towed away from a no-parking area, you may pay as much as thirty dollars to get it back again. And not only parking is expensive, in connection with cars. Automobile insurance if you are student age will cost you practically as much as tuition. Gasoline has become expensive and is liable to get more so by the end of the year.

Bikes are better, not only because they are more efficient in getting you from place to place, and not only because they are cheaper, but because they're good for your body. They give you good exercise, especially if you live on a hill. Most students don't do much exercise, and just sit around getting flabby, so a bike is good for your health as well as everything else. The only bad things about bikes are their habit of getting stolen, but this works out for health too. You toughen up your neck muscles by riding around with a ten pound bike chain for a necklace.

But I haven't said the most important reason that bikes are better than cars. Cars use up petroleum which is in short supply. Bikes use up nothing but the bike riders' excess fat. Car exhaust pollutes the atmosphere and causes respiratory diseases. Bicycles exhaust nobody except the rider. Ecology makes the final reason why a bike is better than a car.

### Two Wheels Are Better Than Four—Number Two
Sharon Rustig

On a large residential campus, like the University of Michigan's, bicycles suit the needs of students more than automobiles do. Buicks and Chevrolets are useful for long trips, or as protection against bad weather, but the daily advantages of Schwinn or Raleigh are far greater. Bicycles save students time; from dormitory to classroom, bike rack to bike rack, will take only five or ten minutes. If students have an hour between classes, they can pedal to the library, lock up, and spend forty minutes in a book on Library Reserve. Or they can do an errand at a nearby store, and return to the classroom in time for the next lecture.

On the other hand, if students were driving an automobile, these alternatives would not be available. Parking makes the difference.

Starting out for class, they would need to allow an extra half hour to look for a parking space. They would need to walk to the library or the store, because they would not be able to count on finding a second or a third parking space. On this campus, cars parked illegally are ticketed and towed, which wastes the student not only time but money. The bicycle, which saves the student parking fines, saves the cost of gasoline as well, and the immense expense of insurance. The practicality of bicycles includes the economy of student finance, as well as the economy of student time.

There is also the economy of student health. Most students work hard at their books, and relax by sitting with their friends at taverns. The student body gets no exercise at all. But the bicyclist uses muscles otherwise unused, and adds to health while subtracting the waste of money and time. The only waste connected with bicycle riding is the epidemic of bicycle thievery; a stout chain prevents theft—and, worn around the neck, contributes to the health of the rider's neck muscles.

Finally, automobiles are detrimental to the health, not only of the sedentary student, but of everyone in the community. It is clear that bicycles are preferable to cars on this campus for purely practical or utilitarian reasons. But we should always ride bicycles, or walk, whenever we can, if an automobile can be avoided. Not only is the world's supply of energy diminishing, requiring us to conserve what energy we can, but the expense of that energy in car exhaust is a present danger to everyone alive. Pollution from carbon monoxide causes respiratory disease. Conservation and ecological danger makes it imperative that all of us make use of two wheels rather than four.

# 4

# *Words*

## THE SMALLEST UNIT

When we study writing we learn to swim by jumping into the lake; some of us swallow much lake water before we paddle to shore. How do we learn to write a paper of five paragraphs when we don't know what a paragraph is? How do we write a paragraph out of seven sentences when the concept of "sentence" remains fuzzy? With writing as with many endeavors, we start at the end because it is the only place where we can make a beginning. We must try everything at once. After we have made a start, only then is it possible to return to beginnings. Now we attend to words, sentences, and paragraphs. Presumably the student comes to this section after writing several essays. In this section we look at the smaller units of writing with the notion that, having sketched out some larger shapes, we can concentrate on language for a while.

## THE INSIDES OF WORDS

### Words Themselves

It may seem difficult, at first, to think of words apart from contexts; *salt* does not stand alone; it is part of "salt and pepper" or "Please pass the salt." Words seem like drops of water in a stream that has its own wholeness and its own motion. But when you write well, each word is accurate and honest and exact in itself, and contributes its special history to the wholeness of the stream of meaning.

The writer must be able to feel words intimately, one at a time. He must also be able to step back, inside his head, and see the flowing sentence. But he starts with the single word. He starts with tens of thousands of these units, and he picks among them. He may end by writing a passage like this account of man's first sleep on the moon:

> It was almost three-thirty in the morning when the astronauts finally prepared for sleep. They pulled down the shades and Aldrin stretched out on the floor, his nose near the moon dust. Armstrong sat on the cover of the ascent engine, his back leaning against one of the walls, his legs supported in a strap he had tied around a vertical bar. In front of his face was the eyepiece of the telescope. The earth was in its field of view, and the earth, "like a big blue eyeball" stared back at him. They could not sleep. Like the eye of a victim just murdered, the earth stared back at him.
>
> Norman Mailer, *Of a Fire on the Moon*

Until the end, this exposition seems simple and straightforward. Simple and straightforward it is, with the power of visual exactness, "his nose near the moon dust," and the unexpected detail, "a strap he had tied around a verticle bar." Mailer cements each word in place exactly and inevitably, with the help of rhythm and sentence structure. For now, just look at how he prepares for the last, emotional image with related words.

This passage, and much of Mailer's book, is about man and machine. The machinery is sophisticated, complex, overwhelming. Men are frail in comparison. The language begins to embody this idea by repeating the names of parts of the body: *nose, back, legs, face.* We have become accustomed to the jerking motions of the puffed-up spacesuits, as if we were watching robots. Now suddenly we see *nose* and *face.* We might be a mother looking at a sleeping child. From *face* we move to the most vulnerable and necessary of sense organs, the *eye,* first by way of a telescope's *eyepiece,* then by a visual comparison, easy to follow, of the earth to a *big blue eyeball,* which stares. We have departed from the astronauts' bodies and moved on to metaphorical bodies. Then, because the eyeball stares, we can leap to the emotional crux: the earth is dead, murdered by the astronauts who leave it behind for another planet, beginning the exploration outward, into the stars. Mailer makes his point not by telling us about it overtly, but by his control of language, his understanding of the insides of words, so that the movement from *nose* to *face* to *eyepiece* and *view* to *victim just murdered* has an inner and emotional necessity.

> All the warm night the secret snow fell so adhesively that every twig in the woods about their little rented house supported a tall slice of white, an upward projection which in the shadowless gloom of early morning lifted depth from the scene, made it seem Chinese, calligraphic, a stiff tapestry hung from the gray sky, a shield of lace interwoven with black thread.
>
> John Updike

This sentence begins a short story called "The Crow in the Wood." Updike exercises the possibilities of our language in rhythm, in variety of sentence structure, and in observation that is dreamy and precise at the same time. He does it with words. Instead of looking at everything he does, let us look at two words that stand out. *Adhesively* is a word we all know, from the noun or adjective *adhesive,* as a longer way of saying *glue* or *sticky.* Here the snow "fell . . . adhesively." Snow really cannot fall like glue, and so we have something apparently inaccurate; yet it is right, because the context prepares us. It is a *warm night;* the snow will be damp. And using *adhesively* rather than *stickily* shows that the snow is not gooey to the fingers, but will readily adhere to something. *Adhesively* by its unusualness draws the right attention to itself.

Then look at the word *slice:* "every twig . . . supported a tall slice of white." Most of us would have said something about snow *piling* or *accumulating* on branches. But "a tall slice of white," besides being pleasing to the ear, is a brilliant image; the sharpness of *slice,* together with the image of whiteness, nearly dazzles the eye. With the word *slice* is an unspoken knife, just out of sight. And I think we have a moment's vision of an upright piece of white-frosted cake.

We could pick many more words for praise in the passages from Mailer and Updike, and maybe for blame as well (we will do that later). But the excellence here is perhaps like all excellence. These writers are *original, as if seeing a thing no one else has seen;* yet they report their vision in a *language that reaches the rest of us.* Here, again, we find the opposites we must combine. For the first quality writers need imagination; for the second skill. Without both qualities, they could not write such a passage. Imagination without skill makes a lively chaos; skill without imagination, a deadly order.

## No Synonyms

To appreciate the word—the *eyepiece*, the *eyeball*, the *slice*, the *adhesively*—writers and readers must first realize that no words can be synonyms. Some words are close to each other in meaning, close enough to reveal that they are not the same. Writers must know not just the surface definitions of words; they must go deeper and realize the families of contexts into which words have extended their associations—like *slice* with *knife* and even *cake.* These families are the connotations of the word and the associations we make with its denotation. We use *denotation* to mean the explicit or literal meaning of a word, *connotation* to mean a word's implications. The verb *to stagger* denotes an unsteady or irregular motion; one of its connotations is drunkenness. Associations are different from connotations. *Pepper* is not a connotation of *salt*, but an association of it. Because we use the whole family, it does not matter that we discriminate connotation from association. But we must know the insides of words; we must be a friend of the family.

The verbs *to emulate, to imitate, to copy,* and *to ape* are synonyms by definition, but when we use them in a sentence, they carry slight differences in meaning. *To emulate* sounds fancy; also, it usually implies that the imitation involves self-improvement. *To imitate* is neutral, except that everyone knows that an imitation is not the real thing; inferiority shadows the word. *To copy* is to reproduce exactly; like *to imitate*, it states a lack of originality. *To ape* is to mimic, and to be comical or mocking about it. If you wanted to say that a young pianist imitated a famous virtuoso, but you carelessly used *ape* instead of *imitate*, you would grant her style the grace of a gorilla. Context is all; the inside of a word must reinforce or continue the force built by the context. When a sportswriter wrote that one middle linebacker aped another middle linebacker, he was being witty.

Dictionaries of synonyms and other books, especially *Roget's Thesaurus*, list words that resemble each other. Experienced writers can sometimes use a thesaurus to joggle their brain to find not a *synonym*, but the *right* word. They will be aware of the insides of the words they discover. The thesaurus can be useful not for supplying words never heard before (we know words only when we have met them in sentences; some dictionaries supply examples of words in use), but to remind writers of words known in the past, but not remembered when needed.

Sometimes an unsophisticated writer finds disaster in such a book. A thesaurus supplies us with words that *resemble* each other, but we must recognize the *differences* among them. When I look up *imitation* in my pocket *Roget*, I find under Verbs:

> imitate, copy, mirror, reflect, reproduce, repeat; do like, echo, re-echo, catch, match, parallel; forge, counterfeit.

> mimic, ape, simulate, impersonate, act, etc. (drama), 599; represent, etc., 554; parody, travesty, caricature, burlesque, take off, mock, borrow.

> follow in the steps (or wake) of, take pattern by, follow suit [colloq.], follow the example of, walk in the shoes of, take after, model after, emulate.

The editors separate the verbs into three categories, which ought to help the cautious writer, but it is difficult sometimes to defend their sorting out. Why does *forge* or *counterfeit* belong among the closer synonyms in the first group and *emulate* among the phrases in the third group? Why is *represent* among the comic or belittling words? Putting *ape* with *travesty* and *parody*, however, reminds us of the comic insides of *ape*. Beginning writers should certainly be wary of a thesaurus, because if they believe in synonyms, they can produce a prose that means something wholly different from what they intend. The sentence

> I walked in the flowers that bordered the garden, sniffing the sweet airs of spring.

could become

> I peregrinated in the flowerets that flounced the orangery, sniffing the saccharine ventilation of the vernal equinox.

Spoken by W. C. Fields, the second version could be perfect for its context, but as an example of how people misuse a thesaurus, it is exaggerated.

Using dictionary synonyms, you can test your sensitivity to the insides of words. Put the adjectives *false, fake, phony,* and *insincere* with the noun *laugh*. Everyone has heard laughs that were unreal, laughs for the sake of flattery, laughs that express the laugher's nervousness, or laughs at jokes that are not funny. If we wrote a description of such a laugh, we might want to write, "His laugh was false," or "His laugh was fake," or "His laugh was phony," or "His laugh was insincere." Each time the exact meaning differs. "His laugh was false" sounds direct and serious, a stern and objective judgment. "His laugh was fake" sounds harsher, a strong indictment of the laugher; it implies that the falseness was deliberate. "His laugh was phony" tells us more about whoever wrote the phrase. The choice of *phony* over *false* or *fake* or *insincere* makes the speaker imply something like, "I am relaxed enough to be slangy." On the other hand, "His laugh was insincere" sounds pompous in its moral judgment—partly pompous, partly naïve.

These attempts to name the associations that words gather, with out setting the context that story or essay bestows, are speculation; but, whatever the context, the words would all be different. Slightly, but genuinely, different. Katherine Anne Porter announced in 1961 that she had discovered "a law" that she put into "a little axiom":

> There is no such thing as an exact synonym and no such thing as an unmixed motive.

## Literalness and Metaphor

Another way to become sensitive to the insides of words is to take them as literally as you can. When you read. "Fog enveloped the city," try seeing a gigantic gray-brown envelope enclosing Los Angeles. You can see some silliness in literal images—but it is a silliness that can increase your sensitivity to words. Puns help too, working through the ear. Literal-mindedness, like all exercises that can improve your writing, can improve your reading as well.

Literal-mindedness exposes mixed metaphors, careless phrases comparing things that are comic or gross or inappropriate when brought together. Metaphors usually become mixed when a writer uses the kind of clichés called "dead metaphors" without noticing their original meanings. Sometimes people write, "The door yawned open"; the would-be comparison of door to mouth is dead from over use. Sometimes people write, "The door beckoned," and the dead metaphor has the door turn into a hand that gestures an invitation. Once a student wrote in a paper, "The door yawned and beckoned." Two clichés make a mixed metaphor, if we are reading the insides of words: first the door is a huge, gaping mouth; suddenly an arm materializes between rows of teeth and motions us to enter.

When we take words literally, we respond to metaphor. We see the fog *compared* to an envelope. A metaphor is a comparison made without being stated. We *state a comparison* as a simile—"like a big blue eyeball"—and we *make* a comparison when we leave out *like* or *as*. Hamlet in his soliloquy wonders if he should "take arms against a sea of troubles." It is futile to fight with the ocean. The futility is what Shakespeare had in mind. If you take the words literally, you can see an armored knight wading into the surf and slashing at the waves with his sword. The image shows an emotion that the abstract word *futility* would only name. The picture—which we receive by literal reading— gives us the emotion without losing the idea.

### Sense Words

Words that carry feeling most strongly are pictures and smells and touches and tastes and noises. Images are details of sense. The more sensuous words are, the more they reach us and move us. Updike embodies feelings of cozy shelter, and of precise observation of the outside world, by using images, not by using words which *tell* us how to feel (like *cozy)* or which abstract ideas from actions (like *observations)*. Mailer gives us an exact visual image of the astronauts trying to sleep on the moon. We feel the astronauts' cramp and discomfort because of the images; he need not say *cramp* and *discomfort*. In the next paragraph, Mailer writes about the failure to sleep, and he writes ideas, but he uses images as well.

> It used to be said that men in the hour of their triumph knew the sleep of the just, but a modern view might argue that men sleep in order to dream, sleep in order to involve that mysterious theater where regions of the unconscious reach into communication with one another, and charts and portraits of the soul and the world outside are subtly retouched from the experience of the day.

"Theater," "charts," "portraits . . . retouched"—Mailer uses images to make his concept clear by a comparison. Not all writing can be sensuous and figurative, but most writing can be. Of course, it is always possible to be safe and boring by stating only the facts, without images and feelings. Mailer could have said that the astronauts arranged themselves to go to sleep but couldn't, perhaps because so much had happened that day. Updike could have said that when his characters woke up, they discovered that it had snowed while they slept.

In his essay "Once More to the Lake," E. B. White needs to let his audience know that his son lacked experience of lakes; he therefore speaks of "my son, who had never had fresh water up his nose and who had seen lily pads only from train windows." Sense words *always* reach the reader with more strength than words of generality, like "lacked experience of lakes."

Sense words carry feeling, and they fulfill purposes appropriate to different kinds of writing: for Mailer, the sense words embody a speculation; for Updike, they convey sensation that will soon body forth fiction to the reader's imagination. For Jane Addams, in this passage from *Twenty Years at Hull House,* images explain a scene at the same time as they express outrage over poverty in Victorian London:

> . . . On Mile End Road, from the top of an omnibus which paused at the end of a dingy street lighted by only occasional flares of gas, we saw two huge masses of ill-clad people clamoring around two hucksters' carts. They were bidding their farthings and ha'pennies for a vegetable held up by the auctioneer, which he at last scornfully flung, with a gibe for its cheapness, to the successful bidder. In the momentary pause only one man detached himself from the groups. He had bidden on a cabbage, and when it struck his hand, he instantly sat down on the curb, tore it with his teeth, and hastily devoured it, unwashed and uncooked as it was. He and his fellows . . . were huddled into ill-fitting, cast-off clothing, the ragged finery which one sees only in East London. Their pale faces were dominated by that most unlovely of human expressions, the cunning and shrewdness of the bargain-hunter who starves if he cannot make a successful trade, and yet the final impression was not of ragged, tawdry clothing nor of pinched and sallow faces, but of myriads of hands, empty, pathetic, nerveless, and workworn, showing white in the uncertain light of the street, and clutching forward for food which was already unfit to eat.

Notice that our sense of outrage, almost without exception, comes from the images chosen; we are not *told*, except when she writes, "that most unlovely of human expressions"; we are *shown*. If Addams used only abstractions like *degradation* and *extreme poverty*, we could forget them easily; we do not forget the man who devours the cabbage *unwashed and uncooked* or the hands clutching at inedible food.

### Misusing the Insides of Words

Just as we can learn to embody feelings by being aware of a word's whole family and by using language that appeals to the senses, so we can misuse words to fool ourselves and other people. By misusing the insides of words, we are insincere. The poet W. B. Yeats wrote, "The rhetorician would deceive his neighbors, / The sentimentalist himself." Sentimentality means faked or exaggerated feeling, emotion that is not genuine. Usually, the rhetorician who wishes to deceive others must first become a sentimentalist who deceives himself. In the advertising business, it is common wisdom that you have to *believe* in your product, so that grown people ride the commuter trains believing that Hotz is superior to all other cold breakfasts. To con others, you begin by conning yourself, or you end that way.

Some propagandists deceive by will. The conscious manipulator sets out to change minds by slanting words to *seem* objective and yet to carry a disguised subjective content. News magazines (*Time, Newsweek, U.S. News and World Report*) often convey subtle editorial comment within their reporting. Newspapers do the same, though the best editors try to keep the editorials editorial and the news objective. But even when you appear objective, you can select with bias. One photograph of candidate Y looks flattering; another makes him look like an ass.

We will never destroy bias, but we can learn to see bias, and not be deceived by reporting that is really editorializing. A few years back, one news magazine blatantly supported one presidential candidate. It openly supported him editorially. And in its news stories it supported him subtly, using the associations of words. Candidate A, it said, "in his rumpled suit slouched into the gleaming limousine." Candidate B, on the other hand, "strode smiling into his black sedan."

Now a sedan may sound expensive, but it may also seem to suit the dignity required of a candidate for high office. *Gleaming limousine* is more lavish, more gloatingly rich. *Rumpled suit* and *smiling* are obvious contrasts. The most telling use of the loaded word is the contrast between *strode* and *slouched.* Who would vote for a man who slouched when he could pick one that strode instead? Yet in all fairness, can we say that the *news* in each sentence is different? In the flattest language, the sentence would read, "The man got in the car." The rhetoricians of the news magazine, playing upon the separation between meaning and expression, flash us the sign: "Vote for B!" Because they pretend to objectivity, their use of sense words to influence opinion is underhanded.

They seem to be doing it consciously, though no one can ever be sure of someone else's consciousness. More dangerous, for anyone who wishes to be honest, are the loaded words we kid ourselves with. We use euphemism to persuade ourselves that one thing is really another; a *janitor* cleans floors, but it sounds more lofty to call him a *custodian.* When we say that someone is *wealthy,* we avoid the plainer word *rich,* which has acquired overtones of vulgarity. If a real estate agent shows you a two-room shack converted from a chicken coop, he does not call it a *house,* he calls it a *home.* A Cadillac is never a *used car;* it is *previously owned.*

Often, a euphemism is more abstract or general than the plain word. The euphemism not only sounds fancier (mortician / undertaker; route salesman / milkman), but it has less color or imagery. H. L. Mencken, in *The American Language,* gave some historical background to American euphemisms.

> The tendency to engaud lowly vocations with names presumably dignified goes back to the Revolution, and has been frequently noted by English travelers, beginning with Thomas Anburey in 1779. In 1784 John Ferdinand Dalziel Smyth observed that the smallest American shopkeepers were calling their establishments *stores,* which indicated a large place to an Englishman. "The different distinct branches of manufacturers," he said, "such as *hosiers, haberdashers, clothiers, linen drapers, grocers, stationers,* etc., are not known here; they are all comprehended in the single name and occupation of *merchant* or *storekeeper.*" By 1846 the American barbershop had begun to be a *shaving salon* and by 1850 a photographer was a *daguerrian artist.* By 1875 barbers were *tonsorial artists* or *tonsorialists,* and in the early 80s presentable saloonkeepers became *restauranters* or *restauranteurs.* By 1901 the *Police Gazette* was carrying on a campaign for the abandonment of the lowly *bartender* and the adoption of either *bar clerk* or *mixologist.*

But euphemism is not only comical. We employ euphemism, frequently, when we want to conceal something painful. When we have a tomcat castrated, we hesitate to admit that we have cut off his testicles or even that we have castrated him; we have had him *altered.* We have a tooth *extracted;* it would be more painful to have it *pulled.*

Politics and political acts of destruction always bring forth the worst in our prose, as we struggle to justify ourselves. Hitler euphemistically labeled his genocide of Jews "the final solution." One of the finest essays on style is George Orwell's "Politics and the English Language," written in the forties. He says:

> Millions of peasants are robbed of their farms and sent trudging along the roads with no more than they can carry: this is called *transfer of population* or *rectification of frontiers.* People are imprisoned for years without trial, or shot in the back of the neck or sent to die of scurvy in Arctic lumber camps; this is called *elimination of undesirable elements.* Such phraseology is needed if we want to name things without calling up mental pictures of them. Consider for instance some comfortable English professor defending Russian totalitarianism. [Geroge Orwell was English and was writing after Stalin's execution of the Kulaks and the mass murders of the Soviet purges of the late thirties.] He cannot say outright, "I believe in killing off your opponents when you can get good results by doing so." Probably, therefore, he will say something like this:
>
> "While freely conceding that the Soviet regime exhibits certain features which the humanitarian may be inclined to deplore, we must, I think, agree that a certain curtailment of the right to political opposition is an unavoidable concomitant of transitional periods, and that the rigors which the Russian people have been called upon to undergo have been amply justified in the sphere of concrete achievement."

Meanwhile, the bullet enters the back of the head. Always be suspicious—as Orwell advises—when the words do not call up a picture. "Terminate with extreme prejudice" does not call to mind the prisoner bound, blindfolded, kneeling, the pistol at the back of his head, the sound, the rush of the body forward, the splatter of brains and blood.

### Avoiding Self-Deceit

Sometimes, then, we use abstractions or euphemisms to avoid or suppress feeling. And sometimes we use sense words in underhanded ways, not so much to evade feeling as to twist it. *Slouched* and *strode* are both verbs of action that make us see. We must decide, by using our brains and our sensitivity, whether the difference between two images is literal description or an emotional nudge disguising itself as objective description. We do not complain that emotions *show;* we complain that the emotions are *disguised.* We do not object to laughter or to anger. We object to laughter that hides anger, expressing gaiety while it means hostility. We can learn to sense the falseness in language—our own or others—as we learn to sense falseness in a gesture or a facial expression. The "examined life" demands it.

If we ourselves have strong opinions or biases, we must be wary, in both reading and writing. If we react instantly to a cliché like *the military-industrial complex*, we are not thinking about it, and we can manipulate ourselves or be manipulated by others. We must become aware of our habits of opinion. We need not alter our convictions; we need only open them to the air—and to our own conscious minds. When we hear a phrase like *iron-curtain countries*, we must not respond like an automation to a pressed button, but like a human being, and decide what the phrase means, if it means anything, in its current context.

Like most of the advice in this book, these notions apply equally to writing and to reading. The more intense our convictions, reading or writing, the more vulnerable we are to self-deceit.

### Collecting Words

We must watch our words to see if we are using them with respect for honest expression. It helps to love words, and a love of words is something that we can develop. The growing writer finds pleasure in becoming a word collector, picking up, examining, and keeping new words (or familiar words seen suddenly, as if for the first time) like seashells or driftwood. Think of the richness in *hogwash* or the exact strength in *rasp*. English is thick with short, strong words. You can collect words from books, of course, but you can also find them in speech; a sense of lively speech adds energy to the best writing. A writer listens to speech—others' and even his own—with a greedy ear. Primitive people and children love words as things in themselves and collect them as ornaments. To become a better writer, rediscover some of the pleasure from words-as-things that you had in your childhood but have probably lost along the way. Patrol the miles of speech looking for words like *flotsam*.

Dictionaries can help, too. A thesaurus or a list of synonyms has the limitations mentioned earlier (page 95). Brief dictionaries have brief definitions, and though they may light up a dark patch in our reading, they often give such a limited definition for the word, so empty of context, that we may misuse the word when we try to say it in a sentence. Good-sized college dictionaries carry more information, and can be a pleasure to read. The more information, the better. The biggest dictionary in the language rewards investigation. Sometime, when you are in the library, take down from the shelves one of the thirteen volumes of the *Oxford English Dictionary* and browse a little. The English poet and novelist Robert Graves says only one book is indispensable to the writer's library: the *OED*. In the thirteen volumes of the original, the editors collected almost all the words you are likely to come across, except for new words and words that at the time of publication were considered unprintable. In 1986 new editors completed a four-volume supplement that added new words and old words newly printable. There is a photographically reduced edition that includes all the pages of the original dictionary, making a two-volume set out of the original thirteen. The price of the two-volume set puts this great dictionary within many people's reach.

It is not the *OED*'s completeness that makes it so valuable; it is the context given for each word—the editors try to supply a context for the earliest example of each shade of meaning for every word; for each word in the language the dictionary provides a small biography. Suppose we look up the word *vegetable*. More than three columns of small print chronicle the life of the word, which began as an adjective meaning "having the vegetating properties of plants; living and growing as a plant or organism endowed with the lowest form of life." The earliest example is from 1400. The poet John Lydgate, a couple of decades later, wrote of the wind (spelling modernized): ". . . that is so comfortable / For to nourish things vegetable." When Andrew Marvell wrote "To His Coy Mistress" two and a half centuries later (1687), he used the adjective in the same way: "My vegetable love should grow / Vaster than empires and more slow." Six examples (complete with small context) comes between Lydgate and Marvell.

Meanwhile, the noun *vegetable* got started in 1582, when an author named J. Hester spoke of "the Hidden Vertues of sondrie Vegitables, Animalles, and Mineralles." The reader can discover thirty-six contexts for the word *vegetable* as a noun from 1582 to modern times—and many shades of meaning. If you take pleasure in words, you will find your sensitivity to the insides of words increasing as you know more about the history of words. So much of our history, external and internal, global and psychic, is coded into our words. The more you know, the more you respect the integrity of the word; integrity means wholeness; a word's wholeness includes all its possibilities: its family, its insides.

### Words as Blanks

A frequent failure in our language, spoken or written, is our use of words that can mean anything the context requires. These words are like blanks for the reader or listener to fill in. Words of vague praise or blame—*lovely, nice,* and *terrible*—are frequent blanks. *Great. Terrific.* What does "nice hair" look like? Is it red or blond or white or black or brown? Long or short? Liveliness is specificity. Obscenities are common words-as-blanks, used without attention to their literal meaning. Vogue words are usually blanks also. *Awesome, wicked, psyched. Fink* was popular a few years ago as a vogue word of contempt, no more precise than the *jerk* or *creep* of earlier generations. Yet once *fink* meant something exact: a man employed to join a labor union and spy for bosses. Words of complex history suddenly come into fashion and lose all color. *Funky* moved from black American speech into television—and no longer has anything to say.

### Words and Associations

Words used as blanks get in the way of writing and thinking and feeling. Words mean things only by our agreement. If we start using *April* to mean *sunset* or *anything pleasant,* it will not be of use to us anymore. Our agreements about words are coded into dictionaries, which of course change as the words shift gradually in meaning because of historical change and the literary genius that adapts old words to new conditions. Our agreements about words are also coded into the dictionary from which we really make our sentences—the dictionary (the computer) of the brain. This mental collection is even more complicated and useful for our writing than the dictionary on the shelf. The thirty thousand associations of the word *April* are stored in it, waiting to be used in the right way at the right time. The inside of a word is a huge room of possibilities, limited—because *April* does not include *August* or *catsup* for most of us—but multiple: flowers and showers, Easter, spring, seeds, vacation from school, Chaucer and Browning and Eliot for readers of poetry, ploughing or manure-spreading for farmers.

Someone might associate April with catsup or cats or soup or a girl in the first grade called April. These associations are private; the few phrases I listed at the end of the preceding paragraph are public or general. A moment's thought will usually reveal to the writer, at least in revision, whether he is using a word privately or generally. "Tulips like catsup" would be a grotesque and inappropriate simile for most of us—despite the real color—though it might be a spontaneous expression of the writer who privately associated April with catsup. A writer must learn to suppress the highly private, because writing must get through to an audience; you are talking to someone besides yourself; you have climbed out of the pure autism of the crib and are trying to make human contact.

### Words and Audience

But we must also remember, in choosing words, that an audience is not *everyone*. The larger the audience we try to reach, the fewer associations we can take for granted and the more circumscribed our room of possibilities. If we are writing for a big newspaper, we probably do not assume that most of our readers associate April with Chaucer, Browning, and Eliot. An idea of the audience is crucial to our choice of words. Everyone makes this sort of choice in conversation: we use words with our best friend that we do not use with our grandmother; if we hitch a ride with a white-haired man wearing a blue suit, our words differ from those we would use if the driver wore reflecting sunglasses and an earring. If our vocabulary stays the same, chances are that we are being hostile in the sacred name of honesty.

To adjust our vocabulary to our audience is honest and not hypocritical; we do not speak of adjusting our opinions or beliefs. Our minds contain multiple possibilities of expression among which we choose. If we do not try to make contact with another, the notion of honest speech is meaningless: for speech is speech only when it reaches another person.

In writing we make the same choices. If we write a letter to the college newspaper, we choose the words from a collection different from the one we choose from when we write a thank-you letter to an aunt. A term paper in business administration requires a vocabulary different from the one for a term paper in literature.

The difficult, necessary task is to adjust your vocabulary to your audience with tact, humility, and appropriateness—but without hypocrisy. Sometimes it is merely a matter of common sense. If you are writing for an audience from the southern hemisphere, you must remember that April connotes autumn and leaves falling, not green and seeds sprouting. But common sense is easy, compared to the difficulties in learning the difference between appropriate tact and gross hypocrisy. When Jim Beck wrote his first essay, the one about "well-rounded individuals" and so on (on pages 10–11), he was writing for an assumed audience. Probably at that moment he did not believe that he could write with honesty for an audience that was a teacher. Probably Jim had no vocabularies to fall back on at that moment but that of high-minded hyprocrisy and that of the boys in the locker room or the dorm, which can be just as hypocritical and one-sided as graduation oratory. By becoming aware of the insides of words, he learned a lot about the insides of Jim Beck; and he learned to make the inside outside—to make connection with other people, to use words for social purposes, to *write.*

### Revising Words

From the first notes for an essay to its final typing, words are the material we work with. When we brainstorm or sprint, we use the associations of words. When we develop ideas, when we expand generalities by detail, our focus on individual words generates more words. But our local concentration on language increases as drafts become later and final. It may be far along before we discover that *wage* may be more appropriate for our context and audience than *salary.* It may take a final draft before we excise the blank word *aspect* and find a useful substitute. At the end we check our sentences both to remove error and to find better language: more exact, more particular, and more original—in a word.

___ **EXERCISES** ___

1. Here are three lists of words similar in meaning. Discuss the varieties of meaning within each list.

ostentatious,showy,conspicuous,exhibitionistic,show-offy,pretentious, preserve, maintain, keep up, support
disease, illness, sickness, infirmity, disorder, indisposition, debility

2. Using a thesaurus, rewrite this passage by substituting a "synonym" for each of the words in italics. See the example on page 95.

I *remember sitting* with my *foot* up on *pillows* on the edge of my *bed* in my *room,* gazing at my *freckled face* in a *hand mirror.* My *face embarrassed* me most of the time and I couldn't *get a comb* through my *mass* of unruly, *tangled red hair.*

Shirley MacLaine, Don't Fall off the Mountain

3. Look past these thesaurus words, and find the proverb:

   a. It requires an entirety of species to fabricate a cosmos.

   b. Precipitousness occasions depletion.

   c. The sum total of matter that scintillates is not necessarily bullion.

4. Here are some headlines or sentences quoted from daily newspapers. Try the tests of "Literalness and Metaphor," pages 96–97. Which writers of the following phrases were conscious of what they were doing? Were any, in your opinion, being deliberately comic?

   a. Unmasked as a faceless automation, he toyed with her affections, and a stormy argument ensued.

   b. AUTO SHOW FANS BASK IN CREAM OF CITY'S CROP

   c. A gush of poetic language cushions these pivotal events until they are nearly—but not quite—camouflaged.

   d. Mushrooming insurance and energy costs represent a double-barreled shotgun pointed at New England ski areas.

   e. PTA OPENS FIRE ON TV VIOLENCE

   f. Off the top of her head she claimed that grass roots were the bottom line.

5. Make up new euphemisms for these professions, events, or actions.

   final exams, Mother's Day, Veterans Day, tackling a quarterback from the blind side, cheating on a quiz, asking for money

6. On page 98 is E. B. White's phrase informing us that his son lacked experience of lakes. Using his sentence as a model, and using sense words, think of two more particulars that could express the same information. You could write "my son, who had never been kept awake by bullfrogs croaking or caught minnows in a sieve. . . ."

7. When prose gets out of control, there is often more than one thing wrong with it. In these passages of bad prose, find words used as blanks and as euphemisms. If you notice other faults, name them.

   a. Thank you for the information you recently provided in connection with your request for Gulf Travel Cards. The information contained in your communication, along with other data developed, has enabled us to reverse our previous decision regarding your Travel Card application.

b. We will be experiencing a development of shower activity.

c. The purpose of this program is to provide opportunities for teachers at undergraduate colleges and universities and at junior and community colleges to work in their areas of interest with distinguished scholars in their fields and to have access to libraries suitable for advanced study.

d. The evidence developed was not corroborative of the allegation on which it was predicated.

8. In this paragraph, underline three words that the author uses with special skill—the way John Updike uses *adhesively* and *slice*—and be prepared to defend your choices in class.

> The top of the hill, pasture for one straggly cow, was clear of brush except for patches of dark juniper, in spreading flat circles ten feet across. Around the tumbled stone walls tall pines and maples held off an advancing army of small gray birch. At one side, by the bouldery path that had once been a town road, a little family graveyard lay on slightly tilted ground. A deer trail ran right through it, bright and twisted between the slate stones, and a birch had fallen and rotted out of its bark, leaving a print like a white hand.
>
> Thomas Williams, *Town Burning*

9. Underline the sense words in this passage from a magazine article. How effective are they? Does the author have the insides of words under control? When he perceives "ten million persons . . . hustling in the . . . carpet," what does he compare them to?

> A blinding splendor sparkling in lazy rhythm to the whine of retarding jet engines welcomes you to Mexico City. The surreal glow seems to extend to the end of the world and it's not hard to believe some ten million persons are rising for the day, hustling in the brilliant carpet of light below.
>
> Sergio Ortiz, "Mexico" (*Playgirl*)

10. Underline examples of euphemism in these passages from a speech about the public relations business:

> So confident were we that a breakthrough was imminent that it became popular to think of changing our name from public relations specialists to communications specialists.
>
> What is new is the role the public relations consultant is beginning to play in relation to the social crises which no one foresaw 10 or 20 years ago. In these new assignments—which represent a small but rapidly growing part of his business—he is no longer primarily a communicator; he is a sort of moderator whose job it is to try to prevent

the crisis from getting out of hand. He may still use the same tools, but the measure of his performance is not how effectively he gets his clients' message across, but how successful he is in avoiding a flare-up which can stop the machinery of his clients' business, how he can help his clients conduct their business in a way that is responsive to the new demands made by concerned scientists, environmentalists, consumerists, minority leaders, underprivileged segments of the community, the young generation.

> David Finn, "Modifying Opinions in the New
> Human Climate" (*Public Relations Quarterly*)

11. Disregarding your own convictions, look in these passages for loaded language, euphemism—the use and misuse of language in general. Underline whatever seems underhanded, and discuss in class.

a. The Great Lakes, which hold one-fifth of all the fresh water on the surface of the earth, have become heavily contaminated. Hundreds of millions of gallons of industrial pollutants are discharged into Lake Superior and flow on into Lake Huron. Lake Michigan drains a huge complex of industries. Lake Erie is described as a "chemical sink." Most of the lake's fish, once a rich harvest, have been killed. In the slow-moving lake water, contaminants have settled to the bottom. Thus, although clean-up efforts are now beginning, experts are far from sure that the lakes can be reclaimed even if further pollution can be halted.

> John Perry, *Our Polluted World*

b. The world needs nuclear energy. The fossil fuels—coal, oil and natural gas—are being consumed at an alarming rate. Many experts believe that by the end of this century half of the world's supply of electric power will come from nuclear stations.

Nuclear fuels are highly concentrated. Operation of a coal-fueled Fermi-2 would require about 3,650,000 tons of coal a year. As a nuclear plant it will consume about 1.25 tons of nuclear fuel annually.

The basic difference between a nuclear and a fossil-fueled power plant is the heat source and method of generating steam. From there on the process is similar to conventional plants: Steam goes to the turbine which spins the rotor of the electric generator. The spent steam is condensed back into feed-water which goes back to the reactor where it is again turned into steam.

Another difference is the very large investment in control, safety and environmental protection systems. If one system fails there is another, and yet another, to take charge and correct the situation. Every effort is made to design, fabricate and construct nuclear plant facilities to the highest quality standards. No other industry has a safety record to match nuclear power.

> The Nuclear Way, "Building Fermi-2"
> (from a publication by Detroit Edison)

c. Before the advent of nuclear energy, medical experience with the internal effects of radiation was very limited, based largely on the fate of several hundred unfortunate women who in the 1920s had used their lips to point up brushes for applying radium-containing luminous paint on watch dials. Standards of radiation exposure were set on the assumption that, at some minimal level, the body would experience no harm at all from radiation, and the AEC used these standards in order to support their claim that fallout was "harmless" to the population as a whole. Later, when it was realized that unlike industrial workers, the general population is unable to escape exposure (for example, by quitting a job) and includes especially susceptible individuals such as children and the aged, the "acceptable" limits were reduced to about three percent of their original value. Finally, experiments show that *every* exposure to radiation, however small, carries with it *some* risk, in the form of genetic damage or cancer.

Barry Commoner, *The Closing Circle*

---

## VERBS

### Action, and the Choice of Style

Verbs act. Verbs move. Verbs do. Verbs strike, soothe, grin, cry, exasperate, decline, fly, hurt, and heal. Verbs make writing go, and they matter more to our language than any other part of speech.

Verbs give energy, if we use them with energy. I could have said, "Verbs are action. Verbs are motion. Verbs are doing." But if I had written the sentences in this second way, I would have written dull prose. I could have gone even further into dullness and written, "Verbs are words that are characterized by action."

Try to use verbs that act. Yet sometimes you will need to write verbs that are less than active. Just as there are no synonyms, there are no two sentences that mean the same thing but are different only in style. A change in style, however slight, is always a change in meaning, however slight. Is it, therefore, possible to make a stylistic generalization at all?

I think that the generalization remains possible, with explanation and with room for exception. Both explanations and exceptions will follow in the sections on verbs and nouns, but let us start with a general explanation. Most of the time, passives and weak verbs evade precision and commitment. Examples follow, in which weak verbs add static to statement and in which passives avoid being wrong by evading definite statement. These habits fuzz our prose with bad brain fuzz. To recommend that we use active forms of active verbs, is to recommend energy and clarity, definite statement and commitment. Style is morals.

### Verbs with Nouns and Adjectives

Usually, a lone verb is stronger and better than a strung-out verb-and-adjective or verb-and-noun combination. People say, "I am aware of this fact," or "I am cognizant of this situation," when they could have said, "I know it." In these examples, we have a weak verb and adjective followed by a noun that means little, but appears to end the sentence, to give the verb an object. The phrases mean something different from "I know it," but the difference is mere pomposity. "I am aware of the fact" differs from "I know it" because it shows us that the speaker thinks well of himself. "I am cognizant of the situation" is so pompous it may sound ironic; it would usually drip from the lips, or leak from the pen, of someone nervous about his intellectual status, like a television executive.

Look out for the verbs *be, is, are,* and *has, have* combined with nouns and adjectives. See if you do not gain by using the verb itself, clear and clean. Edit your writing to simplify your verbs. "He looked outside and became aware of the fact that it was raining" revises easily into "He looked outside and saw that it was raining" or, more simply, "He looked outside. It was raining." Instead of "We had a meeting," try "We met." The meaning is different, slightly, but if the second phrase is accurate, it is better—we save three syllables and add energy to our prose; when we cut to the essential motion, we add vitality. Instead of "They were decisive about the question of . . . ," try "They decided to. . . ."

Now "to be decisive"—if we look at the insides of words—means something quite different from "to decide." The person who "is decisive" has vigor and intellectual intensity; he cuts through the uncertainties that surround a question and makes a choice firmly and quickly. If you are describing a committee meeting in which, after long discussion, the members reached a consensus or took a vote and decided to do something, "they decided" is the clearest phrase to use. "They reached a decision" wastes words, probably; it does imply that it took some work "to arrive at the decision," which by itself would imply more ease, and less struggle, than *reached.* If you feel that the meaning requires *reached* or *arrived,* use the accurate word. But, certainly, in writing about the committee meeting described above, "they were decisive about . . ." would be misuse of words. They weren't decisive at all. They decided. Most of the time, when we use a wordy noun-adjective-verb phrase, we are merely trying to *sound* more complicated. Most of the time, the shade of meaning in *reached* or *arrived* is not needed. We use the longer phrase just to *seem* to be considering fine points. The sensible rule: use the shorter, more direct verb ("they decided") except when the longer variation has a precision that your meaning requires. "They talked for two days about lowering the voting age, without coming to a conclusion. Then Senator Jensen returned from a junket. He spoke briefly. He was decisive. The measure carried by a two-thirds majority."

### Verbs with Participles

The same advice applies to phrases that use verb forms ending in *-ing* (present participles). "They were meeting to discuss" can often become "They met to discuss," and "He is clearing his throat" becomes "He clears his throat." But the participle is different in meaning—it marks a different sort of time—and therefore can be useful when that difference is important. "She'll be comin' 'round the mountain" has more continuous motion in it than "She'll come 'round the mountain." Participles imply continuing action. But be sure that you *intend* the difference and are not just lazy. To say that the group "was deciding a topic" implies that it took some time; if you use this verb phrase, be sure that you mean to use it instead of *decided*. Apparently the mind finds it easier to be pale than to be colorful. Or maybe the mind finds it easier to avoid the extra vocabulary of verbs, sticking to *be* and *has* with nouns and adjectives. Whatever the reason, when we add little words like *is* and *has* to participles, adjectives, and nouns, usually we thin our prose into invisibility.

### Verbs in the Passive Voice

A verb is in the passive voice when it acts upon the subject; for instance, "The passive voice *is used* when the subject *is acted upon* by the verb."

When writers use the passive, they usually subtract meaning from their prose. We say, "A message was received," instead of "They [or *I* or *you* or *he* or *she*] received a message." We suppress identity, which is a particular, and we put hazy distance between implied subject and definite action. The passive voice avoids responsibility, as we sometimes claim that "A dish was dropped in the kitchen" rather than name the dropper. It diminishes a sentence by omitting a doer. It can be politically useful: "Napalm was dropped yesterday on structures in a fire-free zone near the DMZ." Or, as the President said when profits from secret arms sales were covertly diverted to a guerilla army, "Mistakes were made." Many inquired: Who made them?

Sometimes we use the passive from diffidence, or modesty, or false modesty, or all three. It waters the soup. We sound as if we wrote labels for medicine bottles: "Doses may be administered three times daily. Dosage recommended for adults is. . . ." A depressed writer might say, making an argument: "It can be assumed that someone in college is fairly mature. It might be objected that. . . ." Here, passive makes invisible dialogue, a pale argument between people who are not there. Scientific prose uses the passive by convention, establishing an impersonal tone. Sometimes writers on nonscientific subjects achieve a pseudo-scientific tone by using the passive.

Occasionally the passive is right or unavoidable. Passives are used in a textbook whose author advises against passives.

> The author uses passives in the textbook.
> The textbook uses passives.
> Passives are used in the textbook.

In some contexts, the third sentence is best. The second is most terse, but it involves a metaphor—the text must be compared to a person, if it "uses" something—which may weaken the sentence. The first correctly says that the author does the using, but it would be intrusive in some contexts to state the subject when the subject is perfectly obvious; it would be overexplained and wordy. It might be better to use the passive to avoid these other troubles, choosing it as the least of three evils.

Sometimes the passive is useful because we do not know the identity of the doer. The passive (especially if we use it sparingly) can imply this ignorance, which may be part of the meaning of the sentence. Suppose this were the start of a story:

> He walked into his bedroom. Clothes lay in heaps on the floor. Dresser drawers lay upside down on the rug, their contents scattered.

This paragraph describes a scene, mostly in the active voice, with inanimate objects (clothes, dresser drawers) doing active things (lay, lay upside down). It is terse, but it implies no reason for the scene and no response to it. The active voice in this passage is less meaningful than the passive would be:

> He walked into the room. Clothes were heaped on the floor. Dresser drawers were dumped on the rug, and their contents had been scattered.

The scene is the same. We still don't know who did it. But the passives (after the first sentence, which is active) imply that someone else, unknown, has done the damage. They only *imply* it, not *state* it, but the implication is real and further implies shock. The second and third sentences suggest what happens in his mind as he enters the room: "I've been robbed!" To make this last sentence active would sound artificial: "Someone has robbed me!" The writer would be taking as absolute the advice to avoid the passive, which is only a sensible, general rule.

Good writers use the passive for variety in sentence structure, too. Rarely, but they do. In a paragraph about two groups taking opposite sides on an issue, in which all sentences have the active voice, the author looking for stylistic variety might insert the sentence "Arguments were put forward, on both sides, which would make a goat blush." When you use a passive for variety, be certain that you are not using it for any of the reasons that make passives bad: diffidence, false modesty, evading responsibility, or imitating scientific respectability.

### Particular Verbs

I have been writing all along as if there were two classes of verbs: strong ones and weak ones. Of course language is more complicated than that, and not only because weak is sometimes better than strong, as I have argued. Some strong verbs are stronger than others. "He moved" is stronger than "he was in motion." But in a context that admits it, we might say with greater strength, "he crept," or "he slid," or "he hurtled." We would almost always want to say, "he crept" rather than "he moved, creeping." (A difference of meaning might, once, make the second phrase useful.) The first verbs I listed in the paragraph that starts this section are general verbs: *do, move, act.* The second series is particular and more colorful.

### Invisible Verbs

In the prospectus for a dissertation, a Ph.D. candidate wrote this sentence in which he misused verbs; in fact, he managed to write almost *without* verbs.

> Illustrative of what Kornhauser means by constraint imposed on professionals in organizations are the findings of Leo Meltzer in a survey of 3,084 physiologists in the United States.

The sentence has no strong and active verbs. *Means* is the closest. *Illustrative* is an adjective substituted for a verb. *Imposed* is a past participle that suppresses responsibility. *Are* is boring.

To rewrite the sentence in a language not far from the original, but with more vigor and clarity, we can simply cut and rearrange. Edited in revision, the passage could read:

> Leo Meltzer questioned 3,084 physiologists in the United States; his findings demonstrate Kornhauser's contention that organizations constrain professionals.

Maybe *surveyed* is more accurate than *questioned*, but *surveyed* smells of jargon.

The last phrase of this revision may not mean what the original author had in mind. Did he mean that the institution imposed the constraint or that something else, unnamed, chose professionals in organizations, rather than others, to impose restraint on? The ambiguity in the original passage is real and serves no function; it is merely unclear. The second version is clearer, though without context it still raises questions. What is this constraint? What desires are held back? Does the author mean "constraint" as restraint or as compulsion? Does he mean all organizations—like YMCAs, universities, corporations, fraternities, bridge clubs, and nations—or specifically professional ones, like the American Association of University Professors, the Modern Language Association, or the American Medical Association? Clarity comes from vigor combined with detail. Verbs are the most vigorous parts of speech; by particularity, they add detail.

### False Color in Verbs

The search for particularity and color can become obvious, and the prose look silly. In the examples that follow, the faults do not lie in the verbs alone, but in the whole style. Verbs are at the center of the action in our prose, however, for good or for ill. In the play *The Owl and the Pussycat*, a would-be novelist reads the first page of his manuscript to the girl who has invaded his apartment. When he starts by saying the sun *spat* on his protagonist, she flies into a rage. And so should we. Men's action magazines are full of Methedrine prose, violence done to language in the name of violence. In a thriller called *A Clash of Hawks*, the author's second sentence reads:

> The 200-foot-high derrick was a black, latticed steel phallus raping the hot, virginal blue sky.

Tough or sadistic writing is not the only kind of bad overwriting. Maybe pretty writing is worse.

> Songbirds trilled out my window, vines curled at the eaves, and Spring drenched the day with gladness.

Often a beginning writer tries to make the verbs describing dialogue too specific: *he whimpered, she snapped.* Almost always it looks too strenuous. We should use *said*, or nothing at all, most of the time. The emotion should be in the dialogue itself, in the speaker's words; if the reader has to be told, the emotion is not there. The trick is energy with appropriateness. We may need to learn to do too much before we can learn to do the right amount. Newly wakened to verbs, one student wrote this passage:

> The train slammed to a stop in the station. Steam vomited from all apertures. Passengers rushed through the barriers and hurtled into the night.

It was a useful exercise, because the student was searching through his mental dictionary for energetic verbs. The color was more vivid than the actions colored, like photographs in advertisements for food. Steam gushing out at the base of an engine is not like vomiting; *vomiting* is too sick and unpleasant and bad-smelling a word; the writer used it only for its power, not for what it contributed to the picture. Though the general advice—choose color over pallor, energy over lethargy—holds true, one matter overrides all others, in any discussion of style, and that is appropriateness: context is all.

### Fancy Verbs

Some verbs are too fancy for normal use. Writers use them when they think their prose ought to wear fancy clothes. *Depict* is usually inferior to *paint* or *draw* or *describe*. "He depicted a scene of unparalleled magnitude." (W. C. Fields–thesaurus talk again.) Maybe that means, "he painted a big picture," or "he told a good story," or half a dozen other things, but its real meaning is its would-be fanciness. It is a sentence admiring itself in the mirror. *Emulate* would usually be fancy for *copy, ascertain* for *make sure,* and *endeavor* for *try.*

### Made-up Verbs

Then there are the made-up words, neologisms, which sound fancy to the people who use them. When we are tempted to say *finalize,* we would do better to say *end* or *finish.* In general, we should avoid verbs made of an adjective and an *-ize; personalize* is another. Advertising and politics have created many crude verbs, often using nouns as bases instead of adjectives. Some good old English verbs end in *-ize. Scrutinize,* deriving from the noun *scrutiny,* is a useful verb. *Finalize,* on the other hand, is used to sound fancier than *finish* or *end,* to give false complexity to a simple act. Therefore it is bad style, pretending to be something that isn't, a form of euphemism. The writer should search the language for the simplest and most direct way of saying and expressing, not make up a new word when an old one will do.

### Revising Verbs

The section headings of these pages (Verbs with Nouns and Adjectives, Verbs with Participles, Verbs in the Passive Voice, Particular Verbs, Invisible Verbs, False Color in Verbs, Fancy Verbs, Made-up Verbs) can form a checklist for revising the draft of an essay.

### EXERCISES

1. Underline the weak verbs (verb-noun or verb-adjective or verb-participle combinations, invisible verbs, verbs lacking particularity) in these sentences. See if you can substitute strong verbs for those you underline. When you make a substitution, does the meaning of the sentence vary? Can you think of reasons for preferring the weaker verb combinations in any of the sentences?

a. She made the observation that German had been her minor in college.

b. We have endeavored to reach a conclusion that will be satisfactory.

c. We were just starting to sing when the door opened.

d. The committee has been meeting every day for a month.

e. I am trying to be healthy so that I will be playing tennis when I have arrived at eighty.

f. We had gotten around to the subject of getting good grades and got into an argument.

g. A different way of expressing the same idea is that having no commitment to activity, we are engaged upon a course of activity lacking purpose.

h. We were in action right away, moving out into the field on our stomachs until we got to the river.

2. These five sentences contain passives. Underline the passive verbs, and then consider if any are necessary or useful. When the passive is objectionable, figure out why, and revise the sentences so that passive becomes active.

a. Arabella was understood by her neighbors to have cornered the market in soybean futures.

b. People committed to excellence are sought after in the business community.

c. At the picketing sites on North Campus, GEO members were not allowed to use the restrooms.

d. My canoe tipped over, I was thrown out into the water, and I saw the McDonalds ahead of me.

e. Remembering August with Emily in Poughkeepsie, and rereading her letter which arrived this morning, I gradually realized that I had been deceived.

3. (a) Write three sentences of description without using *is, are, was,* or *were.* (b) Find verbs to describe the way wind moves in the leaves of a tree. Perhaps wind *ripples* in leaves or *surges* through them. What else?

4. Here are some fancy verbs. Find simpler verbs that would usually do better.

| | |
|---|---|
| masticate | disseminate |
| cogitate | substantiate |
| commence | estimate |

5. Here is a list of verbs chosen for varieties of tone and degrees of color. With each of them, find alternatives, close synonyms, which might work better in a specific context. For an example, remember the differences among emulate/imitate/copy/ape dis-

cussed on pages 94–96. Make up a context for five of the verbs—
listed and discovered—in which the verb feels appropriate.

| | |
|---|---|
| clutch | communicate |
| exterminate | rasp |
| rattle | split |
| cook | decide |
| act | recommend |

6.   Here are four passages. Underline the verbs and decide in class
how well each author uses them.

a.  When it comes to the actual methods of consumption, asparagus
eaters seem to be roughly divided into two groups. There are those who
assume a crouching position and attack the vegetable with knives and
forks. Lined up against this faction are those who believe the only way
to eat asparagus is to throw back the head, grasp the stalk between
thumb and forefinger and lower it slowly into the mouth, chewing
steadily.

Diane White, "The Noble Asparagus"<br>(The Boston Globe)

b.  A machine gun lashed at him from across the river, and he
ducked in his hole. In the darkness, it spat a vindictive white light like
an acetylene torch, and its sound was terrifying. Croft was holding
himself together by the force of his will. He pressed the trigger of his
gun and it leaped and bucked under his hand. The tracers spewed
wildly into the jungle on the other side of the river.

Norman Mailer, The Naked and the Dead

c.  The service shall be delivered in the following manner: Immediately before commencing to serve, the Server shall stand with both feet
at rest behind the base line, and within the imaginary continuation of
the center mark and side line of the singles court. The Receiver may
stand wherever he pleases behind the service line on his own side of
the net. The Server shall then throw the ball into the air and strike it
with his racket before it hits the ground. Delivery shall be deemed
complete at the moment the racket strikes the ball.

"How Service Is Delivered," Official Tennis Rules

d. Weighing the half-pounds of flour, excluding the scoop, and depos-
iting them dust-free into the thin paper sacks held a simple kind of
adventure for me. I developed an eye for measuring how full a silver-
looking ladle of flour, mash, meal, sugar or corn had to be to push the
scale indicator over to eight ounces or one pound. When I was absolutely accurate our appreciative customers used to admire: "Sister Henderson sure got some smart grandchildrens." If I was off in the Store's
favor, the eagle-eyed women would say, "Put some more in that sack,
child. Don't you try to make your profit offa me."

Maya Angelou, I know Why the Caged Bird Sings

## NOUNS

### Particularity and Choosing a Style

Nouns are the simplest parts of speech, the words least tricky to use. Nouns are the names of things, *things* in the broadest sense: *table, elm, Nancy, rain, noun, Centerville, nation, hunger, nine o'clock.* If verbs supply the energy that makes prose go, nouns are the body of prose. Without nouns, nothing would be doing the going.

Many of the generalizations that apply to verbs also apply to nouns. We prefer as a rule the specific, the sensuous, the strong, the simple, and the colorful over the abstract, the general, the polysyllabic, and the fancy. We prefer *elm* to *tree, Nancy* to *girl,* and *nine o'clock* to *evening.* The more particular the noun, the clearer the pictures we make, and the more accurately we can represent feelings. Pictures carry feelings from writer to reader, as abstract idea-words do not. Particulars make contact. A student wrote,

> I remembered a group of flowers that grew on some land near a relative's house. . .

and revised it to

> I remembered a patch of daisies that grew on a meadow near my Cousin Annie's farm. . .

and the particularity is all gain. The first example was not bad style, but it was pale prose. The second by comparison is vivid.

But we generalize, and we must express reservations. Sometimes the more general noun is more accurate and honest than the specific one. From a distance, you see *a man* or *a woman,* not *a sophomore* or *a mechanic. Town* may be more appropriate, in the right context, than *Centerville,* though it is less specific. We must keep in mind the advice to be specific; but, as ever, we must be wary that our rules do not lead us into absurdity. A student revised some daily writing into

> On Tuesday afternoon, October thirteenth, I read a sentence half-way down the first page of *War and Peace* which. . . .

Maybe in a particular context, such extreme specificity would be useful, but usually it would sound overly precise.

Also, we must remember again that the advice to cultivate one kind of style, at the expense of another, means thinking or seeing things in special ways. *A change in style, however slight, is always a change in meaning, however slight.*

Although most writing improves as particularity increases, there are exceptions to this rule. If we are philosophers seeking generality, *tree* might be preferable to *elm* and *humanity* to *Nancy and David.* For scientific summary, an injunction to *Be particular!* and *Avoid abstraction!* is useless.

> At first cats would not seem to offer a likely clue to human history. Yet when one considers that the writing of adequate histories of human populations began scarcely 200 years ago, that writing itself dates back only about 6,000 years and that for many populations historical, linguistic and cultural records are inadequate or nonexistent, cats appear in a different light. They have been associated with human beings for a long time, but they have never had any economic significance and only rarely have they had much social significance. Genetically they, unlike other domesticated animals, have been left largely to themselves. The study of the population genetics of cats is therefore rewarding not only for what it reveals about the evolution of cats but also for what it suggests about the movements of human populations.
>
> Neil B. Todd, "Cats and Commerce"
> (*Scientific American*)

Todd writes a vigorous expository prose, which must be abstract and concrete by turns to provide appropriate words by which to reach his audience. So too must books about prose style, for that matter.

The wise advice is simply to be as particular as the context allows us; when we are as concrete as possible, we must connect with our audience. Too often, we are vague and general, when we would say much more by discovering the concrete. Instead of saying

> When it got cold the animals looked for shelter.

we could convey much more by a particularity:

> In October there was frost, and the sheep huddled in one corner of the barn for warmth, the cattle in another.

### Abstract and Particular Nouns

Degrees of difference separate the noun at an extreme of abstraction from the noun at an extreme of particularity. S. I. Hayakawa, in his book *Language in Thought and Action,* speaks of moving up a ladder of abstraction, climbing from the most particular level, gradually discarding particularities, and arriving into the thin air around the highest abstraction. The number of rungs on this ladder is limited only by our ingenuity, but we can usefully distinguish three main degrees—the abstract, the general, and the particular.

From the general to the particular, we can move by degrees toward greater particularity. Take "animal, dog, spaniel." One might become still more particular by adding an age and a color and by naming a breed of spaniel: "a five-year-old rust-colored cocker spaniel." On the other hand, one might become more abstract than the general *animal* by climbing the ladder into the thin air of *organism.* Or one might remain general by defining *dog* in scientific classification as *canine* and *quadruped.*

The abstract-general-particular threesome is relative. We can list three words which are all abstract but which move in the direction of the specific: *emotion, love, lust. Love* is certainly an abstraction, but it narrows down the more abstract *emotion.* And *lust* (or *affection*) further specifies the more abstract *love.* The shrewd writer makes choices keeping audience in mind—and with a bias toward the particular.

The more abstract a noun, the more difficult it is to use well. Words like *emotion* (or *love,* for that matter) or *courage* or *hatred* or *responsibility.* To make these nouns work, you must provide a context with anecdote or analogy; you must put flesh on the bones. Usually an adjective in front of an abstraction does not do the work. The abstraction is lazy, retrieved by the writer from the attic of Big Ideas, and the adjective strives to do all the work; but adjectives themselves often are weak, and so we have two weaklings failing to budge the door that one strong noun could burst open. For instance, if you needed to use the abstract word *abstraction,* you could make the analogy that the word was lazy and conclude that "one strong noun could burst" a door open.

Take the word *love* again. *Love* is thin and airy; it is pretty, but what is it about? Our affection for a pet salamander? The feeling of a grandfather for his granddaughter? Bert's obsession with the character of Charles Dickens? Mark and Nancy in the Oldsmobile? Married affection? *Love* is a grab bag of possibilities, only a bit less abstract than *emotion* or *feeling.* If we modify it with the adjective *intense,* we narrow its possibilities a little, but we do not really localize it. If we speak of *young love,* we are more particular—and yet we move toward cliché. Many clichés are adjective-noun combinations in which the adjective is a desperate, though habitual, attempt to rescue a bland abstraction; *blind faith,* for example.

Abstractions are usually lazy. The writer finds it easier to label the general category of a feeling than to search out the particulars that embody the feeling. Sight, taste, smell, touch, and hearing carry feeling from writer to reader—concepts don't. (And most writers using abstractions, we notice instantly, are not using concepts with the precision of a philosopher but vaguely and inaccurately.) Usually, we talk best about *love* when we do not use the word at all. If we use *Nancy,* and *Centerville,* and *a 1979 Pontiac,* and *rain,* and *nine o'clock,* and connect them with strong verbs, the reader may know what we mean by the big hazy word *love*—in this time and in this place.

*Time* and *place* are abstractions. Are they used appropriately here? Sometimes the abstract affords a setting for the concrete, as a black velvet background shows up diamonds. In other contexts, instead of *time* and *place* we would want to use more specific words—*steering wheel, September, elm, Long Lake Road.*

### Abstract Nouns: Beginnings and Endings

An abstraction can be explained by context, by analogy, or by anecdote. Some abstraction or generalization is necessary to any conceptual or argumentative writing. Only fiction, poetry, and autobiography can be free of it, and they do not always stay free. When we revise an essay, we should look most carefully to eliminate abstractions at two points—beginning and ending. Frequently, we introduce a subject with an abstraction—"I am going to tell a story that illustrates inequality"—and then we tell a story that illustrates inequality. If the illustration is clear, the introductory abstraction was unnecessary; what is more, it was probably distracting. When you announce that you are going to tell a funny joke before you tell it, you take the humor away. Let the idea of inequality arise in the reader's mind—by name or not—from your anecdote, and it will be much more powerful. Telling the reader the meaning of what he is going to hear bullies him; he is likely to resist.

Similarly, we often write anecdotes that trail off with an abstraction. Having told a perfectly clear story, we end, "which is an illustration of the inequality so prevalent today." Don't nudge your reader in the ribs, saying, "In case you didn't get it, this is what I mean." We summarize abstractly because we lack confidence in our own writing and in the reader's intelligence. Of course some stories need interpreting; that usually makes them less valuable. If the road is clear, do not put up road markers; they are good only for stumbling over.

### Invisible Nouns

So far, we have been talking about degrees of particularity and color, and we have admitted that some prose needs abstractions. The Preacher could not have said, "All is vanity," if there had been an enforced commandment against abstractions. But some nouns are almost always useless. These nouns are invisible. When someone says, "The snow is gray in color," what is the phrase *in color* doing? It doesn't do anything for meaning or particularity. Maybe it contains a message informing us that the speaker is pompous.

Words like *nature* and *character*, which have perfectly good uses, turn up invisibly in pale prose. Probably the snow was gray in color because of the urban nature of the environment, and the frigid character of the weather. Probably it would have seemed too ordinary to speak of gray snow in the cold, dirty city.

We use invisible nouns with adjectives—much as we use invisible verbs like *be* and *do* and *has* with adjectives or nouns—to make a sentence *sound* grander than it really is, or because we lack the vocabulary. Whatever the reason, we abuse the language. Some other nouns we render invisible: *sense, kind, action, situation, respect, regard, case,* and *element.* Look at this piece of prose from the annual report of a large corporation:

> The President is pleased to report that, despite the unusual nature of the fiscal situation in the past twelve months, earnings have risen substantially above the margin foreseen by the Treasurer's Report of March, 1981. In a marketing sense, the profitable character of the corporation proved itself under trying circumstances.

*Circumstances* is another invisible noun—at least as it is used here. Sensible writers avoid these words unless their contexts provide visible meanings. For instance, a *case* holds papers, *characters* speak parts in plays, and there are five *senses.* Edit invisible nouns out of your prose when you revise.

### Making Bad Nouns from Verbs

The sensible writer also chooses the plain noun, if it is adequate, over the fancy one, and he chooses the old noun rather than making up a new one. On page 117 I mentioned the verb *finalize,* which had been wrenched out of an adjective. It has been wrenched further into a noun: now and then we run across *finalization,* when *end* or *finish* or maybe *finality* would do. Bad stylists know no limits. *Scrutiny* is a fine noun; *scrutinize* is a necessary and traditional verb. But recently a young man wrote on an application form that he submitted documents "for your scrutinization." The word means nothing more than *scrutiny;* it must have sounded more respectable to this writer.

Or maybe his vocubulary failed him. He remembered the verb *scrutinize* but forgot the noun *scrutiny.* And so he made up a new noun out of the verb. When you are tempted to make a new noun from a verb, go to the dictionary first. You know *unify;* when tempted to create *unifization,* go to the dictionary and you will find *unity* and *unification*—and clearer, more eloquent prose.

### Fancy Nouns

Reading bad prose, we find thousands of examples of pomposity or fanciness, either neologism (new words generally invented, when old ones would do, out of a failure of vocabulary) like *scrutinization* or polysyllabic alternatives to simple words like *domicile* for *house* or *cessation* for *end.* These words parallel verbs like *masticate,* substituted for *chew.* The fanciness may arise from diffidence or ignorance or pretension or whatever. Probably we are more often lazy than insincere and simply settle for what we first think of. Whatever our motive or our failing, the result is the same; fanciness separates the thing described and the mental act of perceiving it. Feelings are kept at a distance. Fancy abstractions and clichés enable Orwell's Communist professor to discuss without feelings the murder of innocent people.

### Revising Nouns

In revising, we should look for the lazy abstraction, as well as the invisible noun, the neologism, and the merely fancy noun, and remove them when we find them. Editing and revising, we cut them out. Removing such a word leaves a hole, which we can fill with another noun or a phrase, to specify and bring down to earth the airy word we started with. Lazy abstractions are like clichés and jargon—and the three are usually discovered together—because they are instantly available to the tongue; they lie heaped together with clichés and jargon in the foreroom of the brain; we do not have to search for them with our intelligence or dream for them with our imaginations. Here is a passage from an essay.

Financial problems were coming to a head in my family last spring and we didn't know if my sister and I could have the benefit of higher education. Then my grandfather got the surprise of his life when a large amount of money came his way when he least expected it. He got a sum from the VA which he didn't know was coming to him. Through his generosity, we were enabled to arrange payment for tuition.

As usual with faulty prose, the faults do not lie in one part of speech alone. Some hunks of cliché are ready-made—*financial problems, coming to a head, benefit of higher education, surprise of his life, when he least expected it, arrange payment*—and combine with a dozen other signs of lazy thinking and evasion of feeling. Think of the emotional reality—the anxiety, the jubilation in a family—these phrases obscure with their familiar haze. Instead of *financial problems,* let us forget euphemism and talk about being in debt, or having no money, or losing a job, or payments coming due; *anything* more particular. The ultimate particularity would probably sound as cold as a balance sheet (outstanding indebtedness $27,429.31; assets . . .), but we know a median lies between the bland, evasive euphemism of *financial problems* and the sterile figures. The median is actual circumstances and anecdotes; the median is stronger than the extremes.

Certainly *go to college* or *go on in school* is preferable to *have the benefit of higher education.* Then instead of speaking generally of *surprise*—an abstraction that takes the surprise out of surprise—why not show it happening? Describe the grandfather opening the envelope or picking up the telephone. Use dialogue. Or use some new analogy to express his feelings, instead of a useless cliché. He could be as surprised as someone who finds a pearl in his clam chowder. How much is *a large amount of money* or *a sum?* Both seem genteel evasions for saying a specific figure, like *a check for $5,000.* But perhaps it seems crass to the writer to name the figure. Then at least some phrase could give a better idea of numbers, so that the reader can place the figure between five hundred and five million dollars or judge the amount of money by what it can do: "received a check for enough money to send us both through school."

The phrase *through his generosity* includes an unnecessary, labeling abstraction. We do not need to be told that he is generous. When we are bullied with the notion, we resist it. Maybe the old man just wants to boast that his grandchildren go to college. Finally, the last part of the paragraph has a pair of general nouns and a fancy verb in place of simpler and more natural language. It is pretentious to write, "we were enabled to arrange payment for tuition," when we could write, "we were able to pay for college."

The student, in fact, revised the passage.

> My family was so far in debt last spring that we didn't think my sister and I could go to college. My father had borrowed money to get a fish and chips franchise, and lost it all in six months. My sister and I both took jobs in the summer. I was working twelve hours a day in the mill, and when I came home at night I was so mad and tired I just drank beer and watched the box. Then my grandfather telephoned my father and I saw my father suddenly start crying. The VA had just sent my grandfather a check he didn't know was coming, and it was enough to pay for us both. That night, we bought a bottle of Four Roses.

He changed verbs and other parts of speech, but the revision of his nouns is most useful of all.

## _____ EXERCISES _____

1. Write a paragraph with a highly abstract title—*love, idealism, education, boredom, naïveté, courage*—which does not contain the title word, but which describes a particular occasion that embodies the word. For instance, you might describe someone's apartment so that the reader would understand the loneliness of the tenant. Read your paragraph aloud in class, and see if the class recognizes the abstraction.

2. Take each of these nouns and find two other words to go with it, one more general and one more specific. If you can't find a word, use a short phrase.

| | |
|---|---|
| rodent | cat |
| student | butter |
| lily | book |
| day | spaghetti |
| business | sports car |

3. Collect four or five clichés that combine an abstract noun with an adjective, like *blind faith, basic needs,* and *conflicting desires.* See how many alternatives you can find for each, always realizing that a different context will require a different substitute for these filler phrases. Thus, *basic needs* in different contexts

might be revised into distinctly different phrases—like *minimum nutrition* or *attention and support.* Provide brief contexts, if you need them for clarity.

4. In these sentences, underline the nouns that fail by invisibility, imprecision, fanciness, neologism, or overabstraction. Invent substitutes that improve the sentences.

    a. I chewed the food without swallowing it.

    b. What is the nature of your complaint?

    c. Religion, says Harvey Cox, has undergone privatization.

    d. When I think about my high school, I remember the love I felt for my Spanish teacher and the other feelings I felt for other people.

    e. Precipitation in the form of a thunderstorm situation is expected.

    f. Different aspects of the case of migrant laborers need discussion.

    g. Relationships are a matter of togetherness.

5. Underline the nouns in these passages, and label each as abstract or general or particular, according to the context. In class, compare your judgments with those of other students. Be prepared to argue. These distinctions are often tenuous, but discussing the distinctions will sharpen your eye for the insides of words.

    a. It was formerly the custom in our village, when a poor debtor came out of jail, for his acquaintances to salute him, looking through their fingers, which were crossed to represent the grating of a jail window. "How do you do?" My neighbors did not thus salute me, but looked first at me, and then at another, as if I had returned from a long journey.

Henry David Thoreau,
*"On the Duty of Civil Disobedience"*

    b. At 15,000 feet, its best operating height, the Kittyhawk IA could fly at a maximum speed of only 354 mph and climb to that height in 8.3 minutes, a longer time than the AGM2 Zero took to reach 20,000 feet. Empty weight was 6,350 pounds, normal loaded weight 8,280 pounds, which was the load carried into combat without drop tank or bombs, and maximum permissible weight was 9,200 pounds. Service ceiling was 29,000 feet. The IA climbed best at lower altitudes, but its best rate was only about 2,100 feet per minute at 5,000 feet.

John Vader, *Pacific Hawk*

    c. It is a very small office, most of it taken up by a desk. The desk is placed smack in front of the window—not that it could have been placed anywhere else; this window looks out on the daylight landscape of Bergman's movies. It was gray and glaring the first day I was there, dry and fiery. Leaves kept falling from the trees, each silent descent bringing a little closer the long, dark, Swedish winter. The forest Bergman's characters are always traversing is outside this window and the ominous carriage from which they have yet to escape is still among the properties. I realized, with a small shock, that the landscape of Bergman's mind was simply the landscape in which he had grown up.

James Baldwin, Nobody Knows My Name

6. In the passages just quoted: (a) Discuss each author's use of verbs and how it suits the nouns he uses. (b) Can you find places that might be improved? Try improving one phrase in each passage.

---

## MODIFIERS

### Qualities and Choosing a Style

Modifiers—adjectives, adverbs, participles, and sometimes other words—give quality to nouns and verbs. "The *huge, green* lion leapt *slowly.*" Adjectives and adverbs *modify* nouns and verbs. Participles, and sometimes nouns, work in the same way: "the *grinning* lifeboat," "the hypothesis *constructed* on Thursday," "*rock candy* mountain," "*mouse* music." Used well, modifiers create distinctions in meaning and add particularity to the particular. They discriminate and add precision.

But modifiers give us the greatest trouble of all parts of speech. A writer using clichés assembles prepackaged combinations of nouns and adjectives. A beginning writer, when he tries to write colorfully, may stuff his style into obesity with a diet of fat adjectives.

Overuse or misuse of adjectives and adverbs makes prose weak and lethargic. Because they are qualities rather than actions or things, adjectives and adverbs are inherently weaker parts of speech. Yet once more, choosing a style *means* something. *A change in style, however slight, is a change in meaning, however slight.*

To choose vigor in writing is usually to work with fewer modifiers. A few great writers, like Faulkner, use as many adjectives as any beginner—but use them well and with great originality. Most of the best writers use them sparingly and then make them count. I am not saying that adjectives are unimportant to writing. They are important. But verbs and nouns carry the sentence; if they take charge properly, they liberate adjectives, adverbs, and other modifiers to do their proper work: to make the exact final discriminations necessary to honesty and fullness.

## Using Modifiers Well

Ernest Hemingway is known for using adjectives and adverbs sparingly. Let us look once more at the passage that begins "In Another Country."

> In the fall the war was always there, but we did not go to it any more. It was cold in the fall in Milan and the dark came very early. Then the electric lights came on, and it was pleasant along the streets looking in the windows. There was much game hanging outside the shops, and the snow powdered on the fur of the foxes and the wind blew their tails. The deer hung stiff and heavy and empty, and small birds blew in the wind and the wind turned their feathers. It was a cold fall and the wind came down from the mountains.

Hemingway says *the war,* not *the long war* or *the distant war* or *the bloody, maiming, killing, useless, horrid, revolting war.* He uses *always* and *any more* as adverbs in his simple predicates. *Cold* is an adjective in the second sentence; *electric* is necessary to lights, at a time when electric lights were new—in a country at war they seemed especially unwarlike; *pleasant* is an adjective as restrained as the verbs *was* and *go.* Then the eye of the paragraph turns away from restrained thoughts of war and looks at the dead animals that substitute for dead soldiers; right away the verbs and nouns become stronger and more particular: *game, shops, powdered.* Then the adjectives, exact and strong, come marching in: *stiff and heavy and empty.* The last is especially vigorous. The adjectives used sparingly are used strongly and well.

Let us apply the same standards to the passage quoted before from a story by John Updike.

> All the warm night the secret snow fell so adhesively that every twig in the woods about their little rented house supported a tall slice of white, an upward projection which in the shadowless gloom of early morning lifted depth from the scene, made it seem Chinese, calligraphic, a stiff tapestry hung from the gray sky, a shield of lace interwoven with black thread.

Updike is sometimes condemned by critics for overwriting, for self-indulgence in description, for too much prettiness. Can you find anything here to back up such a charge? We can admire a writer, or a passage of his writing, and still find flaws.

What good does the word *secret* do us? It adds a little to the meaning—a kind of coziness—but to me the word seems there mostly to be pretty. I would like the line better if it read, "All the warm night the snow fell so adhesively. . . ." *Warm* is connected to *adhesively*, but *warm* would be a stronger adjective if it were more isolated, if the next noun, *snow*, did not carry its adjective also. Then later, in one phrase after another, each noun takes one adjective, and although each adjective is defensible in itself, the effect is monotonously pretty: *tall slice, upward projection, shadowless gloom, early morning*. The mixture tastes too sweet. Rearranging clauses, putting an adjective after a noun instead of before it, putting two adjectives with one noun and none with the next—any number of minor reworkings could improve the passage.

The modifier in exposition or argument can help you or hurt you, just as in poetry and fiction. E. B. White, in a brief essay on schools, says that he always went to public ones; by contrast, he says, "my wife was unacquainted with public schools, never having been exposed (in early life) to anything more public than the washroom of Miss Winsor's." The sentence includes several modifiers—*unacquainted, public, exposed, early*, and *public* again—and yet it has vigor and clarity. The words express light disdain for the snobbism that White associates with private schools. The verb phrase *was unacquainted with* is preferable to alternatives like *knew nothing about* because *acquainted* is a word we use in social contexts: "No, I am not acquainted with that person." In the small world of White's sentence, the past participle wears a monocle and looks down at the peasants. *Exposed (in early life)* suggests that public schools are a contagious disease, like measles. And the parenthesis *(in early life)* has a mock formality that agrees with the medical metaphor.

But the adjective with which White plays the best trick is *public*, which he uses twice: first with *schools* and then in the phrase "anything more public than the washroom of Miss Winsor's." *Public* then becomes associated with public lavatories; we wrinkle our nose in disdain. At *Miss Winsor's*—the name sounds snobbish—of course the lavatory would be spotless and relatively private. What's more, it would not be a lavatory, john, W.C., or even bathroom; it would be a *washroom*. By a turn on the adjective *public*—from describing schools to implying lavatories—White makes his point most clearly.

In expository prose, adjectives usually narrow a noun's generality, to make the statement more specific. But if we do not watch ourselves carefully, we'll let the adjective drift into one of its characteristic errors. Here is a passage of exposition from a student essay.

> If you approach the shore of a rocky island, in your kayak, you must paddle slowly and cautiously. Even a gentle breeze may crush the kayak against a sharp rock, and sink the traveler, his vehicle, and all his very precious equipment.

Let us examine the modifiers. *Rocky* is necessary. *Slowly and cautiously* might become only *cautiously,* because *slowly* seems included in the idea of caution. *Sharp* is useful to make the threat more particular. But *very precious* is not so useful; is the equipment any more precious by being called so? Does *very* do anything at all? The sentence would end more vigorously as three nouns in a series: ". . . the traveler, his vehicle, and his equipment."

One adjective in the piece makes a palpable cliché, *gentle breeze.* Yet the writer clearly wants, and needs, to tell us that the winds that can cause this accident need not be gale force. "Why not use 'gentle breeze,' " says the beginning writer, "because 'gentle breeze' is exactly what I mean?" But the problem is not *what I mean,* but *what gets through:* the problem is communication. All problems of writing are problems of audience, of the responses of readers. *Gentle* together with *breeze* simply repeats a commonplace, and the reader is unmoved. We would do better simply to alter the expectation slightly and speak of a *faint breeze, slight breeze,* or *tiny breeze.*

Take another passage:

> The November meeting at the Union League Club was widely reported in the press, which saw evidence of high enthusiasm and sober purpose in the proceedings. A period of feverish activity now ensued. Legal documents were drawn and redrawn (mostly by Choate), potential trustees were sounded out, and advice was solicited. On January 31, 1870, the first board of trustees was elected. The ingredients of this twenty-seven-man founding board were predictable—a pomposity of businessmen and financiers, a clutch of lawyers, a nod of city officials, and a scintillation of writers and architects; less predictable, perhaps, was the inclusion of four practicing artists—the painters John F. Kensett, Frederick E. Church, and Eastman Johnson, and the sculptor J. Q. A. Ward.
>
> Calvin Tomkins, *Merchants and Masterpieces*

Usually a careful writer, Tomkins sounds fatigued. Commonplace combinations of adverb and verb, or adjective and noun, make much of the prose tedious, wordy, and wasteful: *widely reported, high enthusiasm,* and *feverish activity.* The clichés of color are there too: the *ingredients* of the *board* were *predictable.* Other modifiers are decent qualifications, like *November meeting* and *legal documents.* The author moves into color and vivacity at the end with strong nouns, "a pomposity of businessmen and financiers, a clutch of lawyers, a nod of city officials, and a scintillation of writers and architects."

### The Modifier and the Cliché

Beginning writers often misuse modifiers, especially as portions of clichés. In our minds we associate adjectives and nouns in pairs. Our minds are not only computer dictionaries, they are junkyards of cliché. Thus the clichés listed in Exercise 3 on pages 127–128 consist of adjective-noun combinations like *blind faith* and *basic needs. Gentle breeze* is another such combination. Often nouns seem to imply adjectives, and if an adjective is implied by its noun, we should not use the adjective. If we think *grass,* we probably think *green.* We move in worn tracks. If we think *snow,* we think *white.* These weary associations are not really thinking; they are automatic responses to stimuli. The more we can be ourselves, the less we will resemble a machine. If we remember more closely the grass and the snow we are describing, we will describe it precisely, out of our own memories, not out of the sad memory bank of other people's words. We might find an unexpected adjective for grass that is accurate for the grass at that place and that time. We might think of *harsh grass.* Or we might not describe the grass at all, or we might describe it in a clause or in a whole sentence. But we must avoid the description that repeats familiar associations. Only the distinct particular takes our attention. Green snow is news.

Other nouns summon their cousin adjectives by bookish associations. Some of these combinations become comical from overuse or inherent absurdity, like *inscrutable Oriental.* Others have sources not so bookish: *responsible citizen, gracious living.* Whenever you use an adjective that sounds habitual to its noun, try omitting the adjective or recasting the phrase. In avoiding cliché, we have to *think.* We have to decide what we mean by a phrase like *fundamental truth.*

### The Modifier That Weakens the Noun

An adjective gives us the noun's quality or type: *white* snow. An adverb relates to a verb in the same way: he grinned *happily.* But each of these examples would be bad style in most contexts. In each, the modifier diminishes the word it should strengthen. *Snow* is whiter than *white snow. Snow* is white in the brain's computer-dictionary, and so why color it, unless to suggest its opposite? To say *white snow* brings to mind snow that is gray with dirt. This suggestion might be just what the writer wanted: "White snow fell, that morning, on the trash of the old city." The contrast is part of the meaning; *white* takes its place, modifying *snow,* because of the later words *trash* and *city.* But most of the time, when a writer adds *white* to *snow,* he subtracts from his sentence. He adds *white* in an uneasy search for particularity; he lacks confidence in the insides of *snow.* The adjective over-insists on a quality already firm in the word.

If we know that the character grinned, must we be told that he *grinned happily?* It can only bring to mind that he *might* have grinned unhappily, which is a nasty thought; the author reassures us that this supposition is not so, but without the reassurance there would have been no supposition.

A beginning writer often goes through stages with adjectives, and different people have different problems with them. With some beginners, all adjectives are predictable.

> It was a long trip from the high mountains of the frozen north to the desert wastes of sunny Arizona, but it was highly educational and well worthwhile.

Or remember Jim Beck's original impromptu on going to college.

> Education is of paramount importance to today's youth. No one can underestimate the importance of higher education. It makes us well-rounded individuals and. . . .

The problem is not primarily adjectives and adverbs, but thinking (or not thinking) in the old tracks.

### Modifiers as Weak Intensives

We misuse adjectives and adverbs as weak intensifiers. We say, "she moved gracefully," when we might say with more gusto that "she danced" or "she swept" or "she glided." We use vague adjectives in place of specific ones or in place of clauses that could add color and precision. We say, "a tremendous amount," when *amount* is vague and *tremendous* is a weak and unspecific intensifier, or *really huge,* when we might say, *ten million,* or *as long as a supertanker.* Here the specific number of the comparison carries color; the accuracy is one of feeling, not of dimensions.

## Automatic Modifiers

Another misuse of adjectives and adverbs, a more advanced or sophisticated misuse, appears in writers when they suddenly appreciate bright colors in writing, and appears frequently when we begin to write stories and poems. In this misuse, the symptom is not cliché but multiplicity. Nearly every noun carries its adjective, like a tote bag, and every verb wears an adverb for a cape. The style is flashy and overdressed. Here is part of a poem written by a student in a creative writing class.

> I woke suddenly from a ghost-ridden dream
> of old women, to find myself wandering vaguely
> on the far edges of the raw city where white skulls tipped crazily
> in the western sky, and dirty children ran by
> to the cave shelters of abandoned cars. . . .

The lines are improved by mechanically stripping them of modifiers. Should any be kept? Yes. *Abandoned* is necessary to the emotion in *abandoned cars*. If it is merely *cars* that are *shelters*, they could be comfortable, middle-class vehicles in which one drives to the supermarket with one's mother. The *abandoned* makes the children take *shelter* in something like a dump.

Certainly *old women* is different from *women*. The phrase is altered by leaving out the adjective; perhaps we should restore *old*. But the other modifiers are best exterminated. When he revised it, the poem read:

> I woke from a dream
> of old women, to find myself wandering
> on the edges of the city
> where skulls tipped
> in the sky, and children ran
> to the shelters of abandoned cars. . . .

Here only two modifiers remain from the thirteen in the original version. Certainly the spare version is better writing, and it was accomplished wholly by deleting modifiers.

### Nouns as Modifiers

In the phrase *cave shelter, cave* was a noun used as a modifier. Writers use participles and nouns as modifiers—*sheltering cave,* as well as *cave shelter*—with the same dangers, and the same opportunities, which attend plain adjectives. Use them with the same cautions in mind.

It is an advantage of the English language that its grammar is not rigid. In some languages, a noun would have to undergo respelling before it could be used as an adjective. English accepts change. And because it accepts change, in speech and writing, the writer or the speaker can make shades of meaning more precise. Using nouns as modifiers, we can say, *house party, religion committee, death wish.*

We can also say, "this type grammar," or—as in Bergen Evans's example of tediously multiplied nouns-as-modifiers—" . . . he absconded with the River Street fire house Christmas Eve party funds." Because English lacks rigidity, it is subject to chaos and disorganization. *Type* is frequently a filler-noun, and when we use it as a modifier we make even less sense with it than we normally do. With Bergen Evan's example, as with too many sentences that are seriously intended, the proliferation of nouns as modifiers creates heaviness and awkwardness. Here a longer, complex sentence would be preferable: "He absconded with the funds that the River Street fire house had collected for its Christmas Eve party." The noun-modifiers in "River Street fire house" and "Christmas Eve party" are reasonable, and they are not heaped upon each other.

Be careful when you use nouns as modifiers. Sociologists are guiltiest of abusing this device. One hears of the "city group research effort." By the time one reaches the third of these noun-modifiers, one begins to feel afloat in a sea of possibilities. What will go with what? It is as if one were suddenly cast adrift in a Chinese sentence, with no inflections, with no connectives, with no tense or number. Instead, confine yourself to one or two noun-modifiers in a row.

### Revising Modifiers

When you revise your prose, question the need for every adjective and adverb. Can I do without these modifiers? Does the noun (like *postulate* in *basic postulate*) or the verb (like *run* in *run quickly*) do the job without the modifier? Or can I find an exact noun or verb to do the job in one word? Do I avoid a succession of adjective-noun combinations, the monotonous pairs? Do I fall into cliché by joining two words that are commonly used together? Do I, on the other hand, use the modifier when I need it, to make the discrimination, or to add the color, which makes the sentence expressive?

Edit out all unnecessary modifiers; add necessary, useful, colorful ones.

## _____ EXERCISES _____

1. Here are five simple nouns and five simple verbs. Make up ten sentences, using one of the words in each, in which you use an adverb or adjective that would not be a normal association. But let your context make the modifier work: "We bask in the warm concern that radiates from Roger."

| | |
|---|---|
| cut | sand |
| scramble | humility |
| search | concern |
| waver | hut |
| bask | scholar |

2. In these sentences from student essays underline adjectives and adverbs that are useless, either because they are redundant (like *white snow* or *basic postulate*) or because they are weak intensives (like *very cold*).

a. The cat slinks quietly into the room, its sharp claws ready for instant combat.

b. It was a very long examination, with huge one-hour questions to answer completely, and I didn't have the slightest idea how to prepare for it.

c. Whenever a large supertanker approaches a coastal port, concerned environmentalists take special notice.

d. We got to know each other real soon and she is real nice.

e. The forthcoming encounter between these two great teams promises to add luster to the annual classic.

f. It was a spooky horror movie, and we were awfully happy when it finally ended and we could go back home.

3. In these passages from student essays, underline all modifiers. Then see if you can improve the passages by cutting some of them or by substituting other modifiers.

a. Traveling is a great way to learn history. After seeing important places like Bunker Hill and the Smithsonian Institution, national history takes on new and significant meaning.

b. Twenty-four separate and distinct pieces of glass in a metal frame make windows that open outward and dull the landscape with layers of dirt. The factory metal window frame is rusting through the yellow, chipped, peeling paint.

c. Side by side, the swimmers skimmed across the water like swift hydroplanes. The crowd was frantic as it cheered the racing swimmers on.

d. It was a perfect day for skiing, except that the snow was so bright and shiny that it hurt my eyes.

e. Social Security is a regressive tax, harming the old and the poor as much as it helps them.

f. George Washington crossed the Delaware in a rowboat.

4. Underline adverbs and adjectives in these passages. Can you criticize the author's use of modifiers?

a. After the age when hunting was done by males and the gathering of vegetables and small animal food by females—always with close cooperation between men and women—the discovery of planting and herding and then of the animal-drawn plow assured a steadier food supply, which underwrote male enterprises: conquest, the building of cities, trade, and *the stratification of society*. But woman's role continued to be circumscribed by childbearing; whatever a woman did she had to do near home.

Margaret Mead, "Needed: Full Partnership for Women"<br>(Saturday Review)

b. The needs of a society determine its ethics, and in the Black American ghettos the hero is that man who is offered only the crumbs from his country's table but by ingenuity and courage is able to take for himself a Lucullan feast. Hence the janitor who lives in one room but sports a robin's-egg-blue Cadillac is not laughed at but admired, and the domestic who buys forty-dollar shoes is not criticized but is appreciated. We know that they have put to use their full mental and physical powers. Each single gain feeds into the gains of the body collective.

Maya Angelou, "Mr. Red Leg"

c. Nick looked at the burned-over stretch of hillside, where he had expected to find the scattered houses of the town, and then walked down the railroad track to the bridge over the river. The river was there. It swirled against the log spiles of the bridge. Nick looked down into the clear, brown water, colored from the bubbly bottom, and watched the trout keeping themselves steady in the current with wavering fins. As he watched them they changed their position by quick angles, only to hold steady in the fast water again. Nick watched them a long time.

Ernest Hemingway, "Big Two-Hearted River"

d. Personal consideration of various and sundry matters of considerable importance have led numerous observers to ultimately conclude that the final end of Western civilization is certainly closer to a realistic possibility than might earlier have been tentatively assumed.

e. All girls in this period of American Victorianism suffered in an environment that utterly discouraged the healthy development of their emotional lives. However, at least some enterprising girls with a full measure of curiosity were less ignorant—perhaps less virginal—than the popular mythology supposed.

Cynthia Griffin Wolff, *A Feast of Words*

5. You might make more exercises out of the five examples above. Here are some possibilities. (a) Discuss in class the modifiers in each passage. (b) In each passage, look at the verbs and nouns. Are they used well? (c) In example c, put an adjective with every noun that lacks one and an adverb with every verb. Make the additions as apt as you can, and see what you have done. (d) Try to rewrite passage a, omitting adverbs and adjectives. How much, and what, do you lose?

---

## ORIGINAL WORDS: COMPARISONS

### The Need for Originality

When we put words together—adjective with noun, noun with verb, verb with object—we start to talk to each other. We begin to show our own minds, or we show a dull copy of someone else's mind. Originality is clarity and vigor. A source of originality in language is comparison. To talk about metaphoric writing and originality, we must go over some old ground.

Formulas or clichés or trite expressions substitute for the originality that each of us can master. A girl who was mourning the death of her grandfather wrote, starting her first paper of the term, "A tragedy recently occurred at my ancestral home." In a conference with her instructor, the girl wept over the death, she was pale, her hands shook. Moved by her obvious unhappiness, her teacher was sympathetic. At the same time he recognized that her prose style was not adequate to the depth of her feeling. Her body showed her wretchedness, but her prose showed her reading of a weekly country newspaper. No grief was in her phrasing, only the set phrases of headlines or lead sentences in obituaries. Perhaps the formulas came to her pen so that she might avoid the pain that comes with the real feeling. Or perhaps they came because she did not know the difference, in words, between the formula that communicates nothing and the originality that communicates feeling. No feeling reaches her reader. Her audience, instead of feeling moved by her feelings, is bored by her language. Readers' response is almost nothing. Her teacher felt that writing about her grief might help her to understand it, might help her through her mourning. With gentle questions he helped her to criticize her own expression of grief. He suggested that *A tragedy occurred* is a formula that denies the tragic and compared this formula to others, like *a catastrophe was averted* and *a blessed event took place.* They all communicate a journalistic source; but also they all deny feeling, not only by being familiar (the newspaper phrase reminds us of so many similar stories), but by being passive or fancy.

A phrase becomes a formula or a cliché not just because it is used commonly, but because it prevents feeling. The phrase *rain fell* is more common than *a tragedy occurred,* yet we do not think of it as a formula because we do not use it to keep feelings down. A psychiatrist described clichés as "the lies we tell ourselves, that we *want* to hear." When the student wrote, "A tragedy recently occurred at my ancestral home," she was not lying overtly or intending to lie. It was not like saying that she did not chop down a cherry tree when she really did. The lie was internal, the lie of using language to avoid difficult reality, the lie of euphemism.

### Overhearing Your Own Originality

Listen to yourself as you daydream or think idly. Are you reciting newspaper formulas or greeting-card verse? If you overhear yourself, in your own head, thinking trite sentimentality about your love, something is wrong with your loving. Make it new. *Invent.*

In general, trying to *overhear* yourself is a good idea. On some days, you can listen to the dreaming voice easily; on other days, that voice seems mute; it is more likely that you are deaf. The dreaming language is clichés sometimes, sometimes puns or phrases with crazy originality. Sometimes the voice hums the tune from a song; when you remember the lyrics, a coded message is there. You may hear a country-western song about an abandoned lover, when you are feeling lonely or abandoned, or when something inside you feels that you will be lonely soon. The puns and crazy phrases are codes, too. Look at them closely. They have information for you. They are spoken by your original self, looking for attention from your conventional self, the self trained by parents and school and television to think like a train on a track. The crazier the phrase, the more devious the pun, the deeper the source in the self. When the dreaming voice talks in clichés, the train track is getting in the way of the real voice, because the real voice would tell us the truth we would find painful.

*Overhear yourself to know yourself.* Then you can farm your daydreams for original verbal images that express feeling. The crazy image and the pun do not make good writing in themselves—though often they can be the leaping-off point in daily writing—but they do give clues to feelings that the conscious mind can follow. Here is an unrevised passage from a student's daily writing.

> I was taking out the garbage this morning and I heard (in my head) Fanny Davis's voice talking. She has a funny way of talking, Englishy but not really, and I knew it was her. She was saying, "I like to use the word 'to intimate' without any regard for its actual meaning." I kept stuffing the garbage bags into the cans, wondering why I made that up, and why I chose Fanny's voice. It's always sounded affected to me. But that wasn't the sort of thing she says. She talks about her family and the home on the lake up North and going skiing in Switzerland. I was feeling blue. Bob had gone to New York and I knew that Sally was there, his old girlfriend, and I worried about that. Then I started laughing, right at the garbage, because I saw that "to intimate" and "too intimate" are close, but "to intimate" is a long way from the meaning of "too intimate." I was blue because I was too close to Bob, and I could get hurt.

The girl had uncovered something—which she almost knew already—by overhearing a daydream pun and by figuring it out. We may start dreaming, we end up thinking. Now she might be ready to examine her feelings about Bob or her feelings about her feelings.

When you discover something new by subjective scrutiny, paradoxically this inward-look allows outward-expression; for an audience of readers will respond to what is new—and often material that comes from *your* insides will speak to *their* insides. Of course you have to work it over and revise it so that it will make itself clear to an audience.

### Looking for Originality

We can try to activate the daydreaming mind. We will not always succeed. The girl who wrote the paper beginning "A tragedy occurred" was never fully able to write about her grandfather. But her writing and her self-knowledge improved. In her daily writing she returned to the subject many times. The week after her initial paper, she wrote, "A month ago my grandfather died," and went on for a few rather dry sentences. Though the prose was colorless, it communicated much more than tragedies occurring at ancestral homes. Still, it had no images, no pieces of *sense*, no particulars.

Later, thinking about things she could associate with her grandfather, she wrote about *farm implements* that were *unused* and "hanging on the wall of the barn." Then she changed *farm implements* to *rake and hoe.* Then she revised the sentence again and added an image that could come only from the imagination extending itself into the unseen by the probable. "His hoes and rakes hang from pegs in the barn. Spiders will spin webs there while the iron turns red with rust." She had farmed the dreaming part of her self, which imagined the barn, with a selective intelligence, and wrote two sentences that, in their details and associations, began to embody her melancholy and loss.

## Simile and Metaphor

Images are groups of words that give an impression to the senses. Most images are visual, but we can also make images of taste, touch, hearing, and smell. Images communicate feelings and locate them firmly, really making contact between writer and reader. Comparisons in simile and metaphor mostly use images, and become ways for us to show emotions and illustrate ideas.

Similies are comparisons that use *like* or *as*, little words that announce a comparison. Metaphors omit the announcement. We write, "Her face bloomed with affection," and the word *bloomed* compares the girl to a flower; the face-flower is pretty, it is coming into its maturity, and it is associated with spring or summer. The writer may wish to go on talking about the girl in similes that use garden images. Perhaps her dress *rustles like leaves* and her skin is *as soft as petals.* The difference between similes and metaphors is small—a signal is there or not there—but it is real; the simile, because it announces itself, is more reasonable, more conscious of what it is doing.

For clarity, we must distinguish this brief comparison from the word *comparison* as we used it in the last chapter, discussing comparison and contrast as a structure used in exposition; also, we must distinguish it from the grammatical sense—the *comparison of adjectives.* A comparison between the gross national products of Greece and Turkey, or between *less* and *least,* is not like comparing an old cheese to an untidy hog.

Creating a new, verbal comparison—simile, metaphor, and analogy—is our most original act of speech; the originality comes from the dreaming part of the self. Although we cannot always manufacture metaphors at will, we can learn to be alert for comparisons, and we can stimulate their coming. The dead grandfather's funeral happened during a thunderstorm. When the girl tried to write about it, she encountered the trite associations of thunderstorms and death. She began simply.

> The funeral was 2 p.m. He was laid out in the front parlor, which was always closed except for weddings and funerals. Fifty people were there, some crowded into the parlor, others backed into the living room. The minister talked a little and read scripture. Then the sky turned dark.

The prose is simple and direct but it lacks energy. "The minister talked a little and read scripture" would probably be better if it included direct and indirect quotation. "Then the sky turned dark." *How* dark? How did she *feel* about the sky turning dark? We have the sense reading this prose that the feelings (formerly misrepresented in journalistic clichés) are still restricted, held back, reserved.

Suppose the sky turned "as dark as" something. If it turned "as black as the ace of spades," we would be nowhere. What does the ace of spades have to do with her grandfather or her feelings? Even if she had told us that the old man was a poker-playing farmer, the simile is so hackneyed that no one will see the black of the playing card when she says it. The useful comparison will be new. But to say "the sky turned as dark as the soot from a factory chimney" would seem inappropriate; what would a factory have to do with a farm? The comparison must be more than new, it must relate to the context: to her memories of the man, to the funeral, to the idea of death. "The sky turned black as my grandmother's dress" would be a better direction; but maybe that's too black, or the texture is wrong. Or she might want to compare it to something she remembers and associates with the dead farmer: "The sky turned black, like inside the barn after milking." "The sky turned dark as a blueberry."

Sometimes one phrase will not be adequate. You want your comparison to go on longer than that. "The sky turned dark. I could see a black round storm cloud coming. I remembered leaning over the open well, staring down into the round black eye of the water." Here, we find a comparison within the comparison; the water is an *eye*, and the reader alert to the insides of words will reconstruct the dead metaphor: *the eye of the storm*—and revive it—although (or because) the author has not stated it.

### Originality and Memory

To find the right comparison, we must draw on memory and daydream; imagination newly combines old things remembered; it is always present and often hard to discover. Our memory does not consist of things memorized, but of everything that ever happened to us, which we can summon from the storehouse in our minds. We must learn the path to this treasury. Memory is crucial to our writing, thinking, and feeling. By scrutiny of the retained past, we begin to understand and to express that understanding. In the floating world, we connect feelings in the present to feelings about the past. We express these connections mostly by making comparisons. In the uniqueness of each of us, we can find something that the sky grew as dark as.

In speaking of originality and memory, we do not imply that originality applies only to autobiographical writing. Whether we write about grandfathers or the gross national product, dinosaurs or television programs, we need original comparisons to make our prose lively enough to make contact with an audience. The zebra's stripes, in a zoological paper, may be *as dark as* something, although the purpose and audience of most scientific writing requires fewer figures of speech.

In an essay on economics called "The Technostructure," John Kenneth Galbraith contrasts *the man of intelligence* with his opposite; he could have used the abstract noun *stupidity*, parallel to *intelligence*; probably we would have remained content. But instead, he chose to brighten his prose with a figure: " . . . the same for the man of intelligence and for his neighbor who, under medical examination, shows daylight in either ear."

Galbraith remembers a familiar exaggeration of stupidity, as in *airhead*, and rewrites it in his own language by introducing a doctor's office. As we read his complex essay of economic thinking, we are jolted upright by his comedy; it keeps us attentive.

### Analogy

We use the word *analogy* for a comparison that makes or illustrates a point and usually takes longer to say than a metaphor or a simile. An analogy can be extended into a whole essay; ministers' sermons are sometimes analogies—life is like the hundred-yard dash: birth is the starting gun, death is the tape, God is the judge. A whole book, or system of thought, can be based on analogy. Oswald Spengler, in *The Decline of the West*, at the beginning states an analogy that a civilization is an organism, is born, grows old, and dies; then he writes a long book to make a factual case for his analogy.

Analogy often works best within a unit no longer than the paragraph. Frequently, it illustrates the sense in which an abstraction is intended. Analogies may make points; they don't prove them; they show how you feel, or they clarify your use of an ambiguous or all-inclusive word. Suppose we were tempted to support the stick-figure philosophical assertion "Love is better than hate." We would not get far with such a proposition, because it is too vague for support, but we would at least put eyes and ears on our stick figures if we went on, "It is a meadow in the country compared to an alley of garbage and broken glass."

An analogy often runs through a paragraph like a thread in tweed, not separated into patches of assertion followed by comparison, but interwoven. James Thurber wrote this paragraph about working with the editor of *The New Yorker*, Harold Ross:

> Having a manuscript under Ross's scrutiny was like putting your car in the hands of a skilled mechanic, not an automotive engineer with a bachelor of science degree, but a guy who knows what makes a motor go, and sputter, and wheeze, and sometimes come to a dead stop; a man with an ear for the faintest body squeak as well as the loudest engine rattle. When you first gazed, appalled, upon an uncorrected proof of one of your stories or articles, each margin had a thicket of queries and complaints—one writer got a hundred and forty-four on one profile. It was as though you beheld the words of your car spread all over the garage floor, and the job of getting the thing together again and making it work seemed impossible. Then you realize that Ross was trying to make your Model T or old Stutz Bearcat into a Cadillac or Rolls-Royce. He was at work with the tools of his unflagging perfectionism, and, after an exchange of growls or snarls, you set to work to join him in his enterprise.
>
> James Thurber, *The Years with Ross*

Thurber begins by announcing his subject, "Having a manuscript under Ross's scrutiny," departs from it for the rest of a long sentence,
returns to the manuscript for a sentence, then in the final three sentences develops his analogy, makes it funnier, and makes his point
about Ross as an editor. He makes points by contrasts: *mechanic* not
*engineer;* not *automotive engineer* but *guy.* And he makes it by developing his analogy into impossibility (repairing a Model T into a Cadillac), and developing it out of all touch with reality; the customer joins
with the mechanic to rebuild his torn-up machine. The analogy expresses feeling, it is witty, and it is a pleasure to read. Consider this
alternative, omitting the garage and substituting abstraction and generality for analogy:

> Having a manuscript under Ross's scrutiny was an edifying if terri-
> fying experience. He was a skilled editor, not an academic, but a
> practical man. When you first gazed, appalled, upon an uncorrected
> proof of one of your stories or articles, each margin had a thicket of
> queries and complaints—one writer got a hundred and forty-four on
> one profile. You beheld all your work torn apart, and it seemed
> impossible to put it together. Then you realized that Ross was
> trying to make ordinary prose into prose of the highest order. He
> was using his editorial skills with unflagging perfectionism, and,
> after an exchange of growls or snarls, you set to work to join him in
> his enterprise.

This eviscerated version is slightly shorter, but the cutting loses rather
than gains: the paragraph diminishes in energy and expression.

### The Unintended Comparison

With analogy as with other forms of comparison, you must be
wary of the dead, the mixed, and the inadvertently comic. Often a
writer will trap himself in an unconscious analogy expressing an attitude that he really feels but denies to himself. The comic disparity is as
slapstick as a top-hatted man with his trousers missing. Here is an
English critic, writing about American music in the London *Times
Literary Supplement.* He writes in attempted praise of American energy and vitality, but other messages come through his bad prose.

> The American composer is neither enriched nor shackled. He had
> nothing to start from but old rags and bones of European culture
> that, imported to a new environment, soon lost their savor. Then

gradually, in the pulping machine of a polyglot society, the rags and bones began to acquire a taste of their own.

Look at the main analogy, rags and bones. When they were imported here, they "soon lost their savor." Did the gentleman actually expect rags and bones to taste good? His idea of the American stew expresses his distaste by an analogy to eating the product of something like a paper factory: "in the pulping machine . . . the rags and bones began to acquire a taste of their own." The writer expressed his feelings, but he expressed feelings he didn't know he had. He appears to believe that he likes American music, but something unacknowledged inside him is holding its nose.

For another example, we could look at a headnote I wrote in a textbook. Speaking of Virginia Woolf, I wrote, "Handicapped by her sex . . . she persevered against prejudice to refine and develop her abilities." Professor Sandra Donaldson, of the University of North Dakota, wrote me an inquiring letter about my "most puzzling remark." "Did she wear a brace on her arm to help her develop her ability to write, thus overcoming this handicap? Or are there pills women can take, to overcome this curse? Or did she follow a regimen of exercises?" Of course I *intended* to imply that the handicap was male chauvinism; but in my unintended comparison, I revealed my hidden bias. Perhaps my consciousness had been raised, but my unconsciousness nevertheless compared being female to being crippled. I never paused to examine closely what I really said.

To express a feeling without examining it is worthless. Originality combines opposites: we dream—with our eyes open; we are inspired—then we scrutinize and revise. Scrutiny provides the motive for revision. We need to look at words—to see the connection between *rags and bones, savor,* and *taste*—and we will sometimes discover feelings we had not wished to acknowledge. Then we can revise ourselves or our prose or both. We must again float on daydream and memory for new words, and then put the new words under scrutiny again. Only by developing all these mental abilities can we begin to be honest. The paradox is that to be sincere we must struggle; we must struggle to be spontaneous, and then struggle to revise, refine, and order our spontaneity, in order to reach an audience other than ourselves. To speak our most intimate selves into the ears of others, we must revise.

One way to cultivate our sensitivity to the insides of words is to develop an ear for the unintended comparison. (The unintended comparison is often an overt, and sometimes extended, version of the dead metaphor). On a Monday night football broadcast, Howard Cosell said of a new quarterback that he "walked in the wake" of a great predecessor. In this example, the unintended comparison approaches blasphemy.

### Looking for Analogies

We can think out an analogy more easily than we can create the lone metaphor, which, to most writers, seems a gift from the god within us, an inspiration. Suppose you are discussing what makes a love affair succeed. Suppose you decide that it takes a lot of work. The word *work*, itself a metaphor nearly dead, can lead you into analogy. What kind of work is it like? Is it like a nine-to-five job? You can make an analogy in the negative: "This work is no nine-to-five job." Is it like building a house? Rebuilding a destroyed city? Making the sets for a play? Sculpturing a life-sized elephant out of used bubble gum?

Revising writing in order to reach an audience, we can use our clichés as clues leading us toward inventing new analogies and metaphors. If we can learn to identify the worn out, we can create the original. Suppose that when we look over the draft of an essay, we discover the cliché of *clues* that I used above. With a sense of the insides of words, we can discover a mystery story buried in the dead metaphor: clichés are the smoking guns that reveal the murderer—and oddly enough "the murderer" we discover in this analogy will become our original, invented comparison. If we convict the murderer of being a new metaphor, we have won our case. The defense rests.

The liveliest prose moves from analogy to analogy without strain. It takes practice to learn how to invent, and practice to learn when to stop inventing. When analogy shifts abruptly, the effect is usually ridiculous, and comic writers can use these sudden shifts to their advantage; if in one sentence you compare tennis with big-game hunting, do not compare it in the next sentence with knitting unless you want a laugh. Often a sentence or a paragraph of general summary or narrative separates passages of differing analogies, keeping them from clashing.

Here Edward Hoagland begins an essay called "The Courage of Turtles" with a bizarre comparison and goes on to make others.

> Turtles are a kind of bird with the governor turned low. With the same attitude of removal, they cock a glance at what is going on, as if they need only to fly away. Until recently they were also a case of

virtue rewarded, at least in the town where I grew up, because, being humble creatures, there were plenty of them. Even when we still had a few bobcats in the woods the local snapping turtles, growing up to forty pounds, were the largest carnivores. You would see them through the amber water, as big as greeny wash basins at the bottom of the pond, until they faded into the inscrutable mud as if they hadn't existed at all.

(A *governor*, as Hoagland uses the word, is an automatic device attached to an engine to limit its speed.) Hoagland compares a turtle to a bird exactly because the comparison seems impossible. When he provides the bird-turtle with a mechanical device appropriate to tractor-trailers, he makes another impossibility. But by comparing the incomparable, Hoagland shocks us into seeing something freshly: both turtles and birds observe the world with an alert nervousness. When Hoagland goes on to speak of *virtue rewarded*, he makes ironic comparison of turtles with downtrodden humans. He follows with a straightforward but unexpected comparison of turtles to another animal and ends extravagantly by comparing turtles to metallic kitchen utensils which have the power to disappear. The prose's energy derives from its quick assembly of details and outrageous, but accurate, comparisons.

### Revising for Comparison

First, check your sentences to make sure that you are controlling the comparisons you make. Make sure that you do not inadvertently turn a quarterback into a deity or an art form into a bad smell. Second, see that you have not made cliché comparisons that no longer function, like "black as the ace of spades."

Then do the more difficult. *Add* simile, metaphor, and analogy. Most of us in our first drafts lack energy and feeling. Our prose resembles the pale version of Thurber, after the analogy was deleted. The prose is too plain to reach the reader with excitement and precision. Float on memory and daydream to invent; scrutinize with critical intelligence to cut and to improve. Ask yourself if your invention is new, if it is appropriate, if it does not clash with anything else. In a paragraph of exposition, think if you can clarify by analogy. If you find a cliché or a dead metaphor, remake the old into something new. What was it like, to have your prose edited by Ross? What was it like, the day your grandfather died?

_____ **EXERCISES** _____

1. Here are six common comparatives. Taking any three, write sentences in which you make a new simile. Make up comparisons that derive from their subjects. For instance, "The 747 looked as long as the runway of my hometown airport." "The book's cover was as bright as a fresh idea."

| | |
|---|---|
| as long as | as green (or any color) as |
| as bright as | as sour as |
| as wet as | as heavy as |

2. In the Hoagland passage, underline verbs, circle nouns, and draw oblong boxes to enclose modifiers. How do the parts of speech work together—adjective with noun, subject with verb? Do his metaphors and comparisons make use of all parts of speech?

3. These clichés began life as new metaphors. Think of them as they must have sounded when somebody first made them up, when "glued to the spot" implied a puddle of Elmer's in one's chair seat. Then invent a new metaphor that does what the cliché no longer does. Instead of "glued to his chair," say "stapled to his desk."

| | |
|---|---|
| toe the line | a golden opportunity |
| an axe to grind | it dawned on me |
| chip on his shoulder | bathed in sunlight |

4. In these passages, underline analogies, metaphors, and similies. Choose three examples that you particularly like, and explain your reasons for preferring them.

a. But his position was weak. Like a cougar, the army was constantly perched above him, ready to pounce.
John Gerassi, *The Great Fear in Latin America*

b. After thousands of years we're still strangers to darkness, fearful aliens in an enemy camp with our arms crossed over our chests.
Annie Dillard, "Strangers to Darkness"

c. Many of us grow to hate documentaries in school, because the use of movies to teach us something seems a cheat—a pill disguised as candy—and documentaries always seem to be about something we're not interested in.
Pauline Kael, "High School and Other Forms of Madness"
(in *Deeper into Movies*)

d. I lay down on a solitary rock that was like an island in the bottom of the valley, and looked up. The grey sage-brush and the blue-grey rock around me were already in shadow, but high above me the canyon walls were dyed flame-colour with the sunset, and the Cliff City lay in a gold haze against its dark cavern. In a few minutes it, too, was grey, and only the rim rock at the top held the red light. When that was gone, I could still see the copper glow in the piñons along the edge of the top ledges. The arc of sky over the canyon was silvery blue, with its pale yellow moon, and presently stars shivered into it, like crystals dropped into perfectly clear water.

Willa Cather, The Professor's House

e. . . . Women have served all these centuries as looking glasses possessing the magic and delicious power of reflecting the figure of man at twice its natural size. Without that power probably the earth would still be swamp and jungle. The glories of all our wars would be unknown. We should still be scratching the outlines of deer on the remains of mutton bones and bartering flints for sheepskins or whatever simple ornament took our unsophisticated taste. Supermen and Fingers of Destiny would never have existed. The Czar and the Kaiser would never have worn their crowns or lost them. Whatever may be their use in civilised societies, mirrors are essential to all violent and heroic action. That is why Napoleon and Mussolini both insist so emphatically upon the inferiority of women, for if they were not inferior, they would cease to enlarge.

Virginia Woolf, A Room of One's Own

5. Make up three analogies for revising an essay. Thurber's version of Ross as mad mechanic provides an example. Could you construct an analogy from work with a computer? From building a house? Work collectively on this exercise during the class hour.

# 5

## Sentences

### STYLE AND THE SENTENCE

A sentence is a group of words with a period, exclamation point, or question mark at the end. But no definition of the sentence is likely to help us much in writing one. Sentences—the spoken kind—happened first; grammarians named them later. We learn sentence structure by speaking and listening, by reading and writing, more than by studying types of sentences. Still, after studying sentences we can listen more carefully, read more closely, speak more eloquently, and write more clearly. We can learn to *control* the style of our sentences to express feelings and ideas—to make contact with our reader and to hold our reader's interest. We can learn to make sentences that hang together, cohering part with part, achieving unity in the service of clarity. We can learn as well to *vary* our sentences.

### PARTS OF SENTENCES

Before we look into the types of sentences, we need to know something about the parts of sentences and the names of those parts. For convenience we will use standard names for the parts—like *subject* and *predicate;* once learned, the names will save time; *elbow* is both clearer and less wordy than *that joint in the middle of the arm.*

**153**

Sentences have two main parts, subjects and predicates. The *subject* is what we make a statement or ask a question about. Usually the subject is a noun, or a pronoun like *she* or *who;* but on occasion the subject can be something else that substitutes for a noun, like a clause or a phrase. (Even a verb can be a subject: "*Is* is a verb. *Is* is the subject of these sentences.") In these sentences, the subjects are in italics:

> *The frogman* dived.
> *The theory* was valid.
> *Who* committed this brutal crime?
> *Whoever committed this crime* must be insane.
> *Watching pinball machines light up* gave him a headache.

In the following sentence the *simple subject* is *woman,* and the *complete subject* is *the woman in the blue house by the river:*

> The woman in the blue house by the river wrote bizarre sentences on the walls.

The *predicate* is the verb along with its modifiers and complements. The predicate is what the sentence says about the subject; most often, the predicate is the action that goes on in the sentence. In these sentences, the simple predicates are in italics:

> The frogman *dived.*
> The theory *was* valid.
> Who *committed* this brutal crime?
> Watching pinball machines light up *gave* him a headache.

The *simple predicate* in the next sentence is *wrote;* the *complete predicate* is *wrote on the walls with invisible liquids.*

> The woman in the blue house wrote on the walls with invisible liquids.

*Objects* come in four forms: direct objects, indirect objects, objects of prepositions, and complementary objects.

The *direct object* is the part of a sentence that the predicate acts upon. Here, the direct objects are in italics:

> She designed the *atomic reactor.*
> The president washed the *dishes.*
> *What* did the elephant say?
> Underline the *predicates.*

An *indirect object* usually comes before a direct object and tells us to whom or for whom (or to what or for what) the predicate acts.

> She gave the *team* a case of beer.
> Sam wrote *her* a new song.

Most of the time, the indirect object replaces a prepositional phrase using *to* or *for*.

> She gave a case of beer *to the team.*
> Sam wrote a new song *for her.*

In the last two sentences *team* and *her* are *objects of prepositions,* nouns or noun substitutes that a preposition relates to another word or word group. Here are more prepositions followed by objects:

> When you are defenestrated you are thrown *out a window.*
> Dick the Bruiser was barred *from the premises.*

Another construction has two objects, in which the second modifies or describes the first. The second, or *complementary object,* may be a noun or an adjective. In these examples the complementary object is in italics:

> They made her *bartender.*
> He called her a *humbug.*
> Margaret painted the tree *purple.*

*Complements* follow linking verbs like *is* and *become* and *appear.* When they modify or describe the sentence's subject, we call these words *subjective complements.* These words can be adjectives or nouns:

> She's an *artist.*
> They appeared *pretty.*

A *phrase* is a group of words which work together as a unit, but which lack a subject and a predicate. There are several kinds of phrases, defined by the word introducing them:

| | |
|---|---|
| Prepositional phrase | The bat *in the attic* is not a vampire. |
| Verbal phrase | More and more people *will be buying* sub-compact cars as gasoline prices again rise. |
| Infinitive phrase | Hockey fans tend *to enjoy violence.* |

| Gerund phrase | *Establishing a fascist state* requires ruthlessness and ambition. |
| Participial phrase | *Doubting the medical assumptions of his time,* Pasteur sought further knowledge about what causes disease. |

A *clause* is a group of words that contains a subject and a predicate. A clause may be *main* (also called independent) or *subordinate* (also called dependent). A *main clause* can be a simple sentence in itself.

> *The thin dog barked.*

A *subordinate clause* is not a complete sentence and cannot stand by itself; rather, it works as a noun, as an adjective, or as an adverb within a sentence.

| Noun clause | *Whether the new league will flourish* is a question that no one can answer with certainty. |
| Adjective clause | The cricket, *which appeared to be wearing a tiny tuxedo,* did not answer his naïve questions. |
| Adverb clause | She ordered the troops to attack *when it became apparent that to delay any longer would be suicidal.* |

Each of these last two clauses is a *modifier.* A *modifier* is any word, phrase, or clause that functions as an adjective or adverb.

> The bat *in the attic* is not a vampire.

Here the prepositional phrase *in the attic* does something to, *modifies,* *bat;* it tells us *which* bat. If we say, *the vampire bat is in the attic,* then the word vampire is an adjective that modifies *bat.*

> The vampire flew slowly around the room after he assumed the form of a bat.

Here we have three modifiers, all acting as adverbs. One modifier tells us about the way the vampire flew: the single word *slowly;* then a prepositional phrase tells us where: the vampire flew *around the room;* then a subordinate clause tells us when it happened: *after he assumed the form of a bat.* Manner, place, and time.

Now that we have the names of parts, we can examine types of sentences.

## TYPES OF SENTENCES

### Simple Sentences

A sentence is simple as long as it remains one clause, containing one predicate. *John laughed* is a complete, two-word sentence, simple and common in its structure: subject/verb. We could add modifiers, *Big John laughed loudly,* or a prepositional phrase, *John laughed at her,* and the sentence would remain simple.

A sentence can be quite long and yet still be simple. This sentence is simple, but elaborates the predicate with prepositional phrases:

> *Phil runs/with his wife/at Waterman Gymnasium/before classes.*

We can add as many modifiers as we wish; the sentence will remain simple unless we add a subordinate clause.

A subject can be long, too.

> *The ape-man in the gray loincloth, a wooden spear in his hand,* attacked.

Either subject or predicate can be compounded and the sentence remains simple.

> *John and his zebra* cried.
> John *laughed and cried.*

Or the verb can be elaborated.

> The ape-man *attacked swiftly, with a sharp cry, from behind the rocks.*

Or we can have a direct object, and the object can be elaborated.

> The ape-man attacked *the sluggish warriors, those intruders tired from their lengthy searching.*

Or the simple sentence can have all its parts elaborated and remain simple.

> The ape-man in the gray loincloth, a wooden spear in his hand, attacked the sluggish warriors swiftly from behind the rocks, the boulders shining in the hot sun.

The basic sentence is still *The ape-man attacked,* though by this time we have more definition for each of the parts, more information, and too many adjectives.

## Compound Sentences

A compound sentence has two or more main clauses, each containing a subject and a predicate, each describing an action complete in itself. The clauses in the compound sentence are joined by a connective—*and, but, or, nor, yet, for,* or *so*—or by a semicolon or colon.

The economy stagnates and prices rise.

We can lower the price of admission or we can stage fewer plays.

He never went to the snake house again; he had been revolted by the alligator.

The clauses in each of these sentences are independent. Each sentence could become two sentences, with minimal change in meaning.

The economy stagnates. Prices rise.

We can lower the price of admission. We can stage fewer plays.

He never went to the snake house again. He had been revolted by the alligator.

In the compound sentence, notice that the two complete clauses are nearly equal in importance, or *coordinate.* A compound sentence, of course, can have more than two parts.

Clemens pitched a curve, the runner on first sprinted toward second, and Barrett ran to cover the base.

But a string of coordinate clauses is usually boring.

There was more crime in the street, the criminals were running around free, the judges were letting people go, nobody was safe in the streets, criminals were out on bail, murderers were on parole, and nobody did anything.

## Complex Sentences

If, however, one part of the sentence depends on the other—if the one is the cause of the other, for instance—we have a complex rather than a compound sentence. We call the clause that depends upon the other for explanation or completion the *subordinate clause.* A complex sentence would be

*Because the economy stagnates,* high prices find few buyers.

The first clause in this sentence is subordinate. It cannot stand alone.

We can vary sentences even when we use only simple clauses and compounds of equally complete clauses. But the complex sentence provides further variety and allows us to emphasize the relationship of ideas to others in the same sentence. If we combine the two simple sentences

> We were good friends. We saw each other only in the summer.

alternately into two different complex sentences, the results have different meanings:

> We were good friends, although we saw each other only in the summer.

> Although we were good friends, we saw each other only in the summer.

Complex sentences make for a precise relationship among ideas.

Clauses introduced by relative pronouns, *that, which,* or *who*—sometimes called *relative clauses*—are subordinate to a main clause; they depend on it.

> Do you remember the face of the man *who sold you this ticket?*

> The king executed the horse *that had thrown him.*

In other sentences, we attribute cause or sequence, and we do it by a conjunction like *because* or *after.*

> *Because the Girl Scouts had proved to be unscrupulous,* the neighbors burned the cookies they had purchased.

> *After the movie ended,* everyone in the audience left.

Many other conjunctions—like *although, after, if, since,* and *when*—can introduce subordinate clauses, each with its own precise meaning to be used by the careful writer.

### Compound-Complex Sentences

Sometimes we can combine compound and complex sentences, using at least two main clauses and one subordinate clause. In each sentence below, the clause in italics is subordinate; the main clauses are in roman type.

The young heiress jumped under the covers *when her uncle walked in wearing his gorilla suit*, and she refused to come out.

*If you had only proofread the article more carefully*, Mr. Crumbly would not have been so insulted, and we wouldn't have this lawsuit on our hands!

### Incomplete Sentences

Another type of sentence commonly used is the incomplete sentence, or fragment. It is incomplete because it lacks a subject or a predicate. *John laughed* is a brief complete sentence. Neither *John* nor *laughed* would be complete by itself, but we could use either word alone in the proper context.

She thought about whom she might ask to the picnic. Harry? Harry was too grubby. John? John.

When she saw him she covered her mouth and, though she tried to suppress it, laughed. Laughed. He could not believe it.

Often the incomplete sentence is a phrase or a clause of several words.

The essay by Ellsberg shows control of sentence variation. Like the variety in his first paragraph.

Although this combination of sentence and sentence fragment makes sense, we should revise it if we intend to write formal prose. We have several ways of working the meaning of *Like the variety in the first paragraph* into a longer sentence:

Ellsberg's essay shows control of sentence variation, a felicity obvious in his first paragraph.

As we can observe reading his first paragraph, Ellsberg's essay shows control of sentence variaton.

The incomplete sentence is informal and we should usually avoid it when we write essays. Often we use it in speech, where tone of voice or facial expression or gesture completes meaning. But when we write, only the marks on the page carry meaning for us. As writers we must make connections for the reader, fixing meaning with word choice, word order, and punctuation. Frequently the incomplete sentence leaves the reader baffled. But not always. We use the incomplete sentence with many common phrases like *No comment, Not at all, Of course,* and *But not always.*

Student writers usually make sentence fragments accidentally, without noticing that their sentence lacks a main verb. Such fragments creep up on us even when we think we are paying attention.

> Among my favorite foods, English muffins, hot from the oven, dripping butter and honey.

> When I climb onto my moped and drive out of town, away from the noisy dormitories and the silent library, onto the dusty back roads.

> Which she often does, although I don't approve.

> While I was growing up.

These sentence fragments hang in air. They give information which goes nowhere, which holds back from the reader. They leave unanswered questions: *why, where, what?* Each can become a whole sentence when we supply what was missing.

> Among my favorite foods *are* English muffins, hot from the oven, dripping butter and honey.

> When I climb onto my moped, *I* drive out of town, away from the noisy dormitories and the silent library, onto the dusty back roads.

> *She drove home last night,* which she often does, although I don't approve.

> *I fell down and skinned my knees all the time* while I was growing up.

The first rule is clarity.

Students who have difficulty identifying fragments, and who write them without knowing that they are doing it, should look carefully at the review of sentence fragments, pages 378–381, and do the exercises there.

Another possible danger in incomplete sentences is that they tend to avoid committing themselves. If we take notes on a history lecture, using fragments rather than sentences, we may look at them a month later and read something like *Too many wars. Bad economy.* Unless we remember the context, these phrases may leave us puzzled. They could imply that the number of wars, at some time in history, destroyed a nation's economy. Or they could imply that bad economy created the wars. Or both. With neither a verb nor the expected order of subject and object to complete the action, the meaning is left vague. Of course it is ambiguity—not having to make up our mind—which appeals to the part of our mind that likes to absolve itself from responsibility.

> The recession put everybody out of work in Flint. All those rich people in Cadillacs driving past the homes of the unemployed.

Here the sentence fragment avoids responsibility for making connections and leaves the meaning unclear; an incomplete sentence leaves the thought illogical. Are the rich people responsible for the unemployment? Should the rich people take detours to avoid the workers' parts of town?

We must remember, at the same time, that writers *can* use the sentence fragment *when they know what they are doing.* If the prose is informal enough, the sentence fragment is yet another possible variation in rhythm and structure. It isolates a fragment in time, because the period creates a pause longer than the pause inserted by a comma or a semicolon.

> We were going to be consumed by fire once more, and once more the world would let it happen. As usual. What was true yesterday will be true tomorrow.
>
> Elie Wiesel, *A Beggar in Jerusalem*

Only be careful to use incomplete sentences in an informal context, and deliberately, like Elie Wiesel, to establish pause and emphasis. A careless writer may make clauses into sentences (with periods and capital letters) without purpose, and with choppy results.

> He was a writer. Which is a difficult profession.

> She looked tall. Although she was really only 5'3".

Avoid incoherent sentences like these. These sentences need to become complex, with commas replacing periods.

> He was a writer, which is a difficult profession.

> She looked tall, although she was really only 5'3".

## EXERCISES

1. In these sentences, identify subjects, predicates, objects, indirect objects, and objects of prepositions:

a. The Empire State Building is no longer the tallest building in New York.

b. When we sent Ambassador Buntwell to South Africa, we gave the guerrillas tacit support.

c. Which of the fifty states spends least on education?

2. In these sentences, identify phrases as prepositional, verbal, infinitive, gerundive, or participial:

a. Remembering the tradition of the Old South, Rhett was unable to dishonor his name.

b. The senator from Arkansas tried voting the way he felt.

c. In the morning, the sun will be drying the dew off the grass.

3. Combine each of these groups of simple sentences into one compound or complex sentence. In the resulting long sentences, discern any differences in meaning from the originals. Try both compound and complex; is one more effective that the other? Why?

a. The hurricane struck the island at four yesterday afternoon. Mr. Potts couldn't find his Lear jet.

b. Henry ironed his shirts. He ironed pillow cases. He ironed his thumb and a small corner of the wall above the ironing board.

c. The ram was named Chauncy. He butted Mrs.Grace. She carried a bag of groceries. The freezer is now full of mutton.

d. A boa constrictor slowly emerged from the piano. It played a Bach concerto. It went to sleep on the keyboard.

e. Their mother bought Crunchy Bits every Saturday. She went shopping. Crunchy Bits is the only cereal with an inflatable bowl in every box.

f. His shoes squeaked on the linoleum as he walked. Ten people in the library looked up. They frowned angrily.

g. Television antennas bristled from every roof. Pigeons perched on the antennas. They were a nuisance.

h. They met at a party last Saturday night. He likes anchovy pizza. She prefers pepperoni and sausage. They think they have a lot in common.

i. Paul blanched. He gasped. He coughed. He ran into the street.

j. You insist on inviting pumas for dinner. They eat everyone.

4. Identify each sentence as simple, compound, complex, compound-complex, or incomplete. Rewrite each sentence into one of the other types. Decide whether each revision is more or less effective than the original.

a. Because Margaret had brought the elephant into the house, Sandy had to take her sculptures down to the basement.

b. Rose ordered an apricot sour although she had been drinking daiquiris, and winked at her companion as she did.

c. This sentence, for example.

d. Rocking back and forth on her heels, the professor lectured.

e. Although the rainfall is minimal, irrigation waters the valley and nourishes the corn.

f. Australopithecus reasoned, he cooperated, he hunted in large bands, and he used tools.

g. The man in the Foster Grants strolled down the crowded street, a beret on his head, a cane in his hand.

h. Always cheerful, Mr. Sputter the mailman smiled, although a German shepherd hung by its teeth from his sleeve.

i. Without hesitation, thinking only of the trapped ocelot, Branny dashed through the rising flames.

j. He grabbed the chicken feathers and threw them off the cliff, screaming and dancing all the while, although the rites were not yet due to begin and he, a crazed poet, was forbidden to take part.

5. Here are five contexts, each including an incomplete sentence. Which fragments succeed and which fail? Revise the failures into successes.

a. Henry Moore was born in 1898, in a country not known for sculpture since the Middle Ages. Son of a coal miner, raised in Yorkshire, trained to be a teacher, when Moore learned that he could attend an art school on an ex-serviceman's grant.

b. Nevertheless, advocates of strip mining persist in their rhetoric. We hear of "vast untapped natural resources." It makes strip mining sound like pouring a glass of beer. Instead of like destroying the earth.

c. When I came back from Canada, my friends were all tanned. Everybody. I looked like a pale dime in a pile of rich, copper pennies. And I felt like ten cents.

d. They looked up and saw it. The second stage of the launch vehicle.

e. Whenever the Congress decides to tangle with the president, and the people need tax relief or something of that order of magnitude, although the country needs immediate help, and the newspapers are all complaining, except that nothing ever gets done.

6. Here are three passages taken from student essays. What is wrong with the writing? Revise each passage.

a. We used to eat when my father got up. Because he wanted it that way.

b. When inflation rises above 6 percent annually, and the consumer can no longer afford essential services, but the rich can still get whatever they want.

c. We looked at the mountain. Four inches of light snow were on it. It was a good day for skiing.

7. In your daily writing or old papers, find and copy examples of these: (a) A simple, complete sentence. (b) A compound sentence. (c) Three complex sentences of two clauses, in which you use different conjunctions. If you do not have three examples, revise until you do. (d) A compound-complex sentence. (e) An incomplete sentence.

---

## CLARITY, COHERENCE, UNITY

To be understandable, our sentences must hang together. *Clarity* and *coherence* are needed in writing at all levels—from words, to sentences, to paragraphs, to essays, to whole books. We start pursuing clarity when we choose the right word; when we bring that word together with a second word, we begin to pursue coherence. Phrases and clauses must cohere; they must show connectedness in the logic of the sentence and in the larger unity of sentence and paragraph.

We first discover clarity and coherence, most obviously, in the next-to-smallest unit, the sentence. We must make clear sentences before we can make clear paragraphs or clear essays. Unity, clarity, and coherence—we must define these goals before we enumerate ways to reach them.

One way of trying to define a quality—something as abstract as *unity*, as *clarity*, as *coherence*—is to look at its opposite. Here is an incoherent sentence.

> The attention brought to Campus Mangagement's mismanagement of its rental property at 410 Observatory makes a convincing case for the need of a strong and active tenants' organization in Ann Arbor.
>
> From an editorial, *The Michigan Daily*

Nothing holds this sentence together; it lacks unity and sprawls disconnected across the page. When we try to rewrite it, we run into difficulty, because before we revise, we need to know what the writer wants to say. What does he mean when he asserts that "attention" itself "makes a convincing case"? Perhaps he confuses two ideas. (In another chapter, we will look into logic and speak about clarity as it relates to methods of thought. See pages 309–311, 317–318.) Maybe the meaning is something like this: "When we see how this property is mismanaged, we realize that we need a strong and active tenants' organization in Ann Arbor."

Here is another incoherent sentence.

> It seems to be delivering a message right up to the end, but to decipher it, one has to dig deep within his subconscious and then he may not be sure of the nature of the manner in which it has affected him.
>
> From a theater review, *Ann Arbor News*

It is hard to rewrite empty phrases like *the nature of the manner.* Vague, shifty, and incoherent pronouns—*it, one, he*—cause confusion here. Maybe this sentence could become two sentences. If we put a period after "within his subconscious," we could make a sentence like "Even then, one may not be sure of how the filmmakers have done their digging."

Or take a sample from a student paper.

> All these shortages are eventually going to put people in a position which forces them either to take some type of action that will level off the population somewhere, or people are slowly going to make life difficult for the whole human race.

All these examples have faults in punctuation and grammar—but they come to one common result: the sentences are unclear. The writers were unable to use language to make their thoughts clear to another person.

When we speak of unity, clarity, and coherence, and later when we speak of variety, we use different words as approaches toward the same goal. It would be difficult to find a clear sentence that was not also coherent and unified. Coherence makes unity, which is necessary to clarity. Varied sentences can help to win the reader's attention; but we pursue the qualities of unity, clarity, and coherenece all at once, in the act of writing and thinking. In this book, we discuss grammatical errors and proper grammar in the service of these qualities only. When you read advice on not misplacing modifiers, or on avoiding the comma fault or the sentence fragment, remember that the goal is not mere correctness but unity, clarity, and coherence—qualities we cultivate in order to make contact with other people.

## Unity: Coordination and Subordination

The poet W.B. Yeats said that a finished poem made a noise like the click of the lid on a perfectly made box. Prose makes that noise too, only less loudly and clearly than poetry. A good passage of prose resolves rhythm, emotion, and idea into a pleasing whole—a unity.

Our tools for achieving this unity are the types of the English sentence. A good simple sentence is direct and clear; but the simple sentence will not always embody a complete thought. Writers can choose among simple sentences, compound sentences, and complex sentences—and variations within each type and a combination of the latter two types. Beginning writers usually run to simple sentences and collections of simple sentences bound together, which become compound sentences. Usually, the beginning writer needs to practice the art of the complex sentence, the art of subordination.

Subordination, often using conjunctions, saves words and makes connections between ideas. *Coordination* happens when phrases work together like equals, like *co*-workers.

I climbed the mountain and worshipped the sun.

When we use *subordination,* one clause leads the other; the subordinate clause hangs from the main clause, depends on it, is underneath—*sub,* as in *sub*marine—the main clause.

When I climbed the mountain, I worshipped the sun.

Here, *I worshipped the sun* is a main clause and *When I climbed the mountain* is a subordinate clause. The main clause could stand by itself. *I worshipped the sun* could be a perfectly fine, coherent, simple sentence. *When I climbed the mountain,* all by itself, is only a sentence fragment; it does not stand by itself; it hangs from, it depends on, it is subordinate to a main clause.

We could write:

Hamilton was tired of the game. He took out his doughnut cutter.

These sentences are correct, and they are understandable, but too many of them in a row would be boring, and they might not give us a complete idea. We could write:

Hamilton was tired of the game, and he took out his doughnut cutter.

This version is a compound sentence, two whole and simple clauses joined by *and*. If this sentence differs from the earlier version, it differs by enforcing, with its grammar, the notion that the two statements are intimately connected. But with a conjunction and a complex sentence, we could make the connection more explicit.

> When he tired of the game, Hamilton took out his doughnut cutter.

> Because he tired of the game, Hamilton took out his doughnut cutter.

Syntax, like words, has insides. Each arrangement of words into a sentence makes a gesture of meaning. The last two examples, with subordinate clauses beginning with *when* and *because,* make alternatives to the simple sentences or to the compound sentence. They also make alternatives to a sentence using a participle.

> Tired of the game, Hamilton took out his doughnut cutter.

In all the examples but the complex sentences, the closeness of the two notions implies a connection between them, but does not state it. The explicit conjunction makes a statement. If we want to emphasize causation, we can use the conjunction *because.* If we want to emphasize the temporal, we can use the conjunction *when.*

We must always remember the insides, the implications or connotations, of our syntax. In some contexts, *because* might seem over-insistent or bullying. If we write that Bill's best friend has stolen his wife, ruined his business, turned his friends against him, and hired someone to kill him, it is enough to say, "Bill had grown to hate his former friend." If we write, "Because Sam had done these things, Bill had grown to hate his former friend," we have wasted our readers' time. They are likely to feel insulted, because we have slighted their intelligence so. We have no way of deciding, without knowing the context, what form of the sentence about Hamilton and his doughnut cutter would be best. In relaxed, informal writing, the participle might feel right. But the participle might leave questions for the reader that conjunctions like *when* or *because* would answer. The writer has to decide, with each sentence, how much to tell the reader, and with what precision.

### Subordination: The Correct Conjunction

When we make complex sentences using words that imply sequence, cause, or other forms of subordination, our sentences will be whole and solid only if the context supports the idea implicit in the conjunction. We achieve unity only if we are sensitive to the insides of syntax. For this unity, we must use conjunctions responsibly. Beginning writers frequently violate this duty, however. If a writer omits something important, the conjunction may appear illogical; with all the information, the conjunction would have made sense. If we read,

> The work was hard; however, John was an extraordinary worker.

the word *however* is illogical. The hardness of the work should not be a potential contradiction of John's ability. If we read,

> The work was hard; however, the pay was good.

*however* functions logically: pay is compensation for difficulty. The first sentence omits something like this:

> The work was so hard it was difficult to imagine anyone doing it; however, John was an extraordinary worker and therefore he could do it.

Here the protestations in the second half of the sentence (*however . . . extraordinary*) balance the extremity of the first half (*so hard it was difficult to imagine anyone doing it*). The two parts of the sentence go together, and the conjunction earns its place.

A beer commercial (the brand changed) has an interviewer ask, "As a lawyer, what do you think of Fitz's?" The relationship between the two parts of the sentence is mysterious. The possible sentences in this pattern are without limit. We could say, "As a retired major-league relief pitcher, would you tell me the median rainfall in the Canary Islands?" Really, the beer commercial hides the meaning; it only appears to be as pointless as the parody. Its illogic conceals a social statement. Other commercials for that beer include women who don't find beer drinking unfeminine, a black man who identifies himself as a professional artist, and several working-class males. The lawyer finds his way into the series to imply that beer drinking is acceptable among rich chaps, too. He likes beer best after sailing all afternoon in his catamaran. Beer, then, is *not* just lower-class, white, and male, and the interviewer means something by his weird sentence. But he is not allowed to say what he means: "We want to show you that upper-class, professional, chic sailing types drink Fitz's. You are a lawyer who sails. You like Fitz's?" Information is suppressed, and the result is "As a lawyer, what do you think of Fitz's?"

Probably the most important function of conjunctions is to establish relationships and notions of cause and of time. And they save words. Always be careful, however, not to use them falsely, as transitions, when they do not really move from one thing to another. An example is common in the commentary supplied on football games. The announcer blends two sorts of information into one sentence, with brevity but without logic: "And of last year's graduating class two-thirds went on to graduate school while down on the field O'Leary makes three yards on an end-around."

Other forms of subordination—without using conjunctions—save words and strengthen sentences. Subordinate phrases and clauses, used as modifiers, give our prose density and variety.

In the *absolute construction,* we omit the connective and the verb, or sometimes a preposition, and modify directly and clearly. The absolute construction is in italics in this sentence:

> *Day done,* he raised his pitchfork to his shoulder.

Here we have cut from "When day was done" or a longer construction.

> *The desk ordered, pencils sharpened, paper blank,* he was ready for a day of combat with the English language.

> The fullback twisted and plunged, *his legs pistons, his head an iron wedge.*

A construction much like the absolute is the adjective with a prepositional or comparative phrase.

> Spring air, *thick with odor of lilac,* moved through the gardens of Montgomery.

Similar in effect is the *appositive,* a construction that identifies the word preceding it.

> Joe, *the mailman,* said hello.

The appositive is more direct than the adjective with prepositional phrase and briefer than clausal versions: "Fred the horse thief walked in" is more concise than "Fred, who is the horse thief, walked in." In relative phrases not in apposition we can also omit words when the relationship is clear without them; when they can be omitted, they should be. Any unnecessary word, in writing, makes it more likely that the reader will become bored and inattentive. Say "The flowers she picked were lying on the newspaper," not "The flowers that she picked. . . ." This device is often useful in expository prose. "He had taken a position that was both unworthy and untenable" becomes more forceful when we say, "He had taken a position both unworthy and untenable."

The participle is also helpful. Participles are verb forms used as adjectives, *usually* ending in *-ing, -ed,* or *-en.*

> *Breathing heavily,* he plopped down on the bench.

*Breathing* modifies *he.*

> The *broken* umbrella was afraid of the rain.

*Broken* modifies *umbrella.*

> *Impressed* by her credentials, Mr. Jefferson stroked his *unshaven* chin, muttering, "Yes, yes, just what we have in mind."

*Impressed* modifies *Mr. Jefferson,* and *unshaven* modifies *chin.*

To save words, we can frequently use participles in modifying phrases in place of whole subordinate or independent clauses. Of course in saving words we must be careful not to sacrifice meaning; using a participle, we must make clear what it modifies, which is usually the noun nearest it in the independent clause. Participles can be past or present:

> *Tiring* of the game, Hamilton took out his doughnut cutter.
>
> *Tired* of the game. . . .

### Coordination: Punctuating Compounds

We have concentrated on forms of subordination only because subordination is more complicated than coordination and needs more practice to become habitual. But compound or coordinate sentences form an important part of our prose style. And often when we use coordinate clauses, we find ourselves confused about punctuation.

We use a comma, generally, when the two independent clauses in a compound sentence are long.

> The man wore a green bandanna around his neck, but his wife wore a Brooks Brothers suit and a black silk tie.

Short compound sentences, however, need no commas. "He was fat and she was thin." The contradiction inside *but* often suggests a comma's pause, but it is a matter of ear, of judgment, rather than of rule. "He was thin, but he was tall" draws more attention to the speaker's insistence on two opposed ideas than does the same sentence without a comma— "He was thin but he was tall"— which seems more matter-of-fact, more conversational. Context determines choice.

Compound sentences are loosely held together; a semicolon can substitute for the connective *and*. The semicolon implies the close relationship between two clauses, which *and* also implies, but the semicolon makes a different rhythm by substituting a pause for a connective word. It is a useful variation, and it feels more formal. Avoid tacking together random compounds, many clauses all in a row. Prose that repeats the same loose structure comes to feel too lax. We are all familiar with the speaker who cannot pause.

> I saw her and she was carrying a kitten and it had a crooked tail and I think it was part Siamese and . . .

Some of the same boredom afflicts us when the writer multiplies compounds.

> I saw her and she was carrying a kitten. It had a crooked tail and it was part Siamese. The cat was making tiny squeaks and struggling in her arms. She smiled and then she let out a shriek. The cat had clawed her and jumped out of her arms and run away.

It is easy enough, without radical change, to introduce variety; we vary the type of sentence, using some subordination, and we vary the punctuation in the compound sentences.

> When I saw her she was carrying a kitten with a crooked tail. It was part Siamese. The cat struggled in her arms, making tiny squeaks. She smiled. Then she shrieked. The cat had dug its claws into her, jumped out of her arms, and run away.

Without variety we will be bored. But the variety we choose can be more or less expressive. In this small anecdote the action in the last sentence may be best expressed by the three brief clauses, which were there in the original version; however, the long compound has more effect when it follows the two short sentences—two periods make the rhythm choppy with pause—than it had when it followed other compounds. It is like coming from a dark theater into daylight; the light is brighter because we are used to darkness. In a small way, the grammar and the rhythm add to the feeling, or the expression, which is the meaning.

We use conjunctive adverbs—like *however, still, certainly*—to join independent clauses, and not to join subordinate clauses or phrases. Subordinating conjunctions—*although, when, because*—lead to subordinate clauses, and conjunctive adverbs—*moreover, also, finally*—and coordinating conjunctions—*and, but, or*—indicate the equality of independent clauses. When these independent clauses occupy more than a few words, we usually employ a semicolon before the adverb and a comma after it: "Universal Airlines gained two points yesterday; however, it had lost three the day before."

When we join two or more clauses in a compound, we use a connective word or a semicolon, except on rare occasions when we join brief clauses by commas. The classic example is Caesar's "I came, I saw, I conquered," in which the commas make the pauses appropriately brief. Periods—"I came. I saw. I conquered."—make too much space between these clauses. Remember that if the the clauses are long, a comma will not hold them together by itself. We need a comma *and* a connective or a semicolon. In

> The hair fell to the floor of the barbershop, the man with the broom was dozing in the corner.

the comma is misleading. The sentence could be two sentences, with a period and a capital letter. Or a semicolon, which is always a safe choice, could take the place of the comma. Or we could insert the word *and* or *but* after the comma.

The distinction between *long* and *short* in this advice is vague, and must remain so. It is clear that with clauses as brief as

> John blushed, Sara wept, Linda shrieked, the whole class erupted at once.

the commas work. In the bad barbershop example, the comma does not work. When you come to clauses of middling size, you must decide. It could be the comma splice between brief sentences, acceptable in the most informal prose:

> I climbed the hill, Susan climbed with me.

or preferably the semicolon:

> I climbed the hill; Susan climbed with me.

or a subordinate phrase:

> I climbed the hill, Susan with me.

No easy rule will decide among these arrangements. Context and tone as well as audience and purpose should dictate the choice. The writer must become aware of the alternatives, then work to refine his sensitivity to the differences.

Students who make inadvertent comma splices should look at the review section, pages 382–385, which gives advice on how to avoid them and provides exercises.

The insides of syntax and punctuation show themselves in slight differences in meaning. The first version of *I climbed the hill* is rapid and idiomatic and informal. The semicolon in the second example increases the pause slightly and the formality considerably. A period would make the longest pause and create a choppiness, perhaps even an overly simple tone—that boring monosyllabic simplicity we remember from learning to read in the early grades. (All comments on the implication of these forms are generalities, not rules; a context could make the choppiness rhythmically satisfying.) The final example is closest to everyday speech. The first example, by omitting the connection, is a tighter unit.

We have been talking as if *and, but,* or *or* either takes a comma or doesn't, depending on how long the clauses are or on whether the sense will benefit from a pause. Sometimes when the clauses on each (or either) side are long, we may want to use the semicolon, even when we use a connective, so that we can take a longer breath, yet still indicate a close relationship by keeping the two clauses in the same sentence.

> The block was dilapidated, gray, the houses raw and the sidewalks sprouting grass; but he knew he was home.

This semicolon before the connective is more common with *yet* and *so.* We can write:

> The lion was sleeping in the corner of the cage, yet his feeder approached him warily.

But we are more likely to use the greater pause:

> The lion was sleeping in the corner of the cage; yet his feeder approached him warily.

When we use adverbs as connectives—words like *however, therefore,* and *consequently*—we always use a semicolon.

> The lion stirred awake in the corner of the cage; consequently, his feeder threw down the pail of food and ran away.

Notice that the adverb connective takes a semicolon in front of it and a comma after it. Or we can make the two clauses into separate sentences.

___ **EXERCISES** _____

1. Look at these sentences from student papers for clarity, coherence, and unity. Rewrite each of them. If you have to, make assumptions about the writers' intended meanings.

a. It is hard for a graduate student to hold down both a teaching position and work for their degree.

b. He takes one student, Mike, who says he can trust anyone and also that he only has acquaintances and no friends since when is unclear.

c. When a friend of mine, Robert Olds, who I had known for years converted to Christianity in high school and I began to resent him.

2. Make the following sentences more concise.

a. When he had finished eating the birthday cake, he stretched out on the sofa.

b. The magnetic pole, which is not the same as the North Pole, governs the compass.

c. United States Customs destroys tons of food every year. These fruits and meats are illegally imported.

d. A vacuum-cleaner salesman, who was nearly seven feet tall and who smiled continuously, fell down the cellar stairs.

3. Revise each of these passages into one complex sentence. You will have to make your own assumptions about causal and temporal relationships. Do more than one version if you can see diffferent meanings.

a. It was raining. It was about seven o'clock the next morning. The Jeeps sloshed through the street outside the window. We couldn't sleep. We had breakfast. We all felt hungry. All there was was some beans and brown bread left over. We felt better. The sun came out about nine o'clock.

b. She packed her suitcase. It sat open on the bed. She folded a red sweater. She put the sweater in the suitcase. Her mother stood near the window. She looked out at the stark trees. Her arms were crossed in front of her. Her face drooped. She was sad.

c. Mark sits at his desk. His electric typewriter is blue. It is a portable. He received the typewriter on his last birthday. His birthday is in

March. He types five words. He pauses. He drinks coffee. Suddenly he gets an idea.

4.   Analyze two or three of these passages. Decide how each sentence is put together, and identify the variety of sentences in each paragraph. Praise or criticize.

a. Down the hall in Apartment 2 the reporter found a very "strong case." There were holes in both the floor and the ceiling, big enough for the biggest rats. Cockroaches crawled up the kitchen wall. A curtain divided off a section of the room for a bedroom, and out from it peeked an old woman. She smiled at the visitors and watched them with interest. Isabel Sanchez, the head of the house, was pointing out some more ratholes. A teen-age girl sat staring at a television set whose screen was filled with a constantly wavering, almost undistinguishable cowboy movie, spoken in Spanish. The reporter walked to the kitchen to watch the cockroaches, and observed that some dishes were sitting on the table that contained the remains of rice and beans.

Dan Wakefield, *Island in the City*

b.   The greatest sea power in Europe and the greatest land power faced each other in war. The stake was the leadership of Europe. Each was fighting to strengthen her own position at the expense of the other: in the case of the sea power to hold her widely separated empire; in the case of the land power to challenge that empire and win one for herself. Both, as the war began, were uneasily conscious that an important and even decisive factor might be an Asiatic nation, enormous in extent of territory, which had a foothold in Europe and was believed by many to be interested in watching the two chief Western powers weaken and perhaps destroy each other until in the end she herself could easily dominate Europe.

Edith Hamilton, *The Greek Way*

c.   Many women have given their lives to political organizations, laboring anonymously in the background while men of far less ability managed and mismanaged the public trust. These women hung back because they knew the men would not give them a chance. They knew their place and stayed in it. The amount of talent that has been lost to our country that way is appalling.

Shirley Chisholm, *Unbought and Unbossed*

d.   There under a spotlight, two Oriental gentlemen in natty blue suits were doing some amazing things with yo-yos. Tiny, neat men, no bigger than children, they stared abstractedly off into space while yo-yos flew from their hands, zooming in every direction as if under their own power, leaping out from small fists in arcs, circles, and straight lines. I stared open-mouthed as a yo-yo was thrown down and *stayed down*, spinning at the end of its string a fraction of an inch above the floor.

Frank Conroy, *Stop-Time*

e. The American does not enjoy his possessions because sensory enjoyment was not his object, and he lives sparely and thinly among them, in the monastic discipline of Scarsdale or the barracks of Stuyvesant Town. Only among certain groups where franchise, socially speaking, has not been achieved, do pleasure and material splendor constitute a life-object and an occupation. Among the outcasts—Jews, Negroes, Catholics, and homosexuals—excluded from the communion of ascetics, the love of fabrics, gaudy show, and rich possessions still anachronistically flaunts itself. Once a norm has been reached, differing in the different classes, financial ambition itself seems to fade away. The self-made man finds, to his anger, his son uninterested in money; you have shirtsleeves to shirtsleeves in three generations. The great financial empires are a thing of the past. Recent immigrants—movie magnates and gangsters particularly—retain their acquisitiveness, but how long is it since anyone in the general public has murmured, wonderingly, "as rich as Rockefeller"?

Mary McCarthy, "America the Beautiful" in *On the Contrary*

6. Take one of the passages above as a model, and using your own topic—something different from the model's—construct your own sentences imitating the syntax and punctuation of the original.

---

## Grammatical Coherence

The good prose already quoted has exemplified unity in the structure and arrangement of sentences through agreement, consistency, and coherent conjunctions. But we need to consider further various grammatical areas of agreement and consistency essential to good writing. Disagreement and inconsistency can sabotage even the most interesting ideas and alienate the most attentive reader.

*Misplaced Modifiers.* Placing modifiers properly is essential to unity in content and construction. We must always be careful that a clause *does* modify the word that its position makes it appear to modify. As we have seen, the dangling participle, with its often comic effect, destroys unity.

Being six years old and rusted through, I was able to buy the car for a song.

Arranged in this way, the participial phrase *being six years old and rusted through* modifies *I*; it implies that *I* was six years old and rusted through. Here the best solution would be a subordinate stating cause.

> Because it was six years old and rusted through, I was able to buy the car for a song.

A similar mistake is the dangling appositive.

> A good teacher, his superiors saw to it that he was promoted.

This order would imply that *his superiors* were *a good teacher.* Solutions:

> He was a good teacher; his superiors saw to it that he was promoted.

> Because he was a good teacher, his superiors saw to it that he was promoted.

Yet another kind of misplaced modifier is the dangling participle introduced by a preposition.

> On achieving the age of twenty-seven, his parents threw him out of the house.

(The author may have intended the parents to be twenty-seven and expelling a small child; but we would know that much from the context.) Or the dangling phrase can be adjectives.

> Tall and strong, the job was easy for him.

There is a prevalent dangling adverb which is common to everyday speech, but which disfigures formal prose.

> Hopefully, this book will be done by late July.

Does the book really hope? This simplest rewriting would be

> I hope this book will be done by late July.

In all such misreferences, ambiguity is a possible problem; the reader may not be able to tell what we really *did* mean. We lose clarity, we lose coherence. Even if our *intended* meaning is apparent, however, misapplied language is a flaw that cannot be excused as informality. The reader is dismayed by the frayed edge left by incorrect order. We write with correct grammar in order to reach our audience—and grammar (like everything else in language) is a social act.

For the unity of a sentence, nothing is more important than the precise placement of all modifiers. The dangling construction is a common error; everyone falls into it from time to time. We also make mistakes—sometimes amusing ones—merely by misplacing modifiers. For instance, this sentence appeared in the want ads of a newspaper:

> For sale: Piano by owner with large carved legs.

In an earlier edition of this book, I perpetrated this sentence:

> Look at the examples elsewhere in this book of carelessly constructed sentences. . . .

Students who dangle modifiers, or have other problems with agreement (see what follows) should look at the review chapter, especially pages 385 through 396, There is some help on punctuation from 398 to 414.

*Errors in Agreement.* These errors are common when we use indefinite pronouns. *One* and *none* and distributives like *each, every, everybody, nobody,* and *everyone* all take singular verbs. Here are typical errors.

> Everyone says they had a good weekend.
> Everybody had their tennis racket with them.

Common speech accepts most of these errors in agreement; but formal writing rejects them. We should write:

> Everyone says he had a good weekend.
> Everybody had his tennis racket with him.

We should write *he* and *his* to be correct in grammar. Grammar in this standard use of *he* and *his* may, however, conceal sexism. No one has yet found a satisfying alternative that does not seem at times confusing or awkward. We can use *she* or *her* when context and audience allow; we can use the bulky *he and/or she* and *him and/or her;* we can rephrase the sentence to omit pronouns; we can use the plural.

> Everyone should remember to take her personal belongings from the bus.
>
> Everyone should remember to take his or her personal belongings from the bus.
>
> Take all personal belongings from the bus.
>
> People should remember to take their personal belongings from the bus.

Notice how the plural construction in the last sentence seems more vague and general. Perhaps we can only insist that we *know* the traditional rule in order to break it, if we break it, consciously and intelligently.

Frequently our writing becomes awkward, not because we use a singular pronoun together with a plural one, but because we use singular nouns with plural pronouns or other mixtures of singular and plural.

> Although a person may not be hungry, a piece of pastry can stimulate their appetite.

Maybe *his appetite,* maybe *her appetite,* but not *their appetite.* We could say *their appetite,* correctly, if we used a plural in the first part of the sentence:

> Although people may not be hungry, a piece of pastry can stimulate their appetites.

*Vagueness of Pronoun Reference.* This error is more insidious than disagreement, because it is harder to detect in a draft. We misuse *this* and *that* by using them without having a clear connection to something earlier. Thus we destroy unity, clarity, and coherence. We say:

> When I went home at Christmas, the tree wasn't up yet and my dog was sick, my mother had to have an operation, and my father was worried about money. This bothered me.

*What* bothered you? *This* properly refers to one thing, and the reader is forced to choose at random among the items listed. The author might have talked about *This group of circumstances,* for instance. Or we say:

> When the Panama Canal opened for shipping, the elapsed time for sending merchandise coast to coast in the United States diminished by 80 percent, and the cost accordingly. That pleased manufacturers especially.

Was *that* the time? The cost? Both? The last sentence lacks clarity, fades into vagueness and disconnection.

Often we misuse reference by confusing parts of speech and ignoring antecedents.

> My father is a doctor and that is the profession I want to enter.

> Because we put wire fencing around the chicken yard, they cannot escape.

Each of these sentences is understandable, but each is sloppy and improperly connected. *That is the profession* fails to connect: a *doctor* is a person; *medicine* is a profession. In the second example, chickens are not mentioned; *they* can refer to chickens only by association with the phrase *chicken yard.* We reach an audience with these sentences in the sense that people can understand what we are getting at; but part of any reader's response will be annoyance at our sloppiness. This annoyance is an impediment to connection; it gives us a social problem.

The sentences could be revised as follows.

> Because my father is a doctor, I want to enter the profession of medicine.

> Because my father is a doctor, I want to be a doctor.

> Because we put wire fencing around the chicken yard, the chickens cannot escape.

> Because we put wire fencing around their yard, the chickens cannot escape.

*Consistency of Tenses.* The tense, or time, is the form by which a verb signals past, present, or future. We should stick to one verb tense in describing one action. An account of something that happened to us usually sounds best in the past tense, but occasionally fits the present. Summarizing a book, we use either tense, often the present. But it is not choosing past or present that matters most (context decides, as ever); it matters most that we stick to the tense we start with. In careless writing, we drift back and forth without noticing it.

> The maple turned red in September, a bright range of reds from near-gold to near-Chinese. The sky is blue, and the maples show fiercely against it, making the colors more deep. In October the first frost came, and . . .

The second sentence should take the past tense to agree with its neighbors. On rare occasions, and usually at a paragraph break, we can change tenses. A leisurely description moves into sudden action, and a break from past to present signals this change. Be careful if you try this device; and know that you are doing it.

*Consistency of Point of View.* Shifts in tense violate unity, and so too do other sudden shifts. Pronoun disagreement, already discussed, makes a shift in number. We must not shift the person of the sentence, unless there is compelling reason to. We might carelessly write;

> First you put on your skis, one at a time for most people, and then we take a quick look at the slopes.

The *you* and the *we* are inconsistent. Either pronoun will do.

Equally, we do not move from active to passive in the same sentence, unless there is a compelling reason. We need not say:

> We looked forward to the party and it was greatly enjoyed.

Disunity makes unclarity. Instead, say:

> We looked forward to the party and enjoyed it.

Do not shift from one mood of the verb to another; for instance, from an imperative command to an indicative statement of fact. We do not say:

> Keep your eye on the teacher and you should take full notes.

The sentence gains unity if it is one or the other.

> Keep your eye on the teacher and take full notes.

> You should keep your eye on the teacher and you should take full notes.

When it is half each, it is a minor monster.

All these directives ask the writer, for the reader's sake, to keep his voice coming from the same place, in the same tone, with the same number and gender and mood. It is disconcerting—finally impossible to follow—when a voice comes from high and from low in the landscape, from past and from present in time, from singular and from plural in number. As ever, we write well to make connections. Inconsistency and incoherence curse the work of most beginning writers. Here is a paragraph from an essay in which the author lost clarity and coherence by neglecting grammatical unity. He (or she) had no single point of view. The inconsistencies in this passage occur from sentence to sentence in the paragraph, as well as within individual sentences.

> The mountain from a distance is long and low, about eight miles in fact, and when you climb it you find that it is covered with tiny bushes. The climbing itself went easily, and it was fun for every-

body. I was there by 6 A.M., and all through our climb by three in the afternoon.

In revision, the writer found unity, clarity, and coherence:

From a distance the mountain shows itself long and low, eight miles long and only three thousand feet in elevation at its highest. As we drove close to it, and began our climb, we discovered that its sides were dense with small bushes. All of us enjoyed the easy climb, which took us from six in the morning until three in the afternoon, when we drove west again, into the setting sun, and back home.

## EXERCISES

1. Rewrite the following phrases, to give them emphatic unity or to remove errors or ambiguities.

a. Without knowing which one was best, the chocolate-covered one appealed to me most.

b. Having arrived at the airport fifteen minutes ahead of schedule, my friends were nowhere to be seen.

c. A genius at seven, his parents were worried about his relationships with second-grade classmates.

d. Hopefully, some of these exercises are simple.

e. Everyone wore Levi jackets with their names printed on them.

f. While the sunset was beautiful, the aroma of the garden was more beautiful still.

g. In Zambia, Russia, Poland, and in Venezuela . . .

h. When the game was over, when the stands emptied, when the popcorn was swept up, and the lights were extinguished, a vast silence overtook the stadium.

i. Intelligent, pretty, sympathetic, a good friend, Jane was known to everyone in the dormitory.

j. She danced to prove she didn't care, and implying she did.

k. He answered that he didn't care what she did, that he was furious with her, and he would never to speak to her again.

l. Either you come inside, or get a spanking.

2. Rewrite these sentences so that each is consistent and coherent.

a. Everyone went to the picnic and a good time was had by all.

b. He takes off his coat, loosens his tie, and came to the table.

c. Nowadays, everyone buys their own car.

d. Chester's shoes, mud-caked and which were old, was tied together with string.

e. When old, jogging won't seem so easy for me.

f. On entering when the gates are closed, the dogs must remain inside.

g. Driving out past the red house, a fire was discovered.

h. A man with steel-rimmed spectacles comes to the door and said he will buy Rash deodorant soap.

[The following examples have been cited in *Verbatim*, a magazine about language.]

i. The women included their husbands and children in their pot-luck suppers.

j. Even more astonishing was our saving the lives of little babies who formerly died from sheer ignorance.

k. I can't blame you for wanting to go outside and sit on your ten-minute break.

l. In some countries a person cannot slaughter any animal unless rendered unconscious first.

---

## Structural Unity

Many attributes that give stylistic finish and polish come from the organization of the sentence, rather than from the words the writer uses. Ranging from the definable *parallelism* to the intangible *rhythm*, these structural attributes are harder to define than the grammatical unity that is obligatory in good prose. These qualities enhance the writer's connection to the reader because they please the reader: their absence does not prevent connection.

*Parallelism.* Parallelism is essential in formal prose; sometimes we use it in informal prose as well. Parallel constructions are phrases or clauses within the sentence that repeat the same word forms (nouns, verbs, adjectives, and the like) in the same order to perform the same function.

He quit the job because the boss was cruel, the pay was meager, and the work was dangerous.

the boss was cruel / the pay was meager / the work was dangerous

After the conjunction, each subordinate clause follows the pattern of article / noun / past tense verb / predicate adjective. Parallelism is not a grammatical necessity, like agreement. It helps us to manage sentences and to *clarify* grammar. It is a matter of clarity and symmetry, not of correctness.

We use parallelism most obviously when we introduce the parallels with pairs of words: *both/and, either/or, neither/nor, not/but, not only/but also, first/second.* The sentence beginning with one member of these pairs should pivot on the other; and the parallel clauses should use the same form. Do not write:

> Not only did he run into the fire, but also carrying a can of gasoline.

This nonparallel construction is comprehensible, but it feels stylistically uncontrolled. These clauses are not parallel because the second uses a participle instead of an active verb, like the first clause. We could rewrite it:

> Not only did he run into the fire, but also he carried a can of gasoline.

In writing many clauses together, it is confusing to depart from parallelism and destroy unity.

> His reasons amounted to these: first, the overwhelming size of the debt; second, that the company was ill-managed; third, having so little leisure in such a job.

The sentence can be rewritten in numerous ways; for instance,

> His reasons were first, that the debt had grown huge; second, that the firm was ill managed; third, that the job afforded little leisure.

The parallelism would remain the same—and we would still want parallelism—if we dropped the enumerations.

> His reasons were that the debt had grown huge, that the firm was ill managed, and that the job afforded little leisure.

The briefest way to write the sentence would be to make parallels in the predicate subordinate to one *that,* by using the verb *to be* once and then understanding it elsewhere.

> His reasons were that the debt was big, the firm ill managed, and the job onerous.

Context is also important. The writer might properly wish to sound more relaxed and talkative writing a letter to a friend, more concise and clipped composing an official memorandum. The more concise the sentence becomes, the more formal the prose.

With *either/or, not only/but also,* and similar correlative expressions, be sure that by position in the sentence you make the words correlate the same parts of speech in each clause. We frequently misplace our *either*s and *only*s. We say:

> Either she committed the crime or someone else did.

and we are right. This *either* and this *or* correctly refer to *she* and *someone else.* But too often we say:

> Either she ironed all morning, or she watched television.

Because the verbs are being related, the sentence should read:

> She either ironed all morning or watched television.

Here are other ambiguous uses followed by clear ones.

> Either the professor was asleep or drunk. The professor was either asleep or drunk.

> They not only ran to the grocer, but also to the florist. They ran not only to the grocer, but also to the florist.

In making a list, either use an article or a preposition once, at the beginning of the list, or use it throughout. Either

> The soup, spaghetti, lamb, and salad . . .

or

> The soup, the spaghetti, the lamb, and the salad . . .

but not a mixture:

> The soup, spaghetti, the lamb, and salad . . .

At any rate, do not attempt such mixtures in formal prose. For rhythm and emphasis, in informal prose or in a poem, one might depart from parallelism and profit by the departure. Know what you are doing and why you do it.

When one or more prepositional phrases contain several words, parallelism always repeats the preposition. Say:

Through wind, through sleet that stung his cheeks, and through snow . . .

Do not say:

Through wind, sleet that stung his cheeks, and snow . . .

When you use long clauses, introduced by parallel conjunctions, repeat the conjunction. With long clauses, we need the repetition for clarity.

Although the sun had gone down more than twenty minutes ago, and although shadows thickened in the field, he kept on ploughing.

In short clauses, we need only the first conjunction.

Although day was done, and night approaching, he kept on ploughing.

Also, use parallel parts of speech. Verbs go with verbs in a parallel, nouns with nouns, and adjectives with adjectives. We often violate this rule in making lists:

From a distance, he looked tall, gray, well-dressed, and a foreigner.

Instead of *a foreigner,* which is a noun, the sentence should fulfill its unity with the adjective *foreign.* A common departure from parallelism pairs a participle and an infinitive.

He talked to prove he was intelligent and showing off his cultural background.

This writing is stylistically inconsistent, jarring the ear like an untuned piano. We should say:

He talked to prove he was intelligent and to show off his cultural background.

Two participles would be stylistically acceptable, but the infinitives make a more vigorous sentence.

Another frequent lapse in parallelism is to omit a *to* when infinitives follow each other. In formal prose, we preserve the *to* for all infinitives in a series even when simple verbs follow each other. We do not say:

To see, want, and buy is the essence of the American consumer.

We say:

To see, to want, and to buy is the essence of the American consumer.

The longer the clause, the more upsetting it is when we omit a *to*.

> His desires were few: to live on the ocean, to spend at least a portion of each day sketching the sea-birds, to sleep alone, and cook for himself only.

Unity departs when the *to* is omitted before *cook*. Yet in informal prose and speech, we occasionally do something that resembles our practice with articles and prepositions; the *to* remains with the first infinitive and is understood with the rest.

> He wanted to move back, get a job, buy a convertible, and drive through town in style.

As with the rule on prepositions and articles, the word *to*, once omitted after the first use, may not slip back in again.

Constructions on two sides of coordinates should agree. If we find ourselves writing,

> Either he was rotten or a badly misunderstood young man.

we should improve it by keeping the parts of speech parallel:

> He was either rotten or badly misunderstood.

The same rule applies even when pairs like *either/or* aren't used. Sometimes we make sentences like this one:

> He hoped that she would come and she would wear the blue dress.

The first clause uses *that* and the second violates unity by omitting it. The sentence should read:

> He hoped that she would come and that she would wear· the blue dress.

The word *that* can safely be omitted when no parallel clause is used. *He hoped she would come* by itself is fine, but when "he hoped" more than one clause, we need parallel *that*s. In the single clause, follow your ear.

*Emphasis.* Because emphasis works to construct a sentence firmly, emphasis promotes unity. When we use emphasis well, we make a unity between sentence structure and meaning and between sentence structure and appropriate emotional tone. Repetition, order, and contrast are three means of emphasis.

Parallelism is emphatic, and parallelism is a form of *repetition*. Where the politician's speech as a whole gathers speed by repeating a phrase—like "and what is your answer to *this*, Mr. President?"—the sentence gathers firmness by repeating parts and structures. The repetition creates dramatic heightening, like quickening drumbeats on a movie sound track.

> We must agree that *the present administration is* bankrupt, *that it has* no cash reserves of the spirit, *that its morale* is a total liability.

Careful development in the sentence can contribute emphasis. This is emphasis by *order*. For emphasis, we put the most important words in the sentence at the beginning or at the end—and they're best at the end. (See Concluding the Sentence, pages 194–195.) These sentences emphasize beginnings:

> Slowly, as though the engine were harnessed to elderly coolies, we crept out of Granada.
> > Truman Capote, "A Ride through Spain"

> Tears, blinding tears, were running down her face.
> > Thomas Hardy, *Tess of the D'Urbervilles*

These sentences save emphasis for the end:

> I keep wondering if there is an afterlife, and if there is will they be able to break a twenty?
> > Woody Allen, "Selections from the Allen Notebooks"

> One day, perhaps, the earth will have turned into one vast featherbed, with man's body dozing on top of it and his mind underneath, like Desdemona smothered.
> > Aldous Huxley, "Comfort"

> His form had filled out, his wrinkles were gone, the dull eyes had regained their fire, and there, sitting by the fire, and grinning at my surprise, was none other than Sherlock Holmes.
> > Sir Arthur Conan Doyle, "The Man with the Twisted Lip"

When a sentence like Conan Doyle's is long and delays its most crucial or dramatic part for last, we call it a *periodic* sentence. We postpone the most important part of a sentence—often the simple predicate—by using clauses or phrases or parenthetical remarks, in order to build suspense and gain attention. Periodic sentences promise that something is coming, but hold it back, teasing us, so that the resolution comes with power.

> That the spring was late this year, that the dogwood never bloomed, and that the flowers struggled wanly out of the garden, all of these failures must have contributed to the moment when Frederick, suddenly and without warning, shot his wife.

When we have several details or ideas to present in a sentence, the emphatic order is the *crescendo*. If one of the details is a surprise—something that may seem out of place, but really belongs there—it should come last. Otherwise the order is simply that of intensity.

> I would appreciate consideration for any opening on your staff, and believe that I could bring to your firm unusual combinations of energy and caution, originality and reliability, youth and experience.

> The president has tricked the workers, ignored the military, soaked the rich, and plundered the poor.

Departures from an emphatic order destroy unity by appearing accidental. A periodic sentence feels constructed and planned, sturdier than a loose sentence, which trails off into "many other instances of this kind." An emphatic order makes us feel control, not randomness. It is one more device contributing to the click of the box.

Varying sentence types can also become emphatic (and thus variety can lend its power to unity) when we shift suddenly from one sort of sentence to another. This is *contrast*. Most commonly, we see a short sentence provide emphasis after several long sentences.

> We cannot agree that the Cabinet has been ineffective, because as far as we can tell the Cabinet does not exist. If it exists, will someone please tell us if it has met? For we have been unable to discover when it meets, or where, or with whom in attendance, or if the President knows his own Secretaries by name. We think he doesn't.

By contrasting sentence types, we build emphasis into the developing of the paragraph.

*Balance.* Balance and parallelism are related; both have to do with repetition. Both create emphasis. But parallel construction is a matter of maintaining equal grammatical structure, and balance has to do with getting the sentence parts, each with its own weight, where they fit. Balance is style, it is not grammar, nor can it be described grammatically. Parallelism is style, too, but it can be described grammatically. A balanced sentence is one in which the main parts of the sentence have approximately the same rhythm and importance. A balanced sentence need not have two parts in balance; it may have three or four or more.

Balance is similarity and *sense;* parallelism is similarity and *structure.* A balanced sentence is not precisely parallel in detail, in its two or more parts, but its parts must be similar in structure. Here are examples of balance and parallelism, with the parts printed on separate lines.

*Balance*

In his day, Frank built model airplanes of balsa wood and went to the movies on Saturday;

now, at the same age, Jim cruises around in his own car and flies to New York for the weekend.

Freda said it was dangerous,
but Jill insisted on going.

*Balance and parallelism*

The Grogs wanted only to share and be reconciled;
the Kogs wanted only to kill or be killed.

*Parallelism without balance*

We are to have what we have as if it were loaned to us and not given;

to be without proprietary rights to body or soul,
mind or faculties,
worldly goods or honors,
friends,
relations,
houses,
castles,
or anything else.
Meister Eckhart

People possess four things
that are no good at sea:
anchor, rudder, oars,
and the fear of going down.
Antonio Machado

The foxes have their holes and the birds have their nests;
but the Son of Man has no place to lay his head and to rest.
New Testament

The old pine-tree speaks divine wisdom;
the secret bird manifests eternal truth.
Zen proverb

*Rhythm.* Rhythm and resolution, which we name together because they seem related, are more difficult to define or exemplify than
any other words used in this book. By rhythm we mean sounds pleas-
ingly arranged, the sort of emphatic arrangement we might wave our
arms to accompany or want to tap our feet to. The Hemingway passage
quoted on page 15 succeeds by its rhythm. Here is another example of
superb rhythm, quite different from Hemingway's, more lush and energetic.

> Witches, werewolves, imps, demons and hobgoblins plummetted
> from the sky, some on brooms, others on hoops, still others on
> spiders. Osnath, the daughter of Machlath, her fiery hair loosened
> in the wind, her breasts bare and thighs exposed, leaped from chim-
> ney to chimney, and skated along the eaves. Namah, Hurmizah the
> daughter of Aff, and many other she-devils did all sorts of somer-
> saults. Satan himself gave away the bride, while four evil spirits
> held the poles of the canopy, which had turned into writhing py-
> thons. Four dogs escorted the groom.
>     Isaac Bashevis Singer, "The Gentleman from Cracow"

We find pleasure in the rhythmic combination of words, just as we find
pleasure in the rhythms of music or in repetition of line or color in
painting. These rhythms satisfy our elementary need for order, like the
cycling of seasons and tides. But if rhythmic pleasure is essential to the
satisfaction of good style, we must remember that the rhythms of
words cannot be separated from the meanings of words. Sound and
sense go together.

Look at the examples of carelessly constructed sentences elsewhere in this book, as on pages 10–11 and 202–203. In these examples
we can feel the difference between prose that is strong in rhythm and
resolution and prose that is weak in rhythm and resolution. Here are
two sentences from Jim Beck's first draft, rewritten for rhythm and
sense together.

> Therefore I decided when I was young that I would go to college and
> applied myself to studies in high school so that I would be admit-
> ted.

> I've wanted to go to college since I was young, I studied hard in high
> school, and I was admitted last winter.

> Coming here has been a disappointment so far because people are
> not very friendly to freshmen and everyone has their own clique
> and the whole place is too big.

I've been disappointed in college so far; the campus is too big, too unfriendly, too cliquish.

I suspect that writers' ears are their most subtle, and possibly their most valuable, piece of equipment. We acquire a good ear by reading and rereading the great masters until their cadences become part of our minds. The stored memory of a hundred thousand sentences becomes the standard of the writer's own ear, just as all the sentences we have ever heard pattern all the sentences we will speak. Craftsmanship comes from studying the accomplishment of the past and then practicing to equal it. To become potters, beginners must learn about clay, about glazes, about wheels and kilns. But they may also look at pots, even feel them—early Greek vases, American Indian coiled clay cooking pots, Babylonian wine jugs, bowls and basins made by their teachers. They will discover the uses, the shapes, the colors, and the techniques that determine good pots. Then they must make their own. Developing sensitivity to good writing tunes the ears of apprentice writers until they learn to make their own.

*Resolution.* Resolution is the art of ending a thing so that the reader feels satisfied. Resolution partakes of sound, sense, feeling, and emphasis. The periodic sentence, holding back its emphasis until the end, is an obvious method of achieving resolution. Here is another periodic sentence.

> Without schooling, without friends, without money, without the accent that is necessary for success in Britain, he arrived in London.

This device is so pointed that we cannot do it often, and must usually rely on more subtle resolutions. No rules can govern resolution or rhythm, only example and exhortation, because each click of the box is original. The more we know the materials that make style, the more extensive our ability to improvise. Look at the passage by F. Scott Fitzgerald on page 211 and see the slow, rising beginning, the calm plateau at the center, and the slow, peaceful descent at the end. Then contrast it with quicker-moving, informative prose by Garrett Mattingly on pages 211–212. Each sentence is its own little dance, in which variety arrives at unity by way of improvisation; and each sentence relates to each other sentence as part relates to part, so that the paragraph is a round of dances that become one dance.

In talking about rhythm and resolution, we are not so much covering new material as looking at old material from another point of view. Asking you to practice rhythm and resolution is asking you to write well.

*Concluding the Sentence.* I have been speaking—in the sections on emphasis and on resolution—about ending the sentence well. No sentence can have resolution if it trails off in flatness or emptiness. Let us look at some common failures. In conversation and in unedited writing, we frequently start a sentence with high energy and then collapse when we try to conclude it: we have a subject, but we haven't the faintest notion for a predicate. We say,

> The high level of heroin consumption in this country

because we are worried. But we don't know exactly what to say about it, so we reach around for a predicate filler, to end our sentence:

> is a matter of the utmost importance.
>
> requires our immediate attention.
>
> is an aspect of contemporary life that must concern us all.

Sometimes a writer will string such sentences together—all strong subjects with weak predicates.

> The high level of heroin consumption in this country is of paramount concern to us all. The solution will require the utmost in international cooperation. Firm international controls are of the utmost necessity. The identity of heroin-producing nations is a matter of public knowledge. The destruction of crops at their source is one way of dealing with the problem.

Each sentence achieves the art of falling. These dancers trip on their skirts. The writer has a partial idea—like a sentence fragment—but makes it into pseudocomplete sentences with trite predicates. The mind that writes such sentences seems to be disorganized or lazy about organizing. The unresolved, trailing-off sentences communicate a vacuum. Yet, with a little attention, the writer could have talked plainly, with decent whole ideas and an attendant fullness.

> The high level of heroin consumption in this country requires international controls to destroy the crops at their source in the heroin-producing countries.

We used only a third of the words in this version, and the sentence is unified.

Formulas for ending sentences are like other verbal formulas. All formulas should be avoided, but some more than others. The filler predicate is certain to destroy any possibility of a satisfactory coda, an ending that satisfies us by its rhythm and resolution.

___ **EXERCISES** _____

1. Decide whether each of these sentences shows parallelism, balance, both, or neither.

a. Inspiration is the beginning of a poem and it is also its final goal.
Stephen Spender, *The Making of a Poem*

b. I saw a new heaven and a new earth, for the old heaven and the old earth had passed away.
Revelations

c. The superior man understands what is right; the inferior man understands what will sell.
Confucius

d. There are two ways of avoiding fear: one is by persuading ourselves that we are immune from disaster, and the other is by the practice of sheer courage.
Bertrand Russell, *Unpopular Essays*

e. The camera can be lenient; it is also expert at being cruel.
Susan Sontag, *On Photography*

f. Wherever new lines of communication have opened up, wherever ideas new to a people have taken hold of their imagination, people have been able to change.
Margaret Mead, *Aspects of the Present*

g. A man may take to drink because he feels himself to be a failure, and then fail all the more completely because he drinks.
George Orwell, "Politics and the English Language"

2. Choose five of the sentences in Exercise 1 and using them as models, write five sentences of your own. For example, taking sentence (a) as a model: "Understanding is the first step in education and it is also its desired result."

3. Rewrite these sentences from student essays, using parallelism and balance to improve them.

a. Mary Pickford was America's sweetheart in her early films and wore long blonde curls and little girl dresses and a sweet, innocent smile and she was thirty-five years old.

b. The development of nuclear power promises an undreamed of future, and we must be aware of the potential hazards of nuclear waste.

c. Some estimates of adult illiteracy in the United States put it at twenty million, but twenty-five million is the figure favored by others.

d. Television commercials urge children to consume sugar cereals, candy and sweet drinks and the principles of good nutrition are ignored.

e. My little sister stopped being cute at twelve; she borrows my clothes; she whines at my mother; my father buys her anything she wants.

f. Sometimes it is exhilarating to swim in the ocean; I am usually frightened when the waves are dark and choppy.

g. The lead guitarist got his fingers tangled in his guitar strap and then he tripped on his microphone and then broke a string and the crowd went wild.

4. Rewrite these sentences to improve emphasis. For instance, the first sentence might read: "Worst for me among all childhood diseases was measles."

a. I had all the usual childhood diseases, but measles I remember as the worst.

b. Because of the availability of handguns, violent crime in the United States is increasing.

c. I needed glasses and couldn't even see what was written on the blackboard or read the posters behind the lectern.

d. They served exotic fruits for dessert, pomegranates, persimmons, pineapples and mangoes, and I didn't know how to eat them.

5. Revise the following passage so that it has a more satisfying rhythm; for example, the first sentences might become:

The old man lived in the gloomiest part of the forest in a house made of crude bricks.

The old man lived in a house made of crude bricks in the gloomiest part of the forest.

In the gloomiest part of the forest, in a house made of crude bricks, lived the old man.

The old man lived in the gloomiest part of the forest. He had a house there. It was made of crude bricks. All kinds of trees grew around the house. There were oaks, fir trees, and kinds that had no name. They shut out the sun. Only scattered patches and changing shapes of sunlight showed on the ground. The old man didn't mind. He had lived in the city for many long years. He had grown to hate the neurotic scurrying about. And the hypocritic smiles and cement-block faces.

6. Revise these sentences so that they are resolved more concretely.

a. The Boer War was a conflict which was a matter of the utmost importance.

b. *Moby-Dick*, a masterpiece of the nineteenth century, is a great piece of writing.

c. The dark-haired girl that he had only glimpsed before was very attractive.

d. If David and Susan don't manage to compromise somewhat, they'll have trouble.

e. The dog was strangely reserved, almost sinister; Dan didn't like it much.

f. The two of them were excited and pleased with their new car; it performed well.

g. The murder of the senator was a senseless and tragic act.

h. In the face of the increasing violence in our city, drastic measures must be taken.

i. We must try to write better.

j. Racial hatred in this country affects all of us.

---

## Unity of Tone

Earlier, we called some words *fancy,* and we have alluded to formal and informal styles. Now, in a chapter on the sentence, it will be wise to consider the levels of diction, the tones of voice our prose can aim for. By choice of words and syntax, our writing can vary in tone as much as we vary our voices in speech by loudness and pitch. (Think of how "hello" can be said: neutral, questioning, sarcastic, loving, exclamatory—all by the tone with which we pronounce two syllables.) Among other tones, we can in our prose sound calm, precise, strident, humorous, angry, intimate, distant, or reasonable. We think of them now, as we consider unity in sentences, because consistency of tone is another means of holding our writing together, another means to unity. Logically, tone could be part of other chapters, but this place seems most convenient, because unity of tone begins inside the sentence. Tone is the way we fix on our audience, or the way our audience understands and responds to the feelings with which we write.

In the chapter on words, we mentioned formality and informality, fanciness and colloquialism, which pertain to the tone of diction. In this chapter, we mean the tone of syntax and the tone of sentence structure.

*Formality and Informality.* Choosing a tone requires *tact.* You do not use the same vocabulary, sentence structure, or organization of thought on contrasting occasions. Audience determines tone; tone is the writer's choice of a connection with the reader. The doctor delivering a paper to his colleagues writes a formal and scientifically exact prose; the same person, writing an alumni newsletter, writes a relaxed and conversational prose. If one style wandered for a moment into the opposite, we would have disunity.

> The amino acids were observed to disappear from the patient's urine which was a helluva note.

> "Pa" Barker writes that he and his child bride have settled into suburbia where they are expecting obstetric surgery.

The alumni note could be an attempt at humor, much of which depends on disunity. More examples will follow presently.

Of course *formal* and *informal* are relative, and many points fall between the extremes. We must think about three things: first, what distinguishes formal from informal; second, the occasions requiring or suggesting different tones; third, how much unity of tone is appropriate to an essay or a story and how much variety it will tolerate, accept, or enjoy.

It will be good to start with formal and informal prose writings as touchstones or concrete reference points for our abstractions. For formal prose, look at this passage from Ecclesiastes (9:11) in the King James translation of the Bible, which always combines vigor and formality.

> I returned and saw under the sun, that the race is not to the swift, nor the battle to the strong, neither yet bread to the wise, nor yet riches to men of understanding, nor yet favour to men of skill, but time and chance happeneth to them all.

Now look at this passage from a contemporary literary essay, in which the writer has used repetition, parallelism, and appropriate diction to convey controlled feeling and conviction:

> The greatest American industry—why has no one ever said so?—is the industry of using words. We pay tens of millions of people to

spend their lives lying to us, or telling us the truth, or supplying us with a nourishing medicinal compound of the two. All of us are living in the middle of a dark wood—a bright Technicolored forest—of words, words, words. It is a forest in which the wind is never still: there isn't a tree in the forest that is not, for every moment of its life and our lives, persuading or ordering or seducing or overawing us into buying this, believing that, voting for the other.

Randall Jarrell, Kipling, Auden & Co.

For informal prose, here is a passage from James Thurber's *The Years with Ross.*

> Ross began as a dice shooter in the AEF, and ended up with a gambling compulsion. Nobody knows how many thousands of dollars he lost in his time at poker, backgammon and gin rummy, but it ran way up into five figures. He finally gave up sky's-the-limit poker, but would often play all night in Reno or Colorado, on his trips West, in games where the stakes were only a dollar or so. He must have won at poker sometimes, but I don't think he ever really got the hang of the game; certainly he didn't bring to it the intuitive sense he brought to proofs and manuscripts. He once told me about what he called the two goddamdest poker hands he had ever seen laid down on a table. "One guy held a royal flush, and the other had four aces," he said. When I asked, "Who got shot?" he looked puzzled for a moment and then said, "All right, all right, then it was a straight flush, king high, but I've been telling it the other way for ten years." His greatest gambling loss occurred in New York, in 1926, when he plunged into a poker game with a tableful of wealthy men. He got off to a lucky start, and was two thousand dollars ahead and going to drop out when one of the players said, "Winners quitters, eh?" Ross, who was drinking in those days, stayed in the game, kept on drinking, and lost thirty thousand dollars.

In diction, formal prose avoids the slangy, the colloquial, or the novel. A writer attempting a formal style sometimes falls into temporary informality because he cannot think of the appropriate word, because his vocabulary is inadequate, or because he is too lazy to look for the word. Writing a research paper on exports from a small nation, we want to imply that the minister of the treasury lacked financial integrity; but "lacked financial integrity" is a pompous formula. What do we say of him? If we call him "a crook," we will intrude an alien vocabulary upon this paper. The slang is like tactlessness. The best solution is to say something particular, and avoid the generality. Perhaps we can say that he was convicted of taking bribes.

In a more informal context, *crook* might be just the right word, bringing in a slangy touch of roughness, a little asperity. Tact is all. And it is like social tact, which is often called hypocrisy. When you see an old friend for the first time in six months, you may call him all sorts of names that you would not use in front of your priest. When you are introduced to the Rumanian ambassador between the acts of the ballet, you do not use the same epithets you would use with your old friend; you are more apt to say something original, like "How do you do, Mr. Ceascu?" If you called him "you old son of a bitch" (which is no more original, of course), you would have a social problem. Writing a résumé, or a letter applying for a job, if we turn slangy or idiosyncratic—writing *thru* for *through*; saying *guy* or *gal*—we make a noise like someone who does not know how to act, perhaps someone difficult to put up with in the office. Awareness of audience indicates the writer's sensitivity to the world outside the self: to other people.

*Formality Gone Bad.* We can help to define our terms by looking at what they are not. The virtue of informality can slide into the vice of obscurity, wasted words, or vague terms. The virtue of formality can wiggle in a hundred directions into the vices of pomposity, fanciness, pretense, jargon, and meaningless abstraction. George Orwell turned a good formality into a horrid one by rewriting the passage from Ecclesiastes that I quoted earlier. His modern version is the High Abstraction of academic sociology. Orwell takes

> I returned and saw under the sun, that the race is not to the swift, nor the battle to the strong, neither yet bread to the wise, nor yet riches to men of understanding, nor yet favour to men of skill; but time and chance happeneth to them all.

and turns it into

> Objective consideration of contemporary phenomena compels the conclusion that success or failure in competitive activities exhibits no tendency to be commensurate with innate capacity, but that a considerable element of the unpredictable must invariably be taken into account.

Orwell's parody, which would pass for good prose with many people, sounds untouched by human hands, like a monstrous frozen dinner fabricated from sawdust and boiled crayons. The Orwell parody cannot be called formal. Because of its imprecision, it could be called sloppy, but not informal; imprecision is a quality in most bad prose, whether it is formal or informal in its intent. This parody ridicules a stiff prose style that *passes for* formality among many writers.

*Pompous Language.* We use pompous language to paint over a reality we wish to avoid seeing. In Chapter 4, I mentioned euphemisms; sometimes, whole sentences are euphemistic. The airline has the flight attendant say, "Would you care to purchase a cocktail?" instead of "Do you want to buy a drink?" because the second sentence sounds crass, plain, and blunt. For the same reasons, *beverage* is often substituted for *drink*. These words are fancy substitutes for plain talk, and we use them (or they are used on us by commerce) for deceit. They are a vice that formality sometimes supports. But they are not genuinely *more formal. Wealthy* is not more formal than *rich*, it is just fancier. *Rich* is not slang; it belongs in the most formal discourse. It is plain, and formality can include plainness without disunity, as it cannot include slang without upsetting its wholeness of tone. Think of the difference between *crook* and *rich*. And think of the difference between *tool* and *implement*. Like *rich*, *tool* is plain and perfectly suited to formal discourse; *implement* is polysyllabic and general, and often a pompous alternative to *tool*.

Writing a letter to a potential employer, it is easy to fall into pomposity in the effort to avoid slanginess or familiarity. It is best to avoid "so I worked for this gal doing sales pitches for a tiny bit." But do not fall into "Therefore I worked with a female individual in the marketing division for a period of time." Say instead that you worked for the manager of the sales department for two weeks.

*Formal and Informal Sentence Structure.* The question "Do you want to buy a drink?" is neither formal nor informal in itself. "Would you care to purchase a cocktail?" is pompous. "Want to get sloshed?" is slangy, which is not the same as informal. We could use "Do you want to buy a drink?" in a context that was either formal or informal, because its words are plain. Informally:

> The girl came down the aisle looking tidy and cheerful. In back of the makeup and the hair, which looked as if it would break off in chunks if you touched it, perhaps there was a living girl, somebody

with a name like Eileen or Carol. She wanted to say, "Do you want to buy a drink?" But the airline had enameled her talk along with her hair. "Would you care to purchase a cocktail?"

More formally:

When you arrive at the age of fifty, your ability to choose has narrowed, and you find yourself on a narrow road, lacking the old opportunity to expand or wander, facing instead the one bleak point at journey's end. When you were young, you questioned: Do you want to be an actor, or a poet? Will you live in London, New York, or Paris? Now you are no longer young: Will you eat lobster for dinner? Do you want to buy a drink?

The difference here is less a matter of vocabulary than it is of sentence (and paragraph) structure. The difference includes words also, but the difference in vocabulary is relative. *Tidy* and *cheerful* could go in either passage. The idiomatic gesture of *along with* in the first passage is relatively informal; perhaps *as well as* would be the formal equivalent. *Chunks* has an informal sound. But the sentence structure in the second passage—complex, pointed, controlled—mainly accounts for its greater formality.

*Informality Gone Bad.* The fault typical of informal prose, when it goes bad, is incoherence. It does not hang together. (Pompous formal prose, or jargon, at least *seems* to hang together.) Here is a journalist's parody of what the Gettysburg Address would have sounded like if President Eisenhower, who was famous for his meandering style, had delivered it.

I haven't checked these figures but 87 years ago, I think it was, a number of individuals organized a governmental set-up here in this country, I believe it covered certain Eastern areas, with this idea they were following up based on a sort of national independence arrangement and the program that every individual is just as good as every other individual. Well, now, of course, we are dealing with this big difference of opinion, civil disturbance you might say, although I don't like to appear to take sides or name any individuals, and the point is naturally to check up, by actual experience in the field, to see whether any governmental set-up with a basis like the one I was mentioning has any validity and find out whether that dedication by those early individuals will pay off in lasting values and things of that kind.

Well, here we are, at the scene where one of these disturbances between different sides got going. We want to pay our tribute to those loved ones, those departed individuals who made the supreme sacrifice here on the basis of their opinions about how this thing ought to be handled. And I would say this. It is absolutely in order to do this.

But if you look at the over-all picture of this, we can't pay any tribute—we can't sanctify this area, you might say—we can't hallow according to whatever individual creeds or faiths or sort of religious outlooks are involved like I said about this particular area. It was those individuals themselves, including the enlisted men, very brave individuals, who have given this religious character to the area. The way I see it, the rest of the world will not remember any statements issued here but it will never forget how these men put their shoulders to the wheel and carried this idea down the fairway.

Now frankly, our job, the living individuals' job here, is to pick up the burden and sink the putt they made these big efforts here for. It is our job to get on with the assignment—and from these deceased fine individuals to take extra inspiration, you could call it, for the same theories about the set-up for which they made such a big contribution. We have to make up our minds right here and now, as I see it, that they didn't put out all that blood, perspiration and—well—that they didn't just make a dry run here, and that all of us here, under God, that is, the God of our choice, shall beef up this idea about freedom and liberty and those kind of arrangements, and that government of all individuals, by all individuals and for all individuals, shall not pass out of the world-picture.

Oliver Jensen, "The Gettysburg Address in Eisenhowese"

And here, in case you do not remember it, is Lincoln's formal original.

Fourscore and seven years ago our fathers brought forth on this continent a new nation, conceived in liberty, and dedicated to the proposition that all men are created equal.

Now we are engaged in a great civil war, testing whether that nation, or any nation so conceived and so dedicated, can long endure. We are met on a great battlefield of that war. We have come to dedicate a portion of that field as a final resting-place for those who here gave their lives that that nation might live. It is altogether fitting and proper that we should do this.

But in a larger sense, we cannot dedicate—we cannot consecrate—we cannot hallow—this ground. The brave men, living and dead, who struggled here, have consecrated it far above our poor power to add or detract. The world will little note nor long remember what we say here, but it can never forget what they did here. It is for us, the living, rather, to be dedicated here to the unfinished work which they who fought here have thus far so nobly advanced. It is rather for us to be here dedicated to the great task remaining before us—that from these honored dead we take increased devotion to that cause for which they gave the last full measure of devotion; that we here highly resolve that these dead shall not have died in vain; that this nation, under God, shall have a new birth of freedom; and that government of the people, by the people, for the people, shall not perish from the earth.

The parody is twice the length of the original, yet doesn't convey any more information. In fact, it is much less specific—substituting nebulous phrases like "this big difference of opinion, civil disturbance you might say" for clear and simple ones like "a great civil war." The sentences wander and repeat themselves ("It was those individuals themselves, including the enlisted men, very brave individuals . . .").

It would be easy to continue listing the faults, because they were planted deliberately. But it is more important here to notice how they change the effect the statement makes. The writing is so diluted and directionless that we don't feel the speaker cares for the subject; we don't believe that he is genuinely moved. One fault that helps to create this impression—a fault common to many writers—is repeating pointless qualifications like *I think, I believe,* and *I would say.* Many people mistakenly think that such qualifications make writing more informal and natural. But these personalisms are understood without being said, and they make one feel that if the speaker (or writer) is so tentative about speaking his mind, then he is probably not certain of it.

Be wary of becoming careless in trying to be informal. Carelessness is partly a matter of vague words: *individual,* which is jargon for *person,* is vaguer than *person* or *people.* But carelessness is also incoherent sentence and paragraph structure, sentences that wander without resolution and emphasis. Series of simple and compound sentences that bore us are usually careless; parts do not mesh into a whole; there is no consistency. If you write with some respect for variety and unity—if you write with a sense of shape and finish—you will avoid such failings and inhabit some point along the line that stretches from formality to informality.

*Subject and Audience.* We choose a level of diction to fit subject and audience. We know, before we think it over, that a recollection of a family reunion will be more informal than an essay advocating that the U.S. Postal Service be abolished. Content and circumstance determine permissible areas on the line from formal to informal and will determine whether we choose *crook* or *criminal* before we come to it. If a student remembering junior high school writes,

> After a month of missing wallets and empty purses, we decided that somebody in the classroom was a crook.

we read along easily, and the slangy word is vigorous at the end of the sentence. If the student had written,

> After a month of missing wallets and empty purses, we came to the conclusion that someone in the classroom was a criminal.

we would find the style ponderous—*came to the conclusion that*—and serious to the point of comedy. *Criminal* is a heavy word for petty thievery in the junior high.

On the other hand, if the student, in an essay on the traffic in heroin, wrote,

> In 1975, an investigation organized by Interpol showed that high officials in three Mediterranean countries, in which opium grew, in which opium was refined into heroin, and from which illegal shipments started for the United States, were crooks making vast profits by virtue of their public positions.

the word *crooks* would be inappropriately informal in a sentence so formal in diction and structure. *Criminals* would be the better word.

We must learn to look for errors in tact when we revise; we must look for the low word in the high place and for the high word in the low place. When we have used the wrong word or construction, we can revise it out. If we have written *crook* because we could not think of *criminal,* we can consult the dictionary. If we have fallen into repeated compound sentences in a formal context, we can complicate some of them. If, in a modest piece of prose, we have slipped unwittingly into polysyllables and long, complex sentences, we can simplify. But in order to learn to revise we must learn what to look for.

*Mixing Formal and Informal Diction.* We would write more easily if prose were either informal or formal, if nothing lived between the poles. But most good prose lives in the temperate regions on either side of the equator. The informal essay enjoys an occasional periodic sentence or unusual word. The formally deft argument uses a sudden colloquialism with charm and wit.

A sentence by E. B. White exemplifies the mixture a witty writer can make. White has been talking with appropriate disdain about a pamphlet on writing that, among other things, admonishes us, "Whenever possible, personalize your writing by directing it to the reader." *Personalize* is a slimy word. As White says, "a man who likes the word 'personalize' is entitled to his choice, but we wonder whether he should be in the business of giving advice to writers." The word is used commercially to mean an imprinted name—*personalized stationery,* for instance—and does not mean *to make personal* or *to direct toward another person.* White's comment, after he quotes the advice, is the sentence

> As for us, we would as lief Simonize our grandmother as personalize our writing.

The mini-analogy expresses White's feeling: it would be monstrous to *personalize our writing.* He compares the offensive diction to an unnatural act. At the same time, he uses a cunning and *personal* oddity of diction. The plain way to say the sentence is "we would as soon Simonize our grandmother," but Whites uses the old-fashioned *as lief* (we would say *just as soon*). And *lief* nudges against *Simonize,* the old-fashioned word against the trademark. The bizarre mixture of dictions—the *dis*unity—makes its point.

And so the mixture of dictions can be expressive as well as comic. Often it is chiefly comic. W. C. Field's polysyllables are comic because he uses high words in low matters—or for low purposes, like conning people.

*Revising for Unity.* Achieving unity in our writing usually requires revision. Go over your prose, thinking of it as something that ought to be as whole and as shapely as a clay pot or automobile fenders. Maybe a little less shiny and symmetrical than automobile fenders.

Read your sentences aloud to yourself or to a friend. Look for rhythm and resolution, paying special attention to the ends of your sentences. Look for parallelism, emphasis, and balance. Repair any grammatical disunity that may have crept in. Look for places in which your tone shifts for no good reason, and make appropriate repairs.

_____ **EXERCISES** _____

1. Rewrite these sentences as simply as possible. Cut out all the pretentiousness.

  a. He couldn't comprehend how the thermostat mechanism was to be operated.

  b. Surplus will be maximized when these goals are implemented.

  c. Your utilization of the word *sensuality* is improper.

  d. That wedge is merely a portion of the circle's entirety.

  e. We subscribe to the belief that negligence on your part was responsible for the damage incurred by our apartment's furnishings.

  f. My lower appendage does not have a great deal of mobility, confined as it is by the plaster cast.

  g. Indicate the vicinity of my abode.

  h. His investment in the emotional complex of their relationship, which has been ongoing for somewhat over five years, was minuscule.

  i. Due to private considerations the precise nature of which I cannot reveal, I will not be adopting the course of action you proposed as a substitute for my own.

  j. The culinary offerings of this establishment are not of a very high quality.

  k. The thronged multitudes emitted thunderous vibrations from their collective vocal cords at the point in time when the composer emerged into view.

2. Looking into textbooks, magazines, newspapers, college catalogues, find five sentences in which the writer uses a pompous or fancy construction in place of a plainer one. Rewrite for plainness, and speculate on the reasons behind the pomposity.

3. Write ten sentences, five formal and five informal, in which one word stands out as inappropriate to the diction in the sentence. For instance, "The senator, having risen to the platform with difficulty, stated that he believed the measures the Senate had taken in the recent crisis, despite their intentions, were crummy."

4. Take this passage from Ecclesiastes (2:18–19) and make a parody like George Orwell's (see page 200).

And I hated all my labour wherein I laboured under the sun, seeing that I must leave it unto the man that shall be after me. And who knoweth whether he will be a wise man or a fool? Yet will he have rule over all my labour wherein I have laboured, and wherein I have shown myself wise under the sun. This also is vanity.

5  Use the clause or sentence "he never wanted to write again" in two paragraphs, one formal and the other informal.

6.  Write a short account of a real or imagined accident in three tones of voice: for (a) a letter to a relative, (b) an accident report for an insurance company, and (c) a story in the school newspaper.

7.  In these passages, analyze diction and structure for formality and informality. Be prepared to find some mixture.

> a. A dramatic necessity goes deep into the nature of the sentence. Sentences are not different enough to hold the attention unless they are dramatic. No ingenuity of varying structure will do. All that can save them is the speaking tone of voice somehow entangled in the words and fastened to the page for the ear of the imagination. That is all that can save poetry from sing-song, all that can save poetry from itself.
>
> Robert Frost, *Selected Prose of Robert Frost*

> b. "Omit needless words!" cries the author on page 17, and into that imperative Will Strunk really put his heart and soul. In the days when I was sitting in his class, he omitted so many needless words, and omitted them so forcibly and with such eagerness and obvious relish, that he often seemed in the position of having short-changed himself, a man left with nothing more to say yet with time to fill, a radio prophet who had outdistanced the clock. Will Strunk got out of this predicament by a simple trick: he uttered every sentence three times. When he delivered his oration on brevity to the class, he leaned forward over his desk, grasped his coat lapels in his hands, and in a husky, conspiratorial voice said, "Rule Thirteen. Omit needless words! Omit needless words! Omit needless words!"
>
> E. B. White, *The Elements of Style*

> c. This is a society which has little use for anything except gain. All is hacked down in its service, whether people, ideas, or ideals. The writer, say, who achieves some entrance into the mainstream of American letters is almost immediately in jeopardy of being stripped of his insight by the ruffians of "success." A man who writes plays and poems, for instance, is asked to be a civil rights reporter, or write a dopey musical—if he is talked about widely enough—if not, there is no mention of him, and perhaps he is left to rot in some pitiful mistake of a college out in Idaho. A man who writes or makes beautiful music will be asked to immortalize a soap, or make sounds behind the hero while that blond worthy seduces the virgins of our nation's guilt. Even a man who is a great center fielder will still be asked to kick up his heels at Las Vegas.
>
> Leroi Jones, *Home*

## VARIETY AND UNITY

We write varied sentences according to the demands of thought and expression. Subordinate clauses often make appropriate qualifications in longer sentences that in their progress imitate the process of thinking. The succinct sentence embodies the rhythm of a single idea. If our prose has unity, clarity, and coherence, it is usually varied in its sentence structure as well.

But not always. We get in a rut. We lack experience of the long, periodic sentence, or even of the complex sentence, and we tend to fall into a monotony of construction. It helps us, in revision, to look for variety of sentence structure, and if we lack this variety to see if we can appropriately impose it.

Unity and variety need each other. They are the two poles, and the world spins between them. Without variety, there is nothing to be unified. Identically constructed sentences strung together in a row have the unity of chicken wire. When we learn how to read, sentences have this unity, which is perhaps why we want to leave first grade for the second. Paragraphs of successive compound sentences are similarly boring. In this passage from a student essay, the writer, lacking confidence in his ability to use complex sentences, writes chicken-wire prose.

> Student govenment at the high school level is pointless. Principals never allow students any power. School boards are the same. Every year people get elected and nothing happens.

We could revise this passage, for variety, into these words—which also supply greater unity and clarity:

> Student government in high school is pointless because no high school principal is prepared to grant real power to students, and no school board would support a principal who experimented with student power. Although elections take place every year, office without responsibility makes nothing happen.

By using different sentence types, we can vary the speed and style in our prose, and at the same time make it more precise. If for no other reason, we must vary our sentences to keep the reader interested and involved. Monotony destroys attentiveness; if the reader sleeps, our clarity is wasted. But more important than keeping the reader's attention, variation allows us to be subtle; it increases the range and conciseness of our expression. The means are not separate from the ends. *A change in style, however slight, is a change in meaning, however slight.* You will find meanings that you cannot express, cannot convey, unless you can find in your box of varied sentence structures the shape you require.

## Long Sentences

Short sentences are easy. They are also useful when they are mixed with longer sentences of different types. Longer sentences give student writers more trouble; the more parts a machine has, the more things can go wrong. But to become a skillful writer, we must be able to handle varieties of the long sentence.

In the most controlled prose, in the long sentences made by writers being formal, clause follows clause, the sentence is compound as well as complex, and absolutes, participles, and appositives combine with prepositional phrases—a combination of combinations that includes, balances, and ultimately unifies.

If we took the sentence above and separated it into one independent clause for each idea, we might end with something like this:

> Some prose is highly controlled and each sentence is long. This happens when the writer is being formal. There are many clauses. The sentence can be compound and it can also be complex. The sentence can also include absolutes, participles, appositives, and prepositional phrases. This combination makes the sentence inclusive. It gives it balance, and it gives it unity.

This version uses seven sentences and fifty-nine words. The earlier version was one sentence and forty-four words. The gain in brevity is trivial, but the shorter version is more accurate. It is more accurate by its use of subordination, not only in bringing form and content into agreement, but by making direct syntactic connections instead of continually stopping the flow of sense and picking it up again with a pronoun.

But we don't need to make such sentences up; we can find them in the work of many writers. W. H. Auden uses long, formal sentences to define the sea as a symbol in religion and in literature.

> The sea, in fact, is that state of barbaric vagueness and disorder out of which civilization has emerged and into which, unless saved by the effort of gods and men, it is always liable to relapse.
>
> W. H. Auden, *The Enchafèd Flood*

This sentence starts slowly, with *in fact* and *state of,* but ends with a flourish. Auden carries us up the hill, as far as the phrase *and into which,* and then holds us at the summit for a while with "unless saved by the effort of gods and men" before he takes us downhill to resolve the main thought. The parallelism between the prepositions and relatives *out of which* and *into which* finds its action in the exact verbs *emerged* and *relapse,* interrupted, with precise syntactic sense, by the *unless* clause that separates the relative and the verb in the final clause. We might try once more to supply a version of the sentence as someone else might have written it.

> The sea literally depicts a state of being that is barbaric. Also, it is vague, and it does not have any order in it. Civilization is what has come out of the sea. Civilization is always liable to go back into the sea. But civilization is saved by the efforts of gods and men. Or it has been so far, anyway.

Let us find more long sentences, graceful and agile.

> In the early morning the distant image of Cannes, the pink and cream of old fortifications, the purple Alps that bounded Italy, were cast across the water and lay quavering in the ripples and rings sent up by sea-plants through the clear shadows.
>
> F. Scott Fitzgerald, *Tender Is the Night*

The passage begins and ends with prepositional phrases (*In the early morning . . . through the clear shadows*) and in between are more of them, and adjectives, and a varied use of verbs: *bounded, cast, lay quavering.* The verbs, which follow each other in time, have as subject the three phrases and clauses before—an elaborated subject, which includes the verb *bounded* as well as nouns and adjectives. Then we move into more prepositions and nouns, another verb, preposition and noun, preposition, adjective, and noun. At the center stand the verbs that carry the sentence.

Fitzgerald's prose is ornate and well-ordered, but not so formal as the prose of some historians and essayists. Here is a whole paragraph, beginning with a simple sentence.

> Perhaps Philip had not made up his mind either. The English had given him provocation enough: Drake's impudent raid down the Spanish coast and across to the West Indies, Leicester's army in the Netherlands, the worsening fate of the English Catholics for whom, ever since his marriage in England, Philip had felt a special responsibility. The Pope exhorted him to act, the English exile

begged him to hurry, and among his counsellors the war party was
in the ascendant. It may be that Philip was only making haste
slowly because, as he had once written, in so great a matter it was
better to walk with leaden feet.

Garrett Mattingly, *The Defeat of the Spanish Armada*

Here is classic prose that is vigorous and formal at the same time. Try
to recast the second sentence into simple sentences. Notice the colon
used to imply that something follows which has been announced by
the phrase before the colon. Notice how Mattingly starts listing provo-
cations with a long compound subject, varies into a short subject, and
then concludes with a long subject ending with a subordinate clause.
After this long, complex sentence, he varies the pattern by writing a
three-part compound and ends with a longer complex sentence.

The long, complex sentence lends itself to organizing things that
are related to each other, like events in history, plots of stories, or
arguments with several parts.

## Mixing the Types

We can manipulate the types of sentence we use for variety and to
create an expressive effect, to establish a mood, or to emphasize a
point. Here are some examples. Keep in mind that the passages get
their effect not by the sentence structure alone, but by the whole
apparatus built into them—words and ideas. Sometimes, for the sake of
sense or mood, we manipulate phrases to achieve more regularity than
variety.

In a little house on the mountain slopes above Delphi lived an old
woman with her witless son. The house consisted of a single room;
one wall was the mountainside itself, and always dripped with
moisture. It was really not a house at all, but a ramshackle hut
which herdsmen had built for themselves. It stood quite alone
away up in the wild mountain, high above the buildings of the city
and above the sacred precincts of the temple.

Pär Lagerkvist, *The Sybil*

The sentence structure here is simple and stable. The construction is
uncomplicated and regular. All the sentences except the first are regular in word order, beginning subject-verb and continuing evenly, without parenthetical expressions, or phrases set off by commas, or any
other complications in the syntax. The syntax is as undisturbed as the

scene. The sentences are medium in length, and similar in length, establishing a rhythm that reinforces the stability and simplicity in the scene described. We participate in the rhythm of untroubled isolation. That rhythm is established, even more, by the uniform length of the main phrases within the sentences. If we listen to ourselves reading the passage, we will find that natural pauses divide the phrases in this way:

> In a little house on the mountain slopes above Delphi /
> lived an old woman with her witless son. /
> The house consisted of a single room; /
> one wall was the mountainside itself, /
> and always dripped with moisture. /
> It was really not a house at all, /
> but a ramshackle hut which herdsmen had built for
>    themselves. /
> It stood quite alone away up in the wild mountain, /
> high above the buildings of the city /
> and above the sacred precincts of the temple.

It has enough variation to avoid monotony. The even length contributes not only stillness to the scene, but our sense of the narrator's calm, unemotional objectivity.

The following passage from Annie Dillard's *Pilgrim at Tinker Creek* exhibits different sentence constructions, with different effects:

> When I slide under a barbed-wire fence, cross a field, and run over a sycamore trunk felled across the water, I'm on a little island shaped like a tear in the middle of Tinker Creek. On one side of the creek is a steep forested bank; the water is swift and deep on that side of the island. On the other side is the level field I walked through next to the steers' pasture; the water between the field and the island is shallow and sluggish. In summer's low water, flags and bulrushes grow along a series of shallow pools cooled by the lazy current. Water striders patrol the surface film, crayfish hump along the silt bottom eating filth, frogs shout and glare, and shiners and small bream hide among roots from the sulky green heron's eye. I come to this island every month of the year. I walk around it, stopping and staring, or I straddle the sycamore log over the creek, curling my legs out of the water in winter, trying to read. Today I sit on dry grass at the end of the island by the slower side of the creek. I'm drawn to this spot. I come to it as to an oracle; I return to it as a man years later will seek out the battlefield where he lost a leg or an arm.

As with the Lagerkvist passage, we can put the Dillard paragraph into long lines to see its structure more clearly and to understand how her complicated sentences work.

> When I slide under a barbed-wire fence,
>    cross a field,
>    and run over a sycamore trunk felled across the water,
> I'm on a little island shaped like a tear in the middle of
>                                   Tinker Creek.
>
> On one side of the creek is a steep forested bank;
> the water is swift and deep on that side of the island.
> On the other side is the level field
> I walked through next to the steers' pasture;
> the water between the field and the island is shallow and
>    sluggish.
>
> In summer's low water,
> flags and bulrushes grow along a series of shallow pools cooled
>                               by the lazy current.
>
> Water striders patrol the surface film,
> crayfish hump along the silt bottom eating filth,
> frogs shout and glare,
> and shiners and small bream hide among roots from the sulky
>                               green heron's eye.
>
> I come to this island every month of the year.
>
> I walk around it, stopping and staring,
> or I straddle the sycamore log over the creek, curling my legs out of
>                           the water in winter, trying to read.
>
> Today I sit on dry grass at the end of the island by the slower
>                               side of the creek.
>
> I'm drawn to this spot.
>
> I come to it as to an oracle;
> I return to it as a man years later will seek out the battlefield
>                           where he lost a leg or an arm.

Dillard starts with a long complex sentence of description, with three lively verbs in a subordinate clause, and then an elaborated predicate in the main clause. She follows this sophisticated sentence with two simple clauses, a compound joined by a semicolon. The next sentence elaborates the pattern of the second one. The fifth sentence is long and rich, its mass of description tending to obscure the fact that its construction is simple, direct—and compound. Following it is the shortest sentence, and the simplest one so far, in the paragraph. Two sentences later, we find a sentence even shorter and simpler, followed by a compound-complex sentence of great sophistication, and a final image that is startling, almost shattering. Dillard plays the octaves of syntax like a skilled musician improvising at the piano.

### Revising for Variety and Conciseness

Look over your own writing for the construction of sentences. Ask yourself if you vary enough to avoid monotony, if your variations are as expressive as they might be, and if your informal sentences are appropriate and sufficiently precise.

Also, see if you can be more concise. To revise for conciseness often requires compound and complex sentences or conjunction and subordination. Conciseness and precision go together. We ramble on, in our first drafts or in our daily writing, assuming connections and causes but not stating them. If we try to make our prose more concise, by writing complex sentences with precise conjunctions, we often discover that what we wanted to imply does not really derive from what we said. And so this device of revision—by adding the conjunction—becomes another way of testing, and achieving, the identity of expression and meaning. Precision of time and cause is a responsibility that the loose or compound sentence may evade. In an earlier example, a tiny revision illustrated a small gain in brevity and responsibility:

> I saw her and she was carrying a kitten. It had a crooked tail . . .

became

> When I saw her she was carrying a kitten with a crooked tail.

Maybe the greatest change here is in the tone; the writer seems to be controlling something, not merely rattling on.

Here is a passage from a student essay in which the writer dumps things together without showing relationships. He wastes words by repetition, and he wastes the power in those words by poor organization.

> The building was still burning and firemen couldn't put it out. An hour or so went by. The National Guard looked nervous and young.

They drove around in their Jeeps with their guns. They tried to look tough. We didn't know if their guns were loaded or not. They were scary just because they had guns but they looked scared themselves. They were about the same age as the students. Yet they were guarding them.

Because the relationship between remarks is often vague in this passage, we could not rewrite it with certainty unless we knew more facts or the feelings the author tried to express. Reading the passage, we may doubt that the student had arranged the facts in his mind with clarity, or had understood his feelings. Later, he revised the passage, and his sentence structure accounted for much of the improvement—though as always with writing, the *whole* assembles everything we label; the whole is better, partly because of sentence structure.

As we watched the building burn for hours, the firemen standing by helpless, we became aware of the patrolling Jeeps of the National Guard, young men the same age as the students they were guarding, young men who tried to act tough but looked as frightened of their guns as we were.

He gained economy and vividness, and also clarity of thought and feeling.

_____ **EXERCISES** _____

1. Revise this passage to introduce varied sentence structure. Use variation not just for its own sake, but to make the writing more precise. Remember that commas, semicolons, colons, and periods are aids to rhythm and therefore to meaning, to expressiveness, and to clarity.

Every man who worked on the docks had to wear a hard hat. He also had to wear heavy canvas gloves. The hats protected the men from falling objects. Sometimes crates fell into the hole. Sometimes steel beams were swung down to the dock on cables. There was danger of metal splinters and serious abrasions. These dangers were increased because the longshoremen might work for twelve hours straight. They might work from 6 P.M. to 6 A.M. Some of the men also had jobs during the day. And many of the men drank heavily. This was because they got depressed. Sometimes there would be a shipment of whiskey. The men might pretend to have an accident. They would let a crate fall. It would break open. They would stash the unbroken bottles. And they would hide them. They would drink some when the officials were not around. The officials were paid by the shipping companies. They didn't want to be blamed for missing goods.

2. Find and identify, in the passage you made from Exercise 1, a subordinate clause, a main clause, an appositive, a participle, and an adjective with a preposition. If you cannot find one of each, revise the passage to include them.

3. Examine the following passages to discover how sentence structure and variation express content and tone.

a. For purposes of pedagogy, I have sometimes illustrated these tendencies by reference to a technically uncomplicated product, which, unaccountably, neither General Electric nor Westinghouse has yet placed on the market. It is a toaster of standard performance, the pop-up kind, except that it etches on the surface of the toast, in darker carbon, one of a selection of standard messages or designs. For the elegant, an attractive monogram would be available or a coat of arms; for the devout, at breakfast there would be an appropriate devotional message from the Reverend Billy Graham; for the patriotic or worried, there would be an aphorism urging vigilance from Mr. J. Edgar Hoover; for modern painters and economists, there would be a purely abstract design. A restaurant version would sell advertising.

John Kenneth Galbraith, "The Technostructure"

b. The neurobiologists can do all sorts of things in their investigation, and the brain is an organ different from what it seemed twenty-five years ago. Far from being an intricate but ultimately simplifiable mass of electronic circuitry governed by wiring diagrams, it now has the aspect of a fundamentally endocrine tissue, in which the essential reactions, the internal traffic of nerve impulses, are determined by biochemical activators and their suppressors. The technologies available for quantitative study of individual nerve cells are powerful and precise, and the work is now turning toward the functioning of collections of cells, the centers for visual and auditory perception and the like, because work at this level can now be done. It is difficult to think of problems that cannot be studied, ever. The matter of consciousness is argued over, naturally, as a candidate for perpetual unapproachability, but this has more the sound of a philosophical discussion. Nobody has the feeling any longer, as we used to believe, that we can never find out how the brain works.

Lewis Thomas, "Medical Lessons from History"

c. Familiarity has perhaps bred contempt in us Americans: until you have had a washing machine, you cannot imagine how little difference it will make to you. Europeans still believe that money brings happiness, witness the bought journalist, the bought politician, the bought general, the whole venality of European literary life, inconceivable in this country of the dollar. It is true that America produces and consumes more cars, soap, and bathtubs than any other nation, but we live among these objects rather than by them. Americans build skyscrapers; Le Corbusier worships them. Ehrenburg, our Soviet critic, fell in love with the Check-O-Mat in American railway stations, writing home paragraphs of song to this gadget—while deploring American materialism. When an American heiress wants to buy a man, she at once crosses the Atlantic. The only really materialistic people I have ever met have been Europeans.

Mary McCarthy, "America the Beautiful" in *On the Contrary*

# 6

## Paragraphs

### USES OF PARAGRAPHS

The paragraph is a small box of sentences, making a whole shape that is at the same time part of another whole. It is a miniature essay itself, with its own variable structure. The paragraph within the essay makes a sign for the reader; as writers our use of the paragraph alerts the reader to the part-structure of our essay. Paragraphs give signals and directions and help to connect writers with audiences. Paragraphs are partly arbitrary, and will vary in length and purpose according to the essay's occasion. Frequently a writer arrives at the best paragraphing only in late revision.

In that bible for stylists, *Modern English Usage,* H. W. Fowler writes, "The purpose of paragraphing is to give the reader a rest." I called the paragraph a mini-essay; it is also a maxi-sentence: the blank space at the end of the paragraph, before we indent and begin a new one, is like the period ending the sentence, only longer. Paragraphs punctuate by visual arrangement on the page. Like a sentence, a paragraph tells us that something completes itself and that we have come to the end of a group of statements composing a larger statement; now the reader must pause a moment and see what the paragraph was doing.

Look at the preceding paragraph. Its organization is only one of many possible, but it is a common one. It begins with a quotation from

Fowler, which announces its purpose. Then it compares paragraph and sentence. Fowler does not make such a comparison; my strategy develops the comparison from Fowler's word *rest*. The last sentence suggests the function that rest fills. The paragraph elaborates and supports the first sentence, and the pause at the end should grant us a sense of wholeness.

Paragraphs rest the eye as well as the brain. Unbroken print leaves no landmarks for the eye that wanders and returns; we sometimes find ourselves using a finger to keep to the correct line. Though context gives us other reasons for longer or shorter paragraphs, paragraphs are useful as visual aids to comfort in reading. Those little indentations are hand- and footholds in the cliff-face of the essay.

### PARAGRAPHS AS SIGNS FOR READERS

As readers we identify the paragraph by the visual sign of its indented white space. Our eyes register PARAGRAPH before our minds have a chance to consider the writer's reasons for pause, or the content of the new paragraph. But the visual sign is itself information; it begins the new content by alerting us that something changes.

The paragraph holds and shapes; it manipulates the reader's attention. When as writers revising we consider our paragraphing, we must as always imagine ourselves readers. Because the paragraph gives the reader a break, writers can gather their materials into units small enough for separate ingestion, and by separating them can allow each collection its own space as part of the whole essay.

The paragraph is more thoroughly directed to audience than the sentence is: when we write sentences we must also think of audience, but sentences exist as units of expression and even of exploration for writers as well as for readers; we have seen how attention to conjunctions, for instance, can enhance or improve the writer's thought. Maybe our attention to paragraphing improves our thought, if we consider fullness of development a problem not of the essay but of the paragraph; for beginning writers it may be helpful, learning development, to concentrate on the smaller unit; or we may think of the essay's structure as an assemblage of paragraphs in an appropriate order. But paragraphing always includes an element of the arbitrary; finally it is not so much an aid to the writer's thought as a means by which the writer shapes his material, however generated, toward an imagined audience.

Paragraphing therefore tends to find its form in late revision when we realize that one sentence—say, "These opposing views, so diametrical, may be reconciled if we look at diplomatic history"—might perfectly well come at the end of a paragraph that details the opposition *or* at the beginning of the subsequent paragraph that does the reconciling. No rule of paragraphing will decide whether this sentence ends one paragraph or begins another; writers must decide, on the basis of a chosen approach to the reader.

The paragraph is a writerly device for leading the reader by the nose.

The reader, we must remember, has certain expectations: the reader does *not* expect, in the formality of a textbook, paragraphs as short as my last one. When we do such a thing we surprise the reader and therefore we had better have a purpose. Did we?

Nor, on the other hand, does the reader expect to find page after page without any paragraph breaks at all. In some old books, and occasionally in essays by modern writers like John McPhee, readers will find such unexpected solid pages of print—and they may find themselves turning blue from lack of breath. But John McPhee is so skillful at leading readers by the nose with firm but gentle transitions, beguiling them by variety of sentence structure and fresh detail, that he manages the stunt. He performs like the child on the bicycle: "Look, Ma! No paragraphs!"

The tone of discourse makes for different expectations. When we read philosophy, or the history of the Peloponnesian War in the fifth century B.C., we expect longer paragraphs; when we read a news story in an afternoon daily we expect shorter ones.

Always, we expect a paragraph to be a unit; if a brief newspaper story gives one paragraph to each sentence, this very repetitiousness is a unity. (And if it continues long, this unity becomes totally boring.) More likely the paragraph assembles itself as a unit in a familiar way— like an assertion with details following to support the assertion. (We will list and explore familiar paragraph patterns later in this chapter.) Sometimes a paragraph forms part of something ongoing, like a narrative; the break should happen where, if we had to pause for a glass of water, we would pause. (We would *not* pause, say, in the middle of a sentence.) We expect the beginnings and endings of paragraphs, most of the time, to make small signals of starting and stopping. We expect paragraphs to hold together, without loose flapping parts. All of these expectations belong to us as readers; when we become writers, these expectations become devices for our use.

## PURPOSE AND THE PARAGRAPH

Paragraphs can advance the writer's purpose, and their shape must reflect that purpose in the development of the essay. As always, purpose adjusts itself to audience, as the writer improvises a structure. Development by rhetorical patterns, which we return to later in this chapter, often gives paragraphs an appropriate shape—but they are not the only common structures. A frequent paragraph pattern begins with a generalization, makes a necessary qualification, and then reaffirms the generalization by example. "The personal computer, used in conjunction with telephone lines, will revolutionize the habits of American consumers." This topic sentence is defensible, and it acquires more authority if it is accompanied by a modest restriction: "We do not mean that Americans will no longer pick up a quart of milk at a convenience store, or that shopping plazas will become ghost towns." After this qualification, the paragraph will illustrate computer shopping at home with two or three examples.

Another common form of paragraph is the question and answer: "Will consumers find enough choice, if they shop by electronic catalogue?" Questions need not require literal form; the same paragraph could begin, in a more formal prose style, "Some commentators believe that electronic shopping will overly restrict consumer choice." In either paragraph, the sentences offering question or objection may be answered or rebutted by sentences that develop the paragraph.

Many essays profit by several paragraphs in a row constructed on similar principles: query or objection followed by reply or rebuttal. Two or three such paragraphs should suffice; when a whole essay is so constructed, the effect is too mechanical, or perhaps too defensive. It is wise to vary the construction of the paragraphs, and to vary the position of the generalization that the paragraph validates or illustrates. Often a topic sentence can conclude a paragraph; the writer could begin an essay by describing a consumer sitting in a den at the keyboard, shopping for a lawn mower; this opening paragraph could end, after its narrative example: "The personal computer, connected to telephone lines, will revolutionize the habits of the American consumer."

## UNITY IN THE PARAGRAPH

In pursuing unity of thought and of feeling, the paragraph must contain nothing extraneous. The writer must omit the odd fact which happens to be true, but which is extraneous to the topic. The odd fact violates unity and distracts the reader; the paragraph must contain only what is relevant.

> We never had enough time to eat lunch in high school: half of the time I'd get a stomachache from hurriedly wolfing down the food. The food was lousy, anyway, and the kitchen help resented the minimum wage. We complained to the administration, but it didn't do any good. We were often held up in getting into the cafeteria because the lunchroom helpers were slow in getting the tables and the food ready. Then, if you were one of the people who got in toward the end, you would have to wait a long time in line. Sometimes the jocks, who acted as lunchroom police, would hold you up, too, trying to bully you into buying a football schedule.

The sentence about lousy food and dissatisfied kitchen help doesn't fit here; it is a digression from the topic "We never had enough time to each lunch in high school."

We must remain alert to maintain unity of subject matter in our paragraphs, because the associations in our thought, which can lead us to new ideas and perceptions, can also lead us into irrelevance. When we begin to write about a subject, our mind drifts from one thought to another, by personal association. As we have seen in Chapter 3, this random, uncensored thinking can be useful for gathering material. But we must take care that it not lead to rambling disorganization, because our impressions are unified *only* by personal association. Because the reader does not share our private memories and feelings, he cannot see the connections we make—and we fail to make contact. Here is an example from a student paper.

> All the recent concern over the slaughter of whales whose species are nearly extinct has reminded me of my childhood interest in whales and other wild animals, especially animals who prey. I was particularly fascinated by the killer whales, which travel in packs like wolves often attacking larger whales. They will tear off the lips and tongue first, their favorite parts. But man has been almost solely responsible for the dangerous depletion of some of the whale populations, such as the blue whale. Still, I can remember the fear that animals like puff adders, tarantulas, and sharks could inspire in me as a child. So I wonder if, in certain cases, we aren't being hypocritical for blaming the people who actually live in lands inhabited by animals like tigers and wolves for killing them. We might be just as frightened and irrational as they are. But that still doesn't make it right.

The thoughts in this paragraph make connections for the writer, but not for the reader. The writer jumps from the threat to whale populations to his childhood interests, then to the habits of killer whales, then to questions of man's rational and irrational fears of predatory animals. To write a unified paragraph, he would have to decide what the topic of his paragraph ought to be and then stick to that topic. We cannot expect readers to be patient with a rambling, disorganized paragraph, nor can we expect them to read our minds and recognize an order that is personal to us.

Two kinds of writing need especially careful paragraphing. Exposition (which sets forth or explains) and argument (which attempts to convince or persuade) should lead the reader's mind by careful steps to understanding or agreement. Paragraphs in argument or exposition are mini-essays. They deal with one topic, or with closely related data, or with an integral segment of a topic. The paragraph is homogeneous. It is orderly—and we must remember that there are many varieties of order. (See Some Ways of Developing Paragraphs, pages 243–248.)

## Unity and Topic Sentences

Probably the most common paragraph construction begins with a topic sentence, which brings to the paragraph not only order but also unity. The topic sentence announces the topic and an attitude toward it. The other sentences of the paragraph use a consistent order—often moving from the general to the specific—to explain, elaborate, or enumerate examples or analogies supporting the topic sentence. Then a final sentence draws the elaboration to a conclusion in a way that leads to the next paragraph. Here is a paragraph that begins with a topic sentence and moves from a general statement to particular examples.

> Play is older than culture, for culture, however inadequately defined, always presupposes human society, and animals have not waited for man to teach them their playing. We can safely assert, even, that human civilization has added no essential feature to the general idea of play. Animals play just like men. We have only to watch young dogs to see that all the essentials of human play are present in their merry gambols. They invite one another to play by a certain ceremoniousness of attitude and gesture. They keep to the rule that you shall not bite, or not bite hard, your brother's ear. They pretend to get terribly angry. And—what is most important— in all these doings they plainly experience tremendous fun and

enjoyment. Such rompings of young dogs are only one of the simpler forms of animal play. There are other, much more highly developed forms: regular contests and beautiful performances before an
admiring public.

Johan Huizinga, Homo Ludens

Many variations upon this order are possible and are desirable, because
a long essay composed of paragraphs equal in length and identical in
construction would be boring.

Sometimes we find a topic sentence in the middle of a paragraph,
where it provides summary or generalization tying together the particulars that come before and after.

> We hesitated before we stepped into the garden, so heavy was the
> odor of flowering quince. The garden was orderly, comfortable, and
> gorgeous, with little benches artfully placed for the weary guest.
> *Our host, as generous as he was clever, introduced us to his hobby.*
> We toured among hardy perennials, and walked past annual bor-
> ders. We strolled among fig trees, past palms, to a density of shrubs.
> We floated in joy on the tropical air.
>
> Hermann von Kreicke, The Migrant Swan

Sometimes we find a topic sentence ending the paragraph, as a
summary. We can create drama or tension by starting with description
and detail and building to a conclusion.

> Now and then there is a house of brick. But what brick! When it
> is new it is the color of a fried egg. When it has taken on the patina
> of the mills it is the color of an egg long past all hope or caring. Was
> it necessary to adopt that shocking color? No more than it was
> necessary to set all of the houses on end. Red brick, even in a steel
> town, ages with some dignity. Let it become downright black, and
> it is still sightly, especially if its trimmings are of white stone, with
> soot in the depths and the high spots washed by the rain. *But in
> Westmoreland they prefer that uremic yellow, and so they have
> the most loathsome towns and villages ever seen by mortal eye.*
>
> H. L. Mencken, "The Libido for the Ugly"

Notice how this structure involves us. We are pulled into the movement by the piling up of details, not knowing exactly where the argument will lead us. The author carries us with him, and our conclusion
arises from the material presented.

For the opposite effect, look back at the paragraph by Johan Huizinga. Paragraphs that begin with topic sentences differ greatly in

rhythm and in tone from paragraphs that end with them. The Huizinga and Mencken paragraphs have different purposes, which make their different structures appropriate. Huizinga wants to inform and explain. He tells us our destination as we start; he begins with his primary idea and then fleshes it out. Mencken wants to persuade us to share not only his ideas but also his point of view. He keeps us off balance at first and involves us in the accumulating fabric of thought and feeling.

Sometimes we even find a paragraph's topic sentence at the end of the previous paragraph. The paragraph break serves almost as a colon.

> In general, chronology is the most satisfactory organization. *However, we must not rely on it alone.*
> We would reduce our psychological world to the order of the clock. We would become slaves of "then" and "afterward." . . .

The first two sentences in the second paragraph elaborate the negative topic sentence which ends the first paragraph, but which could have introduced the second paragraph just as well.

Sometimes we have no topic sentence, or it is understood or implied as a transition can be understood. A writer may mention that he spent a day in the town of Omaha, then follow with a paragraph:

> The visitor can enjoy the aroma of the stockyards. He can watch the rich sit at their clubs, drinking gin next to pools of chlorine, beside flat golf courses. The visitor can walk up the sides of ugly buildings on dry Sundays. He can watch grass grow, at least in early spring and early fall. He can listen to the medley of rock-station radios in several parks. He can try sleeping for a week or so, until he is able to leave.

He needs no topic sentence; we already know what the topic is. The topic is the place, and the paragraph has unity because we can see that every sentence describes an activity possible in this place.

In argument or exposition, topic sentences often have the flavor of philosophical propositions. For instance:

> When a man needs help, he must know where to turn.

> The nineteenth-century politician's biblical oratory is no longer effective.

> The paragraph is a unit of sense, a discrete idea or topic.

In narrative and descriptive writing, topic sentences often change the scene or introduce signposts in complicated country. Here are some sentences that could be lead-ins to new paragraphs.

Finally, he thought it was time to return.

The weather turned fine.

When they turned the corner, the street changed abruptly.

Election night began with a bad omen.

When he heard footsteps outside in the darkness, he turned off the oil lamps and reached for his gun.

The final chapters seem pointless.

When we revise our prose, it is useful to look into our paragraphs for topic sentences. We do not demand that every paragraph have one—but the *idea* of a topic sentence is a means of focusing and unifying and is therefore essential to clear and forceful prose. We look for the topic sentence of a paragraph—overt or implicit, at beginning, middle, or end—to see if the paragraph is sufficiently unified.

## COHERENCE IN THE PARAGRAPH

Frequently, in unfinished writing, a sentence seems extraneous or irrelevant; the writer has a use for the information, but he has been unable to build the sentence smoothly into his thought. If a fact does not belong in a paragraph, it causes disunity. If it only *seems* not to belong, it causes incoherence.

The writer must learn how to blend his information so that it coheres in a meaningful whole: the relationship between the sentences must be clear, and the paragraph must seem a whole, not just a collection of individual sentences. Here is an incoherent paragraph from some daily writing.

> I had been having severe headaches and frequent dizzy spells. I was terrified of doctors. I went to the health clinic. I waited three days. It was the time of finals and I was very busy. I saw a doctor. He prescribed some pills. The problems continued.

It is impossible to tell what the relationships are between the bits of information related here. Did the speaker wait three days before or after going to the health clinic? Did she wait because of her fear of doctors or because she was busy? Was she busy studying for finals, or doing something else? Not only is the sense confused, but the rhythm is irritatingly choppy. Here is a revised and more coherent version of the passage.

I had been having severe headaches and frequent dizzy spells, but I hesitated to go to the health clinic because I was terrified of doctors. It was the time of finals and I was busy studying for them, so I made the excuse to myself that I didn't have time and that there was nothing the matter with me, just fatigue. Finally, I went, although I waited three days before making an appointment. I saw a doctor, and after he examined me he prescribed some pills. But despite the medication, the problems continued, even after I'd been taking the pills for two weeks.

Notice that much of the coherence comes from using conjunctions and subordinate clauses. Although most facts remain the same, the writer has given the reader much more information, because she has connected the facts in a coherent paragraph, using complex sentences and transitions. The revision illustrates how a writer can take a mere list of facts and, by keeping her audience in mind, build them into a statement that leaves no question unanswered. In revising, the writer found it necessary to add a few facts—that she was busy studying for exams, that she took the pills for two weeks—which she had omitted from the original paragraph, before she had realized that her audience would need to know them.

We achieve coherence in our writing when our paragraphs answer the questions that they raise in the reader's mind. If we merely write,

I was terrified of doctors. I went to the health clinic.

the reader is going to ask, "If you're so afraid of doctors, what compelled you to go?" If we don't answer the invisible question, the paragraph will lack coherence, and the reader will be frustrated or confused.

Similarly, when we make a general assertion, we create the expectation that we will defend it. The reader expects us to justify or explain a statement like "The public was responsible for the war's continuation" or "Statistics show us that the VHS tapes will eventually drive out Betas." The reader does not, presumably, know as much as we know about our chosen subject; we must give the detail, background, statistics, reasons, or explanations that our audience requires and expects of us. We write exposition to deliver information or ideas to other people.

We establish another type of expectation when we use an extended metaphor to enliven and organize a paragraph. Here is a passage from a student paper.

The beast of civil war lay outside the sheepfold, and its roaring could be heard within the gates. At first its voice, as it had begun to slink out of the foothills, had been low and faint. Then, as it drew nearer to the town, the explosions of large artillery shells had been its approaching steps, and the different pitches of the voice—the snarling of machine guns, the howls of mortar shells—had grown distinct. Now the beast clawed at the walls and breathed heavily on the gates with its mouth aflame. The sheep within huddled together, knowing their throats would soon feel the enemy's teeth, knowing the shepherd had fallen asleep.

The extended metaphor compares the enemy to a predatory beast, the city to a sheepfold, and its citizens to helpless sheep. The metaphor makes another kind of coherence, which we would violate if we shifted metaphors in the middle of the paragraph.

> . . . At first its voice, as it had begun to slink out of the foothills, had been low and faint. Then, as it drew nearer, the infernal machine could be heard stomping out death on the plain with the press of bombs, and the different sounds—the grinding of machine gun fire, the chunking of mortars—had grown distinct. Now the beast clawed . . .

### Coherence and Consistency

We should know a few more mechanical ways to maintain coherence in the paragraph. Just as we need agreement within a sentence, we need agreement within a paragraph. We should avoid changes in verb tense. It is easy, if we let our minds wander, to begin writing a passage or paragraph in one tense and then switch to another. We may begin in the present tense to be dramatic and then slip into the past tense because the events described actually occurred in the past.

> He sits on the dock, his feet bare on the warm wood, his eyes half-closed in the hot sun, daydreaming about women in black silk dresses. Suddenly he felt a violent tugging on the pole, and a long shape thrashed in the water ten feet away.

Or we may begin in the past tense and abruptly shift to the present tense, without realizing it, because we want greater immediacy.

> He sat on the dock, his feet bare on the warm wood, his eyes half-closed in the hot sun, and daydreamed about women in black silk dresses. Suddenly he feels a violent tugging on the pole, and sees a long shape thrash in the water only ten feet away.

In rare instances, when skillfully done, a shift in verb tense can serve a purpose—but almost always such shifts are mistakes that proofreading should correct.

Another common violation of coherence is to shift pronouns within a paragraph. If we start with *we*, we should not switch to *you*. We must be careful, if we have chosen to use the formal *one*, that we do not fall back into *I* or *you*.

> But if *one* has experienced the mystical conversion described by adepts in almost every culture in the world, *one* may still fall back into the old dualities and pettinesses. But once *we* have felt that stronger intensity of being, *you* can never again remain satisfied with less. The ghost of that experience haunts *us* like a dead loved one.

Coherence and consistency of paragraphs are goals essential to the final shape and value of the essay. In the stages of writing we may not achieve this coherence and consistency until we have written several drafts. After we have sketched our rough ideas, after we have begun to find phrases and sentences to express the ideas, we must edit and revise, refine and shape, to make a point and to reach an audience by means of coherence and consistency.

### Coherence and the Paragraph: Transitions

Transitions in our writing are devices for moving from one place to another. They range from single words like *but* to phrases like *on the other hand*, and to subtler devices like repetition or parallelism. Transitions are essential to the coherence of paragraph and paper. You might expect to find this topic with the last chapter, on sentences, or further on, in connection with whole essays, but I put it here because transitions happen *within* the paragraph as a way to move from one sentence to another or *between* paragraphs as a way of moving from topic to topic while keeping the essay whole. *Transitions are thus essential to coherence in paragraph and paper.* A prose insufficient in transitions is nervous and obscure. It leaps from subject to subject, without stated or implied connection. The connection remains in the writer's mind.

*Overt Transitions.* Often a transition needs to be obvious to carry the reader along our passage of thought, to make sure we don't lose him. Perhaps we are making an overt contrast. To draw attention to the contrast, we say, "on the one hand . . . on the other"—which is trite but hard to avoid. Or we use the context of our discussion: "Although most transitions are best left implicit, some are properly overt."

Often we need overt transitions when ideas or actions conflict, when the essay's meaning depends upon fully exploiting the reality in that conflict. Or if we are piling detail upon detail, we might want to use a transition that calls attention to our multiplicity: "not only . . . but also." Prose that explains, reasons, or argues frequently uses overt transitions.

> Viewed from a suitable height, the aggregating clusters of medical scientists in the bright sunlight of the boardwalk at Atlantic City, swarmed there from everywhere for the annual meetings, have the look of assemblages of social insects. There is the same vibrating, ionic movement, interrupted by the darting back and forth of jerky individuals to touch antennae and exchange small bits of information; periodically, the mass casts out, like a trout-line, a long single file unerringly toward Childs's. If the boards were not fastened down, it would not be a surprise to see them put together a nest of sorts.
> It is permissible to say this sort of thing about humans. . . .
> Lewis Thomas, "On Societies as Organisms"

Here Lewis Thomas uses "this sort of thing," at the beginning of a new paragraph, as a transitional phrase referring to the comparison made in the preceding paragraph.

*Repeated Words or Phrases.* One way to achieve continuity within a paragraph (or between paragraphs), to make transitions between sentences and between statements, is to repeat words or phrases. One of the simplest of these devices, so simple that we might not think of it as one, is repeating pronouns. We use it for both economy and continuity.

> Not too long ago *a male friend of mine* appeared on the scene fresh from a recent divorce. *He* had one child, who is, of course, with *his* ex-wife. *He* is looking for another wife. As I thought about *him* while I was ironing one evening, it suddenly occurred to me that I, too, would like to have a wife. Why do I want a wife? (Italics added)
> Judy Syfers, "I Want a Wife"

But you should be careful when using a repeated pronoun, because if it is repeated too often, it can become monotonous and confusing. You can get variety and clarity by occasionally using the name the pronoun refers to. A writer also has to make sure that the reader knows what each pronoun refers to. If we say, "Mr. Cortazar saw that the man was following him closely; he stared at him," it is not clear who is doing the staring. Here we may need to be more explicit: "Mr. Cortazar saw that the man was following him closely; Mr. Cortazar stared at him."

Not only pronouns but any word or phrase can be repeated to make effective transitions—if it is important to the meaning or the emotional tenor in the passage.

> If we once accept the premise that we can build a better world by using the different gifts of each *sex*, we shall have two kinds of freedom, freedom to use untapped gifts of each *sex*, and freedom to admit freely and cultivate in each *sex* their special superiorities. We may well find that there are certain fields, such as the physical sciences, mathematics and instrumental music, in which *men* by virtue of their *sex*, as well as by virtue of their qualities as specially gifted human beings, will always have that razor-edge of extra gift which makes all the difference. . . .
>
> This has meant that *men* had to be willing to choose, win, and keep women as *lovers*, protect and provide for them as *husbands*, and protect and provide for their children as *fathers*. It has meant that women have had to be willing to accept *men* as lovers, live with them as wives, and conceive, bear, feed and cherish their children. Any society disappears which fails to make these demands on its members and to receive this much from them.
>
> But from *men*, society has also asked and received something more than this. For thousands of generations *men* have been asked to do something more than be good *lovers* and *husbands* and *fathers*, even with all that that involved of husbandry and organization and protection against attack. . . . (Italics added)
>
> Margaret Mead, *Male and Female*

If we want to avoid monotonous repetition, we can use variations (near-synonyms) for the key words in some places.

> His *sculptures* seem like men and women stripped naked. They are *works of art* that seem to lack all artifice, *plastic creations* which, in their emotional if not in their physical presence, have the feeling of natural, organic creations.

These methods are commonly used for transition *between* paragraphs as well.

. . . and the importance of spatial form in *modern* literature.
   *Modern* thought, as well, has used the metaphor of dimensional-
ity. . . .

*Parallel Constructions.* We can repeat structures as well as words.
Parallel constructions (see Parallelism, pages 184–188) can fulfill a
need for transition that is not only structural and logical, but emotional; passages with parallel sentences can work like sentences with
parallel phrases, to produce a dramatic effect or to maintain emotional
tension.

> Today, now that he is no longer among us, *who can replace* my
> old friend at the gates of this kingdom? *Who will look after* the
> garden until we can get back to it? . . . (Italics added)
>                           Albert Camus, "Encounters with André Gide"

> *We describe* how the poor are plundered *by the rich.* We live
> *among the rich.* Live on the plunder and pander ideas *to the rich.*
> *We have described* the *torture* and we have put our names under
> appeals against *torture*, but we did not stop it. (And we ourselves
> became *torturers* when the higher interests demanded *torture* and
> we became the ideologists of *torture.*) Now *we once more can
> analyze* the world situation and *describe* the wars and explain why
> the many are poor and hungry. But we do no more.
>    *We are not the bearers of consciousness. We are the whores of
> reason.* (Italics added)
>                           Jan Myrdal, *Confessions of a Disloyal European*

Parallel constructions that repeat part of a phrase are common and
useful transitions, especially in exposition and in argument.

> . . . and they never decided whether they were *Bulgarians or Ameri-
> cans, rich or poor, artists or dilettantes.*
>    And we, on our part, could not decide whether they were *heroes
> or frauds.* . . .

*On our part*, in the last sentence, is an overt transition.

*Transitional Words and Phrases.* We use many transitional
phrases to establish the relationship between sentences and between
paragraphs and to prepare the reader for shifts in subject or meaning. The
most common are words like *and, but, or* and *for.* Some are words of
sequence and time—*meanwhile, afterward, before;* of qualification—

*again, also, nonetheless;* and of reasoning—*for example, because, therefore.* Although we often try to avoid phrases like these in fiction or narrative, they are useful and often essential to exposition or argument. Their very commonness and simplicity make them valuable to clarify a sequence of thought. These paragraph openings use common phrases to accomplish transitions; they are taken from *The Naked Ape* by Desmond Morris:

> *Up to this point* I have been concentrating on the social aspects of comfort behaviour in our species. . . .

> *In addition* to problems of keeping clean, the general category of comfort behaviour also includes . . .

> *Because* of his exploratory and opportunist nature, the naked ape's list of prey species is immense. . . .

> *For the next major category,* that of parasites . . .

> *In order to* find the answer to this question we must first assemble some facts. . . .

We commonly use comparison and contrast for transitions, especially in criticism and analysis. The means of transition are relatively simple. We describe one of the objects for examination in one paragraph and then, in a following paragraph, compare and contrast traits of the other. When we turn to the second object, we often begin with one of the transitional phrases that make for comparison or contrast, like *similarly, in the same vein,* or *however, on the other hand, in contrast,* or *contrary to.*

> Freud gave a picture of the unconscious mind as containing primarily memories and the remnants of suppressed desires. He saw the sexual drives as being the foundation of the unconscious.
>
> Jung, *on the other hand,* claimed that Freud's depth psychology wasn't deep enough, that there was another aspect of the unconscious which contained spiritual drives as important as the sexual drives. . . .

Remember that even in expository prose it is better to leave out well-worn phrases *if the sense is just as clear without them.* Many times, we can cut out the obvious direction signals and rely on implicit transition.

Some of the most obvious clues to transition—within the paragraph or between paragraphs—are words of sequence, like *therefore, later, so, then,* and *next.* They are so obvious that it is pleasant to do without them, if we can.

*Implicit Transitions.* The order within the paragraph can itself be a means of transition. It gives the paragraph motion; it gives a reason for one sentence following another: left to right, down to up, smaller to larger; or other sorts of order: color to shape, spring to summer to fall to winter; or orders of ideas: from more obvious to less obvious, from less complex to more complex. These motions are clear enough in themselves to allow the movement from subject to subject without explicit directions. We need not say, "after spring came summer," within a paragraph, unless we are writing for people we can presume unaware of the order the seasons follow. We would be more likely to move from rain and early flowers to the longest day of the year, to hot sun and to swimming and to no school.

Sometimes the rest between paragraphs acts as transition. We take a breath, and we pivot on the pause. It shows that we are moving from one grouping to another. We don't always have to be reminded that we are moving. Sometimes we do, and sometimes we do not. Develop *tact* for transitions. Develop a sense also for the multiple means of transition. A good writer uses implicit, overt, parallel, repetitive, and many other forms of transition, and uses them in rapid sequence as he moves through his paragraphs and from paragraph to paragraph. Transitions in complex expository writing are constant and multiple, overt and implicit. Much that is implied depends on orderly thinking and a clear sense of what the reader needs to know.

Suppose we catalogue everything in a boy's pockets. The next paragraph could begin: "Therefore, his pockets bulged as he walked, and he bumped into tables when he passed them. In fact, he bumped into almost everything. . . ." The paragraph could go on about his *clumsiness.* But the *therefore* at the beginning is unnecessary. It is obvious, if we have catalogued twenty items, that these items bulge out his pockets. Transition can be found in image. No reader need be led by the hand so carefully. The paragraph break could read like this:

> . . . He had on his person two rubber bands, a golf tee, two notes from a teacher, a bottle cap, and a gray-brown handkerchief.
>
> His pockets bulged as he walked, he bumped into tables when he passed them. In fact, he bumped into almost everything. . . .

The word *his*, referring to an antecedent in the previous paragraph, holds the two paragraphs together.

Transitions are a glue that holds parts together. You need enough, or the parts will fall apart. But if you have too much, you will see the glue instead of the parts. The space between the catalogue and the bulging pockets is a sort of invisible glue—but it holds because we have sense enough to know that the objects listed cause the bulging. The next transition, from pockets to clumsiness, is less obvious and more necessary. It takes more doing. The only thing that bulging pockets share with clumsiness is that the little boy possesses both of them. Of course we could use a generality for a transition.

> . . . a bottle cap, and a gray-brown handkerchief.
>     In fact, he was generally rather gross and clumsy. He bumped into everything. . . .

This transition would work, but it is not elegant. It is obvious and general. Suppose in the next paragraph we want to talk about his table manners, do we say again that he was "gross and clumsy"? No, we have used these words up. The stylish transition happens without drawing attention to itself. We move from pockets to bumping into things by picturing the boy bumping into tables with his fat pockets, and then we do a turn on the word *bumping* and we are off into a new subject before the reader knows it. We want to move the reader from one subject to another gently, by the elbow, and if we have done the job well, the reader does not feel the guiding fingers touch his arm.

_____ **EXERCISES** _____

1. These sentences have been extracted from an orderly paragraph and rearranged. Restore them to a sequence that makes sense. You are reader, making the writer's text over for yourself.

a. But within the economics of energy and nature, it is a catastrophe.

b. It is the maintstay of the economy of money.

c. With its array of gadgets and machines, all powered by energies that are destructive of land or air or water, and connected to work, market, school, recreation, etc., by gasoline engines, the modern home is a veritable factory of waste and destruction.

d. It takes in the world's goods and converts them into garbage, sewage, and noxious fumes—for none of which we have found a use.
Wendell Berry, *The Unsettling of America*

2. Decide which sentence functions as a topic sentence in each paragraph. Could it be moved to another place in the paragraph? What would be the effect?

a. Skill is the connection between life and tools, or life and machines. Once, skill was defined ultimately in qualitative terms: How *well* did a person work; how good, durable, and pleasing were his products? But as machines have grown larger and more complex, and as our awe of them and our desire for labor-saving have grown, we have tended more and more to define skill quantitatively: How speedily and cheaply can a person work? We have increasingly wanted a measurable skill. And the more quantifiable skills became, the easier they were to replace with machines. As machines replace skill, they disconnect themselves from life; they come between us and life. They begin to enact our ignorance of value—of essential sources, dependences, and relationships.
Wendell Berry, *The Unsettling of America*

b. From a public point of view, the specialist system is a failure because, though everything is done by an expert, very little is done well. Our typical industrial or professional product is both ingenious and shoddy. The specialist system fails from a personal point of view because a person who can do only one thing can do virtually nothing for himself. In living in the world by his own will and skill, the stupidest peasant or tribesman is more competent than the most intelligent worker or technician or intellectual in a society of specialists.
Wendell Berry, *The Unsettling of America*

3. Analyze these paragraphs for their unity. (a) Do any of these paragraphs have extraneous material? (b) Does each paragraph contain a topic sentence? Underline topic sentences, and discuss in class. (c) What does the position of each topic sentence accomplish, if anything?

a. The sea, autumn mildness, islands bathed in light, fine rain spreading a diaphanous veil over the immortal nakedness of Greece. Happy is the man, I thought, who, before dying, has the good fortune to sail the Aegean Sea.
Many are the joys of this world—women, fruit, ideas. But to cleave that sea in the gentle, autumnal season, murmuring the name of each islet, is to my mind the joy most apt to transport the heart of man into paradise. Nowhere else can one pass so easily and serenely from reality

to dream. The frontiers dwindle, and from the masts of the most ancient ships spring branches and fruits. It is as if here in Greece necessity is the mother of miracles.

Towards noon the rain stopped. The sun parted the clouds and appeared gentle, tender, washed and fresh, and it caressed with its rays the beloved waters and lands. I stood at the prow and let myself be intoxicated with the miracle which was revealed as far as the eye could see.

Nikos Kazantzakis, *Zorba the Greek*

b. A philosopher—is a human being who constantly experiences, sees, hears, suspects, hopes, and dreams extraordinary things; who is struck by his own thoughts as from outside, as from above and below, and by *his* type of experiences and lightning bolts; who is perhaps himself a storm pregnant with new lightnings; a fatal human being around whom there are constant rumblings and growlings, crevices, and uncanny doings. A philosopher—alas, a being that often runs away from itself, often is afraid of itself—but too inquisitive not to "come to" again—always back to himself.

Friedrich Nietzsche, *Beyond Good and Evil*

4. Here are some incoherent paragraphs. (a) Consider the different sorts of incoherence in each paragraph. Which paragraphs can profit by reorganization? In class, reorganize them. (b) Which paragraphs need further development in order to achieve coherence? In class, speculate on the directions development might take. (c) What reasonable readers' expectations do these paragraphs violate?

a. The heavy wooden door was painted red, but the wood showed through in many places where the paint was flaking off. Dandelions covered the lawn, but there were few weeds in the dark grass. A white and black cat lay curled by the door. Three huge oaks threw their shadows across the wide lawn. Far off, a deer was watching from the edge of the woods. There was no knob on the door.

b. The days were unusually hot and humid, even for that part of the state. Joe didn't want to go to the beach. His girlfriend, Linda, did. She wasn't a good swimmer. She loved to swim. Joe was working on his car. He was a fanatical sports enthusiast.

c. He had found that the wolves subsisted mainly on a diet of mice. Farley had been dropped in the middle of the Canadian tundra. He discovered that the hunters were lying, and that they themselves were the insane murderers. Hunters had been complaining that the wolves were slaughtering thousands of caribou for the sheer pleasure of killing. He had made an astonishing discovery. He had been assigned to investigate the killing of caribou by timber wolves.

d. Robert and Daniel crouched in the cave, listening for the sound of approaching footsteps. He thought the troops must have left the area by now. For the moment he was reassured by the silence, but he worried about the sharp pain in his knee, and he wondered if he would be able to walk on it if he had to. He was glad to have his old friend with him. He looked at him. Their gazes meeting, he felt tears come to his eyes from straining to see in the half-darkness, and from thinking where he and his friend had been just yesterday.

c. When the gate opens at last, four thousand music lovers push, crush, and shove each other forward in an immense mass. The sun glares down, the musicians struggle to tune their sweaty instruments, and the ice cream salesman exhausts his stores in twenty minutes. Finally the music started at 1:30.

5. Here are two coherent paragraphs, from the essay in which E. B. White speaks of Simonizing his grandmother. Look at these paragraphs for their unity and their coherence. (a) How does White achieve consistency within these paragraphs? (b) How does he accomplish transitions?

Communication by the written word is a subtler (and more beautiful) thing than Dr. Flesch and General Motors imagine. They contend that the "average reader" is capable of reading only what tests Easy, and that the writer should write at or below this level. This is a presumptuous and degrading idea. There is no average reader, and to reach down toward this mythical character is to deny that each of us is on the way up, is ascending. ("Ascending," by the way, is a word Dr. Flesch advises writers to stay away from. Too unusual.)

It is my belief that no writer can improve his work until he discards the dulcet notion that the reader is feebleminded, for writing is an act of faith, not a trick of grammar. Ascent is at the heart of the matter. A country whose writers are following a calculating machine downstairs is not ascending—if you will pardon the expression—and a writer who questions the capacity of the person at the other end of the line is not a writer at all, merely a schemer. The movies long ago decided that a wider communication could be achieved by a deliberate descent to a lower level, and they walked proudly down until they reached the cellar. Now they are groping for the light switch, hoping to find the way out.

E. B. White, "Calculating Machine"

6. A student writing an essay about a teacher's strike wanted to make these points in one paragraph:

1. Teachers have no legal right to strike.

2. The teachers' union claims the strike is their constitutional right.

3. Some school boards try to fire striking teachers and hire new ones.

4. Striking teachers sometimes find judges who will issue injunctions against this firing and hiring.

5. Picketing disrupts the classes with new teachers.

Here is a first draft of the paragraph.

> Of course it's against the law for teachers to strike anyway. Some teachers say that the law against striking is unconstitutional. So the school board fires the teachers who are striking and hires new teachers who are looking for work. The striking teachers get a judge to make an injunction against the school board. The picketing disrupts classes with the new teachers.

This first attempt was incoherent. Does the paragraph have a topic sentence? Does it have *a topic?* Does one sentence follow from another? Does the last sentence appear to belong in the paragraph? Rewrite this paragraph, paying special attention to coherence. Or write a paragraph of your own using the student's five points as rough notes.

7. Analyze these paragraphs for their transitions, both within paragraphs and between them.

When Saint-Exupéry begins his second paragraph, which word especially links it to the end of the first paragraph? What binds the third paragraph to the second? When the fourth paragraph follows the third, an idea rather than a word makes the transition; underline the words that are intellectually related to each other.

> Once again I had found myself in the presence of a truth and had failed to recognize it. Consider what had happened to me: I had thought myself lost, had touched the very bottom of despair; and then, when the spirit of renunciation had filled me, I had known peace. I know now what I was not conscious of at the time—that in such an hour a man feels that he has finally found himself and has become his own friend. An essential inner need has been satisfied, and against that satisfaction, that self-fulfillment, no external power can prevail. Bonnafous, I imagine, he who spent his life racing before the wind, was acquainted with this serenity of spirit. Guillaumet, too, in his snows. Never shall I forget that, lying buried to the chin in sand, strangled slowly to death by thirst, my heart was infinitely warm beneath the desert stars.
>
> What can men do to make known to themselves this sense of deliverance? Everything about mankind is paradox. He who strives and conquers grows soft. The magnanimous man grown rich becomes mean. The creative artist for whom everything is made easy nods. Every doctrine swears that it can breed men, but none can tell us in advance what sort of men it will breed. Men are not cattle to be fattened for market. On the scales of life an indigent Newton weighs more than a parcel of prosperous nonentities. All of us have had the experience of a sudden joy that came when nothing in the world had forewarned us of its coming—a joy so thrilling that if it was born of misery we remembered even the misery with tenderness. All of us, on seeing old friends

again, have remembered with happiness the trials we lived through with those friends. Of what can we be certain except this—that we are fertilized by mysterious circumstances? Where is man's truth to be found?

Truth is not that which can be demonstrated by the aid of logic. If orange-trees are hardy and rich in fruit in this bit of soil and not that, then this bit of soil is what is truth for orange-trees. If a particular religion, or culture, or scale of values, if one form of activity rather than another, brings self-fulfillment to a man, releases the prince asleep within him unknown to himself, then that scale of values, that culture, that form of activity, constitute his truth. Logic, you say? Let logic wangle its own explanation of life.

Because it is man and not flying that concerns me most, I shall close this book with the story of man's gropings towards self-fulfillment as I witnessed them in the early months of the civil war in Spain. One year after crashing in the desert I made a tour of the Catalan front in order to learn what happens to man when the scaffolding of his traditions suddenly collapses. To Madrid I went for an answer to another question: How does it happen that men are sometimes willing to die?

Antoine de Saint-Exupéry, *Wind, Sand and Stars*

8. In this passage by Michael Walzer, underline the topic sentence of the first paragraph. (a) How does the paragraph grow from this sentence? (b) Is every other sentence in this paragraph related to the topic sentence? (c) How do the sentences proceed? Underline transitions. (d) Do you find implicit transitions in this paragraph, and later between paragraphs? Find the basis for each implicit transition.

Politics is first of all the art of minimizing and controlling violence. It is a taxing and morally dangerous art because violence itself and the threat of violence are two of its instruments. These can be put to use with almost equal ease by the public authorities and by private men and women, but almost always more massively and more effectively by the authorities. So it is best to begin by worrying about them.

War, riot control, law enforcement, "maintenance of order," punishment: all these can involve violence. The word itself calls to mind (to my mind, at least) a charging phalanx of helmeted police, an image fixed, I suppose, as much by the media as by recent events. It is by no means an accurate picture of what it is sometimes said to represent: the state stripped naked. But it does make it impossible to pretend that "the use of physical force to inflict injury" (the dictionary definition of violent behavior) is something other than violent whenever the users are uniformed officials, and it is equally impossible to argue that official violence is somehow presumptively legitimate. Even the justification of punishment, the most ordinary form of official violence, is uncertain and much disputed among philosophers. The intermittent violence of everyday law enforcement is more commonly questioned, especially since historians began to compile the record of police and militia brutality against labor organizers, radical agitators, ethnic and racial minorities. And just as the state's use of violence is often cruel, needless, and illegitimate, so the state possesses no monopoly on legitimate use. We deny its monopoly every time we assert the right of self-defense or of collective resistance to tyranny.

What the state does have and should have is control—in this country it has exclusive control—of the means of massive violence, both human and material: the army and police, planes, tanks, artillery, and so on. Only the ownership of guns is legally the right of individuals in the United States, and this is a right increasingly questioned—for very good reasons. The case for state control of the means of massive violence is so widely accepted that I need not review it here. I have to stress instead that the existence of such control, however justified, also establishes the state as a threat to us all. The threat is simply that violence will be used, as it has been so often in the past, not to protect everyone's rights or to enforce policies democratically agreed upon, but to defend the privileges of some few of us or to interfere with or repress democratic liberties. Obviously, no guarantees are possible here. Official violence is like unofficial violence, at least in this regard: it too inflicts injury, and it needs (in every case) to be justified. From the time of Thomas Hobbes on, the most successful efforts to justify the use of violence have undoubtedly been undertaken on behalf of the state. But these efforts do not free us from the burden of asking ourselves, over and over again, what are the prospects for the use of military and police power? Insofar as we defend state control, we have an obligation to watch over it.

Michael Walzer, *Radical Principles*

9. Find topic sentences in Saint-Exupéry and transitions in Waltzer. In both passages look for purpose and shape, focusing, unity, and coherence.

---

## DEVELOPMENT IN THE PARAGRAPH

Once we pass beyond the single sentence, we become involved in development and its problems. We discussed development in earlier sections of this chapter, when we mentioned using topic sentences to achieve unity and explaining general statements to achieve coherence. The requirements of unity and coherence overlap with the requirements of development. As we must develop paragraphs to substantiate generalizations, so too we must develop paragraphs to make our associations clear to the reader. Frequently, we lack fullness of development because we do not take the reader into account. We put forward a generalization, perhaps, and a conclusion that we have arrived at, but we do not lead the reader through the thinking that proceeds from introduction to conclusion. Perhaps in our own thinking we have leapt from generalization to conclusion by intuition—but the reader will not necessarily leap along with us.

Eventually, as we go over development, we will need to investigate length and order. But first, we must look at methods for developing paragraphs.

### Some Ways of Developing Paragraphs

We can develop a paragraph in countless ways. No list can be comprehensive. But looking at some methods of paragraph development can help us to see the range of possibilities. The type of development we choose—the *how* in the paragraph—depends on the material we are using—the *what* in the paragraph—and the purpose we have in mind—the *why* of the paragraph. If we are listing Paraguay's annual imports, we develop by listing, and not by comparison and contrast. *The container takes its shape from what it contains.* One of our tasks in organizing a paper is to find the means of development that is *most appropriate to our material.*

Earlier we spoke of improvised shape, like generalization followed by qualification followed by example, or question and answer (objection and rebuttal). We have also mentioned chronology and spatial contiguity as useful ways of organizing paragraphs (see also pages 254–255). We need to consider a few more. On occasion the reader must learn *what* something is; the writer must develop a paragraph by means of *definition.* Sometimes a reader needs to know what something is *like* or *not like;* the writer must develop a paragraph of *comparison* or *comparison and contrast.* Sometimes the reader needs to know the *parts* of a thing, what makes it up; the writer must supply *analysis.* Or the writer must use *classification,* he must tell us the species of something, perhaps; is it animal or vegetable? Sometimes we must develop our notion of a thing by discussing its *cause* and its *effect.*

These rhetorical patterns return for lengthier discussion in Chapter 7. They can serve as models for whole essays, but more commonly they provide us shapes for whole paragraphs; certainly these patterns suggest means of development. When we find an unsupported generalization, we discover an opportunity for development, making use of the rhetorical pattern of example. But all processes of writing can help paragraph development. When we revise we should be alert for the journalist's six questions (see pages 59–60), and for opportunities to reach our audience by explaining—which is after all the function of exposition.

We may organize a paragraph to *define* or *elucidate:*

> An addict does not merely pursue a pleasurable experience and need to experience it in order to function normally. He needs to *repeat* it again and again. Something about that particular experience makes life without it less than complete. Other potentially pleasurable experiences are no longer possible, for under the spell of the addictive experience, his life is peculiarly distorted. The addict craves an experience and yet he is never really satisfied. The organism may be temporarily sated, but soon it begins to crave again.
>
> Marie Winn, "Television Addiction"

The paragraph begins in the negative, dispelling a common assumption, and defines by isolating distinctive features.

Or we can develop paragraphs to *compare* and *contrast:*

> In other respects, the film follows Hearst's career with mixed fidelity. The plot adjustments are significant. Both Hearst and Kane were only children, born in 1863, and both were expelled from Harvard. Hearst's father and mother were not, like Kane's, poverty-stricken boardinghouse keepers. George Hearst was a well-to-do farmer's son, whose silver strike at the Comstock lode made him a millionaire, and whose later interest in the Homestake Mine still further increased his massive fortune; he became a senator and earned a respected place in the *American Dictionary of Biography.* In the film these parents are left a deed to the Colorado Lode by a defaulting boarder, Fred Grange, and the Kane fortune is thus founded not by the acumen and push of a paternal figure but by blind chance.
>
> Charles Higham, *The Films of Orson Welles*

Comparison and contrast works when we talk about a relationship or conflict, and are not merely separating facts about two or more subjects. Here, the first sentence states the mixture that is the paragraph's topic, and the rest of the paragraph gives examples of each ingredient in the mixture. Notice that the paragraph, when it compares and contrasts Hearst's life with Kane's, carefully maintains the order in which it first mentions them: Hearst-Kane. This order helps to avoid confusion, and makes for coherence.

Or, to *analyze:*

> The "me decade" did not result from a sudden effusion of selfishness or decadence; it is the logical consequence of a public surface tolerance combined with a loss of individual historical depth. In a sense, people become more like one another (wear the same clothes, go to the same schools, read the same books, are informed by the same media, go to the same parties, are "liberated" into the same mores). In another sense, they lose the social inheritances that, while differentiating them from one another, also instilled in them profound common values. Inwardly, each is animated by nothing more profound than personal preference and idiosyncrasy. Homogenized yet fragmented, the society of the supreme "me" (find yourself, be true to yourself) is the logical expression of a materialistic humanism.
>
> Michael Novak, "On God and Man"

We analyze when we need to explain or to demonstrate the mechanism of a process or an act. We tell how it works rather than what it is. Novak points out possible reasons for the modern cult of the self, and then argues step by step to show the larger causes that underlie the reasons.

We can also develop paragraphs to *classify:*

> We can thus say that while the average human being is a mixture, some people are mainly "digestion-minded," some "muscle-minded," and some "brain-minded," and correspondingly digestion-bodied, muscle-bodied, or brain-bodied. The digestion-bodied people look thick; the muscle-bodied people look wide; and the brain-bodied people look long. This does not mean the taller a man is the brainier he will be. It means that if a man, even a short man, looks long rather than wide or thick, he will often be more concerned about what goes on in his mind than about what he does or what he eats; but the key factor is slenderness and not height. On the other hand, a man who gives the impression of being thick rather than long or wide will usually be more interested in a good steak than in a good idea or a good long walk.
>
> Eric Berne, "Can People Be Judged by Their Appearance?"
> in *A Layman's Guide to Psychiatry and Psychoanalysis*

Berne separates people into groups according to their bodily appearance, relating psychological classifications to physical ones.

This paragraph, from an essay about television advertising, is developed to show *cause and effect:*

> There is good reason to suspect that this manic obsession with cleanliness, fostered, quite naturally, by the giant soap and detergent interests, may bear some responsibility for the cultivated sloppiness of so many of the young in their clothing as well as in their chosen hideouts. The compulsive housewife who spends more time washing and vacuuming and polishing her possessions than communicating to, or stimulating her children creates a kind of sterility that the young would instinctively reject. The impeccably tidy home, the impeccably tidy lawn are—in a very real sense—unnatural and confining. Yet the commercials confront us with broods of happy children, some of whom—believe it or not—notice the new fresh smell their clean, white sweatshirts exhale thanks to Mom's new "softener."
>
> Marya Mannes, "Television Advertising: The Splitting Image"

In her argument, the writer observes negative results of advertising, where an image of cleanliness leads to a slovenly reality.

We may organize a paragraph to *make an assertion and give reasons:*

> The country is vastly indebted to him [Louis Brandeis] for his creative work in the field of labor relations, in dispelling misunderstanding between management and labor, and in making collective bargaining an effective instrument for industrial peace. He successfully arbitrated or conciliated many labor disputes. In 1910 he was arbiter of a serious strike in the New York City garment trade. Not content with settling the immediate dispute, he devised the famous "protocol" for the permanent government of labor relations in the industry, with provision for the preferential union shop, for a Joint Board of Sanitary Control, and for a continuing Board of Arbitration composed of representatives of the public as well as of the employers and the union. The procedures thus developed and successfully tested served as a model in other industries. For several years he served as impartial chairman of this board of arbitration.
>
> Irwin H. Pollock, *The Brandeis Reader*

The writer begins with a contention and then substantiates it by reciting information upon which he bases it.

Or to *make a statement and then give relevant facts:*

> Gandhi recognized that the whites in South Africa thought they needed protection against a majority consisting of Negroes and

Indians. The province of Natal, in 1896, had 400,000 Negro inhabitants, 51,000 Indians, and 50,000 whites. The Cape of Good Hope Colony had 900,000 Negroes, 10,000 Indians, and 400,000 Europeans; the Transvaal Republic 650,000 Negroes, 5,000 Indians, and 120,000 whites. In 1944, the five million Negroes hopelessly outnumbered the million and a quarter whites.

> Louis Fischer, *Gandhi: His Life and Message for the World*

This last category resembles the one before it, except that *facts* (or statistics) take the place of *reasons,* which are arguments based on a value put on events.

Or to *list:*

Now the leadership elements of the Democratic Party began to filter through the suite of the nominee in a parade that was to last the rest of the day, to assist him in making up their mind. First of the big-city leaders to arrive was David Lawrence of Pennsylvania. Following him came the New York crowd—Wagner, Harriman, DeSapio and Prendergast; then William Green of Philadelphia; then DiSalle of Ohio; then Bailey and Ribicoff of Connecticut; then all the others.

> Theodore H. White, *The Making of the President 1960*

First, White tells us what sort of men they are whose names will follow, and then the occasion that brought the men together, and then the names.

Even in the examples chosen, these methods are not exclusive. One paragraph may use more than one method, or one method may involve another. "Relevant facts" usually come in "lists." In the next paragraph, the author develops the idea primarily by an assertion followed by reasons, and his final sentence is a list.

If conventions epitomize the mythology and legendry of American national politics, then Chicago epitomizes the convention city. For one hundred years, ever since the nomination of Abraham Lincoln at the Wigwam, it has been the favorite city of political convention-goers. Counting notches for fourteen Republican and nine Democratic national conventions in the last twenty-five quadrennials, Chicago can boast that here were first named all the following Presidents of the United States: Lincoln, Grant, Garfield, Cleveland, Harrison, Theodore Roosevelt, Harding, Coolidge, Franklin D. Roosevelt, Truman and Eisenhower.

> Theodore H. White, *The Making of the President 1960*

Or to make clear by *elaboration or rephrasing:*

> The "duende," then, is a power and not a construct, is a struggle and not a concept. I have heard an old guitarist, a true virtuoso, remark, "The 'duende' is not in the throat, the 'duende' comes from inside up, up from the very soles of the feet." That is to say, it is not a question of aptitude, but of a true and viable style—of blood, in other words; of what is oldest in culture; of creation made act.
>
> Federico García Lorca,
> "The Duende: Theory and Divertissement"

Here, because the word names something more spiritual than intellectual—something harder to define than a concept—the author does not try so much to define and to elucidate as to name and rename, to offer description and metaphor, until we begin to comprehend the intangible.

Notice that in these quoted paragraphs the progress within the paragraph is the motion of thought. The exact detail, the example that locates the general in the particular, the comparison, the logical steps—these motions develop the thought and unify the paragraph at the same time. Paragraph development makes coherence.

## Development: Length and Completeness

We need here to talk about paragraph length. Our paragraphs will vary in length, folllowing no set rule. The length must be *adequate;* we must take the time and space to flesh out our arguments, to justify our contentions, to explain our theories, or to describe our characters. We discussed this need for completeness in Coherence in the Paragraph, but we must repeat it here. We must never forget that the reader is another person, who must be given reasons if he is to be persuaded of our opinions and must be given details if he is going to see what we see. We must not simply assert, "President Smith is the worst, most dishonest president we've had," and then propose to circumscribe his power. We must tell *why* he is so bad. We must supply reasons, facts, arguments, details *adequate* to the assertion. We must develop the paragraph to make our assertion coherent.

Undeveloped paragraphs bedevil beginning writers. Many times paragraphs remain undeveloped because the writer does not adequately imagine the reader. Here is a paragraph from a student paper.

> When you study dance, you learn either modern or classical ballet. Some people prefer one kind of dance and some another. I learned modern dance and I prefer it.

The writer continued the paper by describing the pleasures of modern dance. But her opening paragraph is undeveloped and lacks a sense of audience, because it begs either for definition or for comparison and contrast. One or two sentences of development, giving the reader an insight into the difference between forms of dance, would establish the necessary background for the discussion of modern dance.

Less frequently, writers are afflicted with too much disorganized detail, so that the writing loses force. As another student wrote in a paper:

> I bought my first car with money I earned working for a summer in a tuna canning factory. I was anxious to keep it running in top condition. It was a 1973 VW bug, with a good engine (from a 1975 VW van) and a pretty good body, with just a little rust below the doors. My friend repainted it for me, bright red, and we rebuilt the engine and almost set the garage on fire. The upholstery is in terrible shape. I change the oil and the oil filter every 1500 miles and the car gets about 25 miles per gallon, but the windshield wipers don't always work, and the insurance costs a lot.

We must keep in mind what is important and what is not. We must give reasons, but not every one we can think of. We must give only so many as we need to make our point. With too many reasons the reader will be confused, bored, or feel bullied.

To decide whether our detail is adequate—neither too little nor too much—we must develop judgment and tact; we must look at what we've written not only as a writer, but as a reader.

Because adequacy always depends on context, it's useless to lay down rules for paragraph length. Different kinds of writing, however, usually need paragraphs of different lengths. The more formal the writing, usually the more lengthy the paragraphing. In narrative and fiction, we use paragraphs with more varied lengths, and in informal writing our paragraphs shorten. Newspaper writing breaks up the solid column of print by making a paragraph out of every sentence or two.

In exposition, or in writing up research, we may move from topic to topic by long paragraphs that introduce a subject, elaborate it, enumerate it, explain it, or conclude it. We may frequently write paragraphs as long as a typewritten page. But if the paragraphs get much longer, we should cut them down. We can always find a place where we can make a break that is not wholly arbitrary and give the reader a rest. One argument could make a six-page paragraph, but it would be tiring to read. If we look back at it, we can find the steps in the argument. We can break between one step and another, even though the pause in reasoning is small. In a long description, we can break between one part of the subject and another. Talking of a barn, we can break between remarks about the colors things have, about the shapes they take, and about the uses they are put to. Talking about a block we grew up on, suppose we want to write equally about ten houses. Ten tiny paragraphs would be too choppy; one paragraph would be two pages of solid print. Here, we can subdivide our houses by talking about one side of the block and then the other or by making a division for three architectural styles, or different shades of paint, or lengths of time houses were occupied by the same tenants.

Some paragraphs must be short. When we write dialogue, we show a change of speaker by indenting a new paragraph.

> "Did you go downtown after lunch?" He was tapping the arm of his chair with his index finger. Behind his glasses his eyes wandered.
> "Yes," she said. "I suppose I did."
> "Why?"

But that paragraphing is mechanical. In descriptive or expository or narrative writing—usual ingredients in essay or autobiography and frequently in story—short paragraphs are choppy, a rash of blurts, like someone who talks in the manner of a machine gun. When we move from dialogue to description or narration, we should provide a change of pace by keeping the paragraphs relatively long. The long paragraph is a rest, a relief after several short ones: here is a bed big enough to lie down on. We do not want

> The room was large, the chairs comfortable. He sat down on the overstuffed sofa.
> All around him the ticking of clocks wove a mesh of sound. There was dust on the windowpane, and the rugs were shabby.
> Dark pictures hung on the walls, and the woodwork was dark.

It is too much like standing up and sitting down all the time. We want to relax and read the description straight.

> The room was large, the chairs comfortable. He sat down on the overstuffed sofa. All around him the ticking of clocks wove a mesh of sound. There was dust on the windowpane, and the rugs were shabby. Dark pictures hung on the walls, and the woodwork was dark.

And the paragraph should continue for another five or six lines.

Sometimes when we chop our prose into too-short paragraphs we may be deceiving ourselves with handwriting, which can make a few words into full-sized paragraphs, and think that we are writing a long paper when we are not. Or perhaps we find it difficult to move from one thing to another within the paragraph, and so we break the paragraph to indicate a switch to another topic. And at times, short paragraphs reveal our laziness. We fail to collect and to develop our thoughts and so write paragraphs that are little more than a sentence announcing a topic, paragraphs lacking detail, elaboration, and support. We need to think of further ideas to support arguments or details to make description carry feeling.

In narrative, the paragraph break is even more arbitrary than it is in exposition. We could justify one after every sentence, we could justify none at all; but neither of these solutions would be tolerable. Therefore we break for a rest when it is most nearly logical, as when the character turns a corner, or sees something new, or understands what is happening.

It is tempting to be dogmatic: "Outside of dialogue, keep your paragraphs between 200 and 250 words." Life would be more comfortable, and writing easier, if simple prescriptions solved our problems. Although a highly formal essay might follow some such rule, most good modern writing has much more variety to it. As it is hard to type the best contemporary stylists as formal or informal, so it is hard to put limits on paragraph size. Although formal writing leads toward a more uniform length of paragraph, it can use something as short as a one-line paragraph. A skillful writer may make a long statement in periodic sentences, a 350-word paragraph that concludes with a flourish, and follow it by a paragraph that reads, in its entirety,

> On the other hand, maybe this reasoning is haphazard.

Then he may write another long paragraph. The one-liner has been a change of pace—at the same time restful, offhand, and revivifying: it keeps us on our toes. We don't know what might come next, we are perpetually a little off balance. Look at this example from a student paper:

> When you approach the city from the east, you enter a down-trodden world with shabby filling stations, electric signs with letters missing, potholes, boarded-over houses, and bars which never close—dark holes of degradation and hopelessness. Next to them

often you see old men asleep in gutters. No one looks young or happy or as if there is any future. The only thing you see which is bright and shiny and new is a police car.

But that is only a part of the city.

To the west and to the north, the lakes attract fine houses. To the south, past the new buildings of prosperous businesses, the farmlands spread in abundance. . . .

Here, the one-line paragraph—which makes a transition between the two longer paragraphs—could easily become a first sentence for the second paragraph, but the student has chosen this rhythmically shocking brevity to underline, to make even more emphatic, the totally changed scene that his prose begins to describe. Because its effect is so dramatic, use the one-line paragraph sparingly.

On the other hand, look at these paragraphs of description, more nearly equal in length:

The river widens; islands appear; but there is no solitude in this heart of Africa. Always there are the little brown settlements in scraped brown yards, the little plantings of maize or banana or sugar cane about huts, the trading dugouts arriving beside the steamer to shouts. In the heat mist the sun, an hour before sunset, can appear round and orange, reflected in an orange band in the water muddy with laterite, the orange reflection broken only by the ripples from the bows of the steamer and the barges. Sometimes at sunset the water will turn violet below a violet sky.

But it is a peopled wilderness. The land of this river basin is land used in the African way. It is burned, cultivated, abandoned. It looks desolate, but its riches and fruits are known; it is a wilderness, but one of monkeys. Bush and blasted trees disappear only toward Kinshasa. It is only after nine hundred miles that earth and laterite give way to igneous rocks, and the land, becoming hilly, with sharp indentations, grows smooth and bare, dark with vegetation only in its hollows.

Plant today, reap tomorrow: this is what they say in Kisangani. But this vast green land, which can feed the continent, barely feeds itself. In Kinshasa the meat and even the vegetables have to be imported from other countries. Eggs and orange juice come from South Africa, in spite of hot official words; and powdered milk and bottled milk come from Europe. The bush is a way of life; and where the bush is so overwhelming, organized agriculture is an illogicality.

V. S. Naipaul, *The Return of Eva Perón*

These even, full, adequate paragraphs march in rank and in good order, helping to convince us—even by their shape itself—that they are calm, logical steps in a progressive statement of thought or opinion. At the same time, the writer creates tension within the paragraphs by setting up contrasts—river and shore, vegetation and cultivation, native agriculture and imported culture.

The variety and unity of the paragraph resemble the variety and unity of the sentence. The effective contrast, when the one-line paragraph follows the complex one, resembles the pleasure we take in a short, simple sentence after a long, complex sentence. A writer can mix a pleasing variety of sentences and paragraphs without violating the unity that holds the essay together.

## Development: Order and Clarity

If we do not want to irritate or confuse the reader, our information or argument must be orderly. Things must follow each other with a sense of purpose. Purpose makes clarity. We cannot say, "Oh, I forgot to say . . . ," or leave out steps in our progress. We must move in an orderly way, from earlier to later, or from less to more important, or from periphery to center, or from smaller to larger, or from larger to smaller. Sometimes we will want to move from center to periphery, from present to past. But we must not scatter our sequence—from larger to smaller to larger to larger to smaller to largest to larger to smallest to large. We may want A B C D E F. On occasion we may want Z Y X W V, but never A Q I X L D.

The order in the following paragraph is fine; we move from generality in the topic sentence to particulars that describe and substantiate it.

> Winter is a catastrophe. Life on skid row is lived out of doors, and the cold and the snow bring with them intense suffering. The men often get drunk enough to lie in the streets in the midst of a storm. The first time one sees a body covered with a light blanket of snow, stretched out on the sidewalk, the sight comes as a shock and a dilemma. Is the man dead or just drunk? Or worse, the habitués are so obsessed and driven that stealing goes on in the dead of winter, and a man who needs a drink will take the shoes of a fellow alcoholic in the middle of January.
>
> Michael Harrington,
> *The Other America: Poverty in the United States*

The following paragraph, organized in a different way, moving from pieces of information to a general conclusion, is also well constructed.

> Last January as he was about to leave office, Lyndon Johnson sent his last report on the economic prospect to the Congress. It was assumed that, in one way or another, the Vietnam War, by which he and his Administration had been destroyed, would come gradually to an end. The question considered by his economists was whether this would bring an increase or a decrease in military spending. The military budget for fiscal 1969 was 78.4 billions; for the year following, including pay increases, it was scheduled to be about three billions higher. Thereafter, assuming peace and a general withdrawal from Asia, there would be a reduction of some six or seven billions. But this was only on the assumption that the Pentagon did not get any major new weapons—that it was content with what had already been authorized. No one really thought this possible. The President's economists noted that plans already existed for "a package" consisting of new aircraft, modern naval vessels, defense installations, and "advanced strategic and general purpose weapons systems" which would cost many billions. This would wipe out any savings from getting out of Vietnam. Peace would now be far more expensive than war.
>
> John Kenneth Galbraith, *How to Control the Military*

The organization in this paragraph, however, is not satisfactory:

> The birds often flock in huge numbers on trees, sometimes breaking limbs off. They may bury a car parked below them in white dung. Starlings can be a terrible nuisance. The dark purplish-black pests may tear up a whole lawn in the process of searching for worms and insects, particularly as winter approaches and live food gets scarce. Their antics can drive a homeowner out of *his* tree. In large enough numbers, they can create a din of voices that blocks out all other sounds in the area. Their cries are strident and irritating.

Here the order is unclear. In this paragraph we move from specific to specific to general to specific to general to specific to specific, without meaningful progression. It would make much better organizational sense to begin, "Starlings can be a terrible nuisance," and to end, "Their antics can drive a homeowner out of *his* tree."

In writing a paragraph we usually have to settle on some controlling principle of order or sequence and then keep to it. Earlier we showed some methods of developing paragraphs for exposition. Two of the simplest and clearest means of ordering, appropriate for all sorts of writing, are simple chronology and spatial proximity, discussed briefly when we looked into transitions. Here we see chronological and spatial development combined in exposition.

> Anchorage has a thin history. Something of a precursor of the modern pipeline camps, it began in 1914 as a collection of tents pitched to shelter workers building the Alaska Railroad. For decades, it was a wooden-sidewalked, gravel-streeted town. Then, remarkably early, as cities go, it developed an urban slum, and both homes and commerce began to abandon its core. The exodus was so rapid that the central business district never wholly consolidated, and downtown Anchorage is even more miscellaneous than outlying parts of the city. There is, for example, a huge J. C. Penney department store filling several blocks in the heart of town, with an interior mall of boutiques and restaurants and a certain degree of chic. A couple of weedy vacant lots separate this complex from five log cabins. Downtown Anchorage from a distance displays an up-reaching skyline that implies great pressure for land. Down below, among the high buildings, are houses, huts, vegetable gardens, and bungalows with tidy front lawns. Anchorage burst out of itself and left these incongruities in the center, and for me they are the most appealing sights in Anchorage. Up against a downtown office building I have seen cordwood stacked for winter.
>
> John McPhee, *Coming into the Country*

Chronology is probably the easiest method for ordering the material in a paragraph and perhaps the most common. At times, in narration and exposition, we want to leap ahead and then catch up. We must use this violation of chronological sequence, however, only when we are fully aware of what we are doing.

> In December 1941, Congress declared war on Japan, Germany, and Italy. The declaration was an immediate result of the Japanese attack on Pearl Harbor, but earlier events had made such a move inevitable. Perhaps the Treaty of Versailles. . . .

Here, the opening sentence states the ultimate topic, an event to be reached by way of causation, and the paragraph develops by reverse chronology. Presumably, the writer will turn around and advance through the twenties and thirties in a conventional forward direction. If this essay began by referring to the earliest event mentioned—that is, if it had followed regular chronology—the reader might have expected, for a moment, that the Treaty of Versailles was the subject.

### Development: Order and Forcefulness

Clarity is not our only consideration when we organize paragraphs; we must also organize for appropriateness and forceful effect. Look again at the paragraphs by Huizinga (pages 224–225) and Mencken (page 225), keeping in mind the discussion of topic sentences. Look at the order in the paragraphs compared with the effects achieved. By their positions the topic sentences give *force* to these paragraphs.

Or take the method that lets us order according to spatial proximity. It can be more than a means to clarity; it can direct the reader's attention significantly and achieve dramatic effect. Here is a passage from *Gandhi* by Louis Fischer.

> At Rajghat, a few hundred feet from the river, a fresh pyre had been built of stone, brick, and earth. It was eight feet square and about two feet high. Long, thin, sandalwood logs sprinkled with incense were stacked on it. Mahatma Gandhi's body lay on the pyre with his head to the north. In that position Buddha met his end.

Notice how the paragraph moves gradually closer to its subject, like a camera that dollies in for a close-up in a film. We start from far back and move gradually closer. If the author had described the body of Gandhi first, and then its surroundings, the passage would be less forceful.

When we consider how we organize our paragraphs, we must always consider our *purpose* in writing. In expository writing, we may want to be sure that the reader knows what we are doing at all times. We may want to avoid listing statistics before telling what they demonstrate. Imagine the other paragraph I quoted about Gandhi with the first sentence placed at the end.

> The province of Natal, in 1896, had 400,000 Negro inhabitants, 51,000 Indians, and 50,000 whites. The Cape of Good Hope Colony had 900,000 Negroes, 10,000 Indians, and 400,000 Europeans; the Transvaal Republic 650,000 Negroes, 5,000 Indians, and 120,000 whites. In 1914, the five million Negroes hopelessly outnumbered the million and a quarter whites. Gandhi recognized that the whites in South Africa thought they needed protection against a majority consisting of Negroes and Indians.

Revised as above, the order makes the paragraph confusing and pointless. The reader does not know what is going on until he finishes reading the paragraph. He will be confused, bored, and inattentive.

And yet if our purpose in writing is to create an ominous or tense atmosphere—in narrative, perhaps, either fictional or autobiographical—we might want to list unexplained details first, waiting for the end of the paragraph to offer an interpretation. This suspenseful order would give our paragraph *force.*

> The forest, all at once, had grown silent. The monkeys had stopped their chattering, and the birds darted their heads apprehensively. The wind in the trees became audible, and then, faintly, the sound of drumming rose from the village enclosure. It could only mean that Godzilla had awakened once more.

Imagine how anticlimactic it would be in a film to show the monster suddenly appearing and then to pan around the trees. It wouldn't make emotional or dramatic sense.

## THE ORDER OF PARAGRAPHS

The developed paragraph is a unit of thought and feeling. The content makes the paragraph, and paragraphs become ways of organizing our complexity (for ourselves and for others) into units we can comprehend. One breakthrough in writing an essay comes when we see which part belongs with which part. We take tiny pieces and assemble them into larger units, and assemble the larger units into the focused paper. The middle unit is the paragraph. It associates detail into order; it concentrates; it begins to narrow our focus. We might start with these notes for an autobiographical essay:

> summer I was eight
> going hunting with my uncle
> gun laws and the NRA
> the bounty on coyotes
> my .22
> killing the coyote pup
> how I felt afterward
> my uncle and the VFW
> Fourth of July parade

Before we can order the whole essay, we must associate these small units with each other in an informal outline. If these notes are on file cards, we can simply make piles of them. Each pile would be a potential paragraph. If the notes are listed on a piece of paper or in a notebook, we can associate one with the other by lettering and numbering each item, linking like to like with the same number. The most obvious order might start with the old summer, and hunting with an uncle and a new .22, then switch moods to tell an anecdote of killing a coyote pup, then consider gun laws and the National Rifle Association; then it might mention a parade of VFW members, including the uncle, carrying rifles. A different order might begin with the recent parade, and return to the memory. Any order is arbitrary, but some orders are better than others. I wish to show here not so much a *best* ordering of the whole, as a useful, preliminary sorting of material into units, small collections of notes, which may turn out to be paragraphs. For instance:

| | |
|---|---|
| $B_1$ | summer I was eight |
| $B_3$ | going hunting with my uncle |
| D | gun laws and the NRA |
| $C_1$ | the bounty on coyotes |
| $B_2$ | my .22 |
| $C_2$ | killing the coyote pup |
| $C_3$ | how I felt afterward |
| $A_2$ | my uncle and the VFW |
| $A_1$ | Fourth of July parade |

This way is only one of many. It is the second ordering suggested, from parade to memory. The units represented by the capital letters are not necessarily single paragraphs. Maybe A would be two paragraphs—first a description of the VFW parading, the uncle puffing along in step, and then a close-up of the uncle, leading to a memory. The items grouped under C—the anecdote about killing a coyote pup and the consequent feelings—might take several paragraphs. But regardless of how many paragraphs each subject takes, the *order* would be

Fourth of July parade
my uncle and the VFW

summer I was eight
my .22
going hunting with my uncle

the bounty on coyotes
killing the coyote pup
how I felt afterward

gun laws and the NRA

Many a beginning writer, or a writer who has not learned to paragraph, might write the essay following the order in which the notes

originally appeared. The result would be chaos, moving back and forth in time by random association. That is the way we talk, thinking of points afterward and crying, "Oh, I forgot to say . . . !" But writing is harder and requires organization. The paragraph is our middle unit of organization between sentences that incorporate raw data and the finished, shapely essay. In developing explanation or narration, the rest or the handhold lets the reader know that a limited subject has been dealt with, finished or postponed, and that we now move to another topic—perhaps arising from the last one, perhaps in contrast to it, certainly different. The paragraph becomes a semantic unit. It carries meaning. The look of it on the page makes a statement; it tells us that a topic, or a detachable unit of an argument, or that an event, or a detachable unit of an event, is complete here. Like commas and sentence structure, paragraphs create meaning in our prose.

In order to make statements with paragraphs, we must be able to construct good ones. The paragraph must have *unity,* and for unity we often require a *topic sentence.* The paragraph must have *coherence* within itself, and a series of paragraphs must cohere to form the essay; coherence requires *transitions.* Finally, we must learn to *develop* the paragraph until it is adequate in its fullness and in its *length,* and until it presents its material in the best possible *order.*

### Revising Paragraphs

Make sure that your paragraphing is useful, to the mind that understands and to the eye that reads. Consider your paragraphs for their unity and variety, their coherence and adequacy of development, and their clarity and effective ordering. Consider their internal organization and their transitions, both internal and between paragraphs, both overt and implicit.

In late drafts of a paper, think of what your paragraphing communicates to a reader. Do your paragraphs give the right signal? Read as if you were someone else, and decide if your paragraph can be improved for clarity's sake—in shape, in wholeness, in development, in transition, in order.

_____ **EXERCISES** _____

1. Rewrite the paragraphs from student papers on page 223. Expand or delete, and organize details as necessary.

2. Develop one of these topic sentences in a short paragraph, using one of the methods discussed in the chapter.

  a. We live in a highly competitive society.

  b. Green is a cool color.

  c. Sitting by the fire on a cold winter night is a pleasure I miss at school.

  d. It is not difficult to make bread.

  e. The man was dressed in a most peculiar fashion.

3. Read these paragraphs and comment on their methods of development. (See pages 243–248)

  a. It's sometimes argued that there's no real progress; that a civilization that kills multitudes in mass warfare, that pollutes the land and oceans with ever larger quantities of debris, that destroys the dignity of individuals by subjecting them to a forced mechanized existence can hardly be called an advance over the simpler hunting and gathering and agricultural existence of prehistoric times. But this argument, though romantically appealing, doesn't hold up. The primitive tribes permitted far less individual freedom than does modern society. Ancient wars were committed with far less moral justification than modern ones. A technology that produces debris can find, and is finding, ways of disposing of it without ecological upset. And the schoolbook pictures of primitive man sometimes omit some of the detractions of his primitive life—the pain, the disease, famine, the hard labor needed just to stay alive. From that agony of bare existence to modern life can be soberly described only as upward progress, and the sole agent for this progress is quite clearly reason itself.

    Robert M. Pirsig, *Zen and the Art of Motorcycle Maintenance*

  b. Now alone in moutains nearly a hundred miles west of Eagle and at least thirty from the nearest human being, I am puzzled by the hour of the day. I have no idea what it is. There has been no dark of night or visible sun. I don't wear a watch. I am like that Frenchman deep in the caves who hadn't a notion of the hour and slept and ate only according to need. I wonder: Could I have prepared and eaten three full meals in only two hours? In twelve? Fifteen? If I could see the sun, the sun would not help. I have neither a map nor a compass with which to assess its position, and now, at the summer solstice, it rides so low above the mountain ridges and dips so briefly behind them that 4 A.M. looks much like nine and noon. All of that is academic anyway. There is a leaden overcast, and the wind is driving a light, cold rain. Tracks are everywhere—wolf, grizzly, caribou. The mountainsides in surrounding view—sixteen doming tundra balds—are green and white, holding the winter and the summer in quilted fields of snow. In this remote landscape, as wild as any in the country—where not so much

as a cabin stands in half a million acres around—my only companions
are a backhoe and a bulldozer.

John McPhee, Coming into the Country

c. We are a practical, inventive people on whom the weight of tradition rests but lightly. In many lands of the world, people confronted
with an unpleasant situation will quietly adjust themselves; in the
United States, a man's first impulse is to change things for the better.
This willingness to experiment came naturally to the pioneers, who
had no precedents on which to build. It has remained a trait of the
industrial pioneers whose ability to adapt and change has laid the basis
for America's supremacy as a manufacturing nation.

Ray Allen Billington, "The Frontier Disappears"

d. So Grant and Lee were in complete contrast, representing two
diametrically opposed elements in American life. Grant was the modern man emerging; beyond him, ready to come on the stage, was the
great age of steel and machinery, of crowded cities and a restless burgeoning vitality. Lee might have ridden down from the old age of
chivalry, lance in hand, silken banner fluttering over his head. Each
man was the perfect champion of his cause, drawing both his strengths
and his weaknesses from the people he led.

Bruce Catton, "Grant and Lee: A Study in Contrasts"

4.  Take this excerpt from the *Detroit Free Press*, tiny newspaper
paragraphs, and copy it out into longer paragraphs, as you would
organize paragraphs in an essay. Break the paragraphs logically and
usefully.

Here's what the historic arms limitation agreements signed here
Friday night in the Kremlin mean.

What they do, essentially, is to freeze a "balance of terror" between
the world's two nuclear superpowers.

Each side, in these agreements, retains the ability to kill millions of
defenseless civilians on the other side.

Washington and Moscow will be defended from nuclear attack with
anti-ballistic missile systems (ABMs).

But Detroit and every other major city in the U.S. will remain unde-
fended. So will Leningrad and Kiev, and other major cities in the Soviet
Union.

Thus each side, in a sense, will hold the civilian population of the
other side hostage—as a means of discouraging the other side from
launching nuclear war.

The fact is, as Henry Kissinger, White House national security ad-
viser, has put it: "Both sides are now vulnerable to each other . . . this
has been a fact now for five or six years."

The new SALT agreements seek to freeze the 25-year-old nuclear
arms race at that point—on the theory that a "balance of terror" is

the best guarantee either side has, in this terrifying age, of preventing war.

But what of other major questions?

How important are the agreements? Can they work? Can they be monitored? Don't the agreements give the Soviets a numerical advantage? What will they mean to the average citizen?

James McCartney

5. Look at the length of paragraphs in these examples. Do the authors provide variety in length and type of paragraph? Do any paragraphs seem choppy? Are transitions adequate? Make notes in the margin for class discussion.

a. What, in our human world, is this power to live? It is the ancient, lost reverence and passion for human personality, joined with the ancient, lost reverence and passion for the earth and its web of life.

This indivisible reverence and passion is what the American Indians almost universally had; and representative groups of them have it still.

They had and have this power for living which our modern world has lost—as world-view and self-view, as tradition and institution, as practical philosophy dominating their societies and as an art supreme among all the arts.

By virtue of this power, the densely populated Inca state, by universal agreement among its people, made the conservation and increase of the earth's resources its foundational national policy. Never before, never since has a nation done what the Inca state did.

By virtue of this same power, the little pueblo of Tesuque, in New Mexico, when threatened by the implacable destroying action of government some twenty-five years ago, starved and let no white friend know it was starving. It asked no help, determined only to defend its spiritual values and institutions and its remnant of land which was holy land.

If our modern world should be able to recapture this power, the earth's natural resources and web of life would not be irrevocably wasted within the twentieth century, which is the prospect now. True democracy, founded in neighborhoods and reaching over the world, would become the realized heaven on earth. And living peace—not just an interlude between wars—would be born and would last through ages.

John Collier, *Indians of the Americas*

b. If we know what we're looking for, why is it so difficult to find? The answer lies in a very simple truth about leadership. People can only be led where they want to go. The leader follows, though a step ahead. Americans *wanted* to climb out of the Depression and needed someone to tell them they could do it, and FDR did. The British believed that they could still win the war after the defeats of 1940, and Churchill told them they were right.

A leader rides the waves, moves with the tides, understands the deepest yearnings of his people. He cannot make a nation that wants peace at any price go to war, or stop a nation determined to fight from doing so. His purpose must match the national mood. His task is to focus the people's energies and desires, to define them in simple terms, to inspire, to make what people already want seem attainable, important, within their grasp.

Above all, he must dignify our desires, convince us that we are taking part in the making of great history, give us a sense of glory about ourselves. Winston Churchill managed, by sheer rhetoric, to turn the British defeat and the evacuation of Dunkirk in 1940 into a major victory. FDR's words turned the sinking of the American fleet at Pearl Harbor into a national rallying cry instead of a humiliating national scandal. A leader must stir our blood, not appeal to our reason.

Michael Korda, "What It Takes to Be a Leader"

6. These phrases might be informal notes for an essay. Arrange them into several groups, each capable of becoming a paragraph. Then write a brief paragraph starting with topic sentence (a) or (b).

    a. Pets should be allowed in the dormitory.

    b. Pets should not be allowed in the dormitory.

       dogs vs. other animals
       sanitation and health laws
       noise, barking during the night
       exercise and traffic
       responsibility for feeding and care
       roommates and allergies
       community considerations
       student life and its demands
       safety
       school vacations and care
       abuse of pets and negligence
       companionship and loneliness

7. Here is a short essay on baseball. I have mixed up the paragraph order and numbered the paragraphs in the mixed-up order. See if you can restore them to their original sequence.

    1. At any one point, there's anticipation, deliberation, preparation: "Now" is a building-up. "Now" is never only for itself. It's cumulative "progresssing," in strife, to form the game's unfolding. Nor are any two games alike, any more than two art works that push themselves into being through the resistance of time, incident by incident, in head-on conflict by two complicated machines designed to win through accidents and opportunity. "What's happening" is contingent. There's a whole game to be gotten through.

2. This is to see baseball as an artwork-in-the-making affair, totally unrehearsed, improvised by more than eighteen men, who thrust in their various skills while the moving parts pass through innings, highlighted by crucial plays, to the conclusion being thereby created.

3. The game in progress is a structure-in-the-becoming; if you see it, through time, as a whole, all the separate episodes can come flashing together, and interlock, to shower aesthetic illumination on a drama of its own devising.

4. Like literature, music, opera, theater, and the dance, baseball takes place in time. (Architecture, sculpture, and painting don't—they're purely spatial.) The performer and the observer, while a game is in progress, look back and look ahead: the present action is laid out in a shifting, dramatic time field. A rhythm, of sorts, weaves its way through the "accidents" on the playing field. A current play, involving positioning and decisions, is affected by what was previous in the game, and is having its effect on what's to come later; the game may be seen as an organic unit. Every pitch has its place in there, somewhere.

Marvin Cohen, *Baseball the Beautiful*

# 7

## Forms for the Essay: Rhetorical Patterns in Exposition

### EXPOSITION

Later we will take up argument and research, but first we must look into the principal form of prose we need to write, not only at the university but elsewhere. Most writing assigned in college is exposition. Exposition is explanation, exposing a subject for an audience, making it clear. The word *exposition* comes from a Latin verb meaning "to set out," and it becomes an English noun meaning "something displayed for public inspection." We write exposition not only in college; most writing required in professional life is expository—in business, in teaching, in technology and science, in law and medicine. When social workers deliver papers, when geologists make reports, when hospital officials release information on new diagnostic equipment, when marketing managers report on the activities of their competition, they write exposition.

In itself, exposition is not argument, although it can form part of an argument. Argument lacking explanation moves toward bombast or harangue because it presents unsubstantiated opinion. Exposition does not tell a story, though it may include narrative to explain something essential. Even pure description may form a necessary task in exposition.

Exposition is usually an essay's foundation. By itself it can make a whole essay. If you spent an exchange year in England, you might feel called upon to write an expository essay explaining baseball or percolator coffee to your teacher and your classmates. If you wrote about Einstein's discoveries in physics, you would need exposition in order to make contact with your audience.

> But there was another consequence which Einstein now brought forward for the first time. If light is produced in a star or in the sun, an area of strong gravity, and then streams down on the earth, an area of weak gravity, its energy will not be dissipated by a reduction of speed, since this is impossible, light always having the same constant speed. What would happen, Einstein postulated, was something very different: the wavelength of the light would be shortened. This "Einstein shift," the assumption that "the spectral lines of sunlight, as compared with the corresponding spectral lines of terrestrial sources of light, must be somewhat displaced toward the red," was spelled out in some detail. However, he was careful to add the qualification that "as other influences [pressure, temperature] affect the position of the centers of the spectral lines, it is difficult to discover whether the enforced influence of the gravitational potential really exists." In fact the Döppler shift, produced by the motion of the stars relative to the solar system, was to provide an additional and even more important complication.
>
> Ronald W. Clark, *Einstein*

Pausing in his biography to explain a scientific discovery, the author analyzes a natural process. *Process analysis* is a rhetorical pattern common to expository writing that answers the question "How does it happen?" or "How does it work?" Now we must look into the many rhetorical patterns—process analysis among others—that recur in exposition and consider the advantages of each, for purpose and audience.

## RHETORICAL PATTERNS

We use rhetorical patterns for purposes. Patterns of rhetoric are ways of thinking; Frank Rodriguez in Chapter 3 used the rhetorical pattern of *comparison and contrast* for a way of thinking, observing differences between two situation comedies about war. Other patterns of rhetoric offer other models of thought. We use these models to reach our readers or listeners, to make contact with other people. Consideration of audience may suggest purpose. Making things clear to an audience, exposing, we need to define terms—and *definition* itself is a prominent rhetorical pattern.

Each of the most common rhetorical patterns answers a question, and these resemble the journalist's six questions. *Example* answers "For instance?" *Classification* answers "What kind is it?" *Division* answers "What are its parts?" *Cause and effect* answers "Why did it happen?" *Process analysis* answers "How does it happen?" *Comparison and contrast* answers "What is it like? What is it unlike?" *Definition* answers "What is it?"

Because these rhetorical patterns give us a paradigm of questions to ask ourselves about a subject, they are doubly useful. In Chapter 3 we introduced them briefly because they can help us in the process of writing—to invent and to get ideas, as well as to organize, to construct, and to develop an essay. Because these patterns provide ways to develop writing that is thin, we discussed them briefly when we spoke in Chapter 6 of developments in the paragraph. Here we need to look at the rhetorical patterns more fully.

Suppose we start with a general topic and wish to generate material. Suppose the topic is community colleges. We could ask ourselves to list *examples* of community colleges, with concrete detail. Or we could jot down various ways to *classify* community colleges, according to size, location, sources of funding, or curricula. We could *divide* one community college into its components—faculty, administration, staff, and student body. We could ask ourselves what social needs *cause* the establishment of community colleges; now that they are established, we could ask what *effects* they have. We could *compare and contrast* community colleges with four-year colleges, with residential colleges, or with technical institutes, and examine the differences. We could investigate the *process* of founding a community college or look at the specific attributes that *define* such an institution. By this time, we would have acquired much material for our essay. Then we would need to investigate the material generated to look for a purpose for our essay, and our purpose would depend on our sense of an audience. Whom do we write for, and why? Probably, a paper on community colleges would use more than one of these rhetorical patterns; it would most likely not use all of them.

As we develop a whole essay using one or more of these rhetorical patterns, so we may develop a paragraph using one or more of them. Each of these devices can structure an entire paper or support one segment of a paper, even as short as a sentence of *example*. Good essays blend rhetorical patterns in a sequence demanded by the essay's purpose. These patterns are neither mutually exclusive nor parallel. If we write a *process analysis* about planting an apple orchard, and we use a term or a concept likely to be unfamiliar to our audience, we will need *definition* within process analysis; when we define a term, one method of definition uses *example:* the definition of a cooking apple may profit from the example of a Gravenstein. Frank Rodriguez used comparison for his rhetorical pattern, yet he ended his essay by suggesting historical or social *cause and effect* as the source of the contrast he found.

Although some assignments require us to use a specific pattern, so that like Frank Rodriguez we look for things to compare and contrast, other assignments suggest a general topic within which we must find a focus and a mode of construction. In life after college, the same opportunities or necessities will appear, although they will not announce themselves in rhetorical terms. Sometimes a report for the manager will necessitate comparison and contrast of two options. The manager making the assignment does not consider the pattern of rhetoric; but if we understand what we are asked to do, we can do it better by understanding rhetorical patterns.

At other times, our investigation of an option, or a book, or a past event may best use process analysis, or classification, or example. The rhetorical patterns are modes of construction that are also modes of thought, and by their shapes they can help us narrow the topic and show us a way to think about it. If Frank's teacher had assigned a topic rather than a pattern—television, for instance—Frank could have used the rhetorical pattern of comparison and contrast to narrow his subject to two contrasting situation comedies. Or he could have used classification to separate types of television programs. Or he could have used division to analyze the repeated structures of one type.

Although we seldom find an essay in a book or magazine that is purely an example of one pattern, it is useful as we study writing to practice using these patterns one at a time. Practice fixes the uses in our minds and keeps the patterns available for future use. But while we practice them in our writing, we must acknowledge: when essayists like Annie Dillard or Edward Hoagland write, they use whatever patterns are useful to their purposes; and in all likelihood they use them without needing to be conscious of using them.

For one more example: suppose we find ourselves charged, in later life, with writing a report on the market for liability insurance in shopping centers. Do we need to use definition? To answer such a question we must consider our audience. If we work for Metropolitan Life Insurance Company, we probably do not need to define "liability insurance." But the term "shopping plaza" may require some limitation for an audience of insurance company executives; maybe we need to use definition at the beginning of our report. We may well need classification, differentiating shopping plazas according to the numbers of units; or we may need division, if sections of plazas require different types of insurance. When we put forward options we may well use example, either historical or hypothetical. Connection between insurance and plaza may require an example that indicates cause and effect. Considering audience and purpose, we may use comparison and contrast.

In mentioning hypothetical topics—community colleges, apple orchards, and insurance for shopping centers—we enter the subject of rhetorical patterns by using example.

### Example

Example or illustration is fundamental to discourse that explains. We say something general, and then we make it clear by locating it in one or more examples. "Students today are more practical than they were fifteen years ago." Such a generalization cries out for an instance. The word *practical* needs a location in the particular world. "They major in subjects that will lead to jobs." This example of practicality suggests examples more particular still; frequently we progress from a broad generalization to an example which remains fairly general to a further example which becomes more specific. "History majors have declined by 40 percent in fifteen years; economics majors have increased by a third, and the new major in computer science has grown by 16 percent a year."

We use example as the first of the rhetorical patterns because it forms part of so many others. When we compare and contrast we often compare and contrast examples; analyzing process, we pin down a generalization of process by example; one of the chief modes of definition is definition by example.

The scale of example is infinite. It can range from one word— "Perennial plants such as geraniums . . ."—to the long historical work that begins with a generalization about the repeated shapes of revolutions in history and spends its length showing the pattern by narrating many examples of revolution. Of course the author would use other rhetorical patterns as well. Within each example of a revolution, the author might analyze historical process; terms would need definition: "An oligarchy is. . . ."

Examples allow the writer to clarify and explain generalizations to a reader, making connection with the audience. When the student used the word *practical,* the word could mean different things to different people. (For someone intending to teach art, art history is practical enough.) Concrete illustrations specify the sense in which *practical* is used. We choose our examples depending on the audience to whom we explain ourselves. If we are addressing the garden club, probably we need not explain "such as geraniums"; our audience can supply its own list of perennial plants.

When teachers complain that an essay lacks detail—a frequent complaint—they usually lament the lack of examples. Someone may write that animal fat contains more calories than a comparable amount of vegetable bulk. It helps to clarify, and the specific is more interesting, if we hear that three ounces of hamburger adds up to two hundred fifty calories, and that three ounces of baked potato amount only to sixty. Examples are necessary to clarify and also to keep the reader from falling asleep. Without generality we lack statement or idea; but without example we lack salt to make the baked idea palatable.

Misuses of example are common, especially in the service of argument or passionate conviction, when we support a generalization with a single example or insufficient detail. (In Chapter 8 we will speak of the argumentative error of generalizing from a particular.) In the expository use of example, we need to consider whether the example fairly represents what we claim. Three ounces of baked potato, if we add butter and sour cream, may grossly exceed the hamburger patty's calories. We must take care, for the sake of honest communication, that the example is truly pertinent to the generality it supports. Sometimes the brief example, like *geraniums,* will explain itself, but often, when we consider audience, we must explain why the example applies. In a generalization about a well-made automobile, we may need to explain by definition *fuel injection* or *independent suspension.* We should avoid the obvious or trite examples as we avoid the cliché in language. When we use a general word like *fruit,* it is unnecessary to give an example "like apples or oranges"; we offend our audience when we condescend to it.

### Thinking by Example

When we generalize in conversation with a friend, saying, "Studying for an exam in psych takes a special kind of brain," we may hear the response, "For example?" To think by using examples, we should take a questioner inside our heads. Example is so fundamental to exposition, we do well to ask ourselves, "For example?" and "For instance?" throughout the process of writing—when we generate notes toward a paper, when we look critically at a draft, and when we give an essay its final polishing revision. Thinking by example will clarify and develop our language and thought. Specificity carries our ideas across the page to our reader.

Suppose Frank Rodriquez had been assigned an essay, not in comparison and contrast, but in example. He would have searched for a generalization to support, and he might still have found his subject on the small screen. Suppose he generalized: "Television helps keep families together because people stay home to watch programs," or "Television impedes mental growth because it does everything for the viewer." The inner critic, responding to either generalization, must ask, "For example? For instance?" Frank could have built an essay by a line of examples supporting either generalization.

### An Example of Example

In a northeastern school a few years back, a teacher in advanced composition assigned his class John McPhee's *Oranges* as a model of good prose for reading and class discussion. Originally a *New Yorker* series of articles, *Oranges* tells everything about the fruit—its history, its botany, its geography, its economics. In the book the author uses various rhetorical patterns many times over. When the teacher spent two weeks of class time on exercises in the rhetorical patterns, she used McPhee as a model and assigned her students exercises and essays using the seven major patterns to discuss the general subject of apples. Because the college sat amid many orchards, she encouraged her students to base their papers on interviews. When she repeated the experiment in the following year, the class became known on campus as "Apples and Oranges." Here is a brief example theme that came from that class:

*The Growth of Orchards*

In the narrow valleys of New England, intensive fruit growing has replaced the general subsistence farm on which a family kept cows, sheep, chickens, and pigs while growing a large vegetable garden. Some farmers now plant a few intensively fertilized acres of strawberries or blueberries, often marketed to customers willing to do their own picking. But such enterprises require nearby cities for their customers. On the sloping hills of northern New England and western Massachusetts, unable to accommodate the farm machinery that makes large herds of milk cattle economical, the family-sized apple orchard provides a common crop.

At Bone's Orchard outside Montague, Massachusetts, the family of Richard Bone tends eight hundred trees including twenty-five varieties from the old McIntosh to the new Empire. The family of five runs its thirty acres as a vertical conglomerate, setting out new trees and cutting down old ones that have slowed down their production, trimming and fertilizing, picking the crop with the assistance of neighbors. Then they sell bushels and pecks of apples, and gallons of apple cider, in front of their house from a roadside stand.

## Classification and Division

We classify to organize the welter of our world. If we do not classify our personal possessions, we can never find anything. Moving into a new house or apartment, we put the bedroom things into the bedroom, the kitchen things in the kitchen. We will never discover our eggbeater if we have mistakenly classified it among the pajamas. In a new dormitory room, most of us will put sweaters with sweaters and shirts with shirts, our books and notes about economics in one place, our chemistry things in another. Similarly, when we must organize our thoughts—to begin a paper about the presidential election of 1984, or to study for an exam about the causes of the 1914–1918 war—we need to classify or divide the information to set it in order, before we can understand or remember it.

Classification is a form of thought. Our minds constantly fit things into categories: apples, towns, automobiles, left-handed people, musical instruments. When we consider friends we have known, towns we have lived in, apples we have eaten, or cars we have driven, our minds tend to classify these things. We group according to similarities, and then we discriminate differences. If we classify voters, we separate people into Republicans, Democrats, Socialists, Prohibitionists, and this discrimination depends on one characteristic: their voting habits. Thinking of cars we have driven, we classify according to mileage, price, country of origin, size, or any other discernible quality; they are all automobiles. Of course classification leads to comparison and often contrast, because the large class depends on similarities—what all seashells or automobiles have in common—and the subdivisions depend on contrasts of striping or handling, size, or horsepower.

Classification keeps our thinking orderly. Essential to good order in classification is parallelism. If we classify forms of literature, we may speak of fiction, drama, and poetry, and the classification remains parallel. If we were tempted to classify literature into novel, drama, short story, poem, and sonnet, our thinking would become muddled: drama is a general category but novel and short story are subcategories of the general notion fiction; poetry is a general category and sonnet a particular form within the category poetry. We must keep classifications parallel.

When we outline a subject, we keep categories parallel by using parallel numbers or letters—roman numeral, capital letter, arabic numeral, lowercase letter:

    I.
      A.
        1.
          a.

Beneath each topic of equal worth, we indent and subclassify or divide. Under the general subject of wartime economics, we might classify

    I. Industry

with further classification into

      A. Production for the military

and

      B. Production for civilians

It might be necessary, under A and B, to divide the subject into geographic areas:

        1. Eastern area
        2. Southern area
        3. Midwestern area

4. Mountain area
5. West Coast area

We might go on to

II. Transportation

and then subdivide into Sea and Land, subdividing Land further into Rail and Highway. Classification and division are modes of thought that supply borders, frames, and containers.

Division is also characteristic of human thought. Classification sets many things in order—apples classified as McIntosh, Delicious, Baldwin, Northern Spy; division separates single things into their parts. Understanding a thing by means of its components is analysis or cutting up. Division gives us the anatomy of an object. An apple, for instance, is composed of skin, stem, flesh, and seeds. To analyze the federal government, we divide it into three parts: executive, legislative, and judicial. To analyze our Buick, we divide it into chassis, engine, and body. When we analyze by division, we analyze a static thing: the finished automobile, the ripe apple. It is important to distinguish between the analysis of a single, static object—for which we use the rhetorical pattern of division—and the narrative analysis of action or process, a pattern we will take up later.

In writing, when we follow the rhetorical pattern of classification or of division, we should be careful not to confuse the two. Sometimes a good writer will begin an essay by classification and end it with division—with thoughtful logic and excellent results. We could classify plays as tragic, comic, historical, and pastoral—and then analyze the anatomy of the tragedy, dividing the one dramatic form into components; Aristotle in his *Poetics,* for instance, distinguished plot, character, diction, thought, spectacle, and song.

But the two patterns are different. Often in careless writing we may start using one pattern and end using the other, not knowing what we do, with monstrous results—as if the Creator's attention had wandered, and He set a robin's head on a daffodil's stem. If we began a paper with an analytic division of the federal government into its components, we would wander into incoherence if we took off from the legislative third of the division and started classifying the different legislatures of the world. Do not wander, like a careless talker, from one pattern to the other without noticing it. The result makes disunity, much as mixed constructions do in individual sentences.

### Thinking by Classification and Division

We cannot think by classification and division until we have ideas, topics, or facts to classify and divide—just as it is difficult to sort our possessions into a house until the moving van has arrived. Therefore we think by classifying after we have first taken notes or brainstormed or written an early draft, after we have generated material to classify. One useful trick is to set outline numbers and letters next to the words and concepts that are parallel, in the margins of notes or drafts; the notion of parallelism in classification is essential to order. If our economics notes list "new freighters 1943," we should recognize a submember of B, Ocean, which is a submember of II, Transportation; when we see a note on "air freight beginning 1944," we should recognize a new category, C, Air, which we had not earlier considered.

Here, classification not only organizes material generated, but also points out a step in thinking; it helps us to generate ideas by creating a third division under "Transportation" that we had not planned on. The writer not wary of classification might include the beginnings of air freight as a hasty addendum to remarks on sea or land transport, and confuse the audience by disorder.

### An Example of Classification and Division

As an exercise in classification and division, one student began:

*Slicing Apples*

We classify apples by the names we give them, by calling them McIntosh, Baldwin, Cortland, and Gravenstein. The names taste good, but only if you can attach a memory to them. Each of these fruits, if we dissect it, is composed after all of the same components—pith or meat, skin, core, and seeds. We tell them apart, for pleasure and nutrition, by taste, smell, and characteristics that suggest their use. But there is more than one way to slice an apple: A McIntosh is smaller than many other apples, sweeter, and does not keep so well; it is best to consume it within thirty-six hours of picking. On the other hand the Cortland. . . .

### Cause and Effect

The rhetorical pattern of cause and effect answers the question "Why did or does or will it happen?" In exposition our explanatory purpose often requires us to assemble causes or to speculate on them. Scientific writing frequently examines phenomena for causes and effects: "Bubonic plague was transmitted by fleas from infected rats." When we explain cause and effect by reciting statistics and scientific facts, we maintain objectivity or at least its appearance. On the other hand historical speculation, though it can lead to conclusions well established, appears less objective. It marshals evidence, usually by means of multiple examples, to suggest causes that led to war, or to defeat for one ruling party and victory for another.

Here the rhetorical pattern of cause and effect approaches persuasion, and indeed this pattern forms a major device in argument and persuasion. When editorial writers tell us, "The death penalty will not serve as a deterrent to murder," they usually argue by cause and effect, citing statistics. We listen for reasonableness in such assertions. If writers wish to convince an audience, they must make their steps in causation logical and support them by detail. Unsupported statements of causal relationship—as if an editorial writer stopped after the one-sentence assertion—will convince no one. (In Chapter 8 we discuss the use of cause and effect in argument.)

Cause and effect is common to most explanation, however, not only to persuasion. A comparison and contrast essay on the utility of bicycles and automobiles, even if in it the writer does not decide for one or the other, will use cause and effect to locate differences. In comparing and contrasting two television comedies, Frank Rodriguez ended by using cause and effect to suggest a reason for the differences he had discovered. Columnists on the business pages of daily newspapers frequently explain by cause and effect. Why have Japanese cars made inroads on the American market? Exposition leads us to encounters with the problem of multiple causation. If we discover four or five possible causes, we must decide the relative importance of each. What accounts for the popularity of Japanese cars? Is it primarily marketing, design, size, convenience, or price? (Notice that the possible causes form a classification.) If you show, by statistics and examples, that price is the primary factor, you may wish, considering your audience, to take the investigation one step further, to inquire into the cause of the cause. Claiming that lower price is the immediate cause for the consumer's choice, one writer argued that it was not the higher salaries of American workers that accounted for the price differential, nor Japanese use of robotics; instead, he said it was the huge range of models offered by each American manufacturer—more than twenty thousand possible options for one model—and contrasted it with the few options offered by Japanese firms; the variety of options, he said, causes the difference in price range.

It was the purpose of this writer, addressing a business audience, to take his cause and effect analysis from one cause (lower price) to a cause further back (simplicity of model range). Audience determines purpose, which determines strategy. Another writer might wish to go further still, to try to determine the causes in national character for the different strategies of the manufacturers.

In exposition we must always remember the needs of an audience. If we seek to explain an increase in arrests of teenagers for drunken driving, perhaps our audience will not be satisfied to learn that statistics show an increase in teenage drinking. We will need to push further, to seek causes for the increase in drinking. If an airplane crashes because of a mechanical malfunction, perhaps we will need to investigate reasons for the malfunction, and not simply demonstrate the cause of the crash by naming the malfunction. Was the cause poor maintenance? Original design? Misuse or abuse?

But when we use the pattern of cause and effect, we must know when to stop. Talking about the causes behind company failure, or war, we could recede historically to the Declaration of Independence, or the Pilgrim Fathers, or the visit to Japan by Admiral Perry—and never arrive at the end of our linked chain. Considering what an audience may reasonably require, we must narrow the focus or the scope of cause and effect; we must recede so far and no further. Otherwise, we will discover that the seeds of the present wars of the Middle East extend backward in history from Mahomet II to Timur, the Crusades, Mahomet I, Constantine, Augustus, Alexander, Moses, and the Pharaohs.

We use the pattern of cause and effect, not only when we talk about what has happened, but when we predict the consequences of actions not yet undertaken. We explain that because our candidate will control health-care costs, the nation's budget deficit will decrease. In business writing, we propose actions based on cause and effect predictions. If we market product X by campaign Y, we will reach market Z. The writer, targeting his audience as the company targets its market, uses examples and statistics to support causal predictions.

### Thinking by Cause and Effect

Explaining by cause and effect is basic to thinking. We assume that every phenomenon, from the sun rising in the morning to a shipwreck to a great painting, results from a cause or, more probable, multiple causes. When we undertake any topic, we should consider the appropriate use of cause and effect. Reading notes or plans or drafts toward an essay, we should encourage the inner critic to ask *why*. Why does this happen or that? And is it relevant to tell our audience why? Does it suit our purpose to carry investigation of sources backward in time, for the sake of the audience we address? Does the audience need explanation of cause for comprehension or clarity?

To think well by cause and effect, be sure that you avoid assertion without evidence or example. Never be satisfied to have found one cause, but consider the possibilities of multiple causation. Making a chain of causes, be careful not to omit a link. Never confuse sequence with cause; forgetting your umbrella did *not* make it rain.

### An Example of Cause and Effect

*Ruinous Health*

When an apple tree has been neglected for some years, disease and undirected growth combine to spoil its fruit. Only worms eat the small, sour apples; people will never touch them. Spraying one spring will keep the insects away, but we will need more than spray to bring the old tree back: the pruning saw must restructure the tree's growth before it will be healthy again.

A tree's natural, healthy growth works against its future health. Vigorous new limbs, growing without our careful attention, keep sunlight and air from reaching the mature limbs. Untended branches rub against each other, breaking the bark, leaving an open sore by which disease may enter the tree's trunk. New shoots start up at the base of the old tree, draining energy from the soil. Eventually, as the new shoots grow into small trees, they extend leaves that rob the old tree of sunlight. Sun makes sugar. When untrimmed branches keep sun from blossom and apple, the result is small apples that never sweeten.

Burgeoning growth is its own undoing. The remedy is the saw, for amputation makes the remaining limbs stronger—open to necessary sunlight, taking necessary energy from soil.

### Comparison and Contrast

We use comparison and contrast to shape our papers—as we saw Frank Rodriguez do in Chapter 3—or we use it as part of the paper. It is a habit of our thought, even at its most abstract, to divide or classify and then to compare and contrast. "There are two kinds of people in the world," we say, or three, or four—and then we use this unlikely generalization as a way to consider and explore human characteristics. Our minds operate by contraries: oasis calls for desert, and nothing brings winter into mind like a summer day.

We use comparison and contrast for clarification within sentences and paragraphs. In an earlier paragraph, I used the caloric count of a hamburger as an example of an example. Perhaps that detail by itself would mean little to most readers; in order to let that detail speak to an audience, I could supply meaning for "two hundred fifty calories" by comparison and contrast.

> Meats are fattening; a hamburger patty two and a half inches across contains about two hundred fifty calories. On the other hand, a medium-sized potato, a member of the starch family often accused of fattening us, contains only sixty calories. On a scale the potato outweighs the hamburger patty two to one; in my metabolism the hamburger alone—without bun, without ketchup, without fried onions—is four times more fattening than the potato.

Here the writer uses comparison and contrast with the clear objective of persuading his audience; purpose is clear, and clear also is the writer's general notion of audience.

Comparison and contrast can be a tool for judgment and decision. We compare sweaters or used cars before we buy one; we compare colleges before we choose where to apply. But we also compare and contrast simply to define or to explain. When we say that a hamburger is fattening, what does the statement mean? Is it fattening compared to a mushroom? Is it fattening compared to a gallon of ice cream? To make the word *fattening* mean anything, we require comparisons; comparison and contrast define one word.

In a paper for a government course, we might compare another country's representative government with America's, to illuminate the differences or to understand our own system better, by seeing its familiar shape against the unfamiliar background of a different system. It is not necessary, in comparison and contrast, to take sides. Although comparison and contrast often contribute to argument, we can use this pattern for exposition alone. So often, in our real lives, it is not clear which alternative is preferable: if we are accepted at three good colleges, it may seem to make no difference which one we attend. Still, we can list differences and characteristics, like locale: rural, urban, small-town; we can find distinctions to compare and contrast, to set matters out for understanding—in the hope that clarity may facilitate choice.

Using comparison and contrast does not imply that we must make a choice among matters compared. Many reports required in the professional world do not require a decision from the reporter. Maybe we are asked to explain the differences among office systems supplied by Wang, IBM, Apple, and Xerox. Studying, classifying, we discern the differences; our bosses will do the choosing. On some occasions comparison and contrast results in a hung jury. On others, the essayist plays the role of researcher and then of decider: we can reach an audience by comparing and contrasting with apparent impartiality, and then explain that we have demonstrated superiority by juxtaposition.

We compare and contrast things which have something in common, and which have some differences as well. *M\*A\*S\*H* and *Hogan's Heroes* are both television shows set during a war, but they also differ. *War and Peace* and *Anna Karenina* are both novels, both by Tolstoy—and they differ considerably. Things compared must have enough in common and enough in contrast, and a purpose must be served in making the comparison. What is this comparison *for?* To compare *War and Peace* and *Love's Latest Gothic,* it may not be enough that both are novels. What purpose do we serve by comparing them? Maybe if we address an audience that cannot tell the difference, our essay serves a purpose.

Whenever we compare and contrast, we face a structural problem. How long do we go on talking about A's qualities before we move to the contrasting qualities of B? If we balance each sentence with a look at both A and B, the alternation will be too swift; our heads snap back and forth as if we were watching Ping-Pong again, and our necks get stiff. A student wrote:

> Green olives are an acquired taste, which I've thought ever since my sister's wedding reception when I got sick after eating twenty of them. Now I like black olives better. Green olives come in three sizes, Large, Extra Large, and Gigantic. Black olives have four, Huge, Colossal, Supercolossal, and Absolutely Enormous. You can buy green olives with pits, or stuffed with those awful little red things, or maybe onions. Black olives are sold with or without pits (so you don't have to hide them under your plate, or in your mother's African violets). Green olives are packed in squatty green jars. Black olives are piled into tall jars or in cans with wild labels.

These sentences give us whiplash. On the other hand, if we talk about A for ten pages before we get to B, we create another problem. When the reader starts seeing, on page eleven, the qualities of B that correspond to the earlier qualities of A, he has forgotten the details ten pages back. Always keep the audience in mind, and beware the confusion of too-swift alternation or of too-distant comparison.

In comparison and contrast the order of the points is essential; we must keep them parallel. If we are comparing and contrasting educational institutions according to admission policy, class size, and tuition, we must be sure that the points proceed in the same order in our speaking of each institution. If we use one order for one institution and a different order for the other, we lose the reader in a jumble of incoherence:

> Alice is taller than her sister Josephine, but Josephine has naturally curly hair like her father, and stands on the short side. Alice's hair is blond and straight like Uncle George's, and she likes to play tennis. Josephine plays the violin, but prefers jazz and disco music.

Because these comparisons jump back and forth, we have difficulty following them.

Analogy is sometimes described as a form of comparison. Analogy compares like and unlike, to make a point. According to Oswald Spengler, civilizations like organisms go through a life span, are born, live, and die. But civilizations, literally speaking, are *not* organisms like mosquitoes and sequoias. Spengler's analogy compares political and social forms with living, growing, breeding, dying organisms, in order to attribute a life span to institutions. Analogy is different enough from ordinary comparison and contrast so that we took it up on pages 145–146, after we discussed simile and metaphor.

### Thinking by Comparison and Contrast

We think by contrasted examples; we define by difference. See hamburgers and potatoes. Probably every essay we write can use comparison and contrast as we develop paragraphs. As a larger tool of thought, comparison and contrast forms a system of perception by opposition that requires us to classify parallel items and juxtapose similarities and differences. The trick in writing, as we present compared and contrasted material to an audience, is to tread a line between too-rapid oscillation and too-separate characterization of each. When we plan an essay of comparison and contrast, and when we look for a structure after generating the material, after the material has been generated and we look for a structure, we may find it especially useful to sketch an informal outline.

## Examples of Comparison and Contrast

### Eating Apples and Cooking Apples

Apples generally fall into one of two categories—those good for eating and those good for cooking. What makes a good eating apple? For one thing the skin should be pleasant to taste—not too thick or waxy and never bitter. The pulp should be pleasantly sweet without added sugar, and the texture should be crisp and moist, not dry or mealy. A perfectly fresh McIntosh is the best eating apple there is—soon after picking. After a couple of days the skin loses its tender crispness and the pulp becomes mushy. The McIntosh is a poor keeper, as the best eating apples tend to be; they are an ephemeral delight.

Because the skin of a cooking apple is usually removed in making apple pastries and sauces, a tough skin is no impediment. The thick and waxy skin of the Rome Beauty covers firm flesh, perhaps a little drier than the McIntosh, so that a Rome Beauty will never turn to mush when it's cooked. In general the drier, firmer-fleshed apples are good keepers that hold their shape in pies and pastries.

Finally, the qualities that make a good eating or cooking apple are a subjective matter. I hate the Delicious apple in all its incarnations, and yet to go to the supermarket in January you would think that it is the only apple that has come down to us from the Garden of Eden. Because she was not making pies that day, Eve was probably reaching for a McIntosh, a Granny Smith, or possibly an Empire—a cross between a McIntosh and a Delicious that has the succulent sweetness of the Mac and the firmness of the Delicious.

### A Choice for the Home Gardener

Old-fashioned apple trees grow twenty-five feet high and nearly as wide. One tree can displace a large portion of a suburban or city garden. But botanists have solved the space problem by grafting standard-variety branches onto the roots of dwarf trees that grow from nine to fifteen feet high.

Saving space is not the only convenience of the smaller trees. Gardeners can put away their ladders; they can prune, spray, and harvest dwarfs and semidwarf apple trees while standing on the ground. Also, these trees are quicker to mature, yielding fruit several years before their standard-sized progenitors.

On the other hand, if you're looking for lots of apples, the standard varieties might be best. Remember that you need good storage facilities, or equipment for making cider, or a market for your produce. But if you simply wish to provide your family with home-grown apples in modest quantities, the smaller trees may serve your purposes better, both for health and for beauty, for pink and white blossoms in the spring, for fresh fruit in the fall.

## Process Analysis

In Chapter 3, when we looked into methods of essay writing, from assignment through note-taking and brainstorming and sprinting, through drafts and revisions, we used the rhetorical pattern of process analysis. Analysis separates things into components; with process analysis we investigate the components (or steps) in a sequence. When we observed the history of Frank Rodriguez writing an essay, we analyzed a process.

Process analysis is the rhetorical tool by which we explain the steps and sequences in an operation. We can separate two common categories of process anlaysis according to their purposes. We give directions by process analysis: how to run a political campaign; how to bake an apple pie; how to improve your jump shot. Or we give information by process analysis: how Nixon was elected in 1972; how Julia Child learned to make knishes. For each, we narrate the steps in a process. Strategy differs according to purpose, according to our relationship to an audience: either we instruct our audience in the art of winning public elections or we tell them how it was done.

Exposition or explanation commonly needs process analysis, which answers the question "How?" *How* is a car manufactured? *How* does the internal combustion engine work? *How* do you change a tire? The answers to these questions differ from one another in tone: the answer to the first would make a scientific article in an encyclopedia; the answer to the second would be a feature story in a newspaper; the answer to the third would be practical directions. But the three are alike in *pattern:* in each answer, exposition analyzes a process, a continuing sequence of events. Process analysis describes sequence or chronology. This pattern demands that we follow chronological order, advancing from a beginning by steps to an end.

When our analysis of process explains how something is made—automobile, perfume, skyscraper—we have something like an encyclopedia article. The writer's task is narrative, and often descriptive; the writer must struggle to clarify scenes and actions for the reader. Where process analysis gives directions—how to change a tire, how to make waffles, how to find an apartment in Manhattan—the writer must take special care to consider the audience's level of knowledge. When we give directions we assume that we know something that our audience does not know. Therefore it behooves us, in a process analysis essay giving directions, to remain aware of audience, especially by defining terms. If we write scientific or mechanical process analysis, we usually require much definition. How do you change a tire? We must define *lug* for a reader who does not know a lug from a roofing nail.

### Thinking with Process Analysis

We must be wary of confusing process analysis with cause and effect. If we write an essay on *why* yeast makes flour and water rise in a bread pan, we write a scientific explanation, in which necessary effect follows particular cause. But if we write an essay on *how* to bake bread, with a recipe and steps of action, we analyze a process. If we intrude the chemistry lab upon the kitchen, mixing up *how* and *why,* the essay may become incoherent through internal disorder. Keep *why* distinct from *how,* cause and effect from process analysis. Or if the shape of your essay requires that you use both patterns one after the other, be certain that you retain control.

Encyclopedia articles often show how exposition works as process analysis—by addressing the *how* of a process. The encyclopedia explains how crude oil becomes gasoline and how gasoline makes the internal combustion engine work. At the same time, the scientific entries in the encyclopedia tell us why gasoline is flammable and why parts of the world are richer in petroleum deposits than others. Cause and effect analysis is analogous to the science of the laboratory; process analysis is analogous to engineering and applied science.

Process analysis, like the other rhetorical patterns, can make a whole essay or a small part of one. Suppose you had a general interest in forms of energy. You might begin a paper by classifying energy according to its sources: oil, fission, wind, coal, water, sun. You might compare and contrast the sources. Focusing on petroleum you might narrate the journey of crude oil from discovery to extraction to refining to transportation to retail sales to vehicle. This narration would be a sequential, chronological analysis of process. This analysis could occupy most of an essay, with much detail; or, cut down with skill, it could become a paragraph or two.

When we revise any paper, we should look through it to recognize the rhetorical pattern of process analysis. Sometimes a writer approaches this pattern without realizing it, and uses it badly by omitting definition or by leaving the analysis incomplete. If we refer to a process we must detail or explain it for an audience that might not be aware of its progress; we must include all the necessary steps. We must consider whether we have defined terms with a clear notion of audience.

### An Example of Process Analysis

#### *Planting an Apple Tree*

The first step is to choose the appropriate site. Apple trees flourish best on rolling land; planting on the sides or tops of hills allows cold air to drain away during potentially damaging frosty spring nights. Hilly terrain also provides good water drainage; apples cannot abide wet feet.

Once the site is chosen, the next step is soil preparation. Where topsoil is shallow the subsoil should be enriched with organic matter, with compost; in sandy soils, we should mix compost with peat.

Plant the young tree no deeper than it grew in the nursery, spreading the roots well in the hole. Put the topsoil back first, and tamp it firmly with your foot. Water well, allowing the water to drain completely into the soil. Then finish filling the hole with the subsoil. If you dug up sod to plant the tree, replace the sod face down, and mulch with three or four inches of hay, straw, or leaf mold. Give the tree another good soak, and don't allow the soil to dry out for at least ten days.

### Definition

To define, we may need to analyze a process, or to adduce an example, or to use other rhetorical patterns—but definition, however we achieve it, is itself a pattern of rhetoric. We list it last because it combines so much. Definition often groups things that are alike and differentiates them from unlike things; in this mode it uses comparison and contrast, or at least comparison, as when a dictionary defining *portal* resorts to synonyms (see pages 94–96) for comparison: *entrance, door, entryway.*

Classification is often crucial to definition. We begin to define something by naming the class it belongs to.

A car is a vehicle. A sparrow hawk is a bird. Then the definition distinguishes the particular species from other members of its genus by means of contrasting examples: a car is mechanical, unlike a horse; it is self-propelled, unlike a bicycle. If we look up *sparrow hawk,* we find first that it is a bird and then, in narrowing details, what sort of a bird it is: its characteristics, its markings, its habits. We go from the broadest classification—*bird*—to the narrowest description of bands of color.

Definition must often move deeply into description. Some portions of definition—like naming the bands that distinguish one bird from another—require exact observation, adjectives of color, details of width in inches or millimeters. An ichthyologist, telling us about a newly discovered Antarctic fish, needs description as much as he needs classification.

Frequently we need definition in exposition to clarify matters for an audience. In analyzing the process of changing a tire, we may realize that the reader needs to know what a lug is. In writing about downhill skiing, perhaps we mention moguls. If we think of our audience, we know that we must define *mogul,* because readers who have not skied may find *mogul* an obscure word.

Always define a word that comes from a particular sport or pastime, discipline or profession. Such definition is invaluable, in the service of clarity. We use simple definition in our writing when we recognize: this is the kind of word that would drive me to the dictionary if I wasn't familiar with its use in this context.

The types of definition illustrated above are simple: we define by near-synonym, by description, and by class. We need simple definitions in order to reach an audience quickly, to clarify with economy, but the brief elucidation of terms is incidental to the larger purposes of an essay. On another level, definition may fill the largest purposes of all. One might call Plato's *Republic* a huge definition of *mind.* Although we would not write a whole essay to define *lug,* as thinking human beings we may write at length to define an abstraction like *courtesy.* Thought about such an abstraction follows the rhetorical pattern of definition. The meaning of *sparrow hawk,* like the meaning of *broadax* or *Abraham Lincoln,* is agreed upon. But suppose we define a subjective or philosophical word: *conservatism* or *imagination* or *romanticism* or *democracy.* We can write an entire essay to define such an idea; we can write a book—we can write a library of books. Definition is the rhetorical form most common to philosophical writers. Wanting to understand *wisdom,* or *good,* or *literature,* or *social class,* we pursue philosophical definition. These definitions require other patterns of rhetoric in arriving at their accomplishment. To define *democracy,* we must compare and contrast it to other forms of government. To define *maturity* we need to classify stages of growth; the movement from one to the next is process analysis. Almost every definition cries out for examples: of *literature,* of *courtesy.* Our thinking's purpose determines our essay's pattern; and purpose as usual requires a sense of audience.

### Thinking by Definition

When we revise, it is imperative to check back for undefined terms. Sometimes we fall into using a special vocabulary incomprehensible to our readers. More often, we use vague words (*conservative, middle class*) without defining them, without allowing our audience to understand how we use them in the context of our thought. For the first lack we can supply quick definitions perhaps by synonyms or classification; the trick is knowing that they are needed. For the second, probably the best revision would replace a vague word with a more particular phrase. But if we cannot discover a particular that does what we require, we can supply a definition for the term. We must take some time to define an abstraction as we use it. Or we can write a whole essay to explore the meaning of the abstraction.

When we write a whole essay of definition, we should reconsider the other rhetorical patterns, to judge which of the modes (possibly two or three of them) will best deliver our understanding to our audience. Defining one word, do not forget to check its etymology in the *Oxford English Dictionary* or in other dictionaries that supply the sources and history of words. (See Chapter 4.) Although essays that open with a reference to the dictionary ("*Webster's* defines *democracy* as . . .") are common to the point of nausea, the curious student will sometimes discover that a word's origins provide the writer with an image, almost an example, which gives color to definition, which helps to make contact with an audience.

## Examples of Definition

*The American Apple Pie*

Apple pie, as we know it in this country, consists of slices of this fruit, mixed with sugar and seasoning, baked inside a crust of dough. Usually cooked and served in a shallow, round dish, this dessert is as common as the flag and as American as apple pie.

*Apples and Evil*

The most useful fruits, apples first discovered their utility in the definition of sin. It was sin, or evil, for man and woman to eat the fruit that God forbade them to eat, the tree that bore the knowledge of good and evil. It seems that the writers of the Old Testament, or at least the authors of Genesis, believed that there is no evil without consciousness of evil. Although it would be illogical therefore to equate consciousness with evil, we can at least acknowledge that after we have eaten the fruit of the knowledge of good and evil, true innocence is no longer possible. Once that consciousness exists, we are moral beings, prone to the evil or sin that we are born to, and subject to the moral universe. Evil is disobedience, and it is also a result of disobedience, but if there were no evil there could be no possibility of good. From early in the history of the Christian church, thinkers have recognized this paradox. If Adam and Eve had not disobeyed God, if man had not fallen, Jesus would have had nothing and no one to redeem. This is the paradox of the fortunate fall, the happy sin, by which traditional Christians find themselves praising the wicked eating of an apple in paradise.

## Narration

With narrative we tell a story; we recount events in succession. Much of our everyday conversation tells stories.

By itself narrative is a form of writing parallel to exposition, description, and argument or persuasion. But narrative is also used in the service of other forms. With process analysis we narrate as we explain by describing a sequence. When we use example, sometimes our example is a story. Narrative (the history of innovative baking, the campaign of Cyrus against the Greeks) may support argument. Much newspaper reporting is narrative, of murders and baseball games. Telling a joke is narrative.

When we tell a story, we must find our way between two extremes. The narrative must have enough detail so that the reader knows what is happening. It must not have so much detail that the reader gets bogged down. The detail must be appropriate; it must have the right quality, as well as the right quantity, and the audience must be able to follow and appreciate the motion of sequence. Here is a fragment from a paper.

> When I heard the doorbell, I stood immediately, my heart pounding. I knew it was her. I didn't answer it quickly, and heard the door opening toward me. I must have forgotten to lock it! I looked around for a second. Then I picked up my suitcase and climbed through the open window.

This was the first version:

> When I heard the doorbell, I placed my hands against the arms of the chair and pushed myself upright immediately. My heart pounded in my chest. I knew it was her. For some reason, I didn't move toward the door right away. I just stood there and stared, my heart pounding, my legs shaking. Then I heard a sound like the doorknob turning, and a creaky noise as she must have started to push the door open. I realized that I had forgotten to lock it when I came in from the drug store. I looked all around to see if there was any way to escape. I saw the window open beside me. Without thinking of what I was doing, I picked up my suitcase, checked the fasteners on it, set it on the windowsill and lowered it to the ground, which was only about 2½ feet down. Then I sat down on the sill myself, swinging my legs through, and pulled the rest of my body after me.

This student was commendably rich in detail. But by the end, we feel as if we have watched someone sleep eight hours. We have stopped paying attention, for total recall is totally boring. We want the essential narrative and nothing more. The revision does it. If the writer had gone further in cutting and had written

> When I heard the doorbell, I climbed out the window.

we would have missed some crucial information. We must always be sensitive to audience—how much is needed? How much is too much?—when we tell a story.

The time we take to tell a story need have little to do with the elapsed time of the event itself. Writing about a football game, we may spend two pages on one play that took only twenty seconds of the game. When we finish narrating this crucial play, we might summarize another fifty-nine minutes and forty seconds in a brief paragraph. Purpose, and clarity for audience, determine narrative—not fidelity to the original duration of things.

The structure or order of narrative is often uncomplicated, a straightforward sequence of events as they happen: first this occurred, then that. But on some occasions we begin our story with its ending, then flash back and tell in chronological order the events that led up to the conclusion. Reading a sports story, no one wishes to wait until the end of the story to find out who won; the journalist's lead paragraph tells us the outcome; then usually the reporter will narrate the progress of the game with detailed attention to crucial moments.

In narrative we need to be aware of the point of view from which we tell the story. If we tell about three people, it is confusing when we skip from one point of view to another. If it is not actually obscure it is incoherent and displeasing. Here is an anecdote with a confused point of view:

> Indignant, the dwarf climbed to the ceiling and perched in the candelabrum, hissing and spitting like a frightened cat. Griselda watched in fascination but with growing terror. Rumpelstiltskin made up his mind to act.

We should stay inside the mind of one or the other. If we must switch from one side to another—if we narrate the siege of Troy, in an epic, we might need to move from Greek intentions to Trojan beliefs—we must pay attention to transition if we are to remain clear to our listeners. When we switch point of view, we must be open about it.

Transitions can be a problem. Telling a story out loud, we may fall into a pattern: ". . . and then . . . and then . . . and then. . . ." Writing it down we should be more careful. We may need *later*; we may need *meanwhile*; a strong narrative makes these words obvious and therefore unnecessary.

Here is a passage from a book by a doctor who spent a year in Vietnam. It begins with exposition and ends with narrative.

> The western perimeter of the camp bordered on a "free-fire zone." Anyone or anything that moves in that area is free game and can be shot, mortared, or bombed. All of the military maps had it marked as such and supposedly all civilians in the area had been informed.
>
> The camp dump was in this "free-fire zone." Each morning at the same time a truck drove out to the dump and all of the tin cans, cardboard containers, wrappers, and garbage from the camp was

dumped about fifty meters inside the zone. Within minutes, the dump was filled with Vietnamese from nearby villes (hamlets) gathering cans and garbage. The marines in the watchtower would fire close to them to frighten them away. A few days earlier, an eight-year-old Vietnamese boy had been wounded by these warning shots and was brought to the aid station where he was kept until his wounds were healed. One day he stole an orange soda from a marine who shot and killed him as he tried to run away.

John A. Parrish, M.D., *12, 20 & 5*

This is a good example of narrative used in exposition and ultimately, as you can see, in an argument that does not need stating. Here narrative has provided an example of war's brutality.

### An Example of Narration

#### *Trouble in the Orchard*

When Richard Bone woke on an October night two years ago, he felt that something was wrong without knowing why he felt as he did. He pulled on a coat over his nightshirt; he pulled long boots lined with felt over his bare feet. Then he set out the back door into his orchard where he had spent a long day with his neighbors picking trees of their ripe apples. At first he saw nothing out of order. Then he made a series of observations in quick succession. First, there was a large bird's nest in an old tree where there had been no bird's nest earlier that afternoon. Second, there was a dog underneath the tree, which made Bone remember that it was a howling sound which had waked him.

But third, he knew that the bird's nest was not a bird's nest, and that the dog was not a dog.

What looked like a bird's nest was a hedgehog come to banquet on his McIntoshes. What looked like a dog was an Eastern coyote or coydog. When Bone returned with his shotgun, the coyote had departed. The hedgehog had not—but it was soon among the departed.

### Description

Description often becomes necessary for clear exposition, and we use it sometimes within rhetorical patterns: in classification, in definition, in comparison and contrast, and in other patterns. Description serves the essayist's purpose, and reaches its audience, when it contrasts the coloring of apples; for this contrast, each apple must be described. Description by itself *evokes* place, scene, or time of day; we feel that we are there. Evocative description, of course, frequently forms a part of fiction and autobiography. Here is how James Agee begins to describe the remembered summer evenings of childhood:

> Supper was at six and was over by half past. There was still daylight, shining softly and with a tarnish, like the lining of a shell; and the carbon lamps lifted at the corners were on in the light, and the locusts were started, and the fire flies were out, and a few frogs were flopping in the dewy grass, by the time the fathers and the children came out.
>
> James Agee, "Knoxville: Summer 1915"

The order we give to details, in description, is usually *spatial.* But words follow each other—they are not simultaneous in the way a picture seems to be—and we necessarily move in words from point to point in a sequence that has to be chronological. So in description we talk about space in a temporal way. In describing a scene, we can begin from the periphery and move to the center or move from the center to the periphery. The order is not crucial: it is crucial that there *be* an order, that we do not move from center to periphery to center to periphery to periphery.

Description moves from extremes of objective measurement (6.5 inches long) to subjective exaggeration (as big as an aircraft carrier). In much writing, we mix these extremes according to purpose and audience. If we write scientifically, we remain objective and exclude the subjective. On the other hand, when we write to make the reader feel with us, we use figures of speech and images to embody emotions and to touch the reader.

Some writers seem to think of description as filler or padding—not only beginning writers, but also professionals who write the less skillful stories in adventure or confession magazines, and are paid by the word. In these places, we will see description used to delay information, to tantalize.

> Rhonda turned from the window, her eyes wet. "Belinda," she said to me, "I could forgive you for Ron. I could forgive you for Bruce. I could even forgive you for Althea. But there is one thing I could never forgive you for!"
>
> She turned back to the window, her eyes flooded with tears. My cheeks suffused with shame. Over her shoulders, I could see the sweet meadows of home, adeck with lilacs and daisies, their sleepy heads waving in the soft breezes of June, while above,

storm clouds gathered to chase away the white puff-ball clouds of early morning.

"They Had a Name for Me," *Real Romance*

Description's main function here seems to be suspense, as a daytime television serial uses an advertisement. To be sure, it also shows a heavy-handed attempt to use description as a good writer does, *for the meaning and the feeling that images carry*. This anonymous writer has the protagonist look at the fields in an attempt to symbolize her past innocence, contrasted to the torment ("storm clouds") of the sinful present.

When you write well, your description cannot seem to approach pure symbolism because then it will not seem to be real description. But there is room for invention, especially when we use comparisons (simile, metaphor, analogy; see pages 142–146) that carry feeling.

In *Ulysses*, James Joyce has Stephen Dedalus look at the sea when he is feeling depressed. "The ring of bog and skyline held a dull green mass of liquid." Though the description is literal enough, it expresses Stephen's emotions. Here is a passage from the book about Vietnam from which I quoted earlier. The author describes finding some bodies washed up on a riverbank.

> Four nude, markedly swollen, water-logged bodies lay side by side on their backs. Each had a massively swollen face. Eyes seemed to try to bulge out of sockets whose contents were as big as apples. Their lips were three times normal size and each mouth was open and round like that of a fish, with a massive splitting tongue protruding skyward. A thin, bloody fluid trickled from their nostrils.
>
> Massive edema and rigor mortis held their arms up and out in front of them with fat fingers reaching toward the clouds. Their scrota were the size of softballs, and their swollen penises stood as if erect. Their knees were bent in identical frog-leg positions. The smell was overwhelming and hundreds of flies circled around those which were already busy inspecting the mouths and nostrils. There was not a mark on the front of their bodies.
>
> John A. Parrish, M.D., *12, 20 & 5*

The accurate description has modifiers that come from observation, not from the worn tracks: *fat* fingers, *frog-leg* positions, *massively swollen*; it has statements of fact and measurement, like "massive edema" and "three times normal size"; it has comparisons that embody feeling, like "mouth . . . open and round like that of a fish," ". . . as big as apples," and "scrota . . . the size of softballs." Parrish's purpose is to move (repel) his audience; he succeeds by the manner of his description.

Statistical accuracy in description must never be confused with emotional accuracy. Again, sometimes we must lie to tell the truth. A contemporary poem ends with a sudden vision: a hundred cows in a field. Reviewing this poem, a hostile critic (carried away by his anger into absurdity) asked *how* the poet could tell that exactly one hundred cows were in the field. He received a postcard from the poet: "I counted the teats and divided by four." The pseudoparticular has a long tradition. It does not lie, because we know that it is not intended to be statistically accurate. When Wordsworth says of daffodils, "Ten thousand saw I at a glance," we do not suspect him of counting. If we write, "The sandwich was as thick as the toe of Italy," we are saying that it was very thick—so thick that it astounded and delighted us. If we say, "The sandwich was two and five-eights inches thick," we are being pedantic, and expressing little astonishment. Mere accuracy is all right, but the exaggeration is a lie that is truer to the feeling than accuracy is. Sometimes in writing you can be accurate in both ways at once; maybe a list of ingredients could be literally true and so carry an astonished reaction to abundance: "salami, bologna, ham, roast beef, corned beef, Swiss cheese, provolone, onions, lettuce, red peppers, olive oil, vinegar, and, I believe, oregano."

Although we use description for many purposes, we also use it purely, and many instructors assign brief descriptive papers or paragraphs for practice in description, much as they assign exercises in the rhetorical patterns. Here is an apple description:

### An Example of Description

*Bone's Orchard*

The orchard faced north on a gentle slope above the farmhouse and the barn. The trees were evenly spaced, and from the hills across the valley the orchard looked like the squares of a quilt. In spring the massive blossoms turned the slope a uniform white. All summer the green leaves of the mature trees blended into the grass of the hill, and the orchard seemed to retreat into a greened shade. In autumn, as one approached the orchard, one became aware of a rich harvest of redness weighing down the old boughs. For a few weeks ladders and apple-pickers poked among the trees, until the fruit was picked clean, packed into crates for shipment to stores, or squeezed into gallons of fresh, tangy cider. In winter the black leafless branches looked starved and skinny against the snow.

Notice that this writer has started close up, moved farther back, and then moved close again—while following the chronological order of the seasons.

_____ **EXERCISES** _____

1. Discuss in class the exposition you have encountered or undertaken so far in this course. In writing essays and exercises, what kinds of exposition have you attempted? What forms or patterns have you found in your assigned reading? What expository devices can you discover in *Writing Well?*

2. Here are ten topics. For each topic, make notes employing one of the rhetorical patterns; among your sets of notes, include all seven rhetorical patterns. For instance, if the topic were thunderstorms, you could *classify* them, discerning sorts of storms; you could tell how they occur, by *process analysis;* or you could *define* a thunderstorm. Discuss in class the purposes served by suggested patterns.

| | |
|---|---|
| pollution | snowmobiles |
| baseball | zoos |
| cousins | freshmen |
| state parks | graveyards |
| supermarkets | shoes |

3. In class discussion, discover ways of using all seven rhetorical patterns, in addition to narrative and description, in writing about one subject. (See the series of apple essays in this chapter.) Try automobiles, houses, books, or fast-food franchises. Discuss the purposes each pattern can serve. Notice how the patterns engender ideas.

This exercise can lead to a written assignment.

4. Divide the class into seven groups, one for each rhetorical pattern. Let each member of each group find in a current newspaper or magazine an example of the assigned pattern.

5. Find rhetorical patterns and forms of exposition in textbooks for other courses. Notice the modes of thought appropriate to different disciplines—history, psychology, business—and the characteristic patterns or forms that these disciplines require. Is history narrative above all? What else is it?

6. Here are four passages from essays. Determine which rhetorical pattern or patterns are employed in each. Determine the purposes for each pattern.

a. To test properly the mechanic removes the plug and lays it against the engine so that the base around the plug is electrically grounded, kicks the starter lever and watches the spark-plug gap for a blue spark. If there isn't any he can conclude one of two things: (a) there is an electrical failure or (b) his experiment is sloppy. If he is experienced he will try it a few more times, checking connections, trying every way he can think of to get that plug to fire. Then, if he can't get it to fire, he finally concludes that *a* is correct, there's an electrical failure, and the experiment is over. He has proved that his hypothesis is correct.

Robert M. Pirsig, *Zen and the Art of Motorcycle Maintenance*

b. So Grant and Lee were in complete contrast, representing two diametrically opposed elements in American life. Grant was the modern man emerging; beyond him, ready to come on the stage, was the great age of steel and machinery, of crowded cities and a restless burgeoning vitality. Lee might have ridden down from the old age of chivalry, lance in hand, silken banner fluttering over his head. Each man was the perfect champion of his cause, drawing both his strengths and his weaknesses from the people he led.

Bruce Catton, "Grant and Lee: A Study in Contrasts,"
in *The American Story*

c. The first baseline in defining Presidential types is *activity-passivity*. How much energy does the man invest in his Presidency? Lyndon Johnson went at his day like a human cyclone, coming to rest long after the sun went down. Calvin Coolidge often slept eleven hours a night and still needed a nap in the middle of the day. In between the Presidents array themselves on the high or low side of the activity line.

The second baseline is *positive-negative affect* toward one's activity—that is, how he feels about what he does. Relatively speaking, does he seem to experience his political life as happy or sad, enjoyable or discouraging, positive or negative in its main effect? The feeling I am after here is not grim satisfaction in a job well done, not some philosophical conclusion. The idea is this: is he someone who, on the surfaces we can see, gives forth the feeling that he has *fun* in political life? Franklin Roosevelt's Secretary of War, Henry L. Stimson, wrote that the Roosevelts "not only understood the *use* of power, they knew the *enjoyment* of power, too. . . . Whether a man is burdened by power or enjoys power; whether he is trapped by responsibility or made free by it; whether he is moved by other people and outer forces or moves them—that is the essence of leadership."

James David Barber, *The Presidential Character*

d. What is pornography to one man is the laughter of genius to another.

The word itself, we are told, means "pertaining to harlots"—the graph of the harlot. But nowadays, what is a harlot? If she was a woman who took money from a man in return for going to bed with him—really, most wives sold themselves, in the past, and plenty of harlots gave themselves, when they felt like it, for nothing. If a woman hasn't got a tiny streak of harlot in her, she's a dry stick as a rule. And probably most harlots had somewhere a streak of womanly generosity. Why be so cut and dried? The law is a dreary thing, and its judgments have nothing to do with life. . . .

One essay on pornography, I remember, comes to the conclusion that pornography in art is that which is calculated to arouse sexual desire, or sexual excitement. And stress is laid on the fact, whether the author or artist *intended to* arouse sexual feelings. It is the old vexed question of intention, become so dull today, when we know how strong and influential our unconscious intentions are. And why a man should be held guilty of his conscious intentions, and innocent of his unconscious intentions, I don't know, since every man is more made up of unconscious intentions than of conscious ones. I am what I am, not merely what I think I am.

D. H. Lawrence, "Pornography,"
in *Pornography and Obscenity*

# 8

## *Argument and Persuasion*

In Chapter 7 I spoke about exposition and rhetorical patterns, then about narrative and description. It is time to look into argument and persuasion, a large category of writing useful throughout our lives. Of course argument and persuasion make use of exposition; without an expository foundation, argumentative writing collapses into bombast or harangue. Exposition provides the foundation for persuasion's structure—and it is not the whole building.

In writing expository prose, we assemble details—facts, anecdotes, descriptions—to understand and to explain, not to take a position and defend it. On occasion, we might seem to argue that something is superior to something else—say, the Cubist painters to the Impressionists—when we are really only giving our personal preference. If we explain our own likes and dislikes, we write exposition; we do not argue that anyone else should feel as we do. Exposing a preference is valid exposition. When I read someone's praise of crocheting, I can enjoy and understand it, without feeling any pressure to make an afghan.

The honest writer avoids some forms of persuasion, or attempted persuasion. "The rhetorician would deceive his neighbors, / The sentimentalist himself"—as I quoted before from W. B. Yeats—and in much dishonest writing the writer is both sentimentalist and, in Yeats's sense, rhetorician. The loaded word—when the dictator's police shoot "unarmed civilians" or "a traitorous rabble"—or loaded syntax—when the beer company's advertisement asks, "As a lawyer, what do you think of Fitz's?"—can combine to make a whole essay into a loaded argument, or propaganda. Words or phrases seem to say one thing and really say another. In good writing, we must avoid such subterfuge.

Persuasion occupies us continually, perceptibly and imperceptibly. We live in a country that promotes a marketplace of goods and ideas; persuasion is one of our national industries. Although political speeches and newspaper editorials are exercises in argument and persuasion, maybe the most prevalent form of persuasion is advertising. We are subject to it daily on television and radio, in newspapers and magazines, over public address systems, and on billboards. Thousands of people spend their working lives trying to persuade us to buy this new car over that one, this red toothpaste over that green one, this diet soft drink instead of that diet soft drink. We are the audience this industry addresses; we are the readers whose responses they predict. As we study argument and persuasion in English composition, it is a side effect of our study that we may better identify and understand the art of persuasion as it is practiced upon us.

Argument is not only external but internal. In our everyday lives, we argue within ourselves as we approach decisions. Should we look for a summer job or enroll in a computer course? Should we major in marketing or Chinese? Should we buy new running shoes or wear our old ones and save the money? Thinking, we engage in argument and persuasion within ourselves—inner argument, dialogue, debate between opposing internal forces.

Knowing how to argue is a useful skill. We use argument within ourselves to arrive at decisions; we use it with others as we discuss business strategies or curriculum changes on committees, as members of a town meeting, a local PTA, a law office, an environmental action group; we use it as fund-raisers for a church or a public television station; we use it in applying for foundation grants and in drafting letters to the editor of a newspaper; we use it when we discuss toxic waste, child abuse, nuclear power, acid rain, tax cuts, bus fares for the elderly, pothole repair, plea bargaining, working mothers, and university investment policies. Our ability to express opinions persuasively will allow us to make differences in shaping public policy.

Most of the time, in writing argument, we work with debatable material. We cannot prove our thesis as a mathematician or a philosophical logician can, by manipulating his own terms. We cannot measure our results in a cyclotron like a physicist. We end with probability and persuasion, not with certainty or proof. We employ an old-fashioned sense of the word *proof,* an exactness that we might call "the agreement of reasonable people."

Matters of fact are rarely arguable. When we disagree about the running time of the Boston Marathon, how many films Clark Gable made, or the population of Minneapolis, we can look it up. About facts, disagreement is pointless. And it is pointless to argue about personal preference. We either do or do not like Hubbard squash, punk rock, jogging, or polyester suits. There is little hope, and usually little purpose, in trying to persuade others to feel as we do.

But opinions—about value or worth, about meaning or interpretation, about solutions to problems—are arguable. People *differ* about two-career marriages, graffiti in subways, bilingual education, entitlement programs, censorship of textbooks, computer literacy in elementary schools, and public assistance. We have our own ideas of what is right, and through persuasion and argument we try to convince our parents, our friends, our employers, our neighbors, our communities, or our congressional representatives.

## AUDIENCE

Market research identifies audiences for manufacturers; writers must do their own. The job is simpler when we stand to speak in front of an audience, and the comparison of speaker's task to writer's can illustrate the writer's difficulties. When we address a group of listeners, we can tell much about our audience by glancing around the room: age, economic status, sex, often degree of education, often social class. As we speak, we can test the success or failure of our efforts by observing the expressions on people's faces, by attention or inattention, by laughter, coughing, or applause.

But when we write an essay we address an unseen audience, and we cannot profit from response—unless we try out our paragraphs on friends or roommates. When we write to persuade, we must work to keep the unseen audience in mind; we must try to visualize them, making a mental comparison between writing and public speaking, so that we can organize information, ideas, and reasons to elicit response from our real readers.

Our tone must meet our audience as equals, as if we were face to face; it must show our argument as fair, as open to modification or to further discussion. Argument must imply the process of dialogue, in which the other side has a voice. Tone of address to audience is fundamental. We lose our chance for a hearing unless we establish rapport and maintain it. Rapport depends first on identifying audience and then on using common sense in addressing it. When we give examples of the occasions for persuasion, we categorize by audience. An argument for breast feeding over formula feeding addressed to suburban American mothers would be very different from one addressed to Third World mothers. An argument for safe toys would require a different emphasis, directed to parents, than it would if it were addressed to toy manufacturers. A plea for more police foot patrols would take a different form if we proposed it to residents of an urban neighborhood with high crime statistics than if we made the suggestion to a suburban neighborhood worried about taxes.

One way to address the problem of the audience, in connection with our argument, is to become the audience. If there is a campus issue at the moment on which student opinion is divided, a little irrational screaming during the class hour will do wonders. Listen to what people say; listen to what you yourself say. Sometimes an instructor has been known to play back on a tape recorder, after a reasonable consensus, the original hot debate. It is notable that when classes break into groups of three to five, consensus arrives more quickly.

## REASONABLENESS IN ARGUMENT

Most of the time, we persuade by being reasonable—and also by seeming so. The *being* is clear thinking; the *seeming* is tone. We will *be* reasonable by writing with clarity and by avoiding typical errors of thinking that I will mention later. We will *seem* reasonable by refusing to be dogmatic, by allowing time to opposing points of view, and by writing with the modesty that distinguishes between fact and opinion. It is not that we should continually qualify our remarks by tagging them with phrases like *in my opinion*; it is more the attitude we take. If it is in fact raining, it will not be dogmatic to assert that the grass is wet. But if we look at a landscape and call it pretty, obviously we are uttering a feeling of our own; nothing *necessarily* follows except within ourselves.

Of course it is natural to mix fact and opinion when we write. We are obligated only for the sake of honest writing, to know which is which. A fact is information that can be documented from historical and scientific sources. ("Truth" is elusive; the scientific "facts" of one century may be illusion to another; a "fact" is what we can reasonably accept as true.) A fact is also a statement of personal experience that can be accepted as reasonable. "It rained all day, May 31, 1984" can be fact; "Hester looked intelligent" is opinion, or surmise, and not fact. When we refer to someone else's documented opinion—"her minister thought that Hester looked intelligent"—we are on the border between fact and opinion. It is a pity that human life is so full of twilights; day and night are so easily distinguishable; but everything human seems to flourish in twilight.

When we quote the minister, we have quoted an outside source, which makes us appear objective, yet we have quoted only an opinion. With this sort of reference, we can write as if the reference were fact if we do not lean on it too heavily. On the other hand, if we make the minister's opinion the fulcrum in our essay ("But contrary to her doctor's statement, we know from her minister that Hester looked intelligent. Therefore . . ."), the opinion will crumble and the essay collapse. We have let ourselves seem to be unreasonable.

For persuasive argument, we must discover a tone that uses fact when it is relevant, inserts opinion modestly and reasonably, allows time and space to doubts, and builds a sequential argument by paragraph steps that the reader can follow. Conviction is one thing, belligerence another. It is the difference between "Let me show you how I think and maybe you will begin to think as I do" and "Agree with me or else!"

In the debate about cutbacks in federal funding for social programs, together with increases in defense spending, it is common for partisans to pretend that their opponents are warmongers who despise the poor or liberals who think that we need no armed forces. Telling arguments acknowledge that the opposition has its points. Here are sentences from two essays with different emphases:

> Although a strong defense is necessary for a country like the United States, which has worldwide interests and influence, we will jeopardize our future security if we neglect the real needs of the poor and education for the next generation of Americans.

> Of course there is a degree of poverty and suffering that any decent government must guarantee to alleviate, but without a believable force for defense, the United States will find itself lacking the prosperity that can supply the alleviation.

In each passage the writer attempts to acknowledge the opponent, and to indicate that the writer's mind is not closed off.

For a purer example of argument, we go to the op-ed page of a newspaper:

### Women's Work Is Never Done

Last week the U.S. Census Bureau reported that the number of women in managerial and administrative jobs rose from 18.5 percent to 30.5 percent between 1970 and 1980. According to the census study, there are more women now in public administration, financial management, personnel and labor relations, accounting and the professions than there were 10 years ago. This may be progress, but on-the-job equality for women is still far from reality.

The percentage of these managerial and professional jobs held by women does not approximate the percentage of women in the work-force. It falls 12 points short of the 42.5 percent of women who work outside the home.

Although the number of women in the professions doubled in some cases in 10 years, only 13.4 percent of doctors, 8.3 percent of architects, 14 percent of lawyers and 4.6 percent of engineers are women. Like women in lower-echelon jobs, these women are paid less than men and bring home paychecks that are about 60 percent of their male counterparts' earnings.

Women are stalled on the corporate ladder as well. An article in this month's *Fortune* magazine points out that no woman is in line to become the president or chief executive officer at any of the country's largest companies, despite the numbers of women advancing into middle management. So much for theories that once women achieved a critical mass in the work force, sex discrimination would end and women would advance at the same rate as men.

Susan Fraker's *Fortune* article suggests that women's lack of progress stems from a persistent failure to treat women equally on the job, to give them the same kind of constructive criticism and frank feedback offered their male colleagues. Affirmative-action programs have been viewed as a way of treating women better than men, of giving them a preferential edge. But if women are not told what they are doing right, what they are doing wrong and how their performance could be improved, there is little chance for progress.

The lingering resistance to women on every rung of the job ladder can be overcome. Phyllis Schlafly is not alone in her wrong-headed assertion that workplace equality for women will only come at men's expense. At recent hearings on comparable worth—

the notion of offering women in traditionally low-paying, female-dominated jobs like teachers, nurses and secretaries the same salaries paid to men in similar jobs—Schlafly testified that comparable worth targets blue-collar men and is "unfair to the traditional family."

   Denying women equality in the workplace is unfair to women. It is unfair to men whose mothers, wives and daughters are denied advancement and fair wages. It is unfair to families—traditional and otherwise—who depend on women's earnings. Denying women equality is also unfair to employers and the nation, which does not benefit from the full range of talent, experience and productivity in the work force.

*The Boston Globe,* April 19, 1984

This essay contains exposition in order to establish grounds for the argument that "Denying women equality in the workplace is unfair. . . ." The explanation provides a basis for advocacy. Then the writer adduces the opposition's arguments and tries to dismiss them by examples and statistics. Notice how the argument concludes with an appeal to the widest possible constituency.

### TIME FOR THE OPPOSITION

   When we hope to persuade, we need to pay court to the opposition—and the opposition is a portion of our audience. We need to imagine possible rebuttals of our position, so that in our argument we can anticipate them. Sometimes we can take on the objections directly. Suppose we are arguing that television news is an abomination. Suppose we argue that television newscasters have become celebrities, that they are hired for looks and personality rather than competence as journalists. We might say, "Networks claim that because television is a visual medium, on-camera appearance is basic to a reporter's ability to communicate with the public. But. . . ." Then we could contradict by means of anecdote, example, or appeal to a hypothesis. To acknowledge possible objections is to weaken their effectiveness.

   Thinking of opposing arguments is also a natural system for generating and gathering ideas. We must put ourselves on the other side, and consider the evidence that argues against our thesis. If we argue that possession of handguns should be illegal, we must consider the argument that Americans have the constitutional right to bear arms. If we contend that impounded dogs and cats should not be used for laboratory experiments, we must answer the argument that by sacrificing unwanted animals we may save human lives. By considering counter-notions, we can develop our argumentative material and discover the form our argument must follow to convince the audience. The internal antagonist is essential to good argument.

As we consult the internal antagonist, this mental debater may answer every assertion with a counterassertion. This back-and-forth is good for generating material but it should not provide form for our essay. A good essay will not bounce the head from left to right like a tennis ball. Such a discussion becomes hard for an audience to follow. Don't say:

> It has been argued that smokers have the right to light up in public places because they are members of the public. But what about the nonsmoking public whose rights to breathe clean air are infringed upon?

Often it is best, in avoiding the tennis match, to lump all opposition ideas together, perhaps in one paragraph, and then answer them in another. Or we can acknowledge and counter an argument in the flow of one sentence:

> Although smokers claim the right to smoke in public places, they forget that nonsmokers have a right to breathe uncontaminated air.

Consulting the inner antagonist, we will find new positive ideas when we think of answers to negative ones, and usually a frontal attack is more forceful than a defense. Suppose we attack the salaries paid to professional football players. Trying to gather examples, we imagine the antagonist answering, "Professional athletes are worth what they are paid because they attract thousands of fans to the games." We can acknowledge and counter this idea by saying, "Surely the multimillion-dollar contracts offered to superstars only ensure more money for the pockets of team owners."

Our most persuasive argument, in the long run, derives from praise of our point of view, rather than blame for the opposition. If we record too many opposing arguments, our own opinion blurs out of focus; we lose unity, and we may lose the sound of conviction. Usually we best deal with opposing views obliquely, raising them in dependent clauses while allowing the main clauses to carry our argument, as in the example about smokers and clean air. This device raises issues that belong to the opposition but keeps our direction clear.

Giving time to the opposition allows us to sound open-minded.

No one wins an argument by asserting that the other point of view is wholly invalid, and that anybody who disagrees with us is ignorant or stupid. We must admit the facts; if we don't, we undercut our own validity and lose our audience, especially the one we want to reach—the misguided fool who disagrees with us.

## THE ORDER OF ARGUMENT

Once we have gathered valid support for our argument, we must organize it. We have spoken about avoiding the tennis match. We must consider kinds of order.

Audience and purpose determine the shape of argument. In any list of argumentative details and evidence, some will make a stronger case than others; some will be more interesting or appealing to our audience. Generally, we save the best for last. One good way to order an argument is by increasing intensity. After we introduce the issue— "The administration claims that the need to raise teachers' salaries and improve facilities will require an increase in students' fees next semester"—we counter it with facts in order of increasing importance, as we see it or as we understand our audience to see it: "But our faculty salaries are already higher than those at other colleges in the state, and the computer center houses equipment that pays its own way with time-sharing. Many students depend on government loans, which become less available, and they will leave school if tuition increases. The administration's well-paid faculty will teach to classrooms full of machines and empty of students." The persuasive effect derives from the crescendo.

Another shape of argument states its main thesis at the beginning, at center stage under spotlights: "Next year's planned increase in tuition and board will contribute to the downfall of this institution." Introducing our argument with a thesis statement, we continue by acknowledging points that argue against our view and by countering them; and then we conclude with a summary that rises to our most persuasive point: "Tuition hikes will deny many students, who have already taken on extensive loans and extra jobs, the opportunity to finish their education. The tuition increase will discriminate against the people whom this university was intended to serve." Conclusion reiterates the force of thesis.

To write argument we frequently use the rhetorical patterns discussed at length in Chapter 7. It will be useful to run through the patterns again, in the context of argument and persuasion.

*Example* is the backbone of argument, the support it requires to become convincing. If we try to persuade people to contribute to the public library system, we may list examples to show what money can achieve:

> to acquire new library materials, from books to computers; to increase hours providing more services; to expand children's programs by adding new staff; to improve facilities allowing community groups to use the library for film festivals and lectures; to preserve old books and manuscripts; and with climate control to prevent further deterioration of the library collection.

We argue by *classification and division:*

> In seeking candidates for membership in the Sierra Club, we look for people who have demonstrated an interest in the outdoors or in protecting the environment. We send you this invitation in the hope that you are such a person. . . . Whether you particularly enjoy hiking, backpacking, camping, canoeing, whitewater rafting, or simply appreciation of nature. . . .
>
> From a letter of solicitation,<br>the Sierra Club

To persuade people to become members of a special group (classification) this letter goes on to identify the characteristics and interests of that group (division).

We argue by *cause and effect:*

> Despite a thirtyfold increase in outlays on social programs for the poor, the condition of impoverished blacks in the United States has been steadily deteriorating since the launching of the War on Poverty and the Great Society in the 1960s. These redistributionist schemes, by destroying incentives for work, thrift, and family support, have created in our inner cities a tragic wreckage of demoralization, rage, unemployment, and crime, raised the illegitimacy rate to fifty-five percent of all black births, and driven fathers altogether out of the ghetto family and national economy.
>
> George Gilder, "But What About Welfare's Grim Side?"<br>*The New York Times*, April 22, 1984

We argue by *comparison and contrast:*

> Unlike the Bulldog I, an expensive proposition for the home computer because it requires a large initial investment, the Mastiff III

plugs into the family television set. It is compatible with many Mastiff programs and can grow with your family, whereas the Bulldog I lacks flexibility.

We argue by *process analysis:*

> Put into practice, computer-aided robotics could mean startling changes in farming before the end of the century. The dairy barn of the future, for example, might look like this:
> Cows wearing identification tags walk through the door and are "recognized" by an electronic sensor. They amble to their permanent feeding stations and eat a ration tailored to their individual needs, weather conditions, and milk production. Sensors implanted in their bodies weigh and check the animals for nutrient levels and early detection of disease.
>
> G. V. Perkins, Jr., "What's New in Agriculture"
> *The New York Times*, March 25, 1984

And we argue by *definition*, which includes other rhetorical patterns:

> Either America is an open society or it isn't. If it is, the country has nothing to fear from such political and literary luminaries as Nobel Prizewinner Gabriel Garcia Marquez, playwright Dario Fo, Salvadoran insurgent leader Guillermo Ungo and Chile's widowed First Lady Hortensia Allende. But the Reagan Administration has refused to grant all of the above—and dozens more—the entry privileges customarily accorded other figures of their stature. The country seems more of a closed company with ever-slamming door. The exclusion of famous people deters thousands of others from the arduous and humiliating application process, where detailed probes are made into political and affectional ties. No particular threat to national security need be divined: radical thinking, organizational affiliation or sexual preference is enough to keep the Administration's critics out.
>
> Editorial, *The Nation*, April 28, 1984

The writer defines open and closed societies by listing controversial visitors to whom our country is a closed door. A society that excludes possible critical visitors is not an open one.

## LOGIC AND EMOTIONALISM

If we wish to persuade, we must be reasonable: we must appear logical. Argument may include feeling but in persuasion the appeal to emotions is dangerous; if it violates reason it may lose its audience. The photograph of a weeping child does not provide a *reason* for doing whatever the caption asks. After all, a caption-writer could use the same melancholy photograph to illustrate the hardship of refugees on either side in any war.

Whether we think publicly or privately, we must avoid illogic in order to think well. All of us know some logic, perhaps without giving it the name; often we use the name of common sense for thought we accept as reasonable. Common sense tells us not to generalize from a particular. Suppose I read in the newspaper about a drunk teenager who killed a pedestrian in a hit-and-run accident. Suppose I told you about it and added, "Therefore, we should raise the drinking age to protect society from drunk teenagers." If you ridiculed my illogic, you would be right. I would have committed an error in logic and in common sense by generalizing from insufficient evidence. One teenager cannot stand for all.

Use of one anecdote or example is not necessarily generalizing from a particular; it depends on how we do it. If I had been modest in my declaration, I could have said, "I know we cannot generalize from a particular, but this sort of news item seems characteristic. At least to my prejudiced eyes, teenagers are always making trouble." Here, the anecdote would serve not as a step in argument, but as a device for introducing personal opinion. There can be no false logic when there is no claim to logic.

When we decry *emotionalism*, we are blaming not feelings but their misuse, as when emotionalism appeals to feeling in order to disguise a defect in thinking. If we say,

> The United States needs a strong defense. Anyone who is against conscription is a traitor to those who have sacrificed their lives to preserve freedom.

we give no reasons to support our claim; we merely name-call with words like *traitor* and *sacrifice*. Charged words persuade only the already persuaded, and alienate those we wish to reach. This writer's opposite number might write,

> Anyone who advocates the peacetime draft wants America to rule the world for the sake of the military-industrial complex.

A writer can defend either position without using loaded language:

> With our commitment to free enterprise or capitalism, in a world that contains many opponents of free enterprise, we would be naive

to reduce our armed forces unless we can be certain that our opponents will do the same. Although all sensible people dread the possibility of war, it can be argued that we can prevent war only by preparing for it.

In this fragment of an argument, the writer carefully avoids the unfairness of loaded words, and gives the antagonist at least the benefit of a dependent clause.

Loaded words, begging the question, and unsupportable claims for cause and effect all contribute to errors in thinking; we may lump them under one general label—*emotionalism pretending to argue.* We must scrutinize ourselves for this kind of bad thinking and bad writing when we take on any heavily charged issue: abortion, capital punishment, prayer in the schools, disarmament, pornography, or freedom of speech.

## STYLE IN ARGUMENT

Loaded words make bad prose. To avoid fooling ourselves and trying to fool others, to appear reasonable, we must apply to argument the stylistic standards of clarity and forcefulness discussed in the chapters on words and sentences. When we use a passive verb instead of an active one, we may detach our subject from responsibility and distort our argument. If we write in the passive mood,

Mistakes were made . . .

or

Toxic wastes were dumped at the site over twelve years . . .

we avoid placing responsibility. The active mood supplies a subject and attributes responsibility:

The Boxtex Company dumped toxic chemical wastes at the site over twelve years . . .

Abstract nouns and euphemisms can combine with the passive to diminish the force of concrete and direct expression:

A process of repatriation was employed . . .

Police and attack dogs drove refugees back over the border.

To argue with clarity, we must use conjunctions carefully; we must not imply cause or sequence that evidence cannot support:

> While the Congress delays additional military aid to Central America, the Soviet Union supplies arms and troops to the rebel forces . . .

It is difficult, in working on a paper in argument, to discover our own errors, especially when we feel strongly about the subject. Often we misuse verb forms and abstract nouns in early drafts of an argument without knowing it. It helps to find a clear-headed friend to read the draft for us. It helps to read our draft checking for unclarity, using the inner critic's eye. Many argumentative errors are not merely mechanical; they are learned errors by which we fool ourselves. Here is some would-be argument from an impromptu essay:

> The governor wants to raise the state drinking age to twenty-one. Adults drink as much as they want and get bombed on cocktails when they get home from the office, but they want to stop kids from having a casual beer. It is true that teenagers are picked up for driving under the influence and getting involved in car accidents. Everybody should be more careful and drunk driving is to be avoided. But there is no reason why teenagers should not relax on weekends with a few beers.

Here there is no argument; assertion and innuendo reek of special pleading. The writer avoids the connections implicit in his sentences; he ought to confront weekend relaxation with highway deaths, but he does not want to make this confrontation. If he wishes to work on his thinking, he can find much to say that is reasonable and even persuasive. If the author revises these sentences for their prose style, the argument will improve. Bad style allows the illogic of emotionalism to wander into common fallacies of thinking—of which we will have more to say.

## COMMON FALLACIES IN THINKING

If we wish to study logic seriously, we should go to the philosophy department. The philosophical study of logic resembles composition-course logic as a computer resembles a pencil. But in studying argument in order to write persuasion, it helps to acknowledge common errors in thinking. Avoiding these errors can help us construct arguments that may persuade a reasonable reader.

Many common fallacies in thinking are misuses of *induction* or *deduction.* We meet them every day in newspapers and advertisements and in presidential campaigns or debates on public policy. *Inductive reasoning,* or *induction,* draws general conclusions from particular examples or evidence—Sherlock Holmes's specialty.

> Because the plums were in the refrigerator when I left, and because George was the only person left in the house, and because the plums have disappeared, and because there are plum pits in the sink, I conclude that George ate the plums.

*Deductive reasoning,* or *deduction,* applies a general truth to a specific instance. We deduce by three-step thinking called the *syllogism.*

> All birds have wings. My parakeet is a bird. My parakeet has wings.
>
> All little brothers are brats. I have a little brother. My little brother is a brat.

Here are some fallacies in thinking that most of us fall into from time to time.

### Generalizing from a Particular

In a common error of induction, we arrive at a general statement from a sole supporting fact, or from too narrow a range of particulars. Remember our earlier example about teenage drunk driving. We are typically silly when we generalize from a particular. We claim that New York City is a rotten apple because one taxi driver was rude to us. We claim that motel chains are dishonest because an aunt was short-changed in San Diego. We generalize poorly when we do not collect sufficient evidence, and we assume that because X happens once or twice, X will always happen.

Advertising plays upon the gullible human tendency to accept a particular as a general truth; in a thirty-second commercial, we watch an actor vacuum a filthy carpet until its cleanliness dazzles us; we are expected to believe that it will do the same for us. If we wish seriously to make generalizations, we need a greater sample; we need to spread the net wide for evidence. And if we cannot support our generalization, we must abandon it, or at least we must admit the worthlessness of limited examples as proof of anything.

These cautions must not be construed as advice to avoid the particular. Often an argument takes on persuasive power because a specific bit of evidence is cautiously presented as *typical* of the generalization. The argument's effectiveness, however, depends upon the general validity of the assertion, for the generalization is never demonstrated by one particular. If we began an essay on public television by describing a nauseating commercial, and said, "Therefore, we must have at least one national network without advertising," we would be illogical. But if, after mentioning the particular commercial, we listed other offensive advertisements, and gave statistics on the programming time devoted to commercials, perhaps we could make a generalization that appeared to follow.

### The Overinclusive Premise

In the furnace of argument, many logical errors are forged from flawed metal like the overinclusive premise or conclusion. All of us are guilty. "Everybody who goes to medical school is out for money." "All people who act like that are Communists." These statements are generalizations (possibly based on a limited sample) that common sense will not tolerate. If we say *some* instead of *all*, we are more sensible—and we have admitted that our charge is not inclusive.

### Guilt by Association

Guilt by association (or holiness by association, for that matter) is another common form of faulty thinking. The Mafia, we believe, is an Italian organization. Whenever we identify someone as Italian, the Mafia may cross our minds. Everyone *knows* this sort of thing is absurd; yet if we do not keep constant scrutiny on ourselves, we fall into it again and again. Politicians thrive on guilt by association. Because socialists believe in free medical care, anyone who believes in free medical care is a socialist. If we attach an emotional negative to the word *socialist*, we can think that we have just argued free medicine down. We have made only an emotional association; we have not *argued* at all.

### Begging the Question

In this error the arguer assumes the truth of a premise that readers may question. The arguer could try to prove the assumption, but does not. He merely repeats it—it is so because it is so. Someone might say, "The rising incidence of lymphatic cancer proves that early advocates of a test-ban treaty were correct." The writer neither demonstrates that lymphatic cancer *is* rising, nor shows that nuclear testing causes lymphatic cancer. Causation asserted but unsupported is common in sloppy thinking. Sometimes misused conjunctions beg the question: "Although middle-aged, he wore Levis."

### Evading the Issue

Cleverly avoiding facing an issue is another favorite tactic of politicians, usually introduced by an assertion that they will *not* evade this issue: "I'm glad you asked that question." Sometimes a politician will say something like, "I believe in freedom of assembly and the freedom of all Americans regardless of race, creed, or color to assemble with people of their own choice." If we look at the context, we may see that the speaker is not defending freedom but segregation, the rights of associations to exclude members on account of race. "Right-to-work" laws are laws against forms of union organizing. "Freedom of the press" is sometimes an umbrella for pornographers. Ignoring the question is frequently a deliberate illogic, an attempt to deceive the public by diverting attention from a real goal, which might seem disreputable, to a substitute goal of which anyone might approve. Evading the issue is euphemism in paragraph form.

### Non Sequitur

*Non sequitur* is Latin for "it does not follow." We use the term for a statement or idea which *appears* to grow out of an earlier one (by causation, by chronology, by logic, or whatever), but which upon examination fails to make the trip:

> He was a doctor and therefore an all-around man.
> She left an hour ago, although her car wouldn't move.

Comedians use the non sequitur to humorous effect. Woody Allen is a master:

> I believe my consumption has grown worse. Also my asthma. The wheezing comes and goes, and I get dizzy more and more frequently. I have taken to violent choking and fainting. My room is damp and I have perpetual chills and palpitations of the heart. I noticed, too, that I am out of napkins.

Non sequiturs sometimes afflict us when we are trying to make complex sentences for conciseness: "My uncle was born in 1902 in Miami where he sells lawnmowers and garden tools." When we use the rhetorical pattern of cause and effect, we sometimes wander carelessly into non sequitur or into the next fallacy.

### Sequence as Cause

*Post hoc ergo propter hoc,* literally "after this, therefore, because of this," is a form of non sequitur. The assumption is that if B follows A, A causes B. This assumption is not logical. "Cousin Eveline visits and I get a headache." We *assume* cause and effect, but we cannot know it.

Again, the politics of paranoia adopts sequence as cause for its argument. "Rudolph Blast was in Newark the day before a bomb went off; therefore. . . ." Such evidence is not even circumstantial, and it does not hold up in court. If a hurricane comes after a bomb test, we cannot safely assume that the bomb test caused it. Sequence is not causation and is inadequate evidence for it.

### The Argument Ad Hominem

*Ad hominem* is Latin for "to the man." Instead of confronting the issue we are discussing, we attack the opponent. We often do so in argument when we lose our tempers or when our thinking doesn't hold up. It is a refinement of evading the issue and of the non sequitur. When someone defends cutting down trees to make a parking lot, we attack *him* instead of questioning the need for additional parking spaces, or the appropriateness of the site proposed. We say, "You're in favor of this plan because you like carbon monoxide more than maples." Name-calling may satisfy something in the name-caller, but it avoids thought. A friend says, "I believe in a socialist form of government, because the profit motive, which is basic to a capitalist system, robs us of our humanity and corrupts our intelligence to serve materialism." We rebut, "You always were nuts."

### The Either-Or Fallacy

For an example of the either-or fallacy, we can look back at the quotation from *The Nation* we used (page 309) for an example of argument by definition. Although the passage defines what it means by a closed society, it begins with an example of the either-or fallacy: "Either America is an open society or it isn't." There is an attractive, no-nonsense tone in this introductory sentence; but in fact it *is* nonsense, for it implies that there are no degrees between one extreme and another. If the United States and the Soviet Union are both closed societies, as the editorial seems to assert, does the writer really wish to imply that there is no difference in the degrees of openness?

We do not necessarily use the words *either* and *or* when we commit this fallacy. "Because Herbert Perkins is not a superb human being he is a rotten wretch."

### Analogy as Fact

Analogies in argument are most useful. They illustrate the sense in which we mean a statement that might otherwise be too tenuous to be understood. They embody attitude and feeling, and they persuade by being exact carriers of feeling. But we can fall into another common form of illogic by arguing from analogy as if it were fact. Suppose we want to write about different civilizations that seem to have features in common—like beginning, development, fulfillment, and decay. To carry this idea to a reader, we invent an analogy: each civilization is like an organism—it is born, it grows up, it matures, it becomes old, and it dies. So far so good. We follow the abstract thought by associating it with concrete things. But many writers become so accustomed to a dominant analogy that they begin to take it literally. Arguing later that our own civilization must end, we say, "Like all organisms, our society must come to death." The argument is invalid because a civilization is not literally an organism, and therefore we have not proved that what is true of an organism will be true of civilization. Or take the common analogy that compares the human body to a machine. The analogy can be useful when we study the principles of bodily function, but the danger is that we will take analogy as fact, identify the human being with the machine, and treat a person as we would a thing. The analogy is not the thing itself.

## THE GENERAL FALLACY: IMPRECISION

Many writers undermine their own arguments by misusing statistics. Some would-be persuaders ignore the differences in mean, median, and average. Others use out-of-date figures; we mislead in 1988 if we speak of northeastern American cities according to the 1970 census.

Some quote statements out of context, distorting their intended meaning; we have all seen movie advertisements or book blurbs that edit reviews to advantage. The critic writes: "It is a work of art in which the flaws outnumber the felicities, with no moments of greatness." The ad reads: " . . . a work of art . . . felicities . . . moments of greatness."

Ambiguity accounts for various imprecisions—misplaced modifiers, pronouns with uncertain antecedents, and words used without definition. A common flaw in argument is the use of one word in several senses. We fool ourselves into thinking that we have said something profound when we have only played with a word. Abstractions lend themselves to ambiguity more readily than concrete words. Some writers use terms so loosely that they can mean anything and therefore mean nothing; "free society" and "democracy" are useless without definition and context. Watch out for prose like this, from a theme about campus politics:

> Jerry was a liberal, but not so liberal as Mary Hunter, who was out in left field. Some of the professors, even the most liberal, were conservative compared to Mary Hunter, who claimed that they didn't deserve to be called liberals at all.

We have no idea what meanings the writer attaches to *liberal* and *conservative*; there is no attempt at definition.

## LOOKING FOR AN ARGUMENT: PROCESS

In Chapter 3 we watched Frank Rodriguez as he worked up a theme comparing and contrasting two television shows. Now we will follow another student part of the way through the writing of a paper in argument. In the spring of 1984, with the Los Angeles Summer Olympics almost upon us, Susan La Belle decided to take on the Olympics for her essay in argument and persuasion. She was annoyed by all the media noise about the Games. She began by rapidly listing negatives:

> Hype!
> athletes not amateurs
> host countries compete to outdo each other
> games become political . . . Hitler 193– (date?), terrorism Munich 1972, Afghanistan boycott, 1980
> drugs artificially boost performance
> endorsement of products, commercialization . . .
> U.S.-Soviet competition makes east-west split *worse* . . .

Then she tried putting herself on the opposite side:

> at Olympics many nations *do* cooperate
> it's a measure of athletic records
> incentives and awards, achievement
> facilities go on to other uses . . .
> ancient tradition
> highest aspiration . . .
> commercial endorsements save money . . .

She did not yet know how to arrange her material; she was not ready to try. Looking for more material, she tried brainstorming, not to begin writing her paper, but to see what came out:

> The Olympics ought to be abolished. They no longer serve any purpose they were intended for. The opposite! They certainly don't promote world peace and understanding! They're nothing but a battlefield for nationalistic hatreds and they emphasize what keeps nations apart rather than what holds them together. Also, they are nothing but advertising for candy bars, orange juice, electric razors, cars, cloth, and goodness knows what else. Swimmers' bods! They're good for nothing except to make money for the athletes, as they get into promotion later on, or sometimes professional athletic careers. But for that matter, these athletes are not amateurs anyway. They all get rich or most of them do. In the Eastern countries they are on perpetual salary and in our country they get payoffs from shoe manufacturers, etc. Besides that, they're all druggies, etc. They artificially pack their blood before a competition so that the chemicals cannot be traced. So much for the spirit of friendly competition and human betterment. When World War III starts, it'll probably be on account of a basketball game.

When she read it over she laughed at herself. Not much Time for the Opposition! Her belligerence, she knew, would never convince a pro-Olympian. She made notes in the margin, where she recognized some of her hasty illogic, emotionalism, and ambiguity. "Develop," she wrote. "Define!" "Argue, don't shout." "Either-or fallacy. . . ."

Then she sat down, with her notes and her sprinted draft, to plan her argument. She noticed that comparison and contrast ought to help her develop her argument; she gave thought to courting an audience who would not necessarily agree with her; she looked for a positive opening. Then she plotted time for the opposition, and then counter-statement with examples in pursuit of persuasion. She wrote another draft.

The Olympic Games enjoyed a long tradition before their revival in this century to promote peace and international understanding through friendly sport. These games have been the scenes of great moments of personal and national triumph for athletes from all over the world. Although some would continue to praise this glorious arena for human endeavor and determination, this gathering of the world's best athletic talent every four years, I wish to suggest that the Games have outlived their purpose.

The Olympic Games today foster hostile competition between East and West. They drain the resources of host nations who try to outshine each other by building bigger and more elaborate facilities to impress spectators and press. Commercialism has invaded the Olympics as manufacturers scramble for endorsements as the *official* Olympic orange juice, sweatshirt, razor, or candy bar. Sucessful athletes receive under-the-counter salaries to use one manufacturer's equipment, and set themselves up for lucrative promotions after the Games are over.

Far from being confined to sportsmanship, the Games have been politicized—as Hitler attempted to politicize the Games in 1936. They have been used to suggest white supremacy, Communist or capitalist superiority, and of course as the stage of international terrorism, most horribly in Munich in 1972, when Palestine terrorists martyred Israeli athletes. The spirit of cooperation and understanding that the Games were meant to encourage is now a hollow front for greed, ambition, and propaganda.

The paper had made a start.

Then the Russians and their allies withdrew from the 1984 Games and her thesis became stronger. She began to think of using the subject for a research paper. For that, she would need to do a lot of work. When did the Games begin? When were they revived? Could she document concrete examples of commercialism and corruption?

She read a column in *The Boston Globe* that gave her some information she required, a few more arguments—and one or two notions on the subject of argument.

The Olympic Games went on for more than a thousand years before Roman Emperor Theodosius, annoyed at their commercialism and corruption, banned them. More than 1,500 years later, a French baron began the Olympic movement all over again, thus proving the axiom that those who forget the past are doomed to repeat it.

The Olympics today are a shoddy carnival of political hypocrisy, amateur exploitation, and commercial profiteering. Two days ago, the Soviet Union pulled out of the Los Angeles Games, complaining about security, smog, crime, commercialism, and politics.

You can say this for the Soviets: They pretty much got it right.

I've attended two Olympiads, the 1976 Montreal Summer Games and the 1980 Lake Placid Winter Games. I saw a few nice events and met a lot of intolerable bureaucrats.

I learned to dislike almost everyone who controls, organizes or promotes the Olympics. I was appalled by the arrogance of the International Olympic Committee, the incompetence of the organizing cities, the buying and selling of the Olympic name.

I lost respect for a great many athletes, most often the successful ones.

The Eastern Bloc athletes are as pampered as prized geese fattened to produce foie gras. The Western athletes are always moaning about the degradation of having to work part-time. They have developed the misguided notion that declaring oneself an Olympic athlete carries with it the inalienable right to be supported by contributions.

By the time I left Lake Placid, I no longer believed the Olympics were of redeeming social value. The Olympics are to sports what pornography is to art.

The Olympics were revived in 1896 by Pierre de Coubertin to promote education, culture and international understanding. They are nothing like that. They are so consumed by politics, terror and drug abuse that merely completing them every four years is a reason to rejoice.

The Olympics are supposed to celebrate amateurism, but few Olympic athletes are pure. Western runners have so many sponsors they should wear sandwich boards instead of shorts. Eastern Bloc weightlifters take so many steroids they set off alarms in health food stores.

The Olympics are supposed to be for the pleasure of the people, but they are really for the gratification of the privileged. Great sums of Olympic money are spent to entertain visiting royalty, government officials, selected sponsors and IOC members.

These people sit in the $95 seats at the basketball and boxing finals, usually for free. Ordinary people sit in the $30 seats at the water polo preliminaries, grateful to pay an unreasonable price.

Above all, the Olympics are supposed to be unconcerned with politics. This has not been true since 1964, when the IOC banned South Africa from the Tokyo Olympics, even though South Africa promised to bring a racially mixed term to the Games.

If fair treatment of minorities were the standard of admission to the Olympics, the IOC would have to ban Great Britain for its treatment of India, the United States for its treatment of blacks, the Soviet Union for its treatment of Jews, Israel for its treatment of Palestinians and Turkey for its treatment of Greeks. That's just a partial list.

Since the 1964 decision, the Olympics have been dominated by bans and boycotts. The bans are placed on politically impotent countries like Rhodesia and Taiwan and the boycotts are imposed by politically important countries like the Soviet Union and the United States.

We blame the USSR for invading Afghanistan. They blame us for invading Grenada. We blame them for human rights violations. They blame us for providing "abnormal" living conditions for athletes. We blame them. They blame us.

We were very proud of ourselves for boycotting the 1980 Moscow Olympics on principle. It seems to me that we should be just as proud of the Soviet Union for boycotting the 1984 Los Angeles Games on principle.

I could only be prouder if every nation would withdraw from the Olympics on principle, an exodus that would bring an end to the modern Olympic movement. What a worthwhile accomplishment that would be.

The Romans had enough sense to know when the Olympics had lost their usefulness. Surely, modern civilization can do as well.

Alan Richman, "Shed No Tears for Olympics,"<br>
*The Boston Globe*, May 10, 1984

We end this chapter on argument and persuasion without allowing Susan to finish her paper. See the first exercise.

_____ **EXERCISES** _____

1. Compare Susan La Belle's draft of an argument with Alan Richman's column. How is Richman's more professional? How is Susan's argument better? What could these writers learn from each other?

2. In class, block out alternate plans for the theme, improving on Susan's beginning. Add information from *The Boston Globe* article, or from the *Encyclopaedia Britannica*. (List your sources.)

3. Write a counterargument. In class, assemble and organize material for an argument praising the Olympics.

4. Here are some lines from advertising copy. Identify the audience addressed.

    a. Is your skin as dry as your Chablis?

    b. When you visit our health spa, you're going to like you.

    c. Today, you're doing more than ever. So should your phone.

    d. Finally, clothing as intelligently designed as you are.

    e. If my car doesn't get noticed, it gets traded.

    f. Your dollar could be the one that beats diabetes.

    g. Trust Tylenol. Hospitals do.

5. Describe the flaws in these arguments.

    a. You're stupid! That's why I'm right.

    b. In 1989, Rupert Hudmill announced that he was no longer associated with the Virgin Vampires. When he decided to destroy the punk rock group, Hudmill gave no reasons.

    c. When Luke hit the first pitch of the game into the left-field stands, it was obvious that Mitchell could no longer pitch.

    d. When we consider the question of aid to underdeveloped nations, we should always consider first that we, too, are an underdeveloped nation.

    e. Since democracy died in Rome with the elevation of Caesar, one can no longer go to the Romans for lessons in the democratic process.

    f. No one who dresses like that could possibly know Mozart from Mantovani.

    g. Warmongers who masquerade as friends of Egypt or Israel attempt to deceive the gullible.

    h. Everybody who votes for Cynthia is a racist.

    i. You can't change human nature.

    j. There will always be conventional warfare.

6. Study the advertising in a selection of magazines: *Time, Mechanix Illustrated, New York Times Magazine, The New Yorker, Penthouse, National Enquirer, Harper's, Ace Comics, The Atlantic, Sport, Fortune, Ms., Family Circle.* Discuss the audience for the ads in each magazine. Write a brief paper explaining how the advertisements persuade different audiences.

7. Look at the op-ed page of a local or college newspaper. Analyze a letter or an editorial for the premise of its argument; for the techniques the writer uses to persuade; for any fallacies in thinking; for charged language that distorts the argument.

8. Write an application to a computer dating service for a friend. Present your friend's qualities (appearance, personality, special talents). Try writing different versions to appeal first to one imagined audience and then another. For instance, direct yourself to a service addressing populations in Boston, Salt Lake City, Atlanta, or any city or area that you know.

9. Pick one of these situations in which to practice the art of persuasion.

a. The city announces plans to route a new highway directly through your residential neighborhood, which will require demolition of well-maintained single-family houses and a park. You head a community action group trying to stop this proposal. Address the city's planning board.

b. Applying for your first job after college, write a cover letter for your résumé to convince your prospective employer. Apply for the best job you can imagine getting.

10. Write a letter to your congressional representative on one of these issues:

a. funding covert political activity in other countries
b. developing defensive weapons in outer space
c. abolishing farm price supports
d. coverage by media of rape trials
e. handgun legislation
f. mandatory retirement age
g. commercials on children's television
h. abolishing government-funded postal service
i. mandatory use of seatbelts in cars
j. bilingual education
k. establishing day-care centers for working mothers
l. prohibiting smoking in public places

11. Here are two passages that argue a point of view. Examine them with these questions in mind: (a) Is the line of argument clear? (b) Is it reasonable? (c) Does it seem balanced, acknowledging the opposite point of view? (d) How is it organized? (e) Does the argument display any logical fallacies? If so, how do they affect the argument?

a. Women's roles have always been more tightly bound than men's to parenthood, more limited by conceptions of reproduction as mysterious, ritually impure, restricting the development of either mind or soul. As a result, women's rebellion against the simple maintenance role that has been their lot is more vivid than men's. Since the beginning of social life, the performance of men's activities, however tedious, dangerous, or humdrum, has been associated with ideas of achievement that both men and women have often mistaken for innate superiority. If men are conscripted and sent to war without ever being consulted by the distant old men who control the corridors of power, they, too, have no more choice over their lives than women without contraceptives have for preventing an unwanted pregnancy.

In this moment of vision, people caught in one kind of life that they have never questioned are getting a glimpse of the way other peoples live; the current questioning of the status of women is part of the whole process of questioning a social order that no longer meets the newly aroused hopes of the people who live within it. The voices of women are combining with voices all over the world against a new worldwide system of political and economic exploitation of the land, the sea, and the air, and the endangered populations that depend upon them.

But there is a difference between women's voices and the voices of all the others who live meaningless lives within a world where they have no part in decisions made too far away. The revolts of the oppressed—slaves, serfs, peons, peasants, manual workers, white-collar workers—are part of the periodic attempts to correct social systems that are seen as exploitative and unfair. But this is the first time in history when the progress made in the control of disease and reproduction has offered to the female half of the population escape from a lifelong role that was defined for every one of them simply by gender. Having one or two children and rearing them together as parents who have chosen parenthood means for men and women—but most of all for women—permission to participate at every level in our highly complex society.

And it is not only women who gain—society gains. Where one half of the best minds were consumed in the performance of small domestic tasks, society can now draw on them. Where women's experiences—inevitably different from men's because women all had mothers with whom they could identify—have been fenced off from contributing to the high-level planning of the world, they can now be used in the attack on such problems as chaotic abuse of food, resources, human settlements, and the total environment. When women are once more able to participate in decisions and are free to be persons as well as parents, they should be able to contribute basic understandings that are presently lacking in the world. These basic new understandings include the fact that food is meant to be used to feed human beings, not to serve as a weapon or commodity; that towns were meant for generations to live in together, not only as barracks or bedrooms; that education can be used to make life meaningful; that we do live in a world community that is here but is unrecognized, in all its interdependence and need for shared responsibility.

Margaret Mead
"Needed: Full Partnership for Women," *Saturday Review*

b. To the Editor:

Your editorial of March 3 decries the potential loss of excellence at the *Harvard Law Review* as a result of its plan to specially choose women or members of racial minorities in addition to picking its staff on the basis of class standing and writing competition.

The myth of the law review, and the corresponding system of job placement accompanying it, is pervasive and wasteful. Each year thousands of students are accepted at the nation's law schools, facing not only three grueling years of study and an equally grueling period of preparation for the bar exam but also the prospect of being precluded from the better law jobs or from any law job at all.

Law firms and corporate law departments in every major city screen job applicants on the basis of first-year law school grades and membership in law reviews, avoiding year after year the burden of attempting to evaluate potential employees on the basis of overall experience and ability.

Employers visiting the top law schools each year grant interviews only to the upper 10 to 15 percent of each class. Some law schools have tried using lottery systems to open up interviews to a few non-law-review students, but the fear that employers will stop coming to such campuses inhibits real changes in the system.

The ability to practice law, to utilize intellect and experience in the representation of clients, does not correspond to the ability to attain top grades in first-year law school classes. The antiquated system of fear, uncertainty and intimidation that characterizes the average first-year curriculum serves more to perpetuate a tradition of trial by fire—similar to the hazing of fraternity pledges—than to teach young lawyers how to succeed in the complex world of law, business and government that they must face after graduation.

Upon attainment of top grades, moreover, law review members in many cases experience two years of intellectual isolation, sharply decreased class attendance and much time spent engaged in two key law review activities—editing one another's papers and socializing. As a result, the nation's top law schools and corporations contain many law associates with limited life experience and business or common sense; it is not unusual for new associates at top New York firms to fail to pass the bar examination on first sitting.

Law review does very little to prepare one for the realities of practice in such industries as banking, energy, transportation, telecommunications and entertainment, to name a few. At the same time, the need is increasingly apparent for training in areas of specialization in order to create lawyers with the necessary skills to do the jobs they must do.

Law reviews do represent a high level of excellence in the intellectual pursuit of legal analysis at America's law schools, and as such constitute a worthy tradition for the bar. Many law reviews serve as well as legal fraternities of value to members throughout their lives. While any employer, as any school, needs some basis for choosing among applicants, the use of law review membership for such a purpose is outmoded and arbitrary, serving as an insult to thousands of bright young graduates frozen out of good jobs by this traditional system.

Rather than bemoan the loss of tradition, we should re-examine the basis for analyzing law school graduates seeking employment to allow for fairer evaluation and fuller utilization of skilled lawyers.

John G. Ives, Letter to the Editor, *The New York Times*

12. Look at Barbara Levine's research paper (on pages 353–372). What is her basic thesis? How does she develop her argument? How could she have organized her information differently? Could she have used different language to change her tone, to argue more persuasively?

# 9

## *Writing Research*

Research is a way to learn things. The research paper, a particular result of the general method, allows us to gather evidence from library investigations and present it documented in an essay.

Although research often supports an argument, our purpose in writing a research paper is first to gather information, assembled from reading. A research paper can answer a question ("How did the United States acquire Alaska?") or bring together current thinking about an issue (disposal of radioactive waste, or photocopying and copyright law). Research is a method of study, a way of learning independently. Skill in research is indispensable to formal, academic study; it can also be useful for the rest of our lives: we can research the voting record of a member of Congress, regional recipes for chicken soup, family history, designs for solar houses, local zoning laws, Japanese business practices, the microchip industry, or the social influence of the potato.

Many composition courses specify a research paper as a final task. Not only does the research paper require students to learn methods of research, but it also provides an ambitious project by which students can demonstrate what they have learned about writing.

When you write a research paper, the first thing you must do is choose a subject: the first thing, and probably the most important. Choosing a subject resembles discovering Chinese boxes, starting with a large box, moving to the smaller one inside it, then to a smaller one

lly we arrive at something of suitable size. We
_it the topic._ Often—maybe _usually_—the hardest
.per is finding a suitable topic and then limiting it.
)wever, is not the only trouble that can afflict a
adness need not be a grievous problem; one can al-
ittle a broad topic down. "Vegetable Gardening" can
ig Organic Tomatoes," and "Voting in a Democracy"
.bsentee Balloting: Its Effects on the Two Parties."
subject is too scientific or too technical, on the other
hand, on., ears of specialized study will prepare a student to write
about it; "The Effects of Gamma Rays on _Drosophila_" is as difficult as
"Genetics." Here, we must abandon our desired topic and look for
something less technical. Other subjects prove impossible because research material is insufficient. "Vampires in Goa" sounds fascinating
enough, but the library is unlikely to provide the necessary sources.
Still another kind of problem is the subject about which there is little
to say—a subject adequately covered by an encyclopedia entry, like the
history of basketball.

In writing a research paper, the most important decision is choosing a manageable topic—a topic neither too large nor too small to be
handled in the assigned number of pages, and a topic neither too technical for a lay audience nor too specialized for the facilities of a university
library. It should be a subject we are interested in: if we have a choice,
we should not write about taconite mining when we really want to
investigate artificial intelligence or Brazilian deforestation.

Sometimes a topic will narrow as we read about it. We concentrate on one feature of a topic and discover this concentration as we
read over our early notes. As we go about finding sources, we must
remain alert to all possibilities of our general subject.

Because the library is the starting point for most research papers,
let us look at some ways of using it.


## USING THE LIBRARY

Libraries hold our collective past. Large university libraries, with
huge collections of books and current periodicals, with microfilm and
microfiche, with special archives of rare books and manuscripts, can
satisfy the most specialized inquiry. But even the smallest library contains more resources than any of us are likely to need in a lifetime.
When we walk into a reference room or into the library book stacks, we

enter a universe of possibilities. The first sight of a big academic library can overwhelm us: *All These Books!* How do we find our way? Many students, entering the largest library they have ever seen, at first want to flee to the dormitory in terror, perhaps to settle down in front of the television set with a bag of potato chips.

But the road maps are there, and people to help. In the next few pages I will talk about library catalogues and reference collections, but first, I want to mention the most obvious things—things sometimes overlooked. Many colleges offer library orientation, and you should never ignore such help. Many also provide a small guide to their facilities, printed or mimeographed, which you can keep and consult when you need to. Finally, there are the librarians—at a desk labeled Information, or at the reference desk, or wherever, who sit there in order to help you out, to advise you, and to acquaint you with the resources stockpiled around you. *Never be afraid to ask a librarian a question.* Whatever you ask, the librarian has probably heard it before: Where do I find out about vampires? What do you have on gene splicing? How do you spell *Drosophila?* Who wrote "Mary Had a Little Lamb"?

The librarian will not find the answer for you, but will show you how to find it for yourself.

## THE LIBRARY CATALOGUE

The library catalogue is a record of everything in the library— books, periodicals, newspapers, government documents, microfilm, microfiche, records, films, and other special materials. Most libraries still use a traditional three-by-five-inch card file, organized alphabetically. Some libraries, however, have switched to computer printouts, access to computer terminals, or a microform that we can read on a viewer. For all these, the organizing principle is the same.

Most books are represented by at least three entries or cards in the catalogue. One is alphabetized under the author's last name; to find *David C. Edwards,* you look under *E* and not under *D.* Another is alphabetized under the first major word of the title; *General Psychology* is found under *G.* A third is alphabetized under the subject PSYCHOLOGY. (Look at the sample author, title, and subject cards on page 332.) Naturally enough, many books are listed under more than one subject; three entries are the *minimum* that will represent each book.

Each library card contains all sorts of useful information. In the upper left-hand margin is the *call number,* which is like a coded ad-

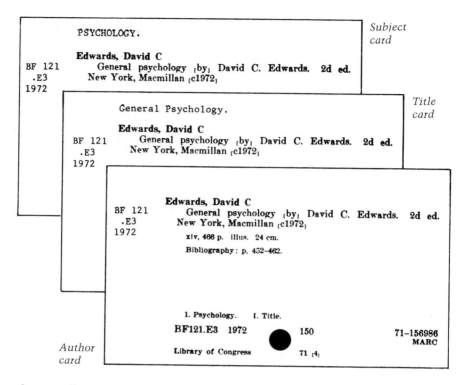

dress, telling us where in the library's stacks we may find the book, grouped on a shelf with others on the same subject. Libraries usually use one of two main systems to classify their collections. The Dewey Decimal System is based on ten number categories; 000s are general topics, 100s philosophy, 200s religion, 300s social sciences, and so on through 900s. The Library of Congress System, a combination of letters and numbers (A for general works; B philosophy, psychology, and religion; C auxiliary sciences of history; D history; and so on through Z), allows more possibilities for subdivision. Many college libraries are changing from Dewey Decimal to Library of Congress because the latter is more flexible and better suited to extensive collections.

The call number on the sample cards uses the Library of Congress System. The mark BF means that the book is classified under psychology (an offshoot of philosophy); 121 means that it is a general work or an advanced textbook; .E3 is the Cutter number, which is derived from the author's last name and groups the title with others on the same subject in alphabetical order by author; 1972 is the date of this edition and is included so that the book will be shelved after any earlier editions the library may already have. If classified in the Dewey system, the call number for Edwards's book would be $\frac{150}{E3}$ because 150 is the classification for psychology.

The catalogue also records the edition of the book if other than the first, publisher, date of publication, number of pages (lowercase roman numerals for introductory material, arabic numerals for text), whether the book has illustrations or special features (Edwards's book has a bibliography from pages 452 to 462), often the author's dates, and, toward the bottom of the card, the other subject headings under which the book is represented in the library catalogue. Those who know how to read a catalogue entry know a good deal about a book before they ever look at it: Is it recent or dated? Is it long or short? What subjects does it touch upon? Preliminary evaluation of a title can save us time and footwork.

When we are doing research, subject entries are especially useful because they bring together at our fingertips the library's resources on a specific topic. But author and title entries are also essential. Sometimes background reading supplies us a title but no author, or we read of an author without reference to books published. Title and author entries provide additional access routes to needed information.

Here are a few things to remember about the organization of the library catalogue:

Most library catalogues are arranged in one alphabet like a dictionary, with author, title, and subject cards interfiled. Occasionally, a library separates its card catalogues into three files for author, title, and subject. Make sure that you understand your own library's organization.

Library catalogues are alphabetized word by word, not letter by letter (*New York* comes before *Newark*), and initial articles (*The, A, An*) are ignored (*A Writer's Reader* is filed under *W*, not *A*). Abbreviated words are alphabetized as if they were spelled out (*St.* as *Saint*) and so too are numbers (*5* as *five*). *Mc* and *M'* are alphabetized as *Mac*, and names with prefixes like *de* and *von* are alphabetized by ignoring the prefix (*von Kreicke* comes under *K*).

Remember that subjects may not always be listed under the words that first occur to us. If we look up "Farming," we may be told "See Agriculture." If there is no entry under the name we have thought of, we should look under near-synonyms. *Roget's Thesaurus* may help, or a librarian can show us the list of subject headings the library uses. Sometimes we may find several titles under our subject; if we look up "Agriculture," we may find an entry that says "See also Livestock," indicating that additional information is under another subject heading.

A writer is an author before he is a subject. Books *by* W. H. Auden will appear before books *about* W. H. Auden.

Subject headings for history are arranged chronologically, not alphabetically. Under "United States—History," "War of 1812" comes *before* "Civil War."

## REFERENCE WORKS

First let us consider a reference book *about* reference books: the comprehensive *Guide to Reference Books* by Eugene T. Sheehy (10th ed.; Chicago: American Library Association, 1986), including sections on computer-readable data sources. (The Sheehy book is known to many librarians as "Winchell," after an earlier editor named Constance M. Winchell.) Most college libraries have this book or others like it, which are worth looking at because they list and describe the enormous range of materials available in a reference room—encyclopedias, dictionaries, yearbooks, almanacs, atlases, gazetteers, and hundreds of specialized reference works.

Here, we can examine only a sampling of the most essential reference sources.

Encyclopedias contain general articles, often with appended bibliographies, on the entire range of human knowledge. The most widely known is the *Encyclopaedia Britannica*, divided in its newest edition into two multivolumed parts. The *Micropaedia* of ten volumes provides short entries and bibliographies for most topics and serves as an index to the detailed, nineteen-volume *Macropaedia*, which includes immense articles on large subjects, some, like the entry on China, as long as a book.

The *Encyclopedia Americana* is another useful general encyclopedia, with a notable emphasis on American topics. Although less scholarly than the *Britannica* or *Americana*, *Collier's Encyclopedia* remains useful. Each of these encyclopedias publishes a yearbook reviewing the previous year's significant events. *The New Columbia Encyclopedia* is a compendious one-volume work for quick reference.

Dictionaries include the historical *Oxford English Dictionary* (see page 103) and *A Dictionary of American English on Historical Principles*, which trace word origins, etymology, and the evolution of meaning and usage. Unabridged general dictionaries include *Webster's Third New International Dictionary, Funk and Wagnall's New Standard Dictionary,* and the *Random House Dictionary.* In addition, there are any number of special dictionaries of slang, dialects, idioms, clichés, usage, synonyms, etymology, and abbreviations.

Dictionaries of quotations contain pithy, often familiar remarks by well-known authors. *Bartlett's Familiar Quotations* and *The Oxford Dictionary of Quotations* arrange quotations chronologically by author and have extensive subject indexes. H. L. Mencken's *A New Dictionary of Quotations,* like many others, arranges quotations by topic and has an index of authors.

When we need biographical information, we can look in several places. Encyclopedias include biography. Biographical dictionaries often include people we do not find in encyclopedias. *Who's Who* gives brief, basic facts about the living, as do *Current Biography* and *Contemporary Authors.* The *Dictionary of National Biography* (DNB) covers British subjects and *The Dictionary of American Biography* (DAB) Americans; *Webster's Biographical Dictionary* and *Chambers's Biographical Dictionary* are international. *Biography Index* and *Biography and Genealogy Master Index* guide the researcher to a wide range of other biographical sources. There are also regional and occupational volumes of *Who's Who,* and specialized compilations like *Notable American Women, Contemporary Poets,* and *American Men and Women of Science.*

Invaluable to anyone researching contemporary problems are the indexes to periodical and newspaper articles. (The library catalogue tells only that the library subscribes to a specific periodical, and sometimes where it is shelved; it does not give information about articles.) Periodical indexes are a record of contemporary thinking on hundreds of topics. The most general periodical index, lined up in thick green volumes, is the *Reader's Guide to Periodical Literature,* which indexes popular and a few specialized and scientific magazines. For more scholarly sources, there are the *Humanities Index* and the *Social Sciences Index* (formerly published together as the *International Index* and then as the *Social Sciences and Humanities Index*). The *New York Times Index* gives a daily index to current events. Other indexes include *Poole's Index to Periodical Literature* and the *Nineteenth Century Readers' Guide to Periodical Literature* for the vast number of periodicals that provided popular entertainment and education in the nineteenth century. Specialized indexes guide us to periodicals in science, technology, art, business, education, psychology, public affairs, and so on.

*The Monthly Catalogue of U.S. Government Publications* indexes titles from the Government Printing Office on an extraordinary variety of topics.

When we want to find a review of a book, we can look in the "Book Review" section at the end of the bound volumes of *Readers' Guide* under the author's last name. Or we can look in two special indexes: *Book Review Digest*, which includes short quotations from reviews as well as full reference information, and *Book Review Index*, which indexes more than three hundred periodicals.

Sometimes it is not a periodical publication we need to find but a book. We should consult a general bibliography like the *United States Catalog* and *Cumulative Book Index*, which together list almost every book printed in the United States for the last eighty years. *Publisher's Trade List Annual, Books in Print*, and *Paperbound Books in Print* record titles that are currently available from publishers. All these sources can help us discover full information on a title in order to request an interlibrary loan.

Yearbooks and almanacs collect statistical material. We mentioned the yearbooks published by the encyclopedias. There are also annual publications like the *World Almanac, Information Please Almanac, Facts on File, Statistical Abstract of the United States*, and the *Guinness Book of World Records*, which record population figures, sports results, world leaders, notable events, economic statistics, and other annual facts.

Basic reference sources for maps and geographic information are the *Encyclopaedia Britannica World Atlas*, the *Rand McNally Cosmopolitan World Atlas*, the *Times Atlas of the World*, and the *National Geographic Atlas of the World*. Historical atlases preserve the geographic past—the route of the Lewis and Clark expedition or Sherman's march to the sea during the Civil War.

When we leave these general categories and become specific, we can find reference books *within* all disciplines: scientific and medical *Who's Who's*; encyclopedias of music and of architecture, of archaeology and of anthropology; and indexes to works of art. Many of these special reference books are listed in the card catalogue under the subject name of the discipline itself. And do not forget to consult the kindly librarian.

Under the subject literature are innumerable reference works, from histories of the literatures of various languages to dictionaries—like the *Oxford* companions to English, American, and world literatures and the *Oxford Classical Dictionary*. *Twentieth Century Authors* has been useful to thousands of students. Some of these books, like the last mentioned, quote criticism of the authors discussed, and most of them include bibliographies of works by the authors and of works written about them.

In almost all fields of study are reference works that can help us with research. I cannot list everything that might come in handy. (Sheehy alone runs to more than eight hundred pages.) A few titles hint at the range that you can expect: Grove's *Dictionary of Music and Musicians; Contemporary Biography; The Dictionary of the History of Ideas; The Timetables of History; Encyclopedia of American Biography; Congressional Record; New Catholic Encyclopedia; McGraw-Hill Encyclopedia of Russia and the Soviet Union; Bibliography of Comparative Literature; Anthropology Today: An Encyclopedia Inventory; Mental Health Book Review Index; International Bibliography of Political Science; Nuclear Science Abstracts; Chambers's Technical Dictionary; Chemical Abstracts; Mathematical Reviews; Encyclopedic Dictionary of Physics*—and on and on and on.

New technology has introduced nonbook materials useful to researchers: microfilms (such as microfilm and microfiche) and direct computer-terminal access to databases (such as ERIC, the Educational Resources Information Center).

When we work on a subject with a local connection, or sometimes on larger topics, we should remember a reference work seldom considered: the telephone book. Frank Rodriguez called a UHF station for the starting dates of two situation comedies (see Chapter 3). The Yellow Pages help us most: when we look into zoning laws, or the mortgage policies of banks, we may find real estate agents or bank officers who are willing to talk to us and supply us with statistics and documentation. Large firms, in manufacturing especially, often include departments of public relations, whose job is to answer questions from the public and to supply information. Always remember that, if we write on a disputed subject, self-interest may inform what our sources tell us, and the information selected for us. The president of a utility company will doubtless view the issue of nuclear power with opinions unlike an environmental activist's.

On many subjects, the United States government listings in the white pages may give you numbers to call—the Internal Revenue Service, the Postal Service, the Department of Agriculture. Remember that state and local agencies may be as useful as federal ones.

Another resource we sometimes overlook is our academic community. Within the college or university, we can find specialists who will help us define a topic by narrowing our focus, and point us toward specific books and articles in the library. From these people we can discover the whereabouts of recent thinking about almost any subject.

Sometimes a personal interview provides fresh information or a perspective too new for print. A tape recording, made with the permission of the informant, may provide accurate quotations for a paper. We may question not only academic specialists, but anyone with special information—even members of our own families. Interviews, after all, are the basis for most journalism, as well as for oral historians. What better source on old logging methods than a seventy-six-year-old neighbor whose father and grandfather were lumbermen? All families have untapped stories to tell. What was it like to work in a munitions factory in World War II? To survive the Great Depression? To patrol Vietnam in 1967? Uncles, aunts, grandparents, and parents are only waiting for us to ask them.

## DOCUMENTATION

As you do your research, you must keep track of your sources. When you write your paper, you must record in parenthetical references and on a list of works cited where quotations and information come from, so that a reader can identify the source and locate it.

Books recommend different systems of documentation, and various disciplines use their own preferred styles. Instructors will require a consistent style of documentation, and many will use the newly revised guidelines adopted by the Modern Language Association: *MLA Handbook for Writers of Research Papers* (2nd ed.; New York, 1984). The new *MLA Handbook* departs from the method of annotation traditionally used in the humanities, which called for full footnotes or endnotes as well as a bibliography repeating much of the same information. Taking its cue from the style rules of the American Psychological Association (APA), widely used in the social sciences, the new edition of the *Handbook* has eliminated the usual footnotes and endnotes altogether. It substitutes simplified parenthetical notes within the body of the text, keyed to a list of works cited, which we add to the end of the research paper and which contains full citations. The *MLA Handbook* has also expanded its coverage of nonprint sources to take account of technological innovations in handling and storing information. It describes how to document films and television programs as well as computer software and databases.

## LIST OF WORKS CITED, OR BIBLIOGRAPHY

The list of works cited includes all the sources a writer has consulted to write a research paper, primarily those mentioned in the parenthetical in-text notes, organized alphabetically by the authors' last names. When we write a research paper we will use a list of works cited by necessity; but we must remember *always* to use a bibliography, or such a list, in *any* paper for which we have consulted *any* sources—a book in the library, an informant in an interview, *Newsweek*, a television program.

As you begin to gather information for your research paper, you will want to make a preliminary list of works cited. Whenever you consult a book, an article in a reference work, a newspaper report—any source at all, even if you think you might not use it—take a note. Make notes also of potential sources you come across in your reading. Three-by-five-inch index cards are handy for this purpose because they are easy to add, discard, and rearrange. Your information will fall into three main units, each separated from the next by a period: author, title, publication information. For each book that you consult, record on one card the whole library call number (not to be included when you type your list of works cited, but helpful if you wish to return to the book), author, full title and subtitle (underlined), place of publication (only the first if there is more than one), publisher and date of publication. The *MLA Handbook* lists shortened forms of publishers' names that simplify our task. Most publishers are represented by one word; any university press adds "UP" to the name of the university. Publishers are listed by the first proper noun of their names: Random House becomes Random; Coward, McCann & Geoghegan becomes Coward; and Farrar, Straus & Giroux becomes Farrar. Exception occurs when the first noun is somebody's first name: William Morrow & Co. becomes Morrow; Alfred A. Knopf becomes Knopf. Be sure to record special information: Is it a second or later edition? A reprint? If a translation, who translated it? Is there more than one volume? For each periodical article, record the author if one is named, title of article (in quotation marks), title of periodical (underlined), volume number (if a scholarly journal), date, and page numbers. Initial accuracy, however tedious, will save work later. Your bibliography cards will contain all the information necessary for your final list of works cited; you can alphabetize your cards and make your list of works cited directly from them. Opposite are some sample working cards for a list.

The *MLA Handbook* includes a thorough discussion of the proper manners to use in a list of works cited. Here are sample citations. Notice punctuation.

*A book with one author:*
Tedlock, Dennis. *The Spoken Word and the Work of Interpretation.* Philadelphia: Pennsylvania UP, 1983.

*A book with two or three authors:*
Cordell, Richard A., and Lowell Matson. *The Off-Broadway Theatre.* New York: Random, 1959.

*A book with more than three authors:*
Leavitt, Emily Stewart, et al., eds. *Animals and Their Legal Rights.* 3rd ed. Washington: Animal Welfare Institute, 1978.

*A book with an editor:*
Henderson, Bill, ed. *The Art of Literary Publishing.* Yonkers: Pushcart, 1980.

*An article from an edited book:*
Lish, Gordon, "True Confessions of a Failed Reader." *The Art of Literary Publishing.* Ed. Bill Henderson. Yonkers: Pushcart, 1980. 230–38.

*A translated book:*
Schulz, Bruno. *The Street of Crocodiles.* Trans. Celina Wieniewska. New York: Penguin, 1977.

*A book in several volumes:*
Johnson, Edgar. *Charles Dickens: His Tragedy and Triumph.* 2 vols. New York: Simon, 1952.

179
F

Fox, Michael

<u>Between Animal and Man</u>

New York: Coward, 1976

see especially chs. 1-3, 9-11

Mason, James B.

"Livestock Factory"

<u>Country Journal</u>    Oct. 1980

pp 58-63

Feed lot finishing of beef

*A new edition:*
Arensberg, Conrad M., and Solon T. Kimball. *Family and Community in Ireland.* 2nd ed. Cambridge: Harvard UP, 1968.

*A periodical article:*
Mumford, Lewis. "The Cult of Anti-Life." *Virginia Quarterly Review* 46 (1970): 198–206.

*An article in a popular (monthly or weekly) magazine:*
Greenwald, John. "The Search for Shelter." *Time* 30 Apr. 1984: 50–51.

*A magazine article with no author given:*
"Talk of the Town." *New Yorker* 22 Nov. 1982: 35–40.

*A newspaper article:*
Perkins, G. V. "What's New in Agriculture." *New York Times* 25 March 1984: F17.

*A lecture:*
Jensen, Jack E. Lecture. Colby-Sawyer College. New London, NH, 25 May 1983.

*An interview:*
Freemont, Helen. Personal interview. 27 June 1983.

*A book review:*
Doctorow, E. L. "Four Characters under Two Tyrannies." Rev. of *Unbearable Lightness of Being,* by Milan Kundera. *New York Times Book Review,* 29 April 1984: 1+.

*A recording:*
Thomas, Dylan. *Dylan Thomas Reading His Complete Recorded Poetry.* Rec. 1949–53. Caedmon, TC 2014, n.d.

*A radio or television program:*
*Prairie Home Companion.* PBS. WGBH, Boston. 12 May 1984.

*Computer software:*
Tobias, Andrew. *Managing Your Money.* Computer software. MECA (Micro Educational Corporation of America), 1984. 128K, one disk drive.

## NOTES

We use parenthetical notes in the body of the text to identify the sources of quotations or paraphrases, facts or opinions that we have derived from others. Because in-text notes refer to the full list of works cited at the end of the research paper, usually the parenthetical citation needs only the last name of the author, or editor or translator, or a short title, and the appropriate page numbers: (Tedlock 43), (*Prairie Home*). It depends on how we enter the source in our list. We can still use foot-notes or endnotes to comment on or to qualify a portion of the text, to mention related but less important information, or to list numerous references (more than three) that would make an in-text parenthesis unmanageably long and disruptive to the attention of the audience. But most documentation appears within the text. The revised *MLA Hand-book*, in its guidelines on documentation, requires a close relationship between the text and the notes. When we mention the author's name in a sentence, we need not repeat it in the note:

> In Tedlock's discussion of the transcription of oral narrative (31–61), he . . .

Here, page numbers are sufficient. If we refer to a whole work, mention-ing the author's name in the sentence eliminates the need for any note:

> Tedlock has continued the discussion of narrative style and struc-ture in storytelling.

A reader can look in the list of works cited, under "Tedlock," to find the work referred to. If we have consulted more than one work by an author, we must add a short title to the note in order to specify the work cited:

> In his latest work (Tedlock, *Spoken Word*), he describes his meth-ods for analyzing and evaluating verbal performance.

These conventions make it easy for readers to locate the source of our ideas, to check the original, or to find the leads for their own research.

The writer need not note material that is general knowledge. When we mention that the horse is a domesticated animal, we need not supply a footnote; the information is generally available. But if we supply information about the evolution of the horse from the eohippus, we should refer to our source.

If we quote an author directly, or paraphrase someone else's idea in our own words, without crediting the source of our information, we are guilty of *plagiarism*—a word that comes from the Latin for "kid-napped." Plagiarism, which is defined and discussed in Chapter 1, is serious business. When we neglect to credit our sources, even uninten-tionally by carelessness, we pass off someone else's words and thoughts as our own. We must always provide notes to acknowledge our indebtedness. Notes certify our honesty and fairness, and record our dependence on ideas other than our own.

For additional advice on notes, consult the *MLA Handbook*. Parenthetical notes should remain simple and concise. Here are some samples of parenthetical notes that correspond with the sample citations on pages 340–342.

*A book with one author:* (Tedlock 43)
*A book with two or three authors:* (Cordell and Matson 148)
*A book with more than three authors:* (Leavitt et al. 15)
*A book with an editor:* (Henderson 126)
*An article from an edited book:* (Lish 235)
*A translated book:* (Schulz 53)
  Unless you are specifically discussing a work as a translation and have entered it in your list of works cited under the translator's name, this note is enough.
*One volume in a multivolume book:* (Johnson 2: 929–40)
*The whole volume:* (Johnson, vol. 2)
*A periodical article:* (Mumford 198)

Some abbreviations frequently used in notes and lists of works cited include:

| | |
|---|---|
| cf. | compare (not "see") |
| ch., chs., chap. | chapter(s) |
| ed., eds. | edition, edited by, editor(s) |
| e.g. | for example |
| et al. | and others |
| i.e. | that is |
| illus. | illustrated by |
| ms., mss. | manuscript(s) |
| n., nn. | note(s) |
| n.d. | no date of publication given in book |
| n.p. | no place of publication or no publisher given |
| rev. | revised |
| trans. | translated by, translator(s) |
| viz. | namely (however, avoid using) |
| rpt. | reprinted by, reprint |
| UP | university press, used in documentation |

## A RESEARCH PROJECT

Barbara Levine rode home on the bus one evening during the spring term of her freshman year, worrying about her research paper assignment, a ten-to-twelve-page paper due in four weeks. She had no idea what to write about. That afternoon, she had talked with her instructor, but she still felt discouraged.

Later that night, after dinner, Barbara sat at her desk. "Write about something you are *interested* in," her instructor had urged her. Well, she liked animals; she thought of studying to be a veterinarian; but veterinary medicine was simply too huge a subject. She remembered an article she had read at the dentist's office, describing how calves were raised for veal in narrow stalls—what was the phrase?—like coffins. She had been shocked; maybe there was a paper on the subject of mistreated veal calves. Was the article in *Smithsonian?* How would she ever find it again?

During a free period the next day, Barbara ventured into the library. She dreaded the thought of looking through all the back issues of *Smithsonian;* what if the article she remembered wasn't even there? She approached the reference librarian, who showed her to the *Readers' Guide to Periodical Literature.* In one of the green volumes, under Animals—*Treatment,* she found what she was looking for:

> **ANIMALS—***Continued*
> **Treatment**
> Scientist helps stir new movement for animal rights [M. Fox] D. Nevin. bibl(p 152) il pors Smithsonian 11:50-9 Ap '80

She wrote "11:50–9"—whatever that meant (it meant the eleventh volume, pages 50 to 59; "il pors" meant "illustrated" and "portraits") and "Ap '80" into her notebook. Down the page she noticed several other possible references: *Animal Experimentation, Hunting— Ethical Aspects; Animals—Protection, Humane Societies, Game Laws, Wildlife Conservation, Trapping.* Suddenly there were many leads to follow; it was exciting—but she would have to focus her search.

When Barbara read the *Smithsonian* article in a bound volume in the stacks, she discovered a bibliography at the end of it (the *Readers' Guide*'s "bibl") listing three books, a magazine article, and a scientific report. All were recent. The animal factory must be a controversial topic.

The next afternoon after class she returned to the library and started looking in encyclopedias for general information on animal factories and animal rights. She found nothing. Then she went to the card catalogue to look up the titles from the bibliography at the end of

*Bibliography card*

> SF
> 51
> M37
>
> Mason, Jim and Peter Singer
>
> <u>Animal Factories</u>
> NY: Crown, 1980
>
> Singer very moral —
> lots of fieldwork here

the *Smithsonian* article, which she had copied into her notebook the day before. Her library owned two of the books.

Reading, she began to compile information and started keeping a list of works cited on three-by-five-inch index cards, one card for each book or article she came across. Under the bibliographic information, she added a note to herself about each source. She kept her cards together with a rubber band, two piles that slowly expanded—one for works cited, another for quotations, summaries, facts, and specific details that she would eventually need to document. She was careful to code her notes to her list of works, to indicate exact page numbers for her references, and to distinguish between quotations and her own summaries, paraphrases, and speculations.

Over the week, Barbara went through the library's catalogue looking at subject cards and tracking down books she found references to. Under *Animals, Treatment,* she found seven titles besides the two she already had, and most of these books provided cross-references to other possibilities. One thing led to another; it was like finding her way through the maze at an amusement park—and sometimes just as confusing. But gradually she began to feel familiar with her topic, and the various pieces of information that she had collected began to fall into place. She jotted down ideas for the shape and purpose of her paper. She didn't try to put her notes in any order, only to gather as many as she could, writing down her fragmentary ideas so that she would not forget them: "... maybe chickens best to write about? . . . legal aspects, laws should be passed? . . . nutrition—for animals *and* people . . . is this agribusiness? . . . "

Gradually she found herself narrowing her topic. As she looked over *Animal Experimentation* and *Hunting—Ethical Aspects*, she decided that she wanted to keep to the specific issue of animal rights on factory farms, which the author of the *Smithsonian* article had sketched. She began to concentrate on cross-references like *Cattle—Confinement Methods* and to pass over references to antivivisectionism.

She started to feel more comfortable in the library's reference room and stacks. It became easier to locate what she wanted. When she could not find one important book in her library, she applied with the aid of a librarian for an interlibrary loan from another college. Another title was being used by someone, but the same librarian at the same circulation desk showed how the library could recall it for her. On one book that sounded important she reached a dead end; the library did not own and could not locate *Animal Machines* by Ruth Harrison. She felt frustrated—but then she found two articles by Ruth Harrison in collections of essays on the subject.

Barbara learned how to use a microfilm machine to read an article from a back issue of *Time*. A librarian showed her how to look up government publications. She found specialized periodical indexes in the reference room and used the *Social Science Index*. At the beginning of her search, Barbara had worried about finding enough information to write a ten-page paper. Now she worried about finding too much. She photocopied magazine articles and essays so that she could take them home with her. She wrote notes in the margins of her copies, and underlined with red marker specific information she wanted to use. When she used portions of books, she photocopied the title page, which contained the author, title, and publishing information she would need, and the pages that contained quotations she might need for her paper. She used a tiny stapler to keep together the pages photocopied from each book.

Taking notes in earnest, she switched to four-by-six-inch index cards because they had room to copy longer quotations and summaries. To save time and avoid recopying, she used some of her cards to index her photocopies: she recorded author's last name, page number, and a rough subject heading. *Cows—Hormones* would lead her to a page about Farrah Faucets, a cow cloned because she was a good milker. For her other notes, she wrote the last name of the author in the upper left-hand corner of the card, adding a short form of the title for authors of more than one book consulted and the page number from which her information came. Usually she jotted a general subject heading in the upper right-hand corner of each card to make sorting easier when she was organizing her thoughts. Most of the time, she summarized or paraphrased important ideas or points related to her argument. One government report said, "In the future, animal breeding programs may be augmented by biotechnology to achieve desired changes with unprecedented speed and selectivity." Barbara summarized, on her index card, "Biotechnology will be a determining factor in how animals are bred in the future." Sometimes she quoted key phrases or opinions directly. She was careful to copy the punctuation and the words exactly and to enclose the quotations in quotation marks so that she wouldn't mistake the words for her own when she was writing.

A week before her paper was due, Barbara began to organize her notes into related groups. She would describe animal factory systems, with examples and evidence, showing them to be unjust and cruel. She had to leave out much that she had learned. The long history of animal mistreatment had fascinated her as she read about it, but she could do no more than allude to a historical background. Although animal factories in America produced all kinds of meat, she would not have room to talk about most of the factory methods. She decided to concentrate on poultry, because factory methods began in the poultry industry; she would find space also to speak about veal calves.

She tried out a brief thesis statement: "Protein factories exploit animals in a cruel way for profit." She consulted her general notes and sketched an informal outline by which she would prove her thesis. When she started the informal outline, she left many spaces between items on her list so that she could backtrack and fill in. Some items she listed twice—first to introduce the subject, later to return and *develop* it. *Animal rights*, for instance, needed to be mentioned at the beginning of the paper, in a context that would lend direction to the exposition of her facts; later, ideas about animal rights (and laws to guarantee them) would form the conclusion to her paper.

When she finished the preliminary loose list of topics, she assigned letters of the alphabet to each of her items so that she could organize her notes into piles listed under a capital letter, instead of the words of her list. As it happened, she found herself with a complete alphabet of items—twenty-six in all.

| A | human-animal history | N | old/new |
|---|---|---|---|
| B | intro.—animal factories | O | James Beard quote |
| C | intro.—animal rights | P | vs. reality |
| D | ecology | Q | crowding |
| E | health | R | anemia |
| F | chicken intro. | S | other animals |
| G | crowding | T | livestock industry |
| H | feeding | U | morals/ |
| I | light | V | money |
| J | "vices" | W | present situation |
| K | cruelty | X | animal rights—THESIS |
| L | deformity | Y | laws |
| M | veal | Z | conclusion |

Then she sat on the floor of her room to sort note cards by subject headings into rough piles corresponding to large divisions of her outline. She put aside several which didn't fit anywhere—or which might be fitted into several places.

Beginning a draft was like swimming: should she wade in slowly to get used to the water, or should she jump off the high board? She wrote: "Humans and animals have lived on the earth together for thousands of years." It sounded obvious but she decided to leave it for the moment. She wrote another general sentence and then moved to her note cards for specific information. She described how factories process chickens, and let facts and statistics speak for themselves; then she discussed the raising of veal calves. As she wrote, using her index cards, she kept track of her sources in parenthetical notes, copying author's name and relevant page numbers from her notes and photocopies.

The day after she finished her first draft, Barbara read it aloud to her mother. By hearing herself read it and by responding to her mother's questions, she found sections where her thinking was unclear or her paragraphs jolted into each other without transitions. She revised—reworking tangled sentences, clarifying confused modifiers, adding ideas to explain transitions. Some quotations were too long. She looked up information on ellipses in quotations (see pages 411–412) and recast sentences so that they took quotations smoothly inside themselves. She consulted the Critic Inside (see Chapter 3) and wrote comments in the margins of her successive drafts, urging herself to greater originality, completeness, and clarity. She tinkered with the order of ideas in her paper, cutting and pasting, shifting paragraphs until she found the

Harrison (in Leavitt)                          LAW – ENGLAND
p. 71

Brambell Committee, set up in mid-sixties
to examine animal husbandry, reported
in 1965:    (legislation, 1968)
    "In principle we disapprove of a degree
of confinement of an animal which
necessarily frustrates most of the major
activities which make up its natural
behaviour."

Note card:
quotation

---

Singer, <u>Animal Liberation</u>          POULTRY
p. 116

"Ultimately, the most convincing way a
bird can indicate that its conditions are
inadequate is by dying."

egg losses run 10–15% per yr. from
crowding and stress

Note card:
quotation
and statistics

---

                                   ANIMAL RIGHTS
Nevin
p. 55

Michael Fox of Institute for Study of
Animal Problems in Washington D.C.:

"rights" – "imply a grasp of the animal's
intrinsic nature and its needs."
To deprive an animal of its natural needs
is as inhumane as causing unnecessary
pain.

Note card:
quotation
and paraphrase

most logical sequence of ideas. Some ideas, and some information, fit nowhere in her paper; with regret she omitted a few favorite items.

The day before it was due, she went back to her last draft and read it through with as much detachment as she could manage. Then she typed the text, rechecked notes to be sure they were accurate and referred clearly to her final list, made a title page, an outline, and her final list of works cited. The title page was easy. Barbara remembered that she was required by her instructor to preface her paper with a title page and an outline. Although she had not worked from an outline, she could easily derive one from the paper. Because she had taken good notes on her index cards, and because she had organized the cards before drafting her paper, she had constructed it clearly. The ordered pile of cards had been her outline.

Here is the paper she handed in. We have added notes in the margin about documentation and transitions.

Animal Rights and Animal Wrongs


by
Barbara Levine


English 101, Section M
Dr. Jensen
April 23, 1984

Animal Rights and Animal Wrongs

Thesis: The way we treat food animals
reflects our exploitative view of the
earth and its resources, which must
change.

I. Introduction
    A. Exploitation of animals
    B. Animal factories
        1. Institutionalized cruelty
        2. Waste and pollution
        3. Health
        4. Agribusiness
II. Examples of factories
    A. Chickens
        1. Factory conditions
           a. Crowding
           b. Lighting
        2. Vices
           a. Aggressive behavior
               (1) Pecking
               (2) Cannibalism
           b. Poor health
        3. Death and the dollar

   B. Veal

      1. Original source

      2. Factory conditions

         a. Crowding

         b. Anemia

   C. Other animals

III. Supporters of factory system

   A. Agribusiness

      1. Animals as "output"

      2. Technology

   B. Feed, equipment, service companies

   C. Agricultural researchers

IV. Protecting animal rights

   A. British example

   B. Direct, indirect benefits of production

      1. Reduce cruelty

      2. Reduce other costs of factory system

V. Conclusion

   A. Compassion and common sense

   B. Regaining our humanity

Animal Rights and Animal Wrongs

When we stopped being animals
and became human, millions of years
ago, we began to exploit the creatures we had been. Using animals for
our profit has been taken as a sign
of being human (Peters 228). We have
used animals as if they existed in order to be our sources of food, clothing, and shelter. We have abused them
for amusement, sport, and luxury.

The belief that human beings
come first is continuous in our history, and today our exploitation of
animals is worse than it ever was.
Modern technology has created the
assembly-line protein factory in
which animals undergo, as protesters
say, "restrictions and manipulations
that would be regarded as atrocities
if practiced on humans" (Mason and
Singer xiii). The American livestock
industry now processes four billion
animals a year by factory methods
(Nevin 56). This vast, institutional-
ized cruelty raises the question: do

*lively title attracts attention and names the paper's subject*

*note credits an idea*

*first paragraph general, followed by more specific paragraph*

*a transition introduces main subjects of animal factories*

*quotation worked into sentence, source noted*

*note credits source of information*

animals have the right to humane treatment? There are other issues as well. Animal factories produce enormous waste and pollution. They use land and energy resources carelessly. They manufacture meat in quantity by compromising quality, which harms human health. Powerful agribusiness conglomerates expropriate the small farmer and contribute to the decline of rural life. They channel to animals large amounts of grain that, if distributed as grain, could relieve hunger throughout the world.

What are these factory systems like? A look behind the scenes—at a factory building for poultry, a veal confinement shed, a cattle feedlot, or a pig "bacon bin"—would be a gruesome eye-opener for anyone. "The modern chicken," say the authors of <u>Animal Factories</u>, "is a business creation" (Mason and Singer 3). Today we take eating chicken for granted, but only the development of factory methods in the poultry industry after World War II[1] has made the chicken in-

*question introduces main section of paper, answered in next eleven paragraphs*

*quotation and source in text*

*endnote 1 refers*

expensive enough for the American table. The chicken is twice as unlucky
as other animals, for we eat its eggs
as well as its flesh. Poultry producers have bred two varieties of the
White Leghorn, one designed for meat,
the other for eggs. Both broilers and
layers are kept in animal factories.

    From ten to fifty thousand, and
in several large West Coast businesses, as many as 90,000 day-old
chicks are brought from hatcheries
and placed in a long windowless building. Often the chicks crowd on concrete floors. Sometimes as many as
four or five are stuffed into tiny
cages, 12 by 18 inches, to prevent
the pile-ups that can suffocate them
if they are loose. These little cages
have no perches because those would
take up room, and chickens stand on
the gridded bottom as best they can.
Standing up is especially hard for
layers because the bottoms of their
cages are often slanted to allow eggs
to roll down to collection shelves.
Bird droppings fall through the wire

*reader to other
sources for
information outside
scope of discussion*

*transition sentence
leads to detailed
description*

to an area below that may not be
cleaned at all until the crop of
birds is finished. One employee can
supervise mechanized food and water
supplies for thousands of birds. The
factory managers manipulate electric
lights, according to the protein they
wish to manufacture: darkness quiets
broilers so that they gain more
weight, and eighteen hours of simu-
lated daylight stimulate layers to
produce more eggs (Singer 100—08;
Smith and Daniel 267—69; Nevin 54—
55).

*note combines sources for information in paragraph*

   Crowding keeps birds from establishing their natural social hierar-
chy and creates boredom and stress.
Stress produces the "vices," as the
manufacturers call them, of pecking
and cannibalism, as well as greater
susceptibility to disease. But instead of cutting down on crowding,
and lowering profits, producers rou-
tinely de-beak chickens with a hot
knife. This mutilation is painful and
makes it difficult or impossible for
some hens to eat. Because layers live

*a descriptive paragraph moves onward to specific abuses, from lesser to greater*

longer, they may have to be de-beaked
a second time. To counter the increased possibility of disease, poultry producers feed their birds a
high-additive feed containing antibiotics, tranquilizers, and appetite
stimulators (Singer 102–04).

Observers have called these
chicken and egg factories "an Inferno
as terrible in its own way as any of
the circles of Dante's hell" (Smith
and Daniel 287). Ultimately, they
frustrate all the birds' natural in-
stincts to walk, scratch, take dust
baths, nest, stretch their wings, defend themselves, and claim a place in
the pecking order. Methods for reviv-
ing fallen-off egg production cause
death from shock. Manure piled underneath cages gives off a searing reek
of ammonia. The wire of the cages dam-
ages feet and claws, in some cases
causing a chicken's foot to grow to
the wire (Singer 111, 114–15).

Because the buildings depend on
automated ventilation systems, a mechanical or electrical failure kills

*quotation used to
introduce writer's
criticism*

thousands of birds. But factory chickens don't live long anyway. Broiler
hens are slaughtered at eight or nine
weeks; egg layers are worn out after
fourteen months and are shipped off
to become chicken pie, soup, and fast
food. By contrast, a free-run chicken
lives up to fifteen or twenty years
(Mason and Singer 5). The moral philosopher Peter Singer observes in his
book, <u>Animal Liberation</u>, that "ultimately, the most convincing way a
bird can indicate that its conditions
are inadequate is by dying," and mortality rates on egg farms run as high
as ten to fifteen percent (116). Even
so, these protein plants remain profitable. A spokesman sums up the industry outlook: "The object of produc-
ing eggs is to make money. When we
forget this objective, we have forgotten what it is all about" (Singer
108).

Gradually over the last thirty
years the barnyard chicken has disap-
peared. Replacing it are industrial-
ized egg machines and additive-filled

*notice transition
from detail to
general information*

*identifying quoted
authority adds
force; author (and
title) mentioned in
text; therefore, note
includes only page
number*

*paragraph sums up
the poultry
business before
turning to veal*

monsters with deformed feet, too
heavy to stand on their own bones and
muscles. Only artificial coloring
makes egg yolks and chicken flesh yellow, allowing the consumer to believe
that nothing has changed.

Compared to the poultry producer, the veal farmer operates on a
much smaller scale. Veal farms usually keep fewer than a hundred animals at a time. Yet Singer calls raising calves for veal the "most morally
repugnant" of all the factory systems
(127). Originally, veal was the naturally pale and tender meat of male
calves killed before weaning. These
calves never weighed much beyond 90
pounds, and killing them for meat was
a practical way for the dairy farmer
to dispose of animals he could not
raise to milk. But expensive restaur-
ants want this meat—and now there
are European methods of raising veal
calves to weigh more than 300 pounds
(Singer 128).

In one of his cookbooks, James
Beard writes:

*transitional
sentence introduces
additional example*

*contrasts of old and
new*

Good veal has always been difficult to find. But recently a
Dutch process has come to our
shores and is giving us limited
quantities of much finer veal
than was generally available before. . . . The process consists
simply of taking calves from
their mothers' milk to small
stalls, where they are fed with
vitamins and powdered milk that
contains no iron to darken the
flesh. Also, the calves are kept
comparatively quiet during their
milk regime. Thus, they have
delicate whitish-pink flesh and
clear fat and are deliciously tender (qtd. in Mason and Singer
126).

Perhaps gourmet cooks and diners
would like to believe this health-spa
description, but the true picture is
horrible. Newborn calves are taken
from their mothers to a windowless
concrete-block building containing
slat-floored wooden stalls only two

*quotation (longer
than four lines)
indented ten
spaces, double-
spaced*

*quotation taken
from a secondary
source; usually it is
preferable to quote
the original*

*transition by
contrast,
descriptive
paragraph*

feet wide. Here the calves stay for
the sixteen short weeks of their
lives. They eat only a high-intensity
liquid diet of nonfat milk, vitamins,
minerals, antibiotics, and drugs for
growth and weight. They have no water
at all. In their thirst they gorge
themselves on their liquid feed and
gain weight faster, making more money
for their owners. They are chained in
their stalls, usually in complete
darkness for twenty-two out of
twenty-four hours to cut down on movement that would toughen their meat.
The slatted floors hurt their legs.
They cannot extend their feet when
they lie down. They cannot groom themselves or turn around.

      Stalls have no straw for bedding
because it contains iron and iron
would darken the calves' meat. The
ideal white, or milk-fed, flesh comes
from acute anemia. By the time the
calves are three and a half months
old, weighing about 330 pounds, they
are seriously ill and would die of
anemia if they were not slaughtered

for restaurant food. Some calves
crave iron so much that they lick
iron stall bars and their own urine,
which contains iron residues.[2]

    The veal industry, finding it
possible and profitable to supply a
steady demand for pale meat, deliberately induces severe anemia, con-
strains movement, and produces an extremely sickly animal, prone to ul-
cers, watery bowel movements, and
pneumonia. The mortality rate of veal
calves runs as high as fifty percent
(Mason and Singer 25). One large veal
producer expresses the industry view:
"Farming is about money production,
not food production" (Singer 130),
and the demand for veal is such that
producers can absorb high calf losses
and still make a solid profit.

    The same exploitation and cru-
elty happens in cattle feedlots and
dairy-cow and pig confinement sheds.[3]
Producers encourage rapid gains in
weight by adding growth stimulators
to grain. Until 1979, these chemicals
included DES, since banned by the

*endnote 2 gathers
sources too long for
inclusion in text*

*another paragraph
of summary, before
moving on*

*endnote 3 refers
reader to further
information on
subject that cannot
be covered here*

Food and Drug Administration as a
cause of cancer (Mason and Singer 61,
69; Robbins 218–19, 224–25). Cows and
pigs are kept immobilized in stalls
and must be bred continually to supply the system. The results are de-
pressingly familiar: bored, aggressive animals showing all the symptoms
of stress.

How did the livestock industry
get like this? It takes a lot of
money to start up. In the last few
years, agribusiness interests have
bought into the system, replacing
smaller independent farmers and producers, because agribusiness has the
capital needed for starting up
(Singer 98). Some factories are opportunities for capital investment, or
ways to reduce taxes, for
nonagricultural companies like Grey-
hound, ITT, and John Hancock Mutual.
These companies make decisions based
on "input and output costs and values" (Mason and Singer 18). Businessmen, wanting a uniform, profitable
end-product, translate animals into

*another question leads to an answer in following paragraphs*

*note credits an idea*

*note credits a direct quotation*

"raw materials" and "conversion units," the value-free vocabulary of technology. We might accept a cost-effective approach in manufacturing plastics or cars, or even in growing fruits and vegetables, but its hard consequences on the lives of animals make cost-effectiveness intolerable in meat production.

Two other groups have encouraged the owners of animal factories: commercial feed, equipment, and services companies find their best customers in agribusiness; agricultural research institutions at our universities, subsidized by tax dollars, find projects and grant money for developing these exploitative systems. On the other hand, small farmers, without the capital for buildings and equipment to compete with large corporations, must sell out and leave the land. Some smaller producers have adopted factory methods with the help of suppliers who sell them feed and stock and buy back the finished animals (Robbins 214–16).

As automation increases, the condition of animals worsens. It is economical to employ fewer human supervisors, but it means less attention to individual animals in distress. Instead of eliminating the methods that cause stress and its problems—aggression, cannibalism, tail—biting, and more disease—farm experts turn to <u>more</u> mechanization, <u>more</u> mutilation, and <u>more</u> genetic manipulation. E. F. Schumacher, economist and advocate of smallness, testifies to the craziness of this approach when he says that it is like trying "to cure a disease by intensifying its causes" (35). The solution to problems caused by technology always seems to be more technology.

*name mentioned in text; only page number necessary*

Scientific methods have already produced anemic calves, neurotic chickens, and bored pigs that gnaw on their own tails. Yet researchers continue to try to "improve" agricultural practices and increase efficiency. A recent project attempts to breed animals that eat and digest faster and sleep less so that they

can put on more weight. Another tries
to make commercial feeds out of animal wastes, cement dust, cardboard,
and newspaper. Another tries to develop chickens without neck feathers
because these feathers declog decapi-
tating machines. Last December, scientists announced the invention of red
contact lenses for poultry, in order
to limit vision and cut down on aggression (Mason and Singer 47—49;
"Egg" 18).

> *transition to conclusion based on research*

> *article without an author uses short title in note*

Mentioning "animal rights" calls
down the wrath of a scientific community heavily involved in laboratory
experimentation with animals. People
who favor humane treatment for animals are dismissed as sentimental.
But Dr. Michael Fox, director of the
Institute for the Study of Animal
Problems in Washington DC, himself a
scientist, says that animal—rights ac-
tivists merely want people "to see
animals as animals and treat them so"
(58). He claims that depriving an animal of its natural needs is as inhumane as inflicting unnecessary pain.

In the mid-sixties, Ruth Harrison alerted the British public to the horrors of factory systems in England. Her book, <u>Animal Machines</u>, prompted the government to investigate. The Brambell Report of 1965, from a specially appointed committee of the British Parliament, acknowledged that animals are capable of suffering and outlined a bill of rights for animals: animals should be able to get up, lie down, turn around, stretch, and groom. In addition, the committee asked that agricultural animals be fed a diet sufficient for health and receive adequate light. The committee condemned slatted floors without bedding, de-beaking, de-tailing, and similar mutilations. It condemned any "degree of confinement of an animal which necessarily frustrates most of the major activities which make up its natural behaviour" (Harrison 71).

Legislation for animal rights became law in England in 1968, setting up minimal codes of practice for ani-

mal factories and an advisory council
to keep watch on practices. So far,
the United States has no similar legislation. Both Holland and France,
the first countries to practice veal
confinement methods, now prohibit
methods still common in the United
States (Nevin 58).

We must pass legislation for animal rights, even if we begin with
small matters. If we only reduce
crowding and allow animals room to
move and socialize, we will eliminate
many of the conditions now treated
with tranquilizers. We must take action. Animal factory systems not only
inflict suffering on animals, but
also impose other hidden costs on all
of us (Mason and Singer 73–93, 127).
They waste huge quantities; 140,000
tons of poultry meat are condemned at
processing plants every year (Mason
and Singer 77). Instead of valuable
nitrogen from the manure of free-
ranging animals, factory systems release potent pollutants, full of antibiotics and chemicals, onto the land

*argument, with facts in support of argument*

and into water supplies. Enormous
amounts of fossil-fuel energy power
the ventilating, heating, and feeding
machines; tons of fertilizer, much of
it petrochemical, go to grow the quantities of grain used for animal feed.
Some scientists have estimated that
if the whole world ate the high-
protein meat diet that Americans do,
the world's petroleum reserves would
give out in only thirteen years
(Pimental et al., 847).

*note for more than
three authors*

    As uninformed consumers, we are
part of a self-perpetuating cycle: we
buy and eat the meat that factory systems produce; our purchases make the
market profitable, and therefore producers build more factory farms.
While the cycle continues, our health
suffers from the additives given animals to make them put on weight, prevent disease, and tranquilize them.
Industry overuse of antibiotics has
produced drug-resistant forms of bac-
teria like salmonella, gonorrhea, and
typhoid (Mason 61; Mason and Singer
83). Research links the high meat con-

*transition from
waste of resources
to waste of health*

sumption of the American diet to
heart disease, diabetes, stroke, and
cancer. The animal factory stands at
the center of a web of intricately related moral and environmental problems.

      If we can magnify cruelty so
thoughtlessly, and end by harming not
only animals but ourselves, perhaps
we can reinvent compassion while using a little common sense. In thinking about the technology which we
invented to serve us and which seems
instead to ruin us and our companions
on earth, we should listen to Wendell
Berry. As a farmer and a poet, he
writes: "our great dangerousness is
that locked in our selfish and myopic
economics, we have been willing to
change or destroy far beyond our
power to understand. We are not humble enough or reverent enough" (85).
With humility and reverence—added to
tough legislation—we can regain our
humanity by respecting nonhuman
rights.

*transition from
negative to positive*

*summary of
argument*

Notes

¹See Smith and Daniel, chs. 12—14.

²Summarized from Singer 127—35; Mason and Singer 13—14, 27—29; Mason 62; Hutchings and Caver 97—98.

*more than three sources go into endnote*

³See Mason 58—63; Singer 118—26, 135—38.

Works Cited

Berry, Wendell. <u>A Continuous Harmony</u>: Essays Cultural and Agricul- tural. New York: Harcourt, 1972.

"The Egg and Eye," <u>Time</u> 29 Dec. 1980: 18.

Fox, Michael W. <u>Between Animal and Man</u>. New York: Coward, 1976

Harrison, Ruth. "Animals in Factory Farms." <u>Animals and Their Legal Rights: A Survey of American Laws from 1641 to 1978</u>. Ed. Emily Stewart Leavitt et al. 3rd ed. Washington: Animal Welfare Institute, 1978. 69–73.

Hutchings, Monica, and Mavis Caver. <u>Man's Dominion: Our Violation of the Animal World</u>. London: Hart-Davis, 1970

Mason, James B. "Livestock Factory." <u>Country Journal</u> Oct. 1980: 58–63.

Mason, Jim, and Peter Singer. <u>Animal Factories</u>. New York: Crown, 1980.

Nevin, David. "Scientist Helps Stir

*notice shortened forms of publishers' names*

*magazine article with no author listed; entered under title*

*one essay quoted from an edited collection; book entered under essay author's name*

*book with two authors*

*magazine article with author listed*

New Movement for Animal Rights."
<u>Smithsonian</u> Apr. 1980: 50–59.

Peters, Michael. "Nature and Culture." <u>Animals, Men and Morals</u>:
<u>An Enquiry into the Maltreatment</u>
<u>of Non-humans</u>. Ed. Stanley
Godlovitch, Roslind Godlovitch,
and John Harris. London: Gol-
lancz, 1971. 213–31.

Pimental, David, et al. "The Potential for Grass-Fed Livestock: Resource Constraints." <u>Science</u> 207
(1980): 843–48.

Robbins, William. <u>The American Food</u>
<u>Scandal</u>. New York: Morrow, 1974.

Schumacher, E. F. <u>Small Is Beautiful</u>.
New York: Harper, 1973.

Singer, Peter. <u>Animal Liberation: A</u>
<u>New Ethics for Our Treatment of</u>
<u>Animals</u>. New York: New York Re-
view, 1975.

Smith, Page, and Charles Daniel. <u>The</u>
<u>Chicken Book</u>. Boston: Little,
1975.

# 10

## A Brief Review of Grammar, Punctuation, and Mechanics

This book is mostly about style and structure, about making writing lively, honest, energetic, and clear. As you move through the text, you find grammar when you need it. Here, I want to make a concentrated review of the most common errors in grammar, punctuation, and mechanics, so that the beginning writer who feels confused—What *is* a whole sentence? When *do* I use a colon?—will have a place to come for answers to questions. It may also serve the writer who, after a summer vacation or a year away from the classroom, needs a quick review of grammar and mechanics concentrating on errors frequently made.

If our grammar is loose and shabby, our punctuation random, and our mechanics haphazard, we will lose our audience. We must put sentences together by rules, because rules describe the readers' expectations. If our language ignores these rules—if we substitute commas for periods or neglect to match parts of sentences to each other—readers will be confused and bored; they will not follow where we want to lead them, even if our ideas are profound and our information fascinating.

When things go wrong in mechanics and grammar, for an inexperienced writer, they go wrong usually because of a few mistakes. If you can follow six general rules, you will avoid most of the errors beginners fall into.

1. Make whole, clear sentences.
2. Match the parts of sentences that need matching.
3. Connect modifiers with what they modify.
4. Keep the sentence consistent.
5. Keep punctuation clear.
6. Keep mechanics conventional.

These rules will become useful only if I do some explaining and give examples. Almost everything mentioned here is repeated from earlier chapters; this chapter is repetitious, but it ought to be useful. It differs from the text in the approach to writing. In the text I talk mostly about the choices a writer can make to express meaning with vigor and clarity. Here, you can read about the swamps that you as a writer can sink into, which keep you from reaching your goal.

Many inexperienced writers have trouble with only one or two of the problems I list and not with the rest. People sitting next to each other in class may have opposite troubles in writing. Neighbor A writes sentence fragments, B uses commas for periods, C mixes up pronouns, and D dangles modifers. None of them has the problem the other has, and each is thoroughly confused by his own problem. With this chapter, each student can go directly to his particular problem; I hope it can help the whole alphabet of writers.

## MAKE WHOLE, CLEAR SENTENCES

### Sentence Fragments

Beginning writers commonly make sentences—groups of words beginning with a capital letter and ending with a period—which don't complete an action. In an essay a student wrote

The effects of World War II.

as if the phrase told us something. But the sentence is incomplete, a sentence fragment. What *about* World War II? Did he want to say

Hungary suffered the effects of World War II.

or

World War II brought prosperity.

or what? In his essay, the writer had said

> The economy began picking up finally in 1939. The effects of World War II.

He needed to connect the sentence fragment to the sentence, making something like this:

> The economy began picking up in 1939 because of World War II.

The best writers sometimes put sentence fragments to good use (see pages 160–162), but when you are inexperienced, you should avoid them entirely. Wait until you have developed a firm and exact feel for the whole sentence's shape. Do not write

> He was a good teacher. Being sympathetic with students and fascinated by his subject.

Instead, write something like

> He was a good teacher, sympathetic with students and fascinated by his subject.

Do not write

> The pumpkins froze. When the blizzard arrived unexpectedly in October.

Instead, write something like

> When the blizzard arrived unexpectedly in October, the pumpkins froze.

Here are some inadvertent sentence fragments, indicated by italics.

> *After the sun finally sank behind the hills.* It was dark and we were ready.

> The principal of my high school was a nice person. *Believing that every kid was potentially all right.*

> *Seeing the Buick with all its tires flat and rusted out in the grass, with no license plates on it.*

> The people at the fair stared at the twins and began to talk about them. *Because they looked different, I guess.*

> Teachers in my opinion do not have the right to strike and miss their classes. *When students have already paid their tuition.*

Inadvertent sentence fragments are mainly of two kinds. Many fragments are subordinate clauses treated as if they were whole sentences. In three of the examples, the sentence fragments begin with *because, after,* and *when.* These words—like *although, since,* and *while*—mean that the clauses they introduce depend on, or hang from, a main clause; they are dependent or subordinate clauses. In the preceding examples, the main clauses (not in italics) make whole sentences themselves. The sentence fragments could become subordinate clauses in complex sentences.

> Teachers in my opinion do not have the right to strike and miss their classes, *when students have already paid their tuition.*

The other category, shown in the second and third examples, is the fragment that modifies a main clause and ought to be separated from it by a comma—not by a period and a capital letter.

> The principal of my high school is a nice person, *believing that every kid is potentially all right.*

Watch out for sentence fragments that begin with an *-ing* word, just as you watch for fragments beginning with *when* or *because.*

You can correct sentence fragments in several ways. You can correct *many* sentence fragments simply by using a comma instead of a period. Or you can add a verb to the fragment and make it a whole sentence, equal to the other.

Here are some alternate repairs for sentence fragments used earlier.

> He was a good teacher. He was sympathetic with students and fascinated by his subject.

> He was a good teacher because he was sympathetic with his students and fascinated by his subject.

> The blizzard arrived unexpectedly in October, freezing the pumpkins.

> The blizzard arrived unexpectedly in October, and the pumpkins froze.

> Because the blizzard arrived unexpectedly in October, the pumpkins froze.

> We saw the Buick with all its tires flat, rusted out in the grass, no license plates on it.

> The principal of my high school was a nice person. He believed that every kid was potentially all right.

The people at the fair stared at the twins and began to talk about them; they looked different, I guess.

After the sun finally sank behind the hills, it was dark and we were ready.

The sun finally sank behind the hills. It was dark and we were ready.

Notice that frequently a sentence fragment can become a whole clear sentence when we remove the subordinating word, like *because,* or change the modifying participle into a subject and a verb—like *we saw* for *seeing.*

## EXERCISES

1. Each of these five passages contains one or more sentence fragments. Identify each fragment, and revise it into a whole sentence in two ways.

a. When the sun rose high in the sky. All of us gathered twigs and fallen branches to make a fire. Then making breakfast for the whole group.

b. No-fault insurance helps all motorists. The good and the bad. Every state should pass no-fault automobile insurance.

c. When the Ford Motor Company named a new car the Pinto, they did a lot of research into the power of names. Names on the final list were largely the names of animals. Based on the discoveries of a market research firm.

d. The morning of our trip to school, the car all packed and ready, the rain falling in sheets outside.

e. Never too late to learn! That is what my high school civics teacher always told us. Which we heard so often that we didn't hear it anymore.

2. Combine the sentence fragments in this paragraph into whole sentences.

When I rented my first apartment, I learned a lot. How to make spaghetti. By the potful. And to keep dirty shirts and socks from piling up on the floor of my closet. I'll never forget the first time I went to the laundromat. Pouring bleach straight on the clothes. Holes in everything. Even my favorite jeans.

## Comma Splices

Comma splices (or comma faults) and run-on sentences are the opposite of sentence fragments. In the comma splice, a comma is forced into the work a period is meant for; in the sentence fragment, a period is pressed into the service a comma is designed for. Here is a typical comma splice, two whole sentences incorrectly joined by a comma:

> The Union stands back from the street about a hundred feet, it was built when land was still cheap.

Substitute a period for the comma, capitalize the next word, and you have two real, whole sentences.

Often the same writer makes sentence fragments and comma splices, because both errors depend on an insecure grasp of what makes a sentence. By reading our prose aloud, pausing according to the punctuation, we can sometimes discover these errors in time to revise them.

The comma splice is confusing to the reader, because two whole ideas are connected (spliced) as if they were not each whole and separate. The writer gives a signal by the comma but the sentence denies the message that the comma carries. The comma gives us the information that we are reading one continuous idea, which conflicts with the wholeness of each of the two spliced sentences. The best writers sometimes use the comma splice to good effect (see pages 173–175), but the beginning writer should avoid the device entirely, until he has developed a firm sense of the sentence.

Writers often make comma splices when they use conjunctive adverbs like *however, moreover, consequently, therefore, besides, then,* and *otherwise.* When these words connect main clauses, we use a semicolon between the clauses, before the adverb, and a comma after the adverb. Do not write

> She was intelligent, moreover she had a Ph.D. from Harvard.

but write

> She was intelligent; moreover, she had a Ph.D. from Harvard.

Here are comma splices taken from student essays.

> The port of New York has minimum safety requirements, some vessels have to dock in Hoboken.

The inevitability of war became obvious to even the most casual observer, maneuvers were constantly being held.

My father grew up on a potato farm in Idaho, he never saw a movie until he was twenty-two years old.

She walked through the door into the dining room, she wore nothing but a bikini.

When they were little, they liked to play in the empty warehouse down the block, it was a spooky and exciting place.

I didn't know where the arboretum was, somebody had to show me.

We were late for the movie, however it started late.

Never eat vegetables from a can which looks puffed up like a balloon, that's something I learned at camp.

Whoever saw the man running away saw the burglar, that's the only possible explanation.

Making a sweater from acrylic gets you into other problems, wool is better when you are beginning.

The canoe started tipping as I approached the falls, I was terrified that I would lose all my gear.

When you correct a comma splice, you have four alternatives. Two of them require only a change in punctuation; two of them require another word.

1. Substituting a semicolon for a comma repairs most comma splices. Making a comma splice often means you want to show a close connection between two whole sentences. You try to move quickly from one to the other, without the long pause implied by a period and a capital letter. The semicolon was invented for just this purpose: to show that two whole sentences follow quickly upon each other and are closely related.

Here are comma splices repaired by semicolons.

The port of New York has minimum safety requirements; some vessels have to dock in Hoboken.

The inevitability of war became obvious to even the most casual observer; maneuvers were constantly being held.

When they were little, they liked to play in the empty warehouse down the block; it was a spooky and exciting place.

2. Or you can use a period and a capital letter; they will always be correct.

> My father grew up on a potato farm in Idaho. He never saw a movie until he was twenty-two years old.

> Never eat vegetables from a can which looks puffed up like a balloon. That's something I learned at camp.

3. On the other hand, you can make a complex sentence, if you find that one sentence can depend on the other, by using a subordinating conjunction.

> When the canoe started tipping as I approached the falls, I was terrified that I would lose all my gear.

4. Or you can connect the two sentences into one compound sentence with *and, but, or, not, yet,* or *so;* the two clauses will be equally strong, or coordinate.

> I didn't know where the arboretum was, so somebody had to show me.

> The port of New York has minimum safety requirements, and some vessels have to dock in Hoboken.

> She walked through the door into the dining room, but she wore nothing but a bikini.

Each of these four solutions makes a slight difference in tone or meaning. In your context, one of the four will be best. Compare these variations of one sentence:

> When they were little, they liked to play in the empty warehouse down the block; it was a spooky and exciting place.

> When they were little, they liked to play in the empty warehouse down the block. It was a spooky and exciting place.

> When they were little, they liked to play in the empty warehouse down the block because it was a spooky and exciting place.

> When they were little, they liked to play in the empty warehouse down the block, and it was a spooky and exciting place.

The writer's choice should depend on mood and rhythm appropriate to context. The semicolon makes a slight pause and the period brings the thought to a full stop. The conjunction *because* makes the second part of the sentence depend on the first, implying cause and effect. The conjunction *and* connects two clauses in an equal partnership.

___ **EXERCISES** _____

1. Here are five passages from student essays. Identify the comma splices, and revise the passages into whole, single sentences. Use any of the four methods listed above. Then revise these passages again, using another of the four methods.

a. Carbon monoxide filled the foggy air, we could breathe only with difficulty.

b. Sunset fell rapidly, we had to hurry to set up our tent.

c. When the waitress removed an empty platter, she was back with a full platter a moment later, I never ate so much in my life, I was so full I thought I would burst.

d. Riding a bike you must never expect someone driving a car to notice you, you must always watch out for yourself.

e. The carrots pulled easily from the wet ground, it had rained for a week.

2. In this paragraph, make whole sentences from the comma splices.

Behind my uncle's barn sat four old cars, they were in various stages of disintegration, most were rusting in the tall weeds. The grille on the '32 Chevy grinned like decayed teeth, I thought when I was little, the doors sagged open. Years of rain had soaked the velour upholstery, the windows were shattered in weblike patterns from kids throwing stones. I would get in on hot summer afternoons, put both hands on the steering wheel, pretend to drive.

_____

## MATCH THE PARTS OF SENTENCES THAT NEED MATCHING

### Matching Subjects with Verbs

When the subject of a sentence is one thing (singular), the verb must be singular also. When the subject is more than one thing (plural), the verb must be plural also. In standard English, we say, "The newspaper covers the waterfront murders," not "The newspaper cover the waterfront murders"; or we say, "The newspapers, which share a reporter, cover the waterfront murders," not "The newspapers covers the waterfront murders."

Here are some frequent pitfalls and how to avoid them.

Sometimes we get into trouble because a phrase comes between the subject and the verb and confuses us. If we have a single subject followed by a prepositional phrase that ends with a plural, we may make the verb plural, because the plural phrase rings in our ears. "The newspaper of the six northern suburbs" is a singular subject. We should say

> The newspaper of the six northern suburbs covers the waterfront murders.

not

> The newspaper of the six northern suburbs cover the waterfront murders.

We should say

> The newspaper with four ace reporters covers the waterfront murders.

not

> The newspaper with four ace reporters cover the waterfront murders.

With words like *anyone, each,* and *everybody* (called indefinite pronouns), we should use a singular verb. It's confusing: *everybody* refers to many people, but it's a single thing, a single "body"—as single as the *one* in *anyone* or *everyone*. We must say, "Everybody hurts this morning"; "Anyone who goes out alone at night takes a chance of being mugged"; and "Each member of the orchestra pays annual dues."

*None* can be either singular or plural, agreeing with a singular or plural noun elsewhere in the sentence. Context decides.

> Many cows are happy, but none is so happy as a cow in spring.

> Many pigs are intelligent, but none are so intelligent as Wilbur and Angeline.

Do not say

> Everybody in town are going to the circus.

> Each of the forty-seven students howl like wolves.

Always find the subject (*everybody, each*) and make sure that the verb agrees.

When you write a sentence that uses *either . . . or, neither . . . nor,* or *not . . . but,* use a singular verb if both subjects are singular.

Either the red-haired witch or her broomstick was on fire.

If one subject is plural and the other singular, the rule says that the verb should agree with the subject closest to it. Thus the rule would allow

Either her two broomsticks or the red-headed witch was on fire.

But such a sentence, technically correct, is stylistically ugly. For style's sake, when one subject is plural and the other is singular, put the plural subject nearer the verb and use a plural verb. Say

Either the red-haired witch or her two broomsticks were on fire.

Do not say

Either her two broomsticks or the red-haired witch were on fire.

or

Either the red-haired witch or her two broomsticks was on fire.

Do not say

Neither the father nor the son want to follow the witch's track.

It should be *wants,* a singular verb. Do not say

Not the Prime Minister but the members of his Cabinet believes in amnesty.

It should be *believe,* a plural verb matching the plural *members.* These sentences are incorrect:

Neither Hitler nor Genghis Khan were conspicuous for humanitarianism.

Not the first potato but the second and the fourth contains the microfilm.

Either the roof or the shingling over the sheds were giving off a putrescent odor.

When your sentence uses a verb like *is* or *are* (a linking verb, a form of *to be*), make sure that the verb matches the subject of the sentence and not a noun that comes afterward. Say

> The best part of the team was its outfielders.

not

> The best part of the team were its outfielders.

Say

> The outfielders were the best part of the team.

not

> The outfielders was the best part of the team.

These sentences are incorrect:

> The middle chapters was the section of the book I liked best.

> The best section of the book were the middle chapters.

Watch out for the agreement of sentences beginning with "There is." Sometimes we begin such a sentence expecting a singular subject, then alter the subject without remembering to alter the verb. It is correct to say

> There is one table in the room.

It would be incorrect and disagreeable to say

> There is one table and one chair in the room.

_____ **EXERCISES** _____

1. Identify and correct the errors in these sentences.

   a. Each of the colored pencils have a different shade.
   b. The store with its aisles of groceries, hardware, soft goods, and paperbacks, rest back from the road.
   c. The green part of Northern Spy apples always taste best.
   d. Neither the horse nor the cows in the barn hears the siren.
   e. Either Bozo or Emmett Kelly get the prize.

2. In this section on matching parts, on pages 386–388, are many incorrect sentences introduced by "Do not say." Correct the errors in these sentences.

3. Rewrite this paragraph, making subjects and verbs agree.

Fifty workers, dressed in gray canvas coveralls and aluminum helmets, descends into the dark, damp caves. Each carry a pail and a small curved knife. They emerge from the elevator and scatters among the earth-filled frames. Slowly, rhythmically, they fan out in groups of five which moves along the frames. Their helmet lights fall in yellow cones on the mushrooms, pale faces clustering in the blackness. There is no sounds except the dull thud of mushrooms tumbling one by one into pails, like soft rain. No clocks, which would measure off the minutes left in a shift, but a siren to tell them when to break for lunch. None of them hurry.

---

## Matching Pronouns with the Words They Refer To

Pronouns (*he, she, it, this, that, you, we*) take their identity from a noun which comes before them, and which they refer to, called their *antecedent*. The noun can come before them in the same sentence, or it can appear in a sentence close enough to have the reference clear. Pronouns must match their nouns both in number (singular or plural) and in gender (male or female).

Mostly, we match pronouns to their antececents without trouble. Here are a few troublesome exceptions.

In formal writing, we use a singular pronoun (*he, she, it*) with an indefinite pronoun like *anybody, everybody, each, none*, and so forth. We say

Everybody carried his tennis racket.

None of the actresses received her paycheck.

Each of the seals extended its flipper.

not

Everybody carried their tennis racket.

None of the actresses received their paycheck.

Each of the seals extended their flipper.

This is a rule of formal writing although we often bend it in informal speech. To avoid *his* as sexist, or to avoid *his or her* as awkward, we sometimes use the incorrect *their* (see pages 179–180). If you do it, know that you are doing it. Perhaps it is best, if possible, to avoid gender entirely.

> Everyone carried a tennis racket.
>
> None of the actresses received a paycheck.
>
> Each of the seals extended a flipper.

Words like *team, committee, jury, class,* and *orchestra* are collective nouns. They are singular words that refer to plural collections of people. Use a singular pronoun when you describe the whole group; use a plural pronoun when you describe the many members. Say

> The team climbed on its bus.
> The team dispersed to their lockers.

Don't say

> The jury went to its separate rooms.
>
> The committee voted to disband themselves.
>
> The team voted to distribute their winnings among twenty-four ballplayers.
>
> The group destroyed their petition to remove the governor.

When a pronoun matches two or more nouns joined by *and*, it is always plural.

> When the boy and his dog wanted supper, they went to the tavern.

When a pronoun matches nouns joined by *or, nor, either . . . or,* or *neither . . . nor* and one of the nouns is plural, the pronoun matches the nearer of the two. When you use such a pair of nouns, the sentence sounds better if the second of the two nouns is the plural. Say

> Although neither Margaret nor the Hamiltons are late, they hurry to the concert hall.

Don't say

> Although neither Margaret nor the Hamiltons are late, she hurries . . .

or

> Although neither the Hamiltons nor Margaret are late, they hurry . . .

Never use a pronoun when it could refer to either of two words before it. We must use pronouns so that the reader will always be *certain* which previous noun they refer to. Uncertainty is confusing and intolerable. Don't say

> When Wilhelmina declared herself to Bertha, she was aghast.

> Leaving his father's house and the dry valley, he was happy to see the last of it.

Both of these sentences lack a clear antecedent to the pronoun. They are ambiguous. Which of the women was aghast? Was he happy to see the last of the house, or of the valley, or of both? To be clear, we should say something like

> Wilhelmina declared herself to Bertha, who was aghast.

> He left the dry valley, happy to see the last of his father's house.

Don't use the pronoun *this* or *that* or *it* to refer to general ideas in a previous sentence or to an antecedent that is not there ("This is true . . ."). Watch out for *this* and *that* when you use them as pronouns. Don't say

> The streetcleaners roared down the street, raising clouds of gritty dust, mowing down the lilac bushes on the corner of the lawn, and dumping gravel all over the grass. That made my mother furious.

*That* lacks a clear antecedent, and the sentence drowns in imprecision.

Here are more examples of pronoun error from student essays. Troublesome pronouns are in italics.

> The state legislature never got around to getting the bill out of committee until October, and *it* was the reason the scholarships were never funded.

> Susan's brother is in his third year at Harvard Medical School, and *this* is the profession she wants to enter.

> The next thing that happened was that the screen door got stuck open and the mosquitoes could get in and the dog would get out whenever he wanted. My mother started crying about *this*.

Preferential voting is fair because it gives the voter a chance to give a graded opinion of the different candidates, and therefore opens the way to third parties. *That* is the real justification for preferential voting.

Down the block from me there was a family that had three cats. One of them was a big red tom named Mio, the biggest cat I ever saw—thirty-four inches long not counting his tail, and twenty-eight pounds. The kids in the neighborhood couldn't get over *this*.

We make another common error when we use a pronoun far removed from its antecedent. The result is more ambiguity, vagueness, and imprecision. Here are two examples.

The partnership of Hudnut and Greenall was breaking up; business had declined, Hudnut's wife was ill, and Greenall's son had run off to Tibet. One Tuesday, *they* suddenly stopped speaking to each other.

When Sharon looked across the classoom, Bill winked and Larry looked away. Outside the window the clouds gathered for rain, and students were beginning to drive off for lunch, many of them carrying no books at all. Suddenly two girls ran toward a car that had stopped to pick them up. *She* saw that *it* was Matt.

## _____ EXERCISES _____

1. In these sentences, underline the errors in pronouns and what they refer to.

a. When the Senate and the House convene, on rare occasions, they do not know how to behave toward each other.

b. Panthers feed on zebras when they can, and zebras feed on grass. As a result of this, panthers live near the grasslands.

c. I was late for registration because my father had the flu and then our car broke down outside Tucson. That made me more nervous than ever.

d. Uncle Bruce is a career man in the navy, stationed in San Diego now, and it makes me think about enlisting myself.

e. The department decided to hold their annual picnic on Riverside Drive.

f. The Boosters Club adjourned its meeting and went to its respective houses.

g. Either Rita or Carole were tardy last Tuesday.

h. Everybody had their ticket to the rock concert.

i. When Rosalyn and Alice finished dinner, she decided to provide dessert.

j. Penelope and Roger had been married seven years. Then Roger met Goneril and fell in love. They did not know what to do.

2. Rewrite the sentences in the first exercise to correct faulty pronouns.

3. Here is a paragraph from a student essay with several examples of pronoun-antecedent and pronoun-verb disagreement. Revise to correct mistakes.

> In their cowboy movies, John Wayne and Gary Cooper each represents the idealized western hero. Walking slowly down the dusty main street of any frontier town, he commands respect. Neither ever flinch in the heavy crossfire of bank robbers or cattle rustlers. The crowd of townsfolk who look on know their sheriff will win the day. None doubt their safety under his leadership. That's why they are examples of courage and social order in a reckless age.

---

## CONNECT MODIFIERS WITH WHAT THEY MODIFY

In most sentences, we write phrases that describe (modify) other things in the sentence. We use prepositional phrases as modifers (to define, to limit).

> the bar *with the lavender paint*
> the girl *in the straw hat*
> the chapter *about grammar*

For similar purposes, we use clauses beginning with words like *that, who, since,* and *because.*

> the worst storm *since the winter of 1978*
> Herbert, *who tipped his homburg*

And we use phrases beginning with *-ing* words (participles), which also modify.

> the chapter *containing the examples*
> *hanging from the skylight,* the plumber

Most of the time we have no trouble controlling these phrases or clauses. We will find no trouble at all if we avoid two common errors.

Make sure that modifiers beginning a sentence really modify what the sentence claims they modify. If we start a sentence "Hanging from the skylight," we tell the reader something; we guarantee that the noun that will begin the main clause is what is hanging.

> Hanging from the skylight, the plumber screamed that he had climbed up there to escape the terrorists.

Too often, we are careless and make a sentence like the next one—which seems to start like the sentence above, and then changes its mind.

> Hanging from the skylight, the plumber looked at the huge spider's web.

Common sense can untangle the mess. The reader will eventually understand that the spider's web is hanging, not the plumber. In the meantime, the reader has been first confused and then annoyed by the misdirection.

Here are more examples of dangling modifiers, which are shown by italics.

> *Being a wreck with no gears at all,* she got the bicycle free.
>
> *Riding in a new car,* the beagle chased me half a mile.
>
> *Driven by his desire to succeed,* the test was easy.
>
> *Before making a reservation,* my roommate recommended a travel agent to me.
>
> *Humbled by circumstances,* the town looked better to him now than it had looked before.

Make sure that your word order says what you want it to say when you place modifiers in a sentence. This advice applies to adverbs and adjectives, as well as to phrases or clauses that modify. The wrong word order can alter your meaning.

> I told her I would gladly lend her my car.

means one thing.

> I told her gladly I would lend her my car.

means something else.

> She heard only the words that hurt.

means one thing.

> She only heard the words that hurt.

means something else.

> He said only that he loved her.

means one thing.

> He only said that he loved her.

means something else. It is the writer's job to know the meaning and to say it. Here are some examples from student papers in which mistakes in word order made sentences that are ambiguous, misleading, or silly.

> Hattie is the cousin who gave me the present in a housecoat.

> Joseph borrowed an egg from a neighbor that was rotten.

> The autobiography tells the exciting life of the man who lived it quickly and modestly.

> The lecturer told us about the problem of alcoholism in room A-14.

### EXERCISES

1. Correct the mistakes in the four sentences that end the preceding section.

2. Discover and correct the errors in these sentences.

a. Desperate, clinging to life, our teacher told us about the surrounded tribe.

b. Igor attempted one last time to climb the hill lacking food and ammunition.

c. Never certain of which side of the road to drive on, American roads drove the Englishman crazy.

d. Full of conceit, the application form looked like a cinch to him.

e. I walked the last five miles to the city tired and full of martinis.

f. She said that animals only burp the way he did.

g. Without his fortune, or his youth, or his good health, the old house looked warm and solid to him.

h. I used the reference section without getting lost because of a librarian's help.

i. We walked on a neighborhood street without coats.

j. Without potholes we walked on a neighborhood street.

3. Discover and correct the misplaced modifiers in this paragraph.

> Walking against rush hour traffic, the worn green raincoat gave the old man a sinister air. He was trying only to find Flossie. He shuffled along the pavement carrying the little red dish calling her name. His bony feet were beginning to hurt him encased in broken leather boots, and the corn throbbed on his toe. Frightened and tired, the police station stood on 104th Street just ahead.

---

## KEEP THE SENTENCE CONSISTENT

Once we start a sentence, we commit ourselves to continue it as we started it. In the second and third sections of this Review, we discussed the commitments to match number and gender and to connect a modifier with what it modifies. We also commit ourselves to other consistencies.

When we write parallelisms, or parallel constructions, as in a series of clauses, we must keep the words grammatically parallel for the sake of consistency. Otherwise, we find our sentences beginning to come apart, to veer off the road into incoherence. We list adjectives or we list nouns, but we do not list three adjectives followed by one noun. Don't say

> He was tall, rich, funny, and a bank robber.

Say something like

> He was tall, rich, funny, and fond of robbing banks.

When one phrase is constructed by one grammatical formula, its parallel phrase must be constructed in the same way. Don't say

> The dog had a long nose, a black tail, and barked loudly.

Instead say

> The dog had a long nose, a black tail, and a loud bark.

Don't say

> The cities are deserted, the countryside parched, the government paralyzed, and the economy not in a healthy condition.

Instead, say something like

The cities are deserted, the countryside parched, the government paralyzed, and the economy ruined.

Here, the sentence must continue with phrases ending in *-ed* words (past participles), or it will be inconsistent.

Consistency is the rule. If you start a sentence—or a linked group of sentences—with one subject or person, be consistent. Don't say

When you get a good grade, one should be proud.

Say either *you* or *one*, and stick to it.

Don't use the active voice in one part of a sentence and shift to the passive in another, when you could perfectly well keep the active and use the same subject.

We could hear raucous sounds from the party as the house was approached.

Be consistent in using the past or present of verbs. Don't say

He went into the room, closed the door, opened the window, and goes to bed.

Remember that we need consistency within related sentences, as well as within the sentence. Here is an inconsistent paragraph.

The median tax on houses in Centerville is $852 a year. You could appeal to the city assessor if you wanted to. But one is well advised not to; he can always hit you for more tax, and you are punished for asking.

_____ **EXERCISES** _____

1. Revise the paragraph at the end of the preceding section so that its sentences are consistent.

2. Locate, name, and correct the inconsistencies in these sentences.

a. She walked like a princess, ate like an ape, and her hair was at least five feet long.

b. If you write a page a day in your notebook, you will discover that one learns from practice.

c. Harriet opened the window to get some fresh air, and we all breathe deeply.

d. Geology is boring, chemistry fatiguing, history overwhelming, but English was a useful class.

e. We lifted the rock, peered into the mud, and a thousand grubs were seen.

3. Rewrite the following paragraph to make the subject singular and the verb tense present.

The banditos waited in the canyon rocks for the evening coach from Sagebrush. They knew it carried bags of gold for the Union army, and they intended to grab the gold and disappear into the hills. At last, a cloud of dust appeared on the horizon. The men tensed, crouched lower against the jagged rocks, and watched intently, guns readied. When they saw the driver cracking his whip over the screaming horses, they opened fire.

---

## KEEP PUNCTUATION CLEAR

Learning to punctuate correctly, we learn the conventions that an experienced reader expects of us. No one can argue that the conventions of English punctuation are ideal. But they are clear, and for the most part they are sensible.

### End Punctuation

At the end of a sentence, we use a period, an exclamation point, or a question mark.

*Period.* Periods end sentences. Periods also indicate abbreviations (*Mr., no., St., etc., i.e., Mass., U.S.A.*). (See pages 414–415.) And periods indicate omissions in quoted material. (See page 411.)

*Exclamation point.* Use exclamation points only for a proper exclamation:

Oh! Zap!

or for a remark almost shouted:

It's Godzilla!

Avoid using them frequently, or they diminish in effect, like a vague intensifier.

I could not make out the face! Then I saw. It was Algernon!

*Question mark.* At the end of a sentence asking a direct question, we use a question mark.

> Did you ask Fernando?
> Have you bought the paper, the pins, and the manila envelopes?

Do not use a question mark to end a sentence that includes a question but does not ask it (an indirect question). These sentences are incorrectly punctuated:

> He asked what time it was?
> I waited to find out where the carnival was?

They should end with periods.

## Commas

The most common mark of punctuation—and the most commonly misused—is the comma. I will not talk here about the comma splice, because I discussed it on pages 382–385. Here are some of the main uses of the comma.

*To separate whole clauses.* In the compound sentence, where two or more whole clauses are connected by *and, or, nor, for,* or *but,* we use a comma just before the connective.

> The faculty senate debated for three hours, but no one could resolve the issue of the blind pig.

When the main clauses are short, the comma is optional. The pause is shorter, and therefore the rhythm different. We can say either

> The wine was old, and we drank it slowly.

or

> The wine was old and we drank it slowly.

On the other hand, we can also opt to use the semicolon, which creates a longer pause, instead of the comma. Sometimes we want this extra pause when the main clauses are especially long, when they themselves contain commas, or when we make strong contrast between the two parts of the sentence.

> The cliff was red, solid, and perpendicular; and the car disappeared into the face of it.

400 A Brief Review of Grammar, Punctuation, and Mechanics

*To separate items in a series.* We use commas to separate words in a series:

> The dress was black, green, and purple.

to separate phrases in a series:

> She wore it to parties, in the bathtub, and at work.

to separate subordinate clauses in a series:

> She explained that it was warm, that it needed washing, that it was comfortable, and that it was in good taste.

and to separate whole clauses in a series:

> She shook her head, she stood up, and she left the room.

When we use *and* with each item in a series, we do not use the comma.

> He touched first and second and third.

It is possible to omit the comma before the *and* in a series of words or short phrases:

> He touched first, second and third.

but it can seem ambiguous, as if the baserunner were able to straddle and touch second and third at the same time.

*To set off introductory words and groups of words.* Adverb clauses, transitional phrases, and phrases introduced by verbals or prepositions, when they come at the beginning of the sentence, usually require a comma to set them off from the main clause. These adverb clauses need a comma:

> *If a dunce applies himself thoroughly,* he can dream of becoming president.

> *When I turned to the left at the end of the lane,* I found the old house intact.

Omitting these commas would leave the sentence hopelessly awkward and confusing. If the order of clauses is reversed, a comma, though possible, is no longer necessary.

> A dunce can dream of becoming president *if he applies himself thoroughly.*

> I found the old house intact *when I turned to the left at the end of the lane.*

An introductory adverb clause, if it is short, need not always carry a comma. A comma is optional in

> *If I lead* he will follow.

Introductory phrases of transition, like *on the other hand*, usually need a comma.

> On the other hand, sometimes they don't.

> In fact they are optional.
> In fact, they are optional.

Retaining the comma is appropriate in formal writing and is acceptable in all writing. Omitting the comma is rhythmically more colloquial. Interjections like *oh* or *shucks*, however, almost always take the comma.

> Gosh, that's not what you said the last time.

We use a comma when the sentence begins with a long phrase governed by a preposition.

> *In the century after the Civil War,* progress in civil rights was almost nil.

When the introductory prepositional or verbal phrase is short, the comma is optional and may be omitted when omission does not cause ambiguity.

> *At twelve* she was full-grown.

> *Having won* they adjourned to a saloon.

> *To avoid ambiguity.* Sometimes we need a comma to indicate a pause which the voice would make, in speech, for clarity, but which is not otherwise necessary.

> Outside the fields spread to the river.

is clearer with a pause:

> Outside, the fields spread to the river.

To find such potential ambiguities in your prose, sometimes it is helpful to read it aloud, pronouncing it as it is written—which means pausing when there is a comma, and *not* pausing when there is *not* a comma.

*To set off nonrestrictive, or parenthetical, clauses.* It is useful to know the difference between a restrictive and a nonrestrictive clause. A restrictive clause describes or limits its subject, providing essential information.

> The knight *who was dressed in black* won all the events in the tourney.

Here, "who was dressed in black" defines the knight, as if we were pointing a finger. The absence of commas lets us know that there were other knights besides the one "who was dressed in black."

> The building *that overlooked the river* was the most popular of all.

In such restrictive clauses as these, no comma separates the clause from the rest of the sentence.

Nonrestrictive clauses, on the other hand, do not define; they could become separate sentences or coordinate clauses, and unless they are very short, they take commas at both ends. We could also write sentences in which the clauses above become nonrestrictive.

> Sir Galahad, *who was dressed in black,* won all the events in the tourney.

This sentence, as opposed to the restrictive example above, could be broken into two sentences, with no violence done to the meaning.

> Sir Galahad was dressed in black. He won all the events in the tourney.

Or, using the clause from the other example, we could have the sentence

> The library building, *which overlooked the river,* was built in 1975.

*To enclose words, phrases, or clauses that are like a parenthesis.* Quotations are common parenthetical elements. So too are phrases and words like *of course, naturally,* and *heavens to Betsy.* When asides or parenthetical expressions appear at the beginning of sentences, place a comma after them. When they appear at the end of sentences, put a comma just before them.

> God knows, the situation is desperate.
> The situation is desperate, God knows.

> Fellow Americans, I speak to you as a concerned citizen.

> I am a representative of the people, of course.

Omitting commas in these examples would make the sentence ambiguous or hard to read.

> God knows the situation is desperate.

Does He?

At times the commas can be omitted with no awkwardness or confusion, and the omission becomes optional. Short sentences in which word order precludes ambiguity give us this option.

> The situation was of course desperate.

On occasion one can take stylistic advantage of the rhythmic speed offered by this option.

Use a comma before and after parenthetical expressions within a sentence.

> I think you're tired, Fred, and hungry.

> The student worked, in a manner of speaking, for three whole days.

> I heard him calling, "There's my bubble gum," to the audience.

*To set off appositives.* Appositives are nouns or noun substitutes placed next to another noun to explain or define that noun.

> Peter, *the flying dwarf,* escorted Tarquina, *his good fairy.*

In many of our first drafts, we use too many commas, or put them where they do not belong. Beginning writers often feel that something is going wrong if they haven't used a comma lately, and so they shake commas over their prose like salt. Here are some sentences, taken from student essays, which have some commas they should *not* have.

> But, it was not too late.
> Clarke came by, later.
> When I left she, followed me.
> The dimensions were, approximately three by five.
> I quickly saw Ed, and Sara.
> He thought she was sickly, and studious.
> The old barn was painted, red.
> A runner, who likes to win, has to train, every day.
> The agency sold, life, fire, and theft, insurance.

_____ **EXERCISES** _____

1. Remove unnecessary commas from the last group of sentences above.

2. The following sentences omit commas necessary to clarity. Add commas where they belong.

a. The indiscreet Martian insensitive to the feelings of Earthlings disintegrated the beagle.

b. "Horrors" I said to the surrounding observers.

c. Of course the narrative begins to become incoherent when Hermione reaches this part of the journey.

d. If there is war in the Middle East within the next decade the winners will be losers.

e. Beyond the river widened.

f. Deciding that cinnamon toast was preferable to fried sardines we looked in the bread box.

g. In a million or two million years the human toenail may disappear.

h. In truth the final dispensation of the profits available to the institution will not be accomplished until the end of the decade.

i. When we take the S-curve at a speed of forty or more miles an hour we hold our lives in our hands as well as the steering wheel.

j. He looked through his pockets and found a comb two matchbooks four paper clips six pennies and a piece of bubble gum.

3. Punctuate and capitalize this paragraph.

for forty years they had come to this house by the lake and for twenty of those Years they had been as they thought a happy family but after Herbie died and Mary Lou went away to school and Joe jr married and started a family of his own it was different they were Strangers to each other and spent whole days staring at the lake stopping only for silent meals and sleepless Naps

## Semicolons

*Semicolons between whole clauses.* Semicolons separate whole clauses, making a pause longer or more emphatic than a comma, but shorter and less definite than a period. The semicolon shows that the clauses follow each other closely, are connected in idea or narrative. We may use the semicolon between two (or more) balanced and equal clauses.

> The sun rose; the sky lightened; day had come.

Or we may use it between clauses of unequal length and different construction.

> The sun rose; instantly, the air was alive with birds singing so happily that anyone who heard them could not help but smile.

These sentences are compound, the semicolon replacing a conjunction.

*Semicolons with series.* Sometimes, in a long sentence, semicolons separate series or divisions, making the divisions clearer than commas would, particularly if commas are already within the divisions.

> There were three sorts of students waiting on table at the Inn: fraternity boys who were dating expensive girls; girls from Detroit whose daddies cut off their allowances because they had moved in with their boy friends; and street people, boys and girls, working for a week or two until they got tired of it.

*Semicolons with conjunctions.* A semicolon used with a conjunction shows more separation or pause between clauses than the comma would show.

> He flew to Denver that night; and we were glad he did.

Adverbs acting as conjunctions in compound sentences (*besides, nevertheless, also, however, indeed, furthermore, still, then*) take a semicolon, as do transitional phrases in the middle of compound sentences (*on the other hand, in fact, in other words, on the contrary*).

> Let us take the matter in hand; however, we must not be foolhardy.

> The sun rose in a clear sky; in fact, the sky was painfully bright.

*Semicolons with incomplete clauses.* Semicolons also separate incomplete clauses when a verb in one of the clauses is omitted but understood.

Poetry is one thing; verse another.

## Apostrophes

*Possessives.* We form the possessive by adding *'s* to singular nouns and most plural nouns (if the additional *s* makes pronunciation difficult, we add only the apostrophe).

The bag was Sara's.
It was the weather's fault.
The technician's car was parked outside.
the hens' feed
Mr. and Mrs. Jones's automobile
the women's club
the Perkins' puppets

An apostrophe does not form part of the possessive of a pronoun. Pronouns have separate possessive forms: *my; your; his, her, its; our; your; their.*

*Contractions.* We also use the apostrophe to show contractions. Use an apostrophe to show that you have omitted one or more letters in a phrase, commonly a combination of a pronoun and a verb. *I'm, she's, he's, who's, we've, you've, they're,* etc; *we'd, you'd, he'd, she'd; he'll, she'll, who'll.* Three contractions become problems. *They're* (a contraction of *they are*) sounds like *their* and *there,* and we may spell one when we mean another. *"Their* out working" is as incorrect as *"there* work" and "working *their."* (Correct: *"They're* out working"; *"their* work"; "working *there."*)

*It's* always means *it is.* It is *not* possessive, like *"its* shadow." Whenever you write or see the apostrophe with these letters—*it's*—remember that the *'s* must stand for *is.* Or memorize the phrase

*It's* afraid of *its* shadow.

*Who's* is another common contraction and once again there is a confusion. *Whose* gets mixed up with *who's.* Again, the *'s* means *is,* and *who's* always stands for *who is,* whereas *whose* is a possessive pronoun.

> *Who's* drinking *whose* soup?

Other common contractions involve a verb and the negative: *isn't, aren't, doesn't, don't, can't, haven't, won't,* which are contractions of *is not, are not, does not, do not, cannot, have not,* and *will not.*

*Plural of numbers.* We use the apostrophe to form the plurals of typographic symbols, words referred to as words, letters, and figures.

> The 7's on the new office typewriter are black as *e*'s, 8's are unreadable, and half the time simple *the*'s are obscure.

Possessive pronouns used without a noun have no apostrophe: *mine; yours; his, hers, its; ours; yours; theirs.*

> *Her* book.
> The book was *hers.*

### EXERCISES

Cross out the incorrect apostrophes in these sentences. Add the missing ones.

> a. Poor dog! Its too late for it's supper.
> b. That Morocco-bound volume of Tolkien was supposed to be her's.
> c. Whose for tennis?
> d. Is'nt English spelling irrational?
> e. It's true he didn't know who's tax he had paid, his wifes or his own.

### Quotation Marks and Punctuating Quotations

The exact words of a speaker or writer, included in a paragraph, are set off by quotation marks. Put a comma at the end of the quotation before the quotation mark, or a period if the quotation ends the sentence. If the quotation ends with a question mark or an exclamation point, these marks of punctuation take the place of the comma and occur inside the quotation marks.

> Al asked Wayne, "Didn't you?"

On the other hand, sometimes we quote in order to exclaim or inquire about the quotation. In such a sentence, the exclamation point or question mark occurs after the quotation mark.

> What did he mean when he said, "Good morning"?
> She had the nerve to say "Hello"!

Notice that the first word of a quoted remark is capitalized. When we quote a passage longer than fifty words, in a research paper for instance, we can use a colon to introduce the quotation and detach the quotation from the text by indenting it. The quotation is not enclosed by quotation marks. Ellipses can help you avoid long, detached quotations.

We use quotation marks to indicate the exact repetition of words from speech or writing.

> As Macbeth would say, "Tomorrow and tomorrow and tomorrow. . . ."

We use them when we cite words as words.

> "Jazz" and "condo" are derogatory words.

In writing that uses many short quotations, as in *Writing Well*, an author may use italics instead of quotation marks: *mine, yours, his, hers, its, ours, yours, theirs.* In writing essays, use the traditional quotation marks.

We also use quotation marks to indicate the titles of songs, television shows, and short literary works, like essays and short stories and poems and chapters or other sections of a longer work. We speak of Tennyson's short poem "Tithonos"; when we refer to a book-length poem by the same author, we use italics instead: *In Memoriam.* We speak of Hemingway's story "A Clean Well-Lighted Place" and his novel *A Farewell to Arms.* "The Dead" is part of James Joyce's *Dubliners.* We use italics for the names of newspapers, magazines, and movies: *The New Haven Register, Blair and Ketcham's Country Journal, Animal House.*

When we quote *within* a quotation, we use single quotation marks: Molly said, "I'd like to read you Wallace Stevens's poem 'The Emperor of Ice Cream.' "

### Other Marks of Punctuation

*Brackets.* Brackets are useful in prose especially in three places, all within or close to quotations. We use them when we add to a quotation material which was not in the original but which is needed for clarity. Sometimes a bracketed word supplies information lacking in the quotation but available in the context. The brackets can contain the antecedent to a pronoun:

> "He [O'Toole] smashed his fist through the window of the bar."

or some important fact:

> "It was in mid-June [1986] that the storm began."

Sometimes, in quoting the spoken word, we use brackets to enclose an indication of action, like a stage direction.

> ". . . and, finally, I want to ask you willingly and cheerfully to share the huge burden of responsibility which the age has thrust upon us all." [Boos.]

Sometimes we use brackets to correct a quotation.

> "It all happened in the early hours of September 20 [actually September 21] when the sun began [to] rise over the boardwalk."

*Colons.* Colons direct our attention to what comes after them. Usually they follow an introductory statement that leads us to expect a follow-up, though sometimes the introduction is implicit, or the colon itself reveals that the clause preceding it was introductory. We use a colon when the second sentence fulfills a kind of promise made by the first. Here are some explicit introductions.

To a long quotation, either included in the text in quotation marks or indented without quotation marks:

> E. B. White wrote of his old professor: "In the days when I was sitting in his class he omitted so many needless words, and omitted them so forcibly and with such eagerness and obvious relish, that. . . ."

To an example:

> The results of the study were as follows: the closer subjects stood to the hoop, the more frequently they were able to make a basket.

To a list:

> Mona asked me to get a few things at the market: potatoes, carrots, and peas.

> When you pack your child's luggage for Camp Winnewaka, please include the following: towels, toiletries, and personal medications.

Less elegantly, to an appositive at the end of a sentence:

> Chosby took off his boots and looked at his toe: a swollen knob of pain.

A comma, here, would be just as correct and perhaps less prone to melodrama.

Sometimes we put a colon instead of a semicolon between two main clauses; it implies that the second clause is a result of the first.

> The hands of the clock seemed never to move: she had never been late before.

Here the colon adds a meaning that the semicolon would lack. The semicolon would present the two statements as closely connected, but without the implication that the second clause derived from the first.

*Dashes.* Use dashes with caution—but use them. Make them on your typed paper by putting two hyphens next to each other.

In the sentence above, the dash shows a hesitation in the voice, followed with a rush by something that seems almost an afterthought. Dashes are informal. For some careless writers, dashes become substitutes for all other forms of punctuation; they not only lose any special meaning dashes may contribute, they also rob other punctuation of its meaning. For instance:

> Yet many people use them too often—they become substitutes for all other forms of punctuation—and thus lose their special meaning—at the same time they rob other punctuation of its meaning—

Two legitimate uses for the dash are the implied afterthought, as in the first sentence of this section, and the informal parenthesis. Marks of parenthesis ( ) look more formal; dashes give a sense of speech. These two sentences illustrate a slight, characteristic difference:

The myth of connotative and denotative meanings was destroyed by Carnap (the logician who taught at the University of Chicago) some twenty-five years ago.

The myth of connotative and denotative meanings was destroyed by a logician and philosopher—I think it was Carnap—about twenty-five years ago.

*Ellipses.* Three dots in a row . . . indicate that you have omitted something from a quotation. Use four dots if the words left out were at the end of a sentence: three to indicate the omission, a fourth for the period.

Ellipses are useful in research papers or arguments using references. Much of a paragraph we want to quote may be irrelevant to our point. To include the whole paragraph in our text would slow the pace and violate the unity in our argument. Therefore we piece-cut the quotation and make it blend smoothly with our essay. Here is the long way to use a quotation:

Marlowe was more direct than Shakespeare and more vigorous. As Professor William Wanger puts it:

If the *Jew of Malta* is Marlowe's *Merchant of Venice,* it is at the same time better and worse than Shakespeare's famous comedy. The lesser-known play has fewer quotable passages, perhaps, and certainly fewer that are quoted; but we must acknowledge that Marlowe's play has more energy than Shakespeare's. What it lacks in finesse it makes up in vigor, and the character of the Jew is surely more complex, and more thoughtfully observed, than the character of the Merchant.

What Professor Wanger says of two plays, we can say of all. . . .

Instead, we can use ellipses and build the necessary quotations into our text:

Marlowe was more direct than Shakespeare and more vigorous.
Comparing comedies by the two men, Professor William Wanger found Marlowe "better and worse than Shakespeare . . . ," lacking "in finesse" but superior in "vigor" and "energy." He found Marlowe's characterization, in one comparison, "more complex, and more thoughtfully observed," than Shakespeare's.

When we are obviously making excerpts, as with single words like *energy* and detached phrases like the last quotation, we do not need ellipses, because ellipses provide information: if we already know that quotations are excerpted, we do not need rows of dots to tell us so. But after *Shakespeare,* earlier in the paragraph, when we cut between a noun and an apostrophe indicating possession, we need the ellipses. On the other hand, we need not use ellipses if we omit words at the beginning of a quote:

> Pelham told the conference, "Every day motorists kill one million animals on American highways."

*Hyphens.* We use hyphens to break a word at the right-hand margin. Dictionaries usually indicate the syllables that make up a word by placing a dot between them (com · pound · ed). Hyphenate only at the syllable break. Write com- / pounded, never comp- / ounded. When the syllable to be isolated is only one or two letters long, avoid division (a-long, man-y, compound-ed). Never hyphenate one-syllable words.

We use the hyphen on occasion to join two adjectives, or words serving as adjectives, modifying a noun. They make a temporary compound word.

> *blood-red* hair
> *mile-long* avenue

Avoid the temptation to multiply hyphenated phrases, which can become a virulent form of adjectivitis.

> The *purple-green cloud-forms sweep-crawl.* . . .

We use hyphens with some temporary compounds. Before *wheel* and *barrow* became the compound word *wheelbarrow,* there may have been a stage at which we wrote *wheel-barrow.* Consult your dictionary when you are in doubt. Hyphens in compounds are a matter of spelling.

We use hyphens in compound numbers from twenty-one through ninety-nine.

We hyphenate fractions.

> a *two-thirds* majority
> *three-quarters* of the population

We use the hyphen to avoid ambiguity. We must spell the word *re-creation* to avoid confusing it with *recreation.*

We use the hyphen with some prefixes and suffixes.

> governor-*elect*
> *ex*-wife
> *self*-determined

We use the hyphen as a typographic device to indicate a manner of speaking, when we indicate that someone is spelling a word by writing it *w-o-r-d*, or when we indicate a stammer, *w-w-word*.

*Italics.* When we type, or write by hand, we show italics by underlining the word: <u>italics</u>. It comes out in type, *italics*.

Use italics for the names of ships: the *Niña*; for the titles of books, films, and plays: *War and Peace*; for the titles of newspapers or magazines: *Sports Illustrated*; and for foreign expressions: *faute de mieux, in medias res.*

Also, we use italics to indicate a special use of a word.

We might call the directory an *encyclopedia* of has-beens.

We use them, from time to time, to indicate emphasis.

Do you really *mean* that?

Using italics for emphasis is tricky, however. Italics are a vague gesture, an attempt to register a tone of voice that often fails because it cannot indicate a *specific* tone of voice. A writer who relies on emphatic italics often is being lazy; a more careful choice of words, a more precise context, and the emphasis will be clear without italics.

*Parentheses.* Use parentheses to enclose material which digresses from or interrupts the main idea of the writing or which explains something but remains a detachable unit.

The minister continued to pace up and down (though he normally slept through the night) and to stare out the window into the darkness.

De Marque points out (not only in the *Treatise*, but in the *Harmonics* as well) that Jolnay was ignorant of Graf.

Fred Papsdorf (Charles Laughton bought his paintings) lives on Jane Street, near East Detroit, in a small bungalow.

She complained that she weighed ten stone (140 pounds; a stone, an English measure of avoirdupois, is fourteen pounds) and had been seven stone a year ago.

Also, use parentheses for numbers or letters that divide parts of a list.

There are three reasons: (1) . . . , (2) . . . , and (3). . . .

_____ **EXERCISES** _____

1. In these sentences, marks of punctuation are used incorrectly or loosely. Discover errors or places where exact punctuation would improve precision or clarity.

   a. Two thirds of the population is semi-literate, and has read nothing more complex than "Readers Digest."

   b. The triumvirate, a ruling-group of three, resembling a contemporary troika, took over from the dying emperor.

   c. The pumpkin stuffing October sun, as the poet (Rarity) called it in his sonnet, *Goose*, pumped calories into the uncoiling sausage of the valley.

   d. "Whatever you do", the potato farmer told me; "remember one thing; eat starch four times a day."

   e. The monk, with the Gucci shoes wearing the new tonsure, spoke, at last with a sigh, "Yes I am Ludwig Babo."

2. Punctuate and capitalize the following paragraph.

   your grandfather a good man but not well educated came to this country when he was twenty two he worked in a dry goods store and then because he was industrious took a job with the greenwood star as a cub reporter he had a motto as he always told us work hard and keep your nose clean

---

## KEEP MECHANICS CONVENTIONAL

Like punctuation marks, the mechanics of English prose are conventions that make life easier. We can argue that the rules of spelling or manuscript form are irrational, and we can make a good case. But if we all agree to abide by the same mechanical conventions—irrational or not—we can more easily understand each other. Here are some remarks about abbreviations, capital letters, manuscript form, numerals, and spelling.

### Abbreviation

For the use of abbreviations in notes and list of works cited, see page 344.

In formal writing, we abbreviate only some words that go with names, like *Mr., Mrs., Ms., Dr., St.* (for *Saint,* not *street*), *Jr., Sr.*; degrees, like *Ph.D.* or *M.A.*; and indications of era or time, like A.D., B.C., A.M., and P.M. (We use the latter two initials only when a specific time is indicated; we speak of "4 P.M.," not "it was the P.M.") We do not abbreviate *Monday* or *August* or *street* or *road* or *volume* or *chemistry* in ordinary writing.

Some writers use *no.* as an abbreviation for *number,* but it looks out of place in formal prose. So too does *U.S.A.* instead of *United States* and *Penna.* or *Pa.* instead of *Pennsylvania, lb.* instead of *pound,* and *oz.* instead of *ounce.*

Some institutions are so commonly called by their initials that it is overly formal to spell them out. The *Federal Bureau of Investigation* seems a pompous way to talk about the *FBI.* On the other hand, consider your audience; many people will need to be told the first time you mention it that *SEATO* is the *Southeast Asia Treaty Organization.*

In conjunction with a figure, *mph* and *rpm* are used in formal writing. We write *50 mph* and *1,000 rpm.* But if we write without figures, we spell them out.

> It is difficult to assess the speed of a space capsule when it is told in *miles per hour.*

Titles like *Governor* can be spelled out or shortened. Frequently, we shorten a title when we give a whole name:

> *Gov.* William Milliken

and spell it out with a last name alone:

> *Governor* Milliken

Any abbreviation of titles is inappropriate to formal prose.

## Capital Letters

Capitalize the names of people, cities, and countries; the titles of people, books, and plays; names of religious or national groups, languages, days of the week, months, holidays, and organizations and their abbreviations; the names of events or eras in history and important documents; and the names of specific structures, like buildings and airplanes and ships. In titles of books, plays, poems, songs, television shows, and movies, capitalize the first word and all subsequent words *except* articles and prepositions.

| | |
|---|---|
| John Doe | June |
| Great Britain | Memorial Day |
| Berlin | General Motors or G.M. |
| Mayor Abe Beame | "Why Do Fools Fall in |
| *Moby-Dick* | Love?" |
| *The Importance of* | Declaration of |
| *Being Earnest* | Independence |
| Methodist | Empire State Building |
| Polish or European or | the *Winnie Mae* |
| Bostonian | the *Titanic* |
| Monday | *Play It Again, Sam* |

Do not capitalize the seasons, or the names of college classes (*freshman, senior*), or general groups like *the lower classes* or *the jet set*. Do not capitalize school subjects or disciplines except languages:

physics
French

Adjectives are capitalized when they derive from proper nouns and still refer to them, like *Shakespearean*. Other nouns or adjectives which derive from names but no longer refer to the person lose their capitals:

boycott
quisling

The title that is capitalized before the proper noun, as

*Mayor* Hermann Garsich

loses its capital when it is used outside of its titling function, as a descriptive word placed after the proper noun:

Hermann Garsich, *mayor* of our town

Sections of a country may take capitals:

the *West*
the *South*

but the same words take lowercase when they are directions:

Go *west*, young man.

Capitalize the first word of a quoted sentence:

Mother said, "Come back soon."

Sentences begin with capitals.

## Manuscript Form

Type if you can.

Double-space on one side of white 8½-by-11-inch twenty-pound bond paper. Never use erasable paper; it won't take inked corrections, it smudges, it sticks together, and it is altogether unpleasant to read. (If you must use it, hand in a photocopy of the finished paper.) Use Ko-Rec-Type, Liquid Paper, or a similar easy device for corrections.

*Always make a carbon or a photocopy.* The most careful graders occasionally lose a paper. The corporations providing stolen papers for rich students make off with manuscripts when they can. Keep a copy to protect yourself.

Make margins of 1 inch to 1½ inches at top, bottom, and sides.

Number pages consecutively, including notes, appendixes, and list of works cited.

Put your name in the upper left-hand corner of the first page.

Type the title, capitalizing the first letter of the first word and of all other words except articles and prepositions, 2 or 3 inches down from the top of the first page. Do not underline or add a period to your title.

If quoted material is short—up to fifty words of prose or two lines of poetry—place it within the paragraph, and use quotation marks. With lines of poetry, use a slash mark (/) to indicate line breaks, and follow the capitalization of the poem.

Of man's first disobedience, and the fruit / Of that forbidden tree. . . .

If quoted material is longer than fifty words or two lines of poetry, detach it from the text. Indent the quotation half an inch to the right of the place where you begin paragraphs, and double-space the quotation. Do not use quotation marks.

## Numerals

In dealing with decimal points and highly precise or technical figures, it is wise to use numerals.

   69.7 decibels

It is acceptable to type dates in numerals also.

   June 14, 1971

The same goes for population figures and addresses.

   104,000 inhabitants
   1715 South University Avenue

   Spell out figures, except when they are long to the point of being ridiculous. If you can write that a town has *one hundred four thousand inhabitants,* it is easy enough to write it out. If necessity requires precision, *104,627* will do; *one hundred four thousand, six hundred and twenty-seven* might look precious.
   Never begin a sentence with a numeral.

   97.6 mph showed on the speedometer.

Either spell out the number (*Ninety-seven and six-tenths*) or rewrite the sentence.

   The speedometer showed 97.6 mph.

The sentence

   30 people stood up.

should certainly be written

   Thirty people stood up.

   It is unnecessary, unless you are a lawyer, to include both spelled-out numbers and figures. Do not write,

   The building was at least twenty (20) stories tall.

Either will do—preferably the written-out word—but both together belong only to legal or business documents.


   **Spelling**

   English spelling is irregular and irrational. There are a few rules of thumb, but the rules always have exceptions. We memorize to learn to spell. By memory we write *there* when it is fitting and *their* when it is fitting. By memory we spell *plough, although, enough,* and *slough.*

Here are some problems in spelling and some suggestions about overcoming them.

All of us have problems of our own, and sometimes we make up our own ways to remember the correct spelling. Suppose you have trouble with the *ite/ate* ending: *definate* is a common mistake for *definite.* Maybe you can remember that it resembles the word *finite:* or maybe the third *i* in *infinity* will help you. Or maybe you write *infinate* by mistake. Remember the antonym *finite* and remember *separate,* as in *"separate* rooms," and not *separite.* (Not *seperate* either, for that matter.)

*I/e, e/i.* People mistakenly write *concieve* instead of *conceive,* and *beleive* instead of *believe.* The old recipe

> *I* before *E*
> Except after *C*
> And when sounded like *ay*
> As in *neighbor* and *weigh.*

is useful. Examples, both ways: *achieve, niece, piece; receipt, ceiling, receive.* Exceptions: *either, seize, weird, leisure, species, foreign.*

*Variant plurals.* Some words change spelling in moving from singular to plural: *wife/wives* (like *knife, life, calf,* and *half*); *man/men* (like *woman, milkman,* etc.); *hero/heroes* (like tomato, potato).

*Dropping a final -e before a vowel.* Most words ending with a silent *-e* drop it when we change them to a participle or other form that begins with a vowel. We spell the verb *move,* and we spell the participle *moving.* The silent *-e* usually remains when the added form begins with a consonant. Exceptions to both generalizations occur (*argue/argument; mile/mileage*), but they are infrequent and the rule is an unusually safe one.

*The final -y.* When *-y* is a final vowel after a consonant (*dry*) it turns to *-ie* before *-s,* and *-i* before other letters, except when the ending is *-ing,* in which case the *y* remains: *dries, drier, drying; beauty, beautiful.* When the *-y* follows another vowel, it generally remains *-y,* as in *joys* and *grayer,* with occasional exceptions, as in *lay/laid.*

*Doubling consonants.* We double a final consonant before *-ed*, *-ing*, *-er*, or *-est* when the original verb or noun ends with a short vowel followed by a single consonant. *Hop* becomes *hopping*. When the vowel is long or a diphthong, we usually show it by a silent *-e* after the single consonant, and a single consonant with the suffix. *Hope* becomes *hoping*. Notice the difference between *plan/planning, plane/planing, slip/slipping, sleep/sleeping*.

*Homonyms.* Words that are pronounced alike but spelled differently present an irritating problem to writers. We have already mentioned *their/there/they're* and *its/it's*. Here are a few more:

affect/effect
accept/except
capital/capitol
principle/principal
gorilla/guerrilla
stationery/stationary
illusion/allusion

Here are some words frequently misspelled.

| | | |
|---|---|---|
| accept | definite | obstacle |
| accommodate | desert | occurred |
| acknowledgment | dessert | piece |
| advice | divide | possession |
| advise | embarrass | principal |
| all right | exaggerate | principle |
| allusion | existence | privilege |
| a lot | explanation | probably |
| annual | friend | professor |
| argument | fulfillment | precede |
| arrangement | grammar | proceed |
| beginning | height | quantity |
| believe | hypocrisy | quite |
| business | irritable | receive |
| capital | its | referred |
| capitol | it's | separate |
| coming | library | shining |
| committee | loneliness | similar |
| complement | lonely | succeed |
| compliment | necessary | surprise |
| decide | nuclear | than |

| then | to, two, too | writing |
| their | villain | written |
| there | who's | |
| they're | whose | |

---

### EXERCISES

1. In this paragraph, circle every mechanical error and correct it in the space between the lines.

During the weeks that I have spent on campus I have learned to except the principal that definate explinations are often to exagerated to beleive in alot. 9 out of 10 students embarass thier professers by not realising the mayor of there towns name, or not being alright in grammer, or not suceeding in reading books like "Moby Dick." Its a disgrase.

2. Correct, capitalize, and punctuate this paragraph:

look at that shot thats ridiculous Graebner tells himself he glances at Carole who has both fists in the air pull yourself together Clark this is a big point Graebner takes off his glasses and wipes them on his dental towel stalling Ashe mumbles while he is waiting he raises his left index finger and slowly pushes his glasses into place across the bridge of his nose just one point Arthur Graebner misses his first serve again Ashe moves in he hits sharply crosscourt Graebner dives for it catches it with a volley then springs up ready at the net Ashe lobs into the sun thinking that was a good get on that volley I didn't think hed get that Graebner punches the ball away with a forehand volley deuce Ashe is rattling the gates but Graebner will not let him in Carole has her hand on the top of her head unbelievable

John McPhee, "Ashe and Graebner"

# A Glossary of Usage and Grammatical Terms

The Glossary entries are of two kinds:

1. Words frequently misused—clichés, commonly confused pairs of words, and words or phrases that should be avoided.

2. Grammatical and rhetorical terms and the names of figures of speech. Each of these entries includes general comments and references to the pages in the text where the subject is discussed.

**A, an**
See **Article.**

**Abbreviation**
See pages 414–415.

**Absolute element**
An absolute element is a word or a group of words which is grammatically independent of the rest of the sentence and which is not joined to it by a relative pronoun or a conjunction. It modifies the whole clause or sentence. Absolute phrases are often made up of a noun followed by a participle.

*All things considered,* he recovered quickly from his injuries.
*Her youth gone,* the old woman passed her days in remembering.

Many absolute constructions are common phrases.

> *Come hell or high water,* I'll get to Dallas by Thursday.
> Neither twin was there, *to tell the truth.*

### Abstract, abstraction

An abstraction is a noun referring to the idea or quality of a thing and not to a thing itself: *redness, courage.*

We use the word *abstract* relatively, referring to more general and less particular words. *Enclosure* is more general, say, than *room* or *cage* or *zoo.*

For remarks on abstractions and prose style, see pages 121–123.

### Accept, except

These words sound alike but mean different things. *Accept* means to receive something voluntarily.

> I *accept* the compliment.

*Except* as a verb means to exclude.

> I *excepted* Jones from the group I wished to congratulate.

*Except* as a preposition is more common.

> I congratulated everyone *except* Jones.

### Acronym

An acronym is an abbreviation, pronounced as a word, which is composed of the first letters of the words in the title or phrase abbreviated.

> *SAC* (Strategic Air Command)
> *snafu* (situation normal, all fouled up)

Use with caution.

### Active voice

Verbs are in the active voice when the subject of the sentence does the action the verb describes.

> Bob *hit* the spider.

When the subject is acted upon, the verb is passive.

> The spider *was hit* by Bob.

See **Passive voice.**

## Adjective

Adjectives describe or limit a noun or a noun substitute. These adjectives describe:

*green* onions
*happiest* year
The man was *old.*

Other adjectives limit in a variety of ways.

Indefinite:

*Some* men walked in the road.

Demonstrative:

*Those* men walked in the road.

Possessive:

*Their* men walked in the road.

Numerical:

*Twelve* men walked in the road.

Interrogative:

*Which* men walked in the road?

Relative:

Nouns can be used as adjectives.

*university* professor

But the writer should beware of using several nouns in a row as adjectives.

For the formation of comparatives, see **Comparison of adjectives and adverbs.** For a stylistic approach to adjectives, see pages 129–137.

## Adjective clause

An adjective clause is a dependent clause used as an adjective.

The man *whose nose is purple* will stand out in a crowd.

## Adjectives frequently misused

Try to avoid the adjective used vaguely. These words once meant specific things: *terror* once inhabited *terrific;* now *terrific* can mean "unusually pleasant."

What a *terrific* summer day!

Some other adjectives are frequently used as vague praise, vague blame, or vague intensives.

| | | | | |
|---|---|---|---|---|
| terrible | nice | cute | real | unbelievable |
| funny | unique | wonderful | fantastic | wicked |
| awful | interesting | incredible | great | obvious |

That *terrible* man with the *cute* name was *awful* to the *nice* girl.

## Adverb

Adverbs describe or limit any words except nouns, pronouns, prepositions, and articles. Adverbs work with verbs, adjectives, other adverbs, verbals, and entire clauses.

Adverbs commonly show degree:

*extremely* hungry

Manner:

ran *slowly*

Place:

hurried *here*

Time:

she *then* left

For stylistic advice on the adverb, see pages 129–137.

## Adverb clause

An adverb clause is a dependent clause used as an adverb.

I'll be gone *before she starts spraying.*

The adverb clause, *before she starts spraying,* modifies the verb *will be gone.*

## Adverbs frequently misused

Most of the adjectives frequently misused become misused adverbs, with an *-ly* added. *Terrible* becomes *terribly,* as in "*terribly* comfortable." Strictly adverbial adjectives are misused also.

| | | | | |
|---|---|---|---|---|
| terrifically | actually | wonderfully | literally | incredibly |
| certainly | very | rather | hopefully | totally |
| absolutely | virtually | practically | really | obviously |

It *certainly* was a *very* hot day and I was *practically* done at the *absolutely* last minute when *actually* a *rather* large man *virtually* beheaded me.

## Advice, advise

*Advice* is a noun; *advise* a verb.

I was *advised* to ignore your *advice.*

## Affect, effect

The two words are commonly confused. These examples illustrate proper uses of them:

Bob *affected* (influenced) the writing of Wright.

Sarah *affected* (assumed) the manner of a Greek tragedian.

The harder spray was *effected* (brought about) by an adjustment of the hose's nozzle.

The *effect* (result) of the new style was unpleasant.

## Agreement

The correspondence in form, or the matching of one word with another. Sentence elements must correspond in number, person, and gender.

*He is* so evil.
*They are* so evil.
*Tom* took *his* crocodile down to the river.
*Tom* and *Maria* took *their* crocodiles down to the river.
The *car* and *its* trailer rounded the corner.

See pages 385–392.

## Agree to, agree with

One *agrees to* a proposal or an action; one *agrees with* a person.

## All ready, already

The words differ in meaning. To say that someone is *all ready* is to say that he is prepared; the word *already* means beforehand in time, as in

He was *already* there.

### All right, alright

*All right* is the correct form. *Alright* means the same thing, but is a recent creation based on an analogy to the old word *already*. In formal writing, stay away from *alright*.

### Allusion, illusion

An allusion is an indirect reference; an illusion is a false belief or perception or a deceptive appearance.

Barnhouse bored us with his *allusions* to his illustrious family.

Under the *illusion* that he was invited, Barnhouse appeared for dinner at seven o'clock.

### Almost, most

*Almost* is an adverb meaning "nearly"; *most* is an adjective meaning "nearly all" or "the greater part of." Avoid using *most* as a shortened form of *almost*.

*Almost* all of us lead lives of quiet desperation.
*Most* men lead lives of quiet desperation.

### Along with

Avoid this wordy and useless phrase, in sentences like

*Along with* tennis, big game hunting is my favorite sport.

MacDowell is my candidate for the presidency, *along with* Vanderschmidt and Creelman-Carr.

Instead, say something like

Big game hunting and tennis are my favorite sports.

For the presidency, I favor MacDowell, Vanderschmidt, or Creelman-Carr.

### A lot

Many people have taken to spelling *a lot* as one word, *alot*. *A lot* is two words, like *all right*.

*A lot* of policemen showed up.

### Although, though

*Although* is preferable in formal writing.

## Altogether, all together

The two do not have the same meaning. *Altogether* means *wholly* or *entirely*. *All together* combines two commonly understood words.

Xavier, Abby, Frank, and Al were *all together* at the table.
Guy Woodhouse was *altogether* disgusting.

## Ambiguity

Writing is ambiguous when it has more than one possible meaning or interpretation.

## Amid, amidst

Avoid these words, which are not common to the American language and which sound stuffy and bookish.

## Among, amongst

*Among* is preferable. *Amongst* is bookish.

## Among, between

Use *between* when you are dealing with two things, *among* for more than two.

*between* you and me
*among* the three of us

In highly informal writing, this distinction is often ignored.

## Amoral, immoral, unmoral

*Amoral* means outside morality, neither moral nor immoral.

Beauty is *amoral.*

*Immoral* is contrary to codes of morality.

Benedict Arnold was *immoral.*

*Unmoral* is a near-synonym for *amoral* and is seldom used. *Amoral* is often used when the assertion is argumentative, *unmoral* when the statement is merely factual.

Dogs and cats are *unmoral.*

## Amount, number

*Amount* refers to a quantity of things viewed as a whole or to the quantity of one item; *number* describes the separate units of a group.

The *amount* of money in his bank account was staggering.
The *number* of dollar bills on the floor was small.
He took a large *amount* of salt a *number* of times.

### Analogy

An analogy is an extended comparison, used for illustration and argument. For examples and stylistic uses, see pages 145–146. For use and abuse in argument, see pages 317–318.

### And / or

This legalism frequently occurs in nonlegal prose where *or* would do just as well.

Cooking with pots *and/or* skillets requires nothing more than a hotplate.

Omit the unnecessary *and*.

### Antecedent

An antecedent is a word or group of words to which a pronoun refers.

As *Kevin* and *Quentin* ran in, *they* dropped the gas pellets.

*Kevin* and *Quentin* are the antecedents of the personal pronoun *they*.

### Antonym

An antonym means the opposite of another word. *Bad* is the antonym of *good*. As there are no exact synonyms, so we must not expect antonyms to be precisely opposite.

### Any, any other

Be careful to use these words properly. If you say

"*King Lear* is more moving than *any other* play in the English language."

you are probably saying what you intend. If you say, however, that

"*King Lear* is more moving than *any* play in the English language."

you imply that *Lear* is not in English—or that *Lear* is better than itself, which would be nonsensical. If you say

"Sophia is sexier than *any* woman in Italy."

you imply that she is not in Italy.

## Anybody, anyone

The words are singular, not plural. They take singular pronouns, as do *every, everyone, everybody.*

*Everyone* charges *his* meal at Alice's.

is formally correct, not

*Everyone* charges *their* meal at Alice's.

But an exception to this rule could make the second example the preferable form of the sentence. When a pronoun has *anybody* as an antecedent, and the gender of the person being discussed is unknown, we may wish to use forms of the plural *they* to avoid deciding between *he* and *she,* because *they* does not indicate gender.

Did *anybody* call? What did *they* say?

## Anyways

This form of *anyway* belongs to informal speech, not to writing.

## Apostrophe

See pages 406–407.

## Appositive

An appositive is a noun, or a noun substitute, which is placed next to another noun and which explains or defines it.

Peter, *the flying dwarf,* escorted Tarquina, his *good fairy.*

*Flying dwarf* is the appositive of *Peter,* and *good fairy* is the appositive of *Tarquina.*

## Apt, liable, likely

*Apt to* means "having a tendency to."

Sarah is *apt to* be discouraged if she doesn't win.

*Likely to* implies "probably going to." Do not say "We will *likely* arrive . . . ," but

We are *likely to* arrive in Cincinnati by early afternoon if the radiator doesn't overheat.

*Liable to* should be used only in situations that imply negative consequences.

That child is *liable to* fall if he leans too far out the window.

## Argument

Writing designed to convince or persuade.

## Article

The definite article is *the,* the indefinites are *a* and *an.* They are adjectives, always indicating that a noun or a noun substitute will follow.

*The* names a particular:

*the* table
*the* abstraction

*A* and *an* name a member of a class:

*a* table
*an* abstraction

The difference in meaning is small but indispensable.

The article *a* is used before words beginning with a consonant sound (even if the letter is a vowel):

*a* train
*a* unit

*An* is used before words beginning with a vowel sound:

*an* imaginative idea
*an* herb

## As, like

*As* is a conjunction, *like* is a preposition. In speech we often find *like* used as a conjunction:

He smiles *like* he felt good.

But in writing, we should avoid using *like* as a conjunction. We should use *as* or *as if* instead. Instead of writing

I write *like* I talk.

we say

I write *as* I talk.
I write *as if* I talked like a Frenchman.

*Like* works as a preposition, in language written or spoken:

He talks *like* a Frenchman.

## Aspect

This noun is commonly used as a blank. Avoid it.

We listened to a lecture on various *aspects* of fishing.

Usually if we remove the word we improve our sentence.

We listened to a lecture on fishing.

## At

Don't use the redundancy "Where are you *at?*" *Where* means "at which place."

## Auxiliaries

Auxiliaries in verb phrases indicate distinctions in tense and person. Common auxiliaries are *will, would, shall, should, be, have, do, can, could, may, might*, and *must*.

We *are* eating the chocolate.
You *would have* done the same.

## Awful, awfully

Literally, if we are *awful*, we are "full of *awe*." We no longer use the word to mean what it means. It is a vague intensive like *terrific, wonderful*, and *horrible*.

## Bad, badly

When we use the adjective *bad* after sensory verbs, in an expression like "I felt *bad* yesterday," we sometimes confuse it with the adverb *badly*. If you claim that you "felt *badly*," your words mean that your sensory apparatus did not function correctly. This use of *bad* holds true for sensory verbs like *feel, taste*, or *sound*, and also for verbs like *seem, appear*, and *look*. In grammatical terms, *bad* in these circumstances is a predicate adjective.

Using *badly* instead of *bad* as a predicate adjective affects gentility but reveals ignorance. It is correct to say

She looked *bad* when she came up to bat.

and incorrect to say

She looked *badly* when she came up to bat.

The latter sentence denigrates her vision. It is correct to say

They seemed *bad* this morning, after the ocean voyage.

referring to the appearance of illness. Do not say

They seemed *badly* this morning after the ocean voyage.

Other constructions require the adverb *badly.*

She played *badly* the first seven innings.

In

She played *bad* the first seven innings.

*bad* is incorrect.

*Badly* has another sense, which is "very much." This sense is colloquial or informal.

They wanted *badly* to be elected.
She was *badly* in need of a drink.

If you mean to employ this colloquialism, be careful of your word order. If you say, "She needed to sing very *badly*," you say something quite different from "She needed very *badly* to sing." If in doubt, be more formal; say

She needed *very much* to sing.

not

She needed to sing *very much.*

### Balanced sentences

See pages 184–191, where I discuss balance and parallelism.

### Being as

A common illiteracy.

Being as it was almost noon. . . .

Rewrite to eliminate. Usually we can substitute *because.*

Because it was almost noon. . . .

**Beside, besides**
Each of these words has several meanings of its own.

She stood *beside* (by the side of) the bureau.
Matt was *beside* himself (almost overwhelmed) with anger.
It's *beside* (not connected with) the point.
No one was awake *besides* (other than) him.
*Besides* (furthermore), it's in questionable taste.

**Between**
See **Among, between.**

**Bibliography**
See pages 339–342.

**Big words**
Never use a big word where a little word will do. Never say *domicile* where you could say *house.* Never say *individual* where you could say *person.* Never say *utilize* where you could say *use.*
See **Genteel words** and **-ize verbs.**

**Brackets**
See page 409.

**Bring, take**
*Bring* (to) implies movement toward.

*Bring* me a cup of coffee.

*Take* (from) implies movement away from.

*Take* the memo to the secretary.

**Can, may**
Both words express possibility. *Can* (or *could*) expresses *physical* possibility.

He *can* go to market because he has the car.
She *could* eat the potato salad, but she doesn't want to.

*May* (or *might*) implies that something is a *chance,* and often implies *volition.*

> He *may* go to Alaska (or he may not).
> She *might* be the last of the clan (or she might not).

Often we can hesitate between the two, and choose the one over the other for the precise shade of meaning. "He *could* take the exam" and "He *might* take the exam" offer different possibilities.

In conversation, and in the most informal writing, *may* often disappears in favor of *can,* and a distinction disappears, which is a loss. Or instead of saying "She *may* read Shakespeare, or Julia Child, or *Young Lust,*" we substitute the wordier "She *can* read Shakespeare, or Julia Child, or *Young Lust,* depending on what she feels like." The final clause supplies the chanciness and the volition implied in *may.*

In asking or granting permission, genteel prose uses *may.*

> *May* I enter?
> Randolph, you *may* not.

But *may* in this usage almost invariably sounds like an effort to be refined.

**Cannot, can not**

The spellings are equally acceptable. *Can not* looks more formal.

**Can't hardly**

Because *hardly,* as Bergen Evans says, "has the force of a negation," *can't hardly* functions as a double negative, or at least as an ambiguity. Does "I *can't hardly* hear you" mean "I *can't* hear you" or "I *can* hear you well" or "I *can hardly* hear you"? Logically, the double negative should make it mean the second, but the speaker probably meant the last. We should increase the clarity of our language by saying simply, "I *can hardly* hear you." The same advice applies to *can't scarcely.*

See **Double negative.**

**Capital letters**

See pages 415–417.

**Case**

See **Inflection.**

**Cf.**

We often find this abbreviation in footnotes and sometimes in parentheses. It tells us to "compare," as in

This decision was an exception (*cf. Toothe v. Carey*).

**Circumlocution**

Circumlocution is taking the long way to say something, using clichés, verbs combined with other parts of speech instead of simple verbs, and filler words and phrases. In

> *Notwithstanding the case of* the seamstress, it is *going to be* obvious that *in general, in a manner of speaking, we do well to remember the observation that a man who* is always in a hurry will lose *something or other in the long run.*

the circumlocution occurs throughout, and phrases typical in circumlocution are in italic. Notice that the last seventeen words might be rendered

Haste makes waste.

**Cite, sight, site**

*Cite* means to quote or to refer to.

They *cited* the constructive things they'd done.

A *sight* is a view:

a moving *sight*

or vision itself.

A *site* is a location:

a building *site*

**Clause**

A clause is a part of a sentence with a subject and a predicate. It may be principal (or main or independent) or subordinate (dependent on a main clause).

*The year ended* and *the year began.*

In the sentence above, two whole clauses are made into a compound sentence by *and*.

The year ended *when it had just begun.*

In this sentence, the italic clause is subordinate.
See page 156.

### Cliché
A cliché is a much used combination of words. *Writing Well* uses and defines this word several times. See pages 5–7, for instance.

### Collective noun
See **Noun.**

### Colon
See pages 409–410.

### Comma
See pages 399–403.

### Comma splice
See pages 382–385.

### Common nouns
See **Noun.**

### Compare to, compare with
To *compare to* shows similarities between things that are obviously different.

He *compared* the sparrow *to* a ten-ton truck.

(Of course by showing similarity, it reveals difference as well.) To *compare with* shows differences between things that are obviously similar.

She *compared* lunch *with* dinner.

(Of course it reveals similarities at the same time.)

### Comparison of adjectives and adverbs
The comparison of adjectives and adverbs indicates relative degree. The three degrees are positive, comparative, and superlative.

| Positive | Comparative | Superlative |
|----------|-------------|-------------|
| good | better | best |
| obnoxious | more obnoxious | most obnoxious |
| quick | quicker | quickest |
| quickly | more quickly | most quickly |

## Comparisons

For a discussion of simile, metaphor, and analogy, see pages 142–146.

## Complement

As a grammatical term, a complement is one or more words that complete the meaning of a verb or an object. A subject complement:

Phyllis is a wicked *girl.*

The predicate noun—*girl*—completes the sense of *Phyllis,* which it refers to. An object complement:

The dog chewed the bone *raw.*

*Raw* modifies and completes *bone.*

## Complement, compliment

A *complement* makes something whole or complete.

Work is the *complement* of play.

A *compliment* is praise.

I paid you a *compliment.*

There is also an archaic meaning in which *compliments* means something like formal politeness, and which survives in the phrase "*compliments* of the season."

## Complex sentence

A complex sentence contains a main clause and a subordinate clause. Here the subordinate (in italics) is a relative:

I whistled at the boy *who hung from the cliff.*

See pages 158–159, 167–171, 209–212.

## Compound sentence

A compound sentence includes two or more main clauses and no subordinate clauses.

> The moon rose at 10:35 P.M. and the stars appeared to recede into the darkness.

See pages 158, 171–175.

## Compound-complex sentence

This sentence type combines, as you might expect, the complex and the compound sentence. It has two main clauses and at least one subordinate clause.

> The snow stopped falling when the sun rose, but the temperature stayed below 10°.

See pages 159–160.

## Compound word

A compound word contains two or more words that are commonly used together as a single word.

> president-elect
> brother-in-law
> blackbird
> wheelbarrow
> handwriting

See a dictionary for current spelling.
See page 412.

## Conjugation

See **Inflection.**

## Conjunction

Conjunctions connect or coordinate (*and, but, for, or,* and occasionally *yet* or *so*) or they subordinate (*after, because, while, when, where, since*). With coordinate conjunctions be careful to preserve unity by keeping the coordinate phrases or clauses parallel (see pages 184–188). With subordinate conjunctions, remain aware of the habits of complex sentences (pages 158–159, 167–171, 209–212). Contrary to the old rule, even the best contemporary writing uses conjunctions at the beginnings of sentences.

**Conjunctive adverb**

A conjunctive adverb can be used to connect main clauses: *then, besides, however, therefore, otherwise.* Use a semicolon between the main clauses (before the adverb) and a comma after the adverb. See pages 174–175.

**Conscience, conscious**

These words mean different things. *Conscience* is a noun meaning the human faculty that distinguishes right from wrong.

After he lied to his boss, his *conscience* would not let him sleep.

*Conscious* is an adjective describing a state of awareness or being awake.

Eleanor was *conscious* of a sharp pain behind her left eye.
The patient became *conscious* after spending a week in a coma.

**Consider . . . as**

Writers frequently misuse the verb *consider* by adding an unnecessary preposition, *as.* Say

She *considered* him handsome.

not

She *considered* him *as* handsome.

Another use of the verb takes *as* appropriately. In the preceding example, *consider* means "believe to be." In the following example, *consider* means "think about" or "talk about."

She *considered* him *as* an administrator and *as* a scholar.

**Consist in, consist of**

*Consist of* refers to the parts that make a whole.

The government *consists of* legislative, executive, and judicial divisions.

*Consist in* refers to inherent qualities:

The value of democracy *consists in* the responsibility with which it endows the citizen.

### Continual, continuous

The two words have slightly different meanings. *Continual* describes an action that is repeated frequently.

He called her *continually* throughout the day.

*Continuous* describes an action done without stopping.

The bleeding was *continuous* for three hours.

### Coordinates

*Coordinate* means equal in rank. Two infinitives are coordinate, for instance, or two main clauses, as in a compound sentence.
See pages 158–159, 167–168, 171–175.

### Correlative conjunctions

*Both . . . and, either . . . or, neither . . . nor,* and *not only . . . but also* are coordinating conjunctions and require parallel forms in the phrases or clauses they coordinate.

### Could have, could of

The correct phrase is *could have. Could of* is a mistake. Don't say

She *could of* been a great actress.

But say

She *could have* been a great actress.

### Counsel, council, consul

*Counsel* is advice, or a lawyer, or someone acting as a lawyer. Though it would be a confusing sentence, one could say

The court-appointed *counsel* gave his client *counsel.*

A different spelling, with the same pronunciation, gives us the word *council,* which is a legislative group.

Harris for City *Council!*

A *consul* represents his government in another country where he keeps residence.

The vice-*consul* was out to lunch.

**Couple**

In the idiomatic sense of *a few*, the word is extremely informal, and in your writing you ought to substitute *two*, or *a few*, or *several*.

**Cutting words from quotations**

See pages 411–412.

**Dangling constructions**

A phrase placed loosely in a sentence dangles. Modifiers dangle frequently and disastrously.
See pages 393–395.

**Dashes**

See pages 410–411.

**Data**

In the most formal prose, we recognize the etymology of *data* as a Latin plural and therefore use the word with a plural verb form. It is correct—if highly formal or scientific—to say

*These* data *convince* us.

rather than

*This* data *convinces* us.

The singular, rarely used, is *datum.*

**Declension**

See **Inflection.**

**Deductive reasoning**

In this form of thinking, we apply a general truth to a specific instance. Thus, if it is true that going through a time warp causes pain, we may *deduce* that if Quasimodo goes through a time warp, he will feel pain.

**Demonstratives**

Demonstratives are adjectives, like *this, that, these,* and *those,* used to point the finger.

*This* is the man who took it; *that's* my basketball.

They can also be pronouns; when they are, they should have clear antecedents. Do not say

> You said that you couldn't read and that you had never learned how. I could not believe *that.*

See pages 391–392.

### Diction
The choice and use of words.

### Different from, different than
*Different from* is usually preferable, especially in formal prose. When a clause follows, *different than* is acceptable.

> This place is *different than* I expected it to be.

### Direct address
A noun or pronoun used to direct a remark to a specific person, set off by commas.

> I was thinking, *Ron,* that you'd like to go up in a balloon.
> *Irving,* close that closet.
> Hey, *you!*

### Direct object
See **Object.**

### Direct quotation
See pages 407–408.

### Discreet, discrete
The two words have different meanings. *Discreet* means "prudent in one's conduct or speech."

> She would never reveal it; she was exceptionally *discreet.*

Discrete means "distinct" or "separate."

> The words are different; they have *discrete* meanings.

### Disinterested, uninterested
These words are frequently confused. To be *uninterested* is to lack fascination about something, even to be bored by it.

I tried to arouse his enthusiasm for a game of golf, but he was *uninterested* in such a pastime.

*Disinterested* is the condition of being impartial or neutral, or of having no stake in an issue. Frequently the word is used positively as a precondition for fairness, as in the phrase "*disinterested* party."

The judge declared his *disinterest* in the matter.

This judge proclaims his ability to judge the case fairly.

### Doesn't, don't

*Don't* goes with *I, you, we,* and *they,* but not with *it, he,* or *she.* It contracts *do not.* It does not contract *does not; doesn't* does.

### Double negative

A double negative occurs in a sentence that uses two negative terms when only one is needed.

He *didn't* say *nothing.*
You *shouldn't never* do that to a bird.

In earlier English such doubling was thought to give emphasis, as in "I never treacherously slew no man" (Bergen Evans's example). But today double negatives are regarded as unacceptable and illogical. If I should *not* never do something, then by implication I should (positively) do it sometime.
See **Can't hardly.**

### Doubt but

Omit *but.* Also omit *but* in *help but.*

They couldn't *doubt but* that the Racquet Club was best.

becomes

They couldn't *doubt* that the Racquet Club was best.

and

They couldn't *help but* know the worst.

becomes

They couldn't *help* knowing the worst.

And always avoid "They couldn't *doubt but* what. . . ."

**Due to**

Never use *due to* for *because of* in adverb phrases. "She won the race *due to* her long legs" sounds unnatural. It is probably best to reserve the word for finance. Sometimes people multiply error by writing, "due to the fact that. . . ."

**Each, every**

*Each* is a pronoun:

*Each* went his own way.

and an adjective:

*Each* package of bubble gum has five pieces.

*Each* means the individual units of a conglomerate:

*Each* of the Boy Scouts

but *every* means the conglomerate itself:

*Every* Boy Scout

In the Boy Scout examples, *each* is a pronoun, *every* an adjective.
When the adjective *each* modifies a singular noun, the following verb and pronouns are singular.

*Each* player *lifts his* bat.

When *each* modifies a plural noun or pronoun and comes before the verb, the verb and pronouns are plural.

They *each go their* own way.

When *each* works as a pronoun, it is usually singular.

*Each goes his* own way.

There are exceptions. In the preceding example, if the pronoun referred to men and women, we might have written

*Each go their* own way.

When *each* refers to two or more singular words, or when a plural word comes between *each* and the verb, the number of the verb is optional. We may say

*Each* of the players *is*

or

*Each* of the players *are*

We may say

When *Mark and Linda* speak, *each* of them *says*

or

When *Mark and Linda* speak, *each* of them *say*

The negative of *each* is *neither*. Do not write *each* with a negative:

*Each* did not speak.

but write

*Neither* spoke.

## Effect, affect
See **Affect, effect.**

## E.g.
This is the abbreviation for a Latin expression that means *for example*. It is usually best to use the English, but on occasion we will find these initials, often in scientific or legal prose.

The review board overlooked significant evidence, *e.g., Baxter v. Baxter.*

## Egoism, egotism
*Egoism* has the connotation of a philosophy, *egotism* of a neurosis. *Egoism* is the other side of *altruism* and is a belief in the value of self-interest. *Egotism* is the necessity to use the word *I* all the time.

## Either
*Either*, like *each*, can be pronoun or adjective.

*Either* path leads us home.
*Either* of the twins . . .

When *either* means one or the other, it takes the singular.

*Either* Rick or Chris *is* lying.

When it means both, it still takes a singular verb.

*Either* of you *is* qualified.

Sometimes *either/or* and *neither/nor* connect a singular and a plural subject. Then the verb agrees with the subject closest to it.

*Either* Peggotty *or* the Steerforths *are* coming to dinner tonight.

As a correlative conjunction, *either* takes *or* and does not take *nor*. *Nor* belongs to *neither*.

### Elicit, illicit

*Elicit* means "to bring out."

We could *elicit* no further response from the members.

*Illicit* means "not permitted."

They were having an *illicit* love affair.

### Ellipses

See pages 411–412.

### Eminent, immanent, imminent

*Eminent* means outstanding.

The *eminent* philosopher . . .

*Immanent* means inherent.

. . . will discuss *immanent* ideas . . .

*Imminent* means impending.

. . . *imminently.*

### Enormity, enormousness

An *enormity* is a moral outrage. *Enormousness* is hugeness.

### Etc.

This abbreviation meaning "and so forth," from the Latin *et cetera*, is out of place in formal prose. In formal and informal prose, it often trails off the end of a sentence into vagueness and avoids extending the brain. Stay away from it in formal prose. Think before you use it in any context.
See **Foreign words and phrases.**

**Etymology**

*Etymology* is the study of the origins and histories of words.

**Euphemism**

Euphemisms are fancy or abstract substitutes for plain words. We use them for social elevation, as when an *undertaker* becomes a *mortician,* or to avoid facing something frightening, as when we say that someone *passed away,* instead of saying that he *died.*

See pages 99–101.

**Everybody, everyone**

*Everybody* and *everyone* take a singular verb.

*Everybody goes* to church.

The words can take a singular pronoun, especially in a formal context:

*Everyone* finds *his* seat and waits for the minister.

or a plural pronoun, especially when it refers to men and women and we wish to avoid the prejudice of picking either *his* or *her.*

*Everybody* waited until *they* caught *their* breath.

See pages 386–388.

**Exclamation point**

See page 398.

**Expletives**

When *it* and *there* fill space in a sentence without contributing to its meaning, we call them expletives.

*There are* thousands of people in the United States who cannot read.

*It is* understood that the rain was falling.

These could be written:

Thousands of people in the United States cannot read.
Rain was falling.

**Exposition**

Writing designed to explain or analyze.

**Fact**

Avoid the phrase *the fact that,* which is wordy and unnecessary.

**Famous, notorious, infamous**

To be *famous* is to be well known or celebrated. To be *notorious* is to be well known for something shady. To be *infamous* is to be well known for something detestable.

He was a *famous* movie star, musician, and second baseman.
He was a *notorious* pirate, extortionist, and linguist.
Bluebeard was an *infamous* character.

**Farther, further**

As "distance to go" the two are interchangeable. Where *further* means "more," *farther* is not a possible alternative.

We have no *further* use for him.

**Few**

See **Less.**

**Field**

A field is a place for growing hay or daisies. Don't use it as a blank, or invisible noun, as in "the field of agriculture."

**Figure**

See **Numeral.**

**Fine**

This adjective is vague and overused.

**Finite verb**

A finite verb is complete, a predicate in itself.

The house *collapses.*

Gerunds, infinitives, and particles are not finite verbs but *verbals.*

**Footnote**

See pages 342–344.

**Foreign words and phrases**

Foreign words and phrases often look pretentious in our writing. In dialogue, they can be useful to characterize someone as foreign or as pretentious. Occasionally nothing in English seems quite so apt as a foreign phrase. But look hard before you give up. If you must use one, italicize it by underlining it.

**Foreword, forward**

The two have different meanings. A *foreword* is a preface, the introductory statement at the beginning of a book. *Forward* is usually a direction. On occasion, *forward* means "bold" or "presumptuous."

> She leaned forward and stuck her tongue out at him; she was very *forward.*

**Fused sentence**

See **Run-on sentence.**

**Gender**

Gender is a grammatical indication of sex. English nouns lack gender except as their own sense indicates. That is, *sister* is feminine, *brother* masculine, and *sibling* can be either. Some pronouns have gender (*he, she*), but most do not (*I, they, you, we*). In some languages, all nouns are assigned a gender. In French, the word for *grass* (*herbe*) is feminine, and the word for *time* (*temps*) is masculine. In English both words are neuter.

**Genteel words**

Some words act as euphemisms by seeming socially preferable to plainer alternatives. People who use them seem to be *trying* to be genteel. Avoid them unless you are making a genuine distinction.

| *Genteel* | *Ordinary* |
|---|---|
| perspire | sweat |
| wealthy | rich |
| home | house |
| luncheon | lunch |

**Gerund**

See **Verbal.**

**Get**

We multiply this little word in our speech; it has small place in our writing. "I went down to *get* some wallpaper" is passable but often imprecise. In writing, it would be better to *choose* or *buy* the wallpaper.

**Good, well**

It is common to use *good* as if it were an adverb, but it is incorrect.

He ran *good.*

When referring to an action, *well* is the right word.

He ran *well.*

Be careful with the word *feels*; to say that a person *feels good* is to say that he is in a pleasant frame of mind; to say that a person *feels well* is to say either that he feels healthy or that his sense of touch is functioning efficiently.

**Grammar**

Grammar describes how words function in a language.

**Guerrilla, gorilla**

A *guerrilla* is an irregular soldier. A *gorilla* is an animal. *Guerrilla* is also used as an adjective and has been used adjectivally to indicate activity in the service of revolution: *guerrilla* theater, *guerrilla* television.

**Had ought**

This combination is clumsy. Instead of writing

We knew he *had ought* to come.

write

We knew he *ought* to come.

**Hanged, hung**

*Hanged* pertains to the execution of human beings, *hung* to the suspension of objects.

Sam Hall was *hanged* in October.
We *hung* the portraits in the hall.

**He, him**

> *He* is a subject, *him* an object.
> Other pronoun pairs, subject and object, are *I/me, they/them, she/her, we/us,* and *who/whom.* (See **Who/whom.**)

> *He* walked to Joe's. *He* and Jane walked to Joe's.
> Joe saw *him.* Joe saw Jane and *him.*

A common error uses the subject when it ought to use the object.

> Joe saw Jane and *I.*

is wrong. You would not say "Joe saw *I*" and therefore you do not say "Joe saw Jane and *I.*" It is correct to say

> Joe saw Jane and *me.*

This error, like many errors, is a false correction. When we are children we may say

> *Me* and Jane went down to Joe's.

We learn to correct this to

> Jane and *I* went down to Joe's.

which is fine because *I* is a subject. Then by mistake we use *I* when we should use the objective *me,* as if we corrected the old error.
   This error happens most often after a preposition like *across, at, behind, between, by, for, from, in, of, on, over, to, under,* and *with.* Prepositions take objects. Always say

> This happened to Jane and *me.*

Never say

> This happened to Jane and *I.*
> This happened to Jane and *he.*
> This happened to Jane and *we.*
> This happened to Jane and *they.*

All of these examples are incorrect.
   The way to remember: if it sounds wrong when you use the preposition alone, as in

> This happened to *I/he/we/they* . . .

then it is wrong when a proper name comes between the preposition (or the verb) and the pronoun.
   Also see **Pronoun.**

**He or she**

This locution is awkward and clumsy. Sometimes we use it to avoid sexism.

See pages 179–180.

**Help but**

See **Doubt but.**

**Homonym**

Homonyms are words that, although pronounced the same, are spelled differently and mean different things.

| | | |
|---|---|---|
| to, too, two | bare, bear | their, there, they're |
| through, threw | blew, blue | heir, air |

**Hopefully**

*Hopefully* is an adverb meaning "full of hope" that frequently becomes a dangling modifier. We say

*Hopefully,* the plane will be on time.

when we do not mean to imply that the plane is full of hope. We could say

*Hopefully,* I awaited her arrival.

We come to use *hopefully* as if it meant "I hope." The first example is meant to say

*I hope* the plane will be on time.

**Hyperbole**

Hyperbole is extreme exaggeration to make a point.

That cat *weighs a ton.*

Use hyperbole with discretion; do not use it, like some writers, a thousand times on every page.

**Hyphen**

See pages 412–413.

**I, me**

See **He/him.**

**I.e.**

*I.e.* abbreviates the Latin *id est,* meaning "that is." We use it sometimes to introduce an explanation or definition of a word or phrase.

> She was nonessential, *i.e.,* they didn't need to employ her.

Usually, the expression seems overprecise and too much like legal or scientific writing. The sentence above can omit the Latinism and use instead a colon or a semicolon.

> She was nonessential: they didn't need to employ her.

**Immigrant, emigrant**

An *immigrant* is someone who enters a country; an *emigrant* leaves one. Our ancestors had to emigrate ~~before they could immi-~~ grate.

**Incredible, unbelievable**

In theory, these words are synonymous. In practice, *unbelievable* holds up better.

> The charges were *unbelievable*

states rather straightforwardly the disbelief.

> The charges were *incredible*

suffers from the use of *incredible* as a vague intensive.

> Those hamburgers were *incredible*

simply praises the hamburgers in hyperbole from which constant use has withdrawn the strength. *Unbelievable* undergoes some of the same diminishment:

> . . . *unbelievably* rare

and may also lose its utility in time.

**Indefinite pronoun**

See **Pronoun** and pages 389–392.

**Independent clause**

See **Clause.**

**Indirect object**
> See **Object.**

**Indirect quotation**
> We use indirect quotations when we attribute a remark without claiming to use exact words and without using quotation marks.

> > The congressman from Ohio then claimed that he had heard enough.

> > She said that Herbert was the nicest boy she had ever met.

> When we indirectly quote information taken from a source, we should footnote it just as we would a direct quotation.

**Inductive reasoning**
> This form of thought draws general conclusions from particular examples or evidence.

> > As a result of these experiments we conclude that if water temperature falls below 32 degrees the water will freeze.

**Infer, imply**
> We *infer* or understand from what a speaker or writer *implies* to us. *Infer* means "conclude"; *imply* means "suggest."

> > From the tone of her voice on the telephone, I *inferred* her terror.
> > She *implied* that she had seen a face at the window.

> We cannot say that another person *inferred* something to us. He or she *implied* it, and we *inferred* a meaning in the implication.

**Inferior to, inferior than**
> *Inferior than* is incorrect. Say either *inferior to* or *worse than*.

**Infinitive**
> See **Verbal.**

**Inflection**
> Inflection is the change in the form of a word to indicate a change in meaning or grammatical relationship. The inflection of nouns and pronouns is called *declension;* of verbs, *conjugation;* and of adjectives and adverbs, *comparison.*

Inflection of nouns indicates *number* and *case.*

aardvark, aardvarks, aardvark's, aardvarks'; man, men, man's, men's

Inflection of pronouns indicates *case, person,* and *number.*

she, her, hers; who, whom, whose; they, them, their

Inflection of verbs indicates *tense, person,* and *mood.*

laugh, laughing, laughs, laughed
spring, springing, springs, sprung

Inflection of modifiers indicates *comparison* and *number.*

thin, thinner, thinnest
this dog, that dog, these dogs, those dogs

## In regard to, in regards to

*In regard to* is preferable. The good stylist rewrites to avoid either. Instead of

In regard to your letter of May 9 . . .

we might say

Answering your letter of May 9 . . .

## Intensive pronoun

See **pronoun.**

## Intransitive verb

An intransitive verb neither has an object nor is passive in form.

I *was* at Annette's house in Santa Fe at the time.
Quaker *has been waiting* on the flagpole for hours.

## Irony

Intentional irony is a conscious statement intended to convey the opposite of what it seems to say. It can be used humorously; it can be gentle or sarcastic and biting. We can say that the weather is marvelous when we are standing in a downpour. Our irony is obvious. When Jonathan Swift wrote his satirical "Modest Proposal," he suggested that Irish babies be slaughtered and eaten, as a convenience to the English. He did not intend the suggestion literally. Most of his readers perceived his irony.

### Irregardless

Use *regardless*. *Irregardless* is a redundancy, made in error on the model of *irrespective*.

### Italics

See page 413.

### Its, it's

*It's* always stands for *it is*. *Its* is possessive.

*It's* eating *its* supper.

See pages 406–407.

### -ize verbs

Avoid making new verbs ending in *-ize*, like "*tomato-ize* the spaghetti." Avoid using some recent coinages too: *utilize* (say "use"), *personalize, finalize, prioritize.*

### Jargon

Jargon is the argot of a profession, or a peer group, like educationists' jargon, or astronauts', or rock musicians'. Businessmen fall into a jargon frequently. Sometimes they *firm up* a deal before they *finalize* it. Sometimes two negotiators are not *in the same ballpark;* one of them, however, may *come out of left field.*

Slang makes jargon too, and every campus—every year, every term—invents a local dialect of student jargon.

Jargon is a language by which we attempt to prove that *we* are the initiated and to keep noninitiates in confusion and befuddlement. It is language not to communicate but to exclude.

Jargon has a real purpose when it is the precise shorthand of a science. But for most of us most of the time, jargon has a tendency to be considerably vaguer than the larger language we share.

### Kind of

This phrase is misused, and even used properly is often not helpful. When we say "*kind of* big" we are qualifying *big,* as if we said "*rather* big." It is a misuse of the word *kind. Kind* means species.

It is a *kind of* pine tree.

This usage works, but we often slide into vague species-making.

She is a *kind of* blonde I can't stand.

The sentence cannot be rewritten; it must be rethought. What exactly is it that you cannot stand? Name it.

I do not like a blonde who has red eyebrows.

The same remarks apply to *sort of.*

## Lay, lie

*Lay/laid/laid,* meaning to put or place, applies to the following uses: "she *lays* an egg"; "you *laid* the book on the table"; "I *laid* my pen on this paid." *Lay* takes a direct object. The present tense of *lie* is *lay,* which is a source of confusion. *Lie/lay/lain,* meaning to rest or recline, applies to these uses: I *lie* on the grass; she *lay* on the bed all day; we *had lain* in the sun. *Lie* never takes a direct object.

## Lead, led

*Lead* is present tense, *led* is past, and *lead*—when pronounced like *led*—is the metal.

Yesterday I *led* the class.
Today I *lead* the escape.

## Leave, let

*Leave* means "to go away"; *let* means "to allow."

*Leave* me. (Go away from me.)
*Let* me. (Allow me to.)
*Leave* me out. (Don't include me.)
*Let* me out. (Allow me to go.)

## Less

This word is frequently misused where *fewer* would be correct.

There are *less* flowers in the vase today.

should be

There are *fewer* flowers in the vase today.

*Fewer* refers to actual numbers; *less* refers to quantity in general.

The powerful nations are *fewer* than they used to be.
Nations have *less* power.

### Lie, lay

See **Lay, lie.**

### Like, as

See **As, like.**

### Likewise

This expression is a clumsy transition, almost always a piece of bone in the hamburger.

### Linking verb

A linking verb expresses the relationship between the subject and the predicate noun or predicate adjective. The principal linking verbs are *appear, be, become, seem,* and verbs used for sensations (*feel, smell, sound, taste, look*).

Lorca *is* magnificent.
Rose *became* a mother.
Joe *looks* sick.
The steak *smells* rotten.

### Literally

We often say *literally* when we mean the opposite: *figuratively.* We use a metaphor, but we realize that it is dead and we play Dr. Frankenstein to the monster by applying the cathodes of *literally* (or *literal*).

She was *literally* as big as a house.
He was a *literal* man of straw.
He hit the ball *literally* a thousand miles.

The monster never walks. Use *literally* only to emphasize that you mean just what you say.

When the police broke into the warehouse, they found the prime minister *literally* weeping tears of gratitude.

*Literal* means "according to the letter" or "as it actually appears." Never use it unless you mean it literally. When you find yourself misusing it for the purposes above, you can either omit it and settle for the corpse of your metaphor, or you can make a new metaphor, "She was as big as. . . ."

## Litotes

Litotes is a figure of speech understating something by saying the negative of its opposite. Saying "It's not a beauty" may mean "It's ugly."

## Little

Often we misuse this word—which is necessary to common speech in its literal meaning—as a vague qualifier.

He's a *little* late.

We misuse *pretty* in the same way, without considering its meaning. James Thurber tormented his editor on *The New Yorker* by writing that something was "a little big" and "pretty ugly."

## Logic

See **Deductive reasoning** and **Inductive reasoning.** Also see pages 299–322 for some remarks about persuasion and an account of some common errors in thinking.

For further reading, consult Manuel Bilsky's *Patterns of Argument.*

## Loose, lose

Different spellings make different words.

The dog is *loose.*
I *lose* the dog.
The *loose* rope *loses* the dog.

## Lot, lots

These are informal substitutes for other quantitative words: *a great many, a number of.* Avoid in formal writing.

## Mad, angry

*Mad* means "crazy" or "insane," but popular speech has made it synonymous with *angry:* "I'm *mad* at you" means "I'm *angry* with you." Use *angry* in formal writing.

## Main clause

A *main clause* can stand by itself. It can be a whole, simple sentence.

They built an armadillo.

Two *main clauses* can make a compound sentence.

They built an armadillo and they traded it for a VW.

In a complex sentence, the main clause (in italics) governs a subordinate clause.

When night fell, *they built an armadillo.*

## Man who . . .

A common circumlocution uses a noun (like *man* or *woman* or *person* or *senator* or *typist*) in a relative clause when the extra words serve no function.

He was *a man who* drank half a bottle of Scotch before breakfast.
She was *a woman who* knew better.
She was *a senator who* always filibustered.

If this last sentence gave us the information that she was a senator, it would be justified.

He was *a typist who* never typed more than twenty-seven words a minute.

These sentences can become

*He drank* half a bottle of Scotch before breakfast.
*She knew* better.
*She always* filibustered.
*He never typed* more than twenty-seven words a minute.

## Manuscript form

See page 417.

## May, can

See **Can, may.**

## Metaphor

See pages 142–144.

## Mixed constructions

Avoid sentences that begin as if they will follow one form, switch forms, and become mixed and confusing. Do not say

> Because the annual snowfall reaches eighty inches causes everybody to keep a supply of food.

This example uses a dependent clause as a subject. It could be repaired into

> Because the annual snowfall reaches eighty inches, everyone keeps a supply of food.

Here is a mixed construction in which an adverb clause is used as a noun.

> A Fourth of July celebration is when you have fireworks and picnics.

This can be changed to

> At a Fourth of July celebration, you have fireworks and picnics.

## Modifier

Any word or group of words that describes or qualifies another word or group of words is a modifier.

For a general account of adjectives, adverbs, and other modifiers, see pages 129–137. For attention to some problems common in the use of modifiers, see pages 393–395.

## Momentary, momentous

*Momentary* has to do with time. It refers to something that lasts only a moment or happens at any moment. *Momentous* means of extraordinary importance, as in the cliché "a *momentous* occasion."

> The affliction was *momentous.*
> She looked west, awaiting his *momentary* arrival.

## Mood

The mood (or mode) of the verb indicates an attitude on the part of the writer. The mood may be indicative, imperative, or subjunctive. The *indicative* mood states a fact or asks a question.

> Jim Rice *is* here.
> *Was* Bill Walton there?

The *imperative* mood gives a command, gives directions, or makes a request.

> *Beware* of darkness.
> *Turn* right at Golgotha.
> *Mend* my parachute, please.

The *subjunctive* mood expresses uncertainty, contradiction, wishfulness, regret, or speculation. It is most common in contrary-to-fact clauses beginning with *if* ("If it *were* possible, I would fly") and after certain verbs such as *move* ("I move that the meeting *be* postponed") and *demand* ("They demanded that the bail *be* fixed").

### Morale, moral

*Moral* is a matter of ethics, *morale* of high or low spirits.

> Their *morals* were low, but their *morale* was high.
> Murder is not a *moral* act, usually.

### Ms.

A recently invented title, on the analogy of *Mr., Mrs.,* and *Miss, Ms.* reveals female gender while it conceals marital status.

### Myself

Do not use *myself* as a substitute for *I* or *me.* Do not say

> Richard and *myself* went to the circus.
> The elephant paused a few yards downwind from *myself.*

Do say

> Richard and *I* went to the circus.
> The elephant paused a few yards downwind from *me.*

### Narration

Writing that tells a story in a connected series of events.

### N.b.

This common abbreviation from the Latin means "Notice well!" and draws our attention to something.

### Neither

See **Either.**

## Neologism

A neologism is a made-up word, often used out of laziness or affectation when an old word would do. *Finalize* is a neologism; *end* or *finish* are the old words.

## None

*None* can be either singular or plural, depending on context and intention.

> *None* of the other guys *were* going to the game.
> *None* of his fellow senators *was* likely to take so strong a stand on the war.

## Nonrestrictive modifier

A nonrestrictive modifier is a parenthetical expression that does not limit the noun or pronoun modified. It can be a nonrestrictive clause:

> The Buick, *which was a car new to my neighborhood,* was the object of fascination.

or a phrase:

> The banana, *a fruit new to our taste,* was divided evenly.

See page 378.

## No one, nobody

These words take a singular verb. Third-person pronouns, singular and plural, can refer to them: *he, his, him, she, hers, her, they, them.* We use *they* and *them* when we feel that the gender of the pronoun would be invidious.

## Not un-

Eschew the habit of writing *not un-*'s

> A *not un*distinguished gentleman, in a *not un*elegant dinner jacket, *not un*gracefully strode past the *not un*chic lady.

## Noun

There are several types of nouns. *Common* nouns belong to one of a class of people, places, or things (*woman, country, table*). *Proper* nouns are names of specific people, places, or things (*Max von*

*Sydow, Liv Ullmann, Casablanca, Ann Arbor, Statue of Liberty).*
*Concrete* nouns name something that can be perceived by the senses
(*acid, trees, eggs, horses*). *Abstract* nouns name a general idea or
quality (*terror, love, harshness, agony*). *Collective* nouns refer to a
group as a unit (*band, team, council, league*). These categories are
not mutually exclusive; a word like *tree* is common and concrete.

Nouns, whatever their funtions in a sentence, retain their basic
form, varying it only in forming the plural and the possessive. The
plural of most nouns is formed by adding *-s* to the singular, the
possessive by adding an apostrophe and an *-s* to the singular or an
apostrophe after the *-s* of the plural: *hen, hens, hen's, hens'; house,
houses, house's, houses'.* Some nouns add *-es* for the plural: *hero,
heroes, hero's, heroes'.* A few nouns change their internal spelling
for the plural: *man, men; woman, women;* here, the possessive is
formed by an apostrophe and an *-s,* in singular and in plural (*man's,
men's*). Other nouns with an irregular plural are listed on page 419.

For stylistic advice about nouns, see pages 120–127.

### Nouns commonly used as blanks

Many nouns, which are perfectly useful when spoken with care,
are frequently used imprecisely, wordily, and without utility—
nouns used as blanks: *aspect, case, character, factor, fact, field,
element, effect, experience, nature, manner, respect, situation,* and
*feature.*

> Some *aspects* in the *case* of Rumpelstiltskin have the *character* of
> *elements* that seem sinister in *nature.* The *fact* that the enraged
> dwarf was a *factor* in the *nature* of the King's *manner* is a *feature*
> with *respect* to which we can not distinguish the *effect.*

This paragraph has the consistency of mud or an annual report.

### Noun substitute

A noun substitute, whether clause or phrase or pronoun, functions as a noun.

### Number

See **Inflection.**

### Numeral

See pages 417–418.

**Object**
A complete sentence needs a subject and a verb; it need not have an object.

The cat screeched.

is a complete sentence.

The cat clawed *Herbert.*

includes an object. An object is something a verb acts upon.

Objects are direct and indirect. A *direct object* is any noun (or noun substitute) that answers the question "What?" or "Whom?" after a transitive verb. Direct objects are the objects of the verb's action.

She toppled *the giant.*
He knows *what she wants.*

An *indirect object* is a noun or noun substitute which is indirectly affected by the verb's action and which tells *to whom* or *for whom* the action is done.

She gave *him* a karate chop.

*Him* is the indirect object, *karate chop* the direct object.

**Object complement**
See **Complement.**

**Of**
We often use *of* when we don't have to.

outside *of* the house
off *of* the ground
inside *of* the room

The phrases read more stylishly as

outside the house
off the ground
inside the room

Keep the *of* when the extra preposition changes meaning. *Outside of* can mean "to the exclusion *of,*" and we are correct to say "Outside *of* scientific speculation, there is no use for such calibration."

468  *A Glossary of Usage and Grammatical Terms*

*Inside of* can mean "in less than." "*Inside of* an hour, he had finished the work."

**One, you**

Be careful not to use *one* in place of *you* so much that it sounds awkward or pretentious.

Should *one* be careful to avoid the use of the word "one" when *one* is speaking to a woman whom *one* loves?

As suggested by this example, context is important when you consider using *one*. It is useful at times, but it has a way of seeming affected. Never use it as an obvious disguise for *I*.

*One* took an amusing jaunt to Cedar Point last summer.

Finally, be careful not to mix *one* and *you* or *I* in the same sentence.

**One of the most . . .**

This cliché is drained of meaning.

She is *one of the most* lovable people in the world.
The rodeo was *one of the most* exciting experiences of my life.

If you use this phrase, cross it out and consider the particulars to which you refer. One example, showing the character *being* lovable, is worth ten thousand assertions. An exciting anecdote from the rodeo makes assertion unnecessary.

Show, don't tell.

**Parallelism**

See pages 184–188.

**Parentheses**

See page 413.

**Participle**

See **Verbal.**

**Passive voice**

A verb is in the passive voice when it *acts upon* the subject.

LeFlore *was hit* by the pitch.

See **Active voice.**

**Period**

See page 398.

**Person**

In grammar, the person of a verb or a pronoun shows that someone is speaking (in *first person*), or is spoken to (*second person*), or is spoken about (*third person*). In *I see, you see, he sees,* the person of the pronoun changes each time; the verb form of the first person and the second person happens to be the same, but the verb form changes to indicate the third person. With a few verbs, the form changes with each change of person (I *am,* you *are,* he *is*).

**Phrase**

Phrases function as a part of speech and do not have a subject and a predicate.

An *infinitive* phrase:

I studied *to learn Greek.*

A *prepositional* phrase:

The flower grows *in the mountain.*

A *verb* phrase:

The zebra *is catching up.*

A *participial* phrase:

*Sliding into second,* Zarido tore a ligament.

**Plagiarism**

Plagiarism is using other people's work, whether it is a published source used without acknowledgment or a friend's old paper or a term paper bought from an entrepreneur.

**Possessive**

For the possessive of nouns, see **Noun.** For the possessive of pronouns, see **Pronoun.**

**Precede, proceed**

To *precede* is to "go before" or "in front of."

The Pirates *preceded* the Reds onto the field.

To *proceed* is to "continue" or to "begin again."

> After the game, they *proceeded* to the airport.

## Predicate

A predicate is the part of the sentence *about* the subject. It includes verbs and, on occasion, adverbs, direct objects, indirect objects, and clauses attached to the predicate.
See page 154.

## Predicate adjective
See **Complement.**

## Predicate noun
See **Complement.**

## Preposition

Prepositions show the relationship between a noun or noun equivalent and another word in the sentence. Some of the most commonly used prepositions are *across, after, at, behind, between, by, for, from, of, on, over, to, under,* and *with.*

> Tom hid *in* the attic.

The preposition *in* relates the noun *attic* to the verb *hid.*

## Presently

This word means "in a little while," not "now" or "currently." Say

> He is *at present* a milkman.

not

> He is *presently* a milkman.

But say

> He will come back to Chicago *presently.*

## Pretty
See **Little.**

**Principal, principle**

*Principle* is a noun meaning a general truth (the *principles* of physics) or moral ideas (she had the highest *principles*). The adjective *principal* means "the foremost." One could speak of the *principal principle* of a science or a philosophy. The noun *principal* means the chief officer.

Alex Emerson is the *principal* of Bob's school.

**Pronoun**

A pronoun is a word used in place of a noun.

*Personal* pronouns:

I, you, he, she, we, etc.

*Relative* pronouns:

who, which, that

*Demonstrative* pronouns:

this, that, these, those

*Indefinite* pronouns:

each, either, any, some, someone, all, etc.

*Reciprocal* pronouns:

each other, one another

*Reflexive*, or *intensive*, pronouns:

myself, yourself, etc.

For pronoun usage, subject and object, see **He/him.**

**Proper noun**

See **Noun.**

**Prophesy, prophecy**

The word with the *s* is the verb, the word with the *c* the noun.

The priest *prophesied* doom.
It was an accurate *prophecy.*

**Proved, proven**

*Proved* is the regular past participle form of *prove* and is preferred in American usage. *Proven* is a Scottish version of the participle, sometimes found in current usage.

### Punctuation

See pages 398–413.

### Quotation marks

See pages 407–408.

### Rational, rationale

*Rational* means "reasonable and sensible." It is an adjective. *Rationale* is a noun meaning "the whole system of reasons behind an idea, a position, or an action."

> His arguments were *rational.*
> Her *rationale* for the program was easy to discern.

### Real, really

Conversational usage accepts *real* as an adverb, but it will not do in writing. Write

> The boat was *really* handsome!
> Josephine seemed to be a *really* happy girl.

Don't write

> The boat was *real* handsome.
> Josephine seemed to be a *real* happy girl.

*Real* as an adjective survives.

> It was a *real* boat.

Frequently, we use *real* and *really* as weak intensifiers, but our sentences will be stronger without them.

### Reason is because, reason why

Don't use these constructions. If you must use *reason is,* have it be "*reason is that. . . .*"

### Relative clause

See **Subordinate clause.**

**Relative pronoun**
  See **Pronoun.**

**Respectfully, respectively**
  *Respectfully* is an adverb that modifies an action full of respect.

  I remain, yours *respectfully,*

  *Respectively* pertains to each of a number, in an order.

  He swore that he saw Ted and Joan wearing a flower and a bowler, *respectively.*

  Therefore to end a letter "Yours *respectively*" makes no sense.

**Restrictive clause or modifier**
  A restrictive modifier is a clause or a phrase essential to the identity of what is modified.

  Everybody *who wants* can get to the top.

  See **Nonrestrictive modifier** for contrast.

**Rhetoric**
  Rhetoric is the art of discourse, either spoken or written. The use of *rhetoric* to mean "inflated or exaggerated speech" is recent.

  The politician's promises were mere *rhetoric.*

**Rhetorical question**
  The rhetorical question is a frequent device of argument or persuasion. We ask a question, not to be answered, but to affect the listener or reader.

  Are we born, to suffer and to die, only to satisfy the whims of rich warmongers?

  Must we write themes forever?

**Run-on sentence**
  A run-on sentence fuses two sentences.

  I was eight my brother was ten.

is a run-on or fused sentence. It should read

I was eight. My brother was ten.

### Satire

*Satire* is a form of literature, either prose or poetry, that uses ridicule to expose and to judge behavior or ideas that the satirist finds foolish, or wicked, or both.

### Seldom ever

This phrase is redundant. *Seldom* will do. Instead of

He *seldom ever* brushed his hair.

say

He *seldom* brushed his hair.

### Semantics

The study of the meanings and associations of words. A good book on semantics is S. I. Hayakawa, *Language in Thought and Action.*

### Semicolon

See pages 405–406.

### Sensual, sensuous

The two words have different meanings. *Sensual* has unfavorable connotations and means "preoccupied with or inclined to the gratification of the senses or appetites."

He was wholly *sensual* in his priorities; his gluttony came first.

*Sensuous* has complimentary connotations and describes things that give pleasure to the senses.

The passage is one of the most *sensuous* in all literature.

### Sentence fragment

See pages 160–162, 378–381.

### Sentence types

See **Compound-complex sentence, Compound sentence, Complex sentence,** and **Simple sentence.**

**Shall, will**

In common speech and most writing, we make small distinction between the words. Formally, *I shall* expresses a person's belief about his future.

*I shall* be twenty-one in December.

*I will* expresses his will power, his wish.

*I will* get to Japan before I die!

**She/her**

See **He/him.**

**Should, would**

*Should* expresses obligation.

You *should* be ashamed.

It is confused with *would* when it is used in other senses.

I *should* not have reached Chicago without your loan.

When we use the past of *shall* in an indirect quotation, formal prose requires *should* instead of *would.*

I said that you *should* be ready before eight.

*Would* commonly expresses habitual activities.

He *would* visit the lake and fish from dawn to dusk.

When another phrase (like "every summer," if it were added to the last sentence) expresses habit, we can drop the *would* and use the past tense alone.

He visited the lake every summer and fished from dawn to dusk.

**Should have, should of**

The words are *should have,* which can be pronounced *should've. Should of* does not make sense.

**Sic**

Pronounced "sick," this Latin word appears in quotations, enclosed in brackets, to signify that an error was made in the source material, not by the writer copying the quotation.

Studebaker writes, "I would rather be Thoreu [*sic*] unhappy than a contented pig."

### Simile

A figure of speech in which comparison is openly made, usually by *like* or *as.*

He walks *like* a turkey.
The fabric was soft *as* a baby's bottom.

### Simple sentence

A simple sentence has one main clause and no subordinate clauses.

She barked at the full moon.

See page 157.

### Slang

The special, idiosyncratic vocabulary or jargon associated with a culture or subculture. Slang words have been absorbed into English from various ethnic groups ("Fred is such a *klutz*, his career is *kaput*"), from sports ("It's your *ballgame*"), and, most recently, from technology ("I asked him to give me some *input* on that"). Most slang is short-lived. Avoid using it in formal prose.

### So

This word is a stylistic pitfall for many beginning writers. As a coordinating conjunction, *so* is often boring and repetitious, leading the writer into dull compound sentences.

She was tall *so* he asked her how she liked the weather up there.
She was tired of hearing that question *so* she knocked him flat.

As a vague intensive, *so* is as useless as *wonderful* and *terrible*, though it occupies less space.

The building was *so* tall.
I am *so* glad to see you!

### Sort of

See **Kind of.**

**Spelling**
>   See pages 418–421.

**Split infinitive**
>   An infinitive is the form of the verb that uses *to*, as in *to run, to think, to scratch*. When we place another word (commonly an adverb) in the middle of an infinitive, we are splitting the infinitive.

>   to *quickly* run
>   to *occasionally* think
>   to *from time to time* scratch

>   Grammarians used to insist that the infinitive never be split. People split them anyway.

>   Remember *to never split* the infinitive!

>   Now, most grammarians consider a prohibition against split infinitives fussy. But careful writers rarely split them.

**Stationary, stationery**
>   *Stationary* is an adjective that means "standing still." *Stationery* means "writing materials."

**Style**
>   See especially Chapters 4–6. See also William Strunk and E. B. White, *The Elements of Style;* Bergen Evans, *A Dictionary of Contemporary American Usage;* and *A Dictionary of Modern English Usage* by H. W. Fowler, rev. and ed. by Sir Ernest Gowers. See also *The Modern Stylists*, ed. by Donald Hall, a collection of essays and excerpts by George Orwell, Ernest Hemingway, Ezra Pound, Edmund Wilson, James Thurber, and others.

**Subject**
>   A subject is a noun, or a noun substitute, about which something is stated or questioned. The subject usually comes before the predicate. The complete subject is the subject and all the words (modifiers, etc.) that belong to it.

>   *The grinning barbarian, his teeth clenched,* looked into the barnyard.

*Barbarian* is the simple subject; the first six words make the complete subject.

### Subjunctive
See **Mood.**

### Subordinate clause
A subordinate (or dependent) clause cannot stand by itself and make a whole sentence. It depends upon a main clause.

> I cannot see *who it is.*
> The claws are not lethal, *because he was de-clawed.*

### Substantive
A *substantive* is a word or group of words used as a noun; it may be a noun, pronoun, phrase, or noun clause.

### Suppose, supposed
The past tense often disappears, and meaning disappears with it. See **Used to, use to.**

### Syntax
Syntax is the way in which words are put together to form larger units, phrases, clauses, or sentences. It is also the part of grammar that describes this putting together.

### Tense
The tense of a verb shows the time in which an action takes place. In the last sentence, *shows* is in the present tense. In

> I *showed* you.

*showed* is in the past tense.

> I *will show* you.

uses the future tense.

### Than, then
These words are different in spelling, meaning, and function. *Then* refers to time, and *than* makes a comparison.

We were nice *then*.
She was taller *than* he was.

## That, which, who

We use the word *that* in a number of ways.

It is a demonstrative, as in "*that* cat."

Many writers are confused about when to use *that* and when to use *which* in introducing clauses. Nonrestrictive (nondefining) clauses take *which*.

The old car, *which* was struggling through the winter, seemed younger when spring arrived.

When the clause is restrictive or defining, we use *that* when it is possible, which is most of the time.

The old car *that* Mr. Hornback owned was struggling up the hill.

*Which* is possible in this last sentence, but seems overprecise or rigid, and is stylistically inferior. However, when a sentence requires several restrictive clauses in a row, *that* can become confusing, and we had better revert to *which*.

The old car *which* Mr. Hornback owned, *which* had one headlight dangling loose, and *which* smelled perpetually of gasoline chugged struggling up the hill.

Remember that *who* applies to people, whether the clause is restrictive or nonrestrictive, and *which* never applies to people.

The folks *which* lived next door.

is incorrect. Some writers, informally, substitute *that* for *who* on occasions when the person is seen as if from a distance.

The man *that* stood outside the door was tall and fortyish.

## Then

In a familiar balance, within a sentence, we use *then* after *if*.

*If* statistics imply the opposite, *then* the statistics are incorrect.

## Their, there, they're

See page 406.

**They, them**
>See **He/him.**

**Through, thru**
>*Thru* is incorrect, merely a labor-saving device, adopted by sign painters, advertisers, and the fabricators of headlines.

**To, too, two**
>These homonyms are sometimes confused. *Two* is only a number. *Too* is only an excess: *too* much is *too* much. *To* is a preposition (I handed the book *to* Geronimo) or part of an infinitive (*to* be or not *to* be . . .).

**Toward, towards**
>Either is possible. *Toward* is more American, *towards* more British.

**Transitive verb**
>A transitive verb *must* have a direct object to fill out its meaning.

>He *put the book* down.

>*Book* is the direct object of the transitive verb *put.*

**Try and**

>*Try and see* if she's home.

is a long way to say

>*See* if she's home.

**Type**
>*Type* is another word to stay away from. Even used grammatically, it is usually filler.

>It was a strange *type* of animal.

boils down nicely to

>It was a strange animal.

Occasionally, as with *sort* or *kind,* we actually mean something by the word.

Never use it next to a noun, without the preposition *of* coming between. It is useless to say:

| | |
|---|---|
| a new *type* soft drink | their *type* business |
| a long *type* Buick | that *type* handsomeness |

In all these examples, an *of* would make the phrases more acceptable; but in the first three, omission of *type* would be the better solution. We save a word. In the fourth example, the idea of *type* (or *sort* or *kind*) has more meaning, but could benefit from greater specificity.

### Unthinkable, inconceivable

Something that is literally *unthinkable* is probably literally unmentionable. We use *unthinkable* as hyperbole, usually to describe something that we deplore.

His conduct was *unthinkable.*

*Inconceivable* means "impossible to imagine or explain."

Her absence was *inconceivable.*

### Until, till

We say *till*, but we write *until. Till* looks stilted and literary on the page.

### Used to, use to

The correct form is *used to.*

I *used to* see her every morning at nine o'clock.

Probably because of our slovenly pronunciation, we sometimes drift into

I *use* to see her every morning at nine o'clock.

when we write it down. We should use the correct form to make temporal sense. The same is true of *supposed to.*

### Verb

For advice on style and the verb, see pages 110–117. Also see **Active voice, Intransitive verb, Mood, Object, Passive voice, Predicate,** and **Transitive verb.**

**Verbal**

Verbals are words derived from verbs but used as nouns or adjectives and sometimes as adverbs. Verbals are *gerunds, participles,* and *infinitives.*

*Gerunds* always end in *-ing* and are used as nouns.

*Flying* is fun.
*Running* is good exercise.
Neal and Liz have benefited from their *running.*

*Participles* (past and present) are used as adjectives.

This *flying* manual is essential.
His *shattered* hip was mending slowly.
"The *rising* cost of living" is a common phrase.

*Infinitives* are used primarily as nouns, but sometimes as adjectives or adverbs. They are composed of *to* and a verb.

We started *to run* from Godzilla.
*To fail* is a pleasure he can't afford.
He dropped out *to begin* his career as a clown.

**Vocative**

See **Direct address.**

**We/us**

See **He/him.**

**When**

Don't use *when* as an introduction to definitions.

Loneliness is *when* you play the radio just to hear the announcer's voice.

You could say instead

You are lonely *when* you play the radio just to hear the announcer's voice.

or

It is a definition of loneliness to play the radio just to hear the announcer's voice.

**Where**
> See **When.** The same injunction applies.

**Which, that**
> See **That, which, who.**

**While**
> The word means "at the same time" or "during the time that."
Sometimes writers use it in place of *although*, and it can work.

> *While* John is large, his stomach is not excessive.

But this usage is prone to ambiguity.

> Winter is warm in the southern hemisphere, *while* summer is
> cold.

Think about this sentence for a moment; it is absurd.

**Who, whom**
> *Who* is a subject, *whom* an object.

> *Who's* on first?
> *To whom* should I deliver the testimony?

In the last sentence, *whom* is the object of the preposition *to.* In
formal writing, always say *whom* when it is an object—of a verb or
of a preposition.
  Sometimes position leads us into error. When a pronoun precedes
a verb, it sounds as if it were a subject; it isn't always. We may be
tempted to write

> From *who* is the noise coming?

but the phrase is *from whom,* and *the noise* (not *who*) is the subject
of *is.* We should write

> From *whom* is the noise coming?

Sometimes a clause separates the subject *who* from its verb, and we
misuse *whom* for *who.* We write

> Herbert, *whom* she said would be here at 6:30, strolled in at 8:00.

In this sentence the three noun-verb combinations make a box within a box within a box. "Herbert . . . strolled" is the outside box, "who . . . would be here" is the middle box, and "she said" the inside box.

When *whom* comes before a preposition of which it is the object, it is correct but highly formal.

> *Whom* am I looking at?

Here, we always write *who* in informal writing. Frequently, *whom* will sound too formal even in an essay that is mostly formal. Use your judgment. The position of the pronoun makes the problem, which comes up when it is the object of a verb as well as when it is the object of a preposition.

> *Whom* do I see?
> *Who* do I see?

The first is correct and the second incorrect—technically—but it would take a highly formal context to accept the "correct" form without creating a moment of stuffiness.

**Whose, who's**

See pages 406–407.

**-wise**

Stylewise, avoid this syllable in combination with words with which it has not been combined before. *Clockwise* and *otherwise* are parts of the language. Avoid *literarywise, poetrywise, intelligence quotientwise, Septemberwise, costwise, Sallywise, ecologywise*—and anything similar.

**Woman, women**

People sometimes forget that the two spellings show a difference in number. *Woman* is singular, *women* plural.

*Annie Dillard.* Quotation on page 213 from *Pilgrim at Tinker Creek,* pages 4-5, by Annie Dillard. Copyright © 1974 by Annie Dillard. Reprinted by permission of Harper & Row, Publishers, Inc., and Blanche C. Gregory, Inc.

*Robert Frost.* "Stopping by Woods on a Snowy Evening" on page 33. Copyright 1923, © 1969 by Holt, Rinehart and Winston. Copyright 1951 by Robert Frost. Reprinted from *The Poetry of Robert Frost* edited by Edward Connery Lathem, by permission of Henry Holt and Company, Inc. and Jonathan Cape Ltd.

*George Gildner.* Quotation on page 308 from "But What About Welfare's Grim Side?" *The New York Times,* April 22, 1984. Copyright © 1984 by The New York Times Company. Reprinted by permission.

*Edward Hoagland.* "Walking the Dog" on page 41, "There Go the Clowns" on pages 48–49 from *The New York Times,* April 16, 1979 and March 30, 1979. Copyright © 1979 by The New York Times Company. "Banking for Winter" on pages 49–50 from *The New York Times,* November 16, 1980. Copyright © 1980 by the New York Times Company. Reprinted by permission. Quotation on pages 148–149 from "The Courage of Turtles" from *The Courage of Turtles,* by Edward Hoagland. Copyright © 1970 by Edward Hoagland. Reprinted by permission of Random House, Inc.

*John G. Ives.* "Questionable Role of Law Review in Evaluating Young Lawyers" on pages 326–327, a letter to the editor of *The New York Times,* March 11, 1981. Copyright © 1981 by The New York Times Company. Reprinted by permission.

*Randall Jarrell.* Quotation on pages 198–199 from *A Sad Heart at the Supermarket: Essays and Fables by Randall Jarrell.* Copyright © 1962 by Randall Jarrell. Reprinted by permission.

*Oliver Jensen.* "The Gettysburg Address in Eisenhowerese" by Oliver Jensen on pages 202–203, previously published in *The Territorial Enterprise* and *The New Republic,* June 17, 1957. Reprinted by permission of the author.

*The Journal Transcript.* "Downtown Merchants Association" on pages 44–45 from *The Journal Transcript,* January 28, 1987. Reprinted by permission of The Journal Transcript, Franklin, N.H.

*Michael Korda.* Quotation on pages 263–264 from "How to Be a Leader," *Newsweek,* January 5, 1981. Reprinted by permission of the author.

*Andrew Kopkind.* Quotation on page 309 excerpted from Andrew Kopkind, "U.S. to Critics: Keep Out!" *The Nation,* April 28, 1984. Copyright 1984 The Nation Company, Inc. Reprinted by permission.

*D. H. Lawrence.* Quotation on pages 296–297 from *Pornography and Obscenity,* by D. H. Lawrence. Copyright 1930 by Alfred A. Knopf, Inc. Reprinted by permission of Alfred A. Knopf, Inc., Laurence Pollinger Ltd., and the Estate of the late Mrs. Frieda Lawrence Ravagli.

*Mary McCarthy.* Quotations on pages 177 and 217–218 excerpted from "America the Beautiful" in *On the Contrary.* Copyright © 1957, 1961 by Mary McCarthy. Reprinted by permission.

*John McPhee.* Quotations on pages 255 and 260–261 reprinted by permission of Farrar, Straus and Giroux, Inc., and Hamish Hamilton Ltd. from *Coming into the Country* by John McPhee. Copyright © 1976, 1977 by John McPhee. Quotation on page 241 (selection retitled "Ashe and Graebner") reprinted by permission of Farrar, Straus and Giroux, Inc. from *Levels of the Game* by John McPhee. Copyright © 1969 by John McPhee. Material by John McPhee originally appeared in *The New Yorker.*

*Antonio Machado.* Quotation on page 191 from *The Sea and the Honeycomb* by Antonio Machado, translated by Robert Bly. Copyright © 1971 by Robert Bly. Reprinted by permission.

*Margaret Mead.* Quotation on page 232 from *Male and Female* by Margaret Mead. Copyright 1949, © 1955 by Margaret Mead. By permission of William Morrow & Company. Quotations on pages 138 and 324–325 from "Needed: Full Partnerships for Women" by Margaret Mead, *Saturday Review*, June 14, 1975, © 1975 by Saturday Review/World, Inc. Reprinted by permission of the Institute of Intercultural Studies.

*H. L. Mencken.* Quotation on page 100 from *The American Language,* abridged ed., by H. L. Mencken. Copyright 1936, © 1963 by Alfred A. Knopf, Inc., and renewed 1964 by August Mencken and Mercantile-Safe Deposit and Trust Company. Reprinted by permission of the publisher. Quotation on page 225 from "A Libido for the Ugly" in *A Mencken Chrestomathy* by H. L. Mencken. Copyright 1949 by Alfred A. Knopf, Inc. Reprinted by permission of the publisher.

*V. S. Naipaul.* Quotation on page 252 from *The Return of Eva Peron with the Killings in Trinidad,* by V. S. Naipaul. Copyright © 1980 by V. S. Naipaul. Reprinted by permission of Alfred A. Knopf, Inc.

*Michael Novak.* Quotation on page 245 from *Solzhenitsyn at Harvard: The Address, Twelve Early Responses, and Six Later Reflections,* edited by Ronald Berman, Ethics and Public Policy Center (1211 Connecticut Avenue, N.W., Washington, D.C. 20036), 1980. Reprinted by permission.

*John A. Parrish.* Quotations on pages 290–291 and 293 from *12, 20 & 5: A Doctor's Year in Vietnam* by John A. Parrish, M.D. Copyright © 1974 by John A. Parrish, M.D. Reprinted by permission of the publisher, E. P. Dutton, Inc., and Gerard McCauley Agency.

*G. V. Perkins, Jr.* Quotation on page 309 from "What's New in Agriculture," *The New York Times,* March 25, 1984. Copyright © 1984 by The New York Times Company. Reprinted by permission.

*Robert M. Pirsig.* Quotations on pages 260 and 296 from *Zen and the Art of Motorcycle Maintenance* by Robert M. Pirsig. Copyright © 1974 by Robert M. Pirsig. By permission of William Morrow & Company and The Bodley Head Ltd.

*Readers' Guide to Periodical Literature.* Quotation on page 345 from the August 1980 *Readers Guide to Pediodical Literature.* Copyright © 1980 by the H. W. Wilson Company. Material reproduced by permission of the publisher.

*Alan Richman.* "Shed No Tears for Olympics" on pages 320–322 from *The Boston Globe,* May 10, 1984. Reprinted courtesy of The Boston Globe.

*Antoine de Saint-Exupéry.* Quotation on pages 240–241 from *Wind, Sand and Stars,* copyright 1939 by Antoine de Saint-Exupéry; renewed 1967 by Lewis Galantiere. Reprinted by permission of Harcourt Brace Jovanovich, Inc.

*James Thurber.* Quotation on pages 145 and 199 copyright 1959 by James Thurber. From *The Years with Ross,* published by Atlantic-Little, Brown. Originally appeared in the *Atlantic Monthly.*

*Michael Walzer.* Quotation on pages 241–242 from *Radical Principles: Reflections of an Unreconstructed Democrat,* by Michael Walzer. Copyright © 1980 by Basic Books, Inc. Reprinted by permission of Basic Books, Inc., Publishers.

*Diane White.* Quotation on page 119 from "The Noble Asparagus" by Diane White, *The Boston Globe*, May 26, 1977. Reprinted by permission.

*E. B. White.* Quotation on page 239 from "Calculating Machine" in *Poems and Sketches of E. B. White* (1981). Copyright 1951, 1979 by E. B. White. Reprinted by permission of Harper & Row, Publishers, Inc.

# AUTHOR AND TITLE INDEX

# SUBJECT INDEX

To the Student:

Part of our job as educational publishers is to try to improve the textbooks we publish. Thus, when revising we take into account the experience of both instructors and students with the previous edition. At some time your instructor will be asked to comment extensively on *Writing Well*, Sixth Edition, but right now we want to hear from you. After all, though your instructor assigned this book you are the one who paid for it.

Please help us by completing this questionnaire and returning it to College Division, Scott, Foresman/Little, Brown and Company, 34 Beacon Street, Boston, Mass. 02108.


School:_____Course Title: _____

Instructor's Name: _____

1.  What parts of *Writing Well*, Sixth Edition, were most useful to you?

    Why?_____

    _____

    _____

    _____

    _____

    _____

2.  What parts did you find least helpful? Why? _____

    _____

    _____

    _____

    _____

    _____

3. Did you use "A Brief Review of Grammar, Punctuation, and Mechanics?" _____

   Did you find it useful? _____

4. Did you find the Glossary helpful? _____

   _____

   _____

   _____

   _____

5. Any suggestions for improving *Writing Well*? _____

   _____

   _____

   _____

   _____

   _____

   _____

   _____

   _____

   _____

6. Will you keep this book for future reference? _____

   _____

   Date                          Name

   _____

   Mailing Address

   *Thanks for your help.*